Critical Realism and Marxism

Critical realism is gaining ground in the social sciences and humanities, and critical realist orientated scholars are to be found in economics, gender studies, geography, history, law, organisation and management studies, sociology, social theory and philosophy. Marxism not only refuses to go away, it remains one of the key intellectual perspectives – a point conceded even by many of its opponents. Moreover, many of those caught in the recent upsurge of 'anti-capitalist' sentiment are discovering the valuable lessons available from a body of thought that has been staunchly 'anti-capitalist' for 150 years.

Critical Realism and Marxism is the first book to address the controversial debates between critical realism and Marxism, and it does so from a wide range of disciplines. The authors argue that whilst one book cannot answer all the questions about the relationship between critical realism and Marxism, this book does provide some significant answers. In so doing, *Critical Realism and Marxism* reveals a potentially fruitful relationship, deepens our understanding of the social world, and thereby makes a contribution towards eliminating the barbarism that accompanies contemporary capitalism.

Andrew Brown is a lecturer in economics at the University of Leeds. He is the co-author of *The Euro: Evolution and Prospects*. **Steve Fleetwood** is a lecturer in employment studies at Lancaster University. He is the author of *Hayek's Political Economy: The Socio-Economics of Order*, editor of *Critical Realism in Economics: Development and Debate*, and co-editor of *Realist Perspectives on Organisation and Management*. **John Michael Roberts** is currently a research associate in the Department of Sociology at the University of Manchester.

Critical realism: interventions
Edited by Margaret Archer, Roy Bhaskar, Andrew Collier, Tony Lawson and Alan Norrie

Critical realism is one of the most influential new developments in the philosophy of science and in the social sciences, providing a powerful alternative to positivism and post modernism. This series will explore the critical realist position in philosophy and across the social sciences.

Critical Realism
Essential readings
Edited by Margaret Archer, Roy Bhaskar, Andrew Collier, Tony Lawson and Alan Norrie

The Possibility of Naturalism 3rd edition
A philosophical critique of the contemporary human sciences
Roy Bhaskar

Being & Worth
Andrew Collier

Quantum Theory and the Flight from Realism
Philosophical responses to quantum mechanics
Christopher Norris

From East to West
Odyssey of a soul
Roy Bhaskar

Realism and Racism
Concepts of race in sociological research
Bob Carter

Rational Choice Theory
Resisting colonisation
Edited by Margaret Archer and Jonathan Q Tritter

Explaining Society
Critical realism in the social sciences
Berth Danermark, Mats Ekström, Jan Ch Karlsson and Liselotte Jakobsen

Critical Realism and Marxism
Edited by Andrew Brown, Steve Fleetwood and John Michael Roberts

Critical Realism in Economics
Edited by Steve Fleetwood

Realist Perspectives on Management and Organisations
Edited by Stephen Ackroyd and Steve Fleetwood

Also published by Routledge

Routledge studies in critical realism
Edited by Margaret Archer, Roy Bhaskar, Andrew Collier,
Tony Lawson and Alan Norrie

Critical Realism and Marxism

Edited by Andrew Brown,
Steve Fleetwood and
John Michael Roberts

London and New York

First published 2002 by Routledge
11 New Fetter Lane, London EC4P 4EE

Simultaneously published in the USA and Canada
by Routledge
29 West 35th Street, New York, NY 10001

Routledge is an imprint of the Taylor & Francis Group

© 2002 selection and editorial matter, Andrew Brown, Steve Fleetwood
and John Michael Roberts; individual chapters, the contributors

Typeset in Baskerville by BC Typesetting, Bristol
Printed and bound in Great Britain by
MPG Books Ltd, Bodmin

British Library Cataloguing in Publication Data
A catalogue record for this book is available from the British Library

Library of Congress Cataloging in Publication Data
Critical realism and Marxism/edited by Andrew Brown, Steve Fleetwood,
and Michael Roberts.
        p.   cm.
   Includes bibliographical references and index.
   1. Communism and social sciences. 2. Cricial realism. 3. Philosophy,
Marxist. I. Brown, Andrew. II. Fleetwood, Steve, 1955–
III. Roberts, Michael, 1971–

HX541.5.C75 2001
335.4′01–dc21   2001031756

ISBN 0–415–25012–9 (hbk)
ISBN 0–415–25013–7 (pbk)

Contents

Illustrations

Figure

Tables

Contributors

Christopher J. Arthur is a former lecturer in philosophy at the University of Sussex. He is the author of *Dialectics of Labour*. He edited Marx and Engels *The German Ideology*; *Marx's Capital: A Student Edition*; *Friedrich Engels: A Centenary Appreciation*; and (with G. Reuten) *The Circulation of Capital*.

Andrew Brown is a lecturer in economics at the University of Leeds. His research interests include economic methodology, value theory and the economics of the Euro. He is associate editor of *Historical Materialism* and co-author (with Philip Arestis and Malcolm Sawyer) of *The Euro: Evolution and Prospects*.

Noel Castree is a reader in human geography at Manchester University. Co-editor (with Bruce Braun) of *Remaking Reality* (Routledge) and *Social Nature* (Blackwell), he has published extensively on Marxian political economy. His current research focuses on genomics and intellectual property rights in living organisms.

Andrew Collier is Professor of Philosophy at Southampton University and a trustee of the Centre for Critical Realism. His books include *Scientific Realism and Socialist Thought* (Harvester, 1988), *Socialist Reasoning* (Pluto, 1990), *Critical Realism* (Verso, 1994) and *Being and Worth* (Routledge, 1999).

Sean Creaven teaches sociology at Leeds Metropolitan University. He is the author of *Marxism and Realism: a materialistic application of realism in the social sciences* (Routledge, 2000). His current research interests include social theory, historical sociology and stratification.

Neil Curry is currently completing his Ph.D. at University College Chichester on Marxism, Post-Marxism and the Discourse of Postmodernity: with specific reference to the work of Roy Bhaskar, Fredric Jameson and Ernesto Laclau.

Hans G. Ehrbar is a German-born Marxist teaching economics and econometrics at the University of Utah in Salt Lake City. He regularly teaches courses about Marx's *Capital* on the internet and is writing a detailed commentary to *Capital* which can be downloaded from his web page.

Steve Fleetwood is a lecturer in employment studies in Lancaster University. He is author of *Hayek's Political Economy: The Socio Economics of Order* (Routledge, 1995), editor of *Critical Realism in Economics: Development and Debate* (Routledge, 1998), and co-editor (with Stephen Ackroyd) of *Realist Perspectives on Organisation and Management* (Routledge, 2000). His current research focuses on the sociology of work, HRM, employment relations and the economics of the labour market.

Bob Jessop is Professor of Sociology at Lancaster University. He is best known for his work on state theory, the political economy of post-war Britain, radical political economy and the regulation approach (especially Fordism and post-Fordism), and the restructuring of welfare regimes. His book *The Future of the Capitalist State* will be published by Polity Press in 2002.

Jonathan Joseph teaches social science at the Open University and Goldsmiths College, University of London. He has written a number of articles on critical realism, Marxism, hegemony and deconstruction.

John Michael Roberts is currently a research associate in the Department of Sociology at the University of Manchester working on a project that explores new forms of democracy and participation in the UK. He is co-editor (with Nick Crossley) of *After Habermas: New Perspectives on the Public Sphere* (Blackwell, forthcoming) and is currently writing a book, *Rethinking the Public Sphere: The Aesthetics of Free Speech* (Liverpool University Press).

Preface

This collection started life as a project to collect, into one volume, papers that were already in print elsewhere. However, as we (Andrew Brown, Steve Fleetwood and John Roberts) began to discuss this project, between ourselves and with colleagues, it became apparent that many people were keen to make new contributions exploring the possible relation between critical realism and Marxism. Hence *Critical Realism and Marxism* was born.

This brings us to an important question: is there a relation between critical realism and Marxism, and if so, what is the nature of this relation? As we explored this potential relationship three broad viewpoints began to crystallise: critical realism can add to Marxism without taking anything away; Marxism is in no need of the services of critical realism; and Marxism and critical realism have something to gain from one another. Whilst there is a clear affinity between the first and third of these viewpoints, even those who feel critical realism has little to offer Marxism are not totally dismissive. Their (understandable) worry that critical realism might lead Marxism on (another) fruitless journey, is tempered by two factors. First, they recognise that critical realist orientated Marxists are prepared to engage in the kinds of debates, and on the kinds of topics that, at the very least, encourage Marxists to sharpen their own categories and, therefore, help in clarifying Marxism. Second, they realise that many critical realists are serious Marxists and, therefore, have a desire to develop Marxism.

Whilst one collection cannot possibly complete the task of exploring the relation between critical realism and Marxism it can, at least, make a start. It is the hope of the editors that *Critical Realism and Marxism* will encourage others to engage in this project and that dialogue will develop, thereby, deepening our understanding of the social and natural world.

It is, we think, worth adding that all contributors have conducted themselves not only with scholarship, but also with collegiality and amiability. All contributors have accepted that those with whom they disagree, often fundamentally, are not to be dismissed dogmatically, but are to be treated as serious scholars, committed to the task of furthering our knowledge. Moreover, the very existence of such scholarly debate is a fair indication that both critical realism and Marxism are in a good state of intellectual health. This bodes well for two bodies of thought that, ultimately, see their role as making a small contribution towards eliminating the barbarism that accompanies contemporary capitalism.

Acknowledgements

The editors and publisher wish to thank the following journals for their permission to use copyright material and to reprint articles: Capital & Class for Steve Fleetwood, 'What kind of *theory* is Marx's labour *theory* of value? A critical realist inquiry', *Capital & Class* 73 (2001): 41–77; and Radical Philosophy for Christopher Arthur, 'The spectral ontology of value', *Radical Philosophy* May 2001.

Special thanks go to Anne Fleetwood for her patient work in collecting the disparate contributions, getting them all into house style, and ruthlessly hunting out gremlins wherever they appeared.

1 The marriage of critical realism and Marxism

Happy, unhappy or on the rocks?

*Andrew Brown, Steve Fleetwood and
John Michael Roberts*

Introduction

Critical realism is steadily gaining ground in the social sciences and
humanities. Critical realist orientated scholars are to be found in many
areas such as: sociology and social theory, organisation and management
studies, feminism, geography, law and economics. Marxism, despite having
been unfashionable for several decades, refuses to go away and remains one
of the key intellectual perspectives – a point recognised by many of its
opponents. Moreover, many of those caught in the recent upsurge of 'anti-
capitalist' sentiment are discovering the valuable lessons available from a
body of thought that has been staunchly 'anti-capitalist' for a century and a
half. The purpose of this collection, then, is to explore the relationship
between critical realism and Marxism.

Broadly speaking there appear to be three (not entirely mutually exclusive) viewpoints on the nature of this relation: critical realism can add to
Marxism without taking anything away; Marxism is in no need of the
services of critical realism; and Marxism and critical realism have something
to gain from one another. This introductory chapter consists of Steve Fleetwood (SF), John Roberts (JR) and Andrew Brown (AB) elaborating these
three viewpoints, in order to give the reader a flavour of the kind of debates
that are currently taking place between critical realists and Marxists. It
might be added that the very existence of serious, and amicable, scholarly
debate of this kind is a fair indication that both critical realism and Marxism
are in a good state of intellectual health.

Critical realism: augmenting Marxism
(Steve Fleetwood)

Before seeking a possible relationship between two entities, a basis for comparison must be established otherwise the search may end up inadvertently
trying to seek a relationship between chalk and cheese – with conceptual

confusion following almost inevitably. In this confusion we might conclude either that a relationship exists where actually there is none, or that no relationship exists where actually there is one. The same goes for seeking a possible relationship between Marxism and critical realism. Let us consider Marxism and critical realism in turn to see if we can establish a basis for comparison.

Comparing like with like

Marxism is a body of thought which, at least in the hands of its keenest scholars, has always sought to consistently span three levels: philosophical, theoretical and practical. Dialectical materialism has generally been understood as a philosophy that grounds theoretical pronouncements such as the necessity of the value form, and the emancipatory role of the working class. In turn, these theoretical pronouncements, have been used to inform political practice. What is hardly ever recognised, however, is that a range of political practices are consistent with a range of theoretical pronouncements, and a range of theoretical pronouncements are consistent with dialectical materialism. One might, for example, subscribe to dialectical materialism and to the theory that (a) the working class has been defeated, or (b) the working class is alive and well. Clearly a range of political practices will follow from the theoretical position adopted. Theory (a) leads to political support for things like new social movements whereas theory (b) leads to political support for things like the vanguard party. There is, therefore, *no one-to-one mapping between a particular (Marxist) political practice, a particular (Marxist) theory and a particular (dialectical materialist) philosophy*. The truth of this proposition lies in the (probably uncontroversial) fact that there are several competing Marxist theories (about various phenomena) and several Marxist political programmes, all perfectly compatible with dialectical materialist philosophy.

Critical realism is located at the level of philosophy and, unlike Marxism, it does not try to span three levels. Precisely because it licenses no particular political programme and particular theory, critical realism often comes in for criticism from Marxists on the ground that it is theoretically and politically sterile, or worse, that it sponsors anti-Marxist theories. If, however, there is no one-to-one mapping between a particular (Marxist) political practice, a particular (Marxist) theory and a particular (dialectical materialist) philosophy, then criticisms based upon critical realism's alleged sterility apply to any philosophy, including one belonging to Marxism. It is, therefore, erroneous to seek a possible relationship between critical realism and Marxist *theory* or Marxist *political practice*, but not between critical realism and Marxism *at the level of philosophy*. That is to say, if a relationship exists between critical realism and Marxism, it is located at the philosophical level. Let us, therefore, approach philosophy with a little more precision.

Critical realism: a full-blown philosophy of science

Whilst critical realism has many things to teach us about philosophy (and many of those things are elaborated in the chapters of this collection) it is, primarily, a *philosophy of science*. Moreover, critical realism focuses neither on one, or a small number, of topics in the philosophy of science, but is wide ranging, covering topics such as: ontology, epistemology, modes of inference, nature of causality, nature of laws/tendencies, role of abstraction, distinction between essence and appearance, criterion for theory evaluation, and so on. For brevity, I refer to such an all-encompassing philosophy of science as *full-blown*. And critical realism is a *full-blown* philosophy of science. Now, whilst Marxist philosophy is not short of papers and books dedicated to various *topics* in the philosophy of science, there have been relatively few attempts to elaborate a *full-blown* philosophy of science compatible with Marxism or, as I will refer to it, a Marxist philosophy of science.

Let me tread with caution here. I am not claiming there has been no work on various *topics* in Marxist philosophy of science: I am claiming that there has been very little work that attempts to combine these various topics to elaborate a *full-blown* Marxist philosophy of science. Whilst the likes of Ruben (1979), Murray (1988), Sayer (1983) and Zeleny (1980) spring to mind, even here there seems to be more of an emphasis on repeating and re-interpreting some of Marx's own scattered ideas than on elaborating a *full-blown* Marxist philosophy of science. Moreover, there have been very few attempts to elaborate a Marxist philosophy of science that can neutralise attacks from current philosophies of science, especially recent versions of positivism and, more recently, postmodernist and poststructuralist versions. At this point, I wish to make three claims.

Only a *full-blown* Marxist philosophy of science can be used to place Marxist theories and political practices on a secure footing. This is not, of course, to claim any one-to-one mapping between critical realism, theory and practice. It is merely to recognise that a *full-blown* Marxist philosophy of science can assist in formulating the *kinds* of theories deemed appropriate by Marxists.[1]

Only a *full-blown* Marxist philosophy of science can successfully neutralise attacks from current philosophies of science, because many of the latter are full-blown (*non*-Marxist) philosophies of science. Marxists may not like to think that positivism is a full-blown philosophy of science but, like it or not, positivism does have an inclusive position on topics such as ontology, epistemology, causality, law, mode of inference, and has criteria for theory evaluation. The fact that it may have an inappropriate position on all these topics is beside the point here. The ability to successfully neutralise attacks from current philosophies of science is not merely a matter of scholarly and/or academic interest. The absence of a full-blown Marxist philosophy of science has allowed a vacuum to develop in the Marxist canon, which is often filled by Marxists borrowing topics from non-Marxist philosophies of science – with damaging consequences for Marxism.

Critical realism can supply the *full-blown* philosophy of science lacking in Marxism. This does not imply critical realism is replacing dialectical materialism, it is simply doing something else, it is adding to it.[2]

These claims could be established in various ways. For example, I could demonstrate how positivism has encouraged debates on the so-called 'transformation problem'; the (mis)use of rational choice models; the (mis)use of econometrics to test hypotheses such as the falling rate of profit. Alternatively, I could demonstrate how postmodernism and poststructuralism have encouraged the, arguably, anti-Marxist perspective referred to as post-Marxism. I will, however, try to establish these claims via one example, namely the notion of 'tendency'.

Laws or tendencies

It is well known that Marx conceives of laws in terms of tendencies. In discussing the tendency for profit rates to equalise, for example, he suggests that this equalisation be 'viewed as a tendency *like all other economic laws*' (1984: 175, emphasis added). Moreover, the conception of law as tendency has permeated much Marxist economics ever since. The problem, however, is that the exact meaning of the term 'tendency' within the Marxist canon is ambiguous. Marx himself left few clues and, whilst latter day Marxists have discussed tendencies, most discussions have taken the form of (often not un-illuminating) asides to other issues.[3] As MacBride puts it:

> These laws [i.e. tendencies] are, presumably, nothing but accurate high-level generalisations concerning a wide range of phenomena (although, to be candid, the failure to say very much about the meaning of the term 'law' as he uses it is one of the most gaping lacunae in Marx's all too brief discussions of methodology.
>
> (1977: 59, see also 123–6)

Whilst it will become clear below that it is misleading to refer to tendencies as 'high level generalisations', MacBride's instinct is essentially correct: there has been a failure to develop a systematic, explicit and unambiguous conception of tendency in Marxism. Ruben sees no future in the critical realist attempt to disentangle law from tendency, being:

> genuinely worried that the tendency v. empirical regularity debate, if pushed hard enough, might well collapse into little more than a quibble about the use of the term 'law'.
>
> (1979: 207)

Far from a mere 'quibble', the tendency v. empirical law debate is instructive in illuminating just how critical realism can place the notion of tendency on a more secure footing than it is now, and therefore, demonstrate how critical realism can add to Marxist theory without taking anything away. To do this, I take the following issues as read.

Critical realists reject (a) event regularities, and hence (Humean) laws styled as 'whenever event x then event y', as most unlikely features of social reality and (b) the (Humean) notion of causality as event regularity. The critical realist is, therefore, free to (i) seek the cause of an event in something other than the event with which it is (allegedly) conjoined, and (ii) to employ a notion of causation as powers of forces. Attention thus turns away from the flux of perceived and actual events towards the *mechanisms, social structures, powers and relations* that causally govern these events. Thus is the ontology referred to as *stratified*: underlying the domain of the empirical are the domains of the actual and the 'deep'. Because of the openness of socio-economic systems, results, consequences, or outcomes *cannot* be successfully predicted but the mechanisms, social structures, powers and relations that causally govern the flux of events *can*, however, be uncovered and *explained*. Explanation usurps prediction, as the goal of science. Explanatory content provides a criterion for evaluating theories. One can now understand my reason for calling the method 'causal/explanatory'. To *explain* a phenomenon is to give an account of its *causal* history (cf. Lipton 1993: 33). Significantly, this account is not couched in terms of the event(s) that just happens to precede the phenomenon to be explained, but in terms of the underlying, *mechanisms, social structures, powers and relations* that causally govern the phenomenon. The following section puts these critical realist categories to work to elaborate a sophisticated notion of tendency.

Structures, powers, mechanisms, relations and tendencies

A complex entity possesses an intrinsic *structure* (or combinations of structures) which makes it the kind of thing it is and not another thing. The structure also endows the entity with dispositions, capacities, potentials, abilities to act in certain ways. In short, the structure endows the entity with *powers* to do certain things, but not others. And powers may *be possessed, exercised* or *actualised*.

a A power is *possessed* by an entity in virtue of its intrinsic structure, and this power endures whether or not it is exercised or actualised. The power acts transfactually.

b A power *exercised* is a power that has been triggered, and is generating an effect in an open system. Due to interference from the effects of other exercised powers, however, one can never know *a priori*, what the outcome of any particular power will be. The exercised power acts transfactually.

c   A power *actualised* is an exercised power generating its effect in an open
    system. The power is, however, not deflected or counteracted by the
    effects of other exercised powers. The actualised power does not act trans-
    factually but factually in the sense that the power generates its effect
    constantly.

Let us consider these distinctions in a little more depth via the simple
example of a bicycle.

a   Once structures such as wheels, frame, saddle and handlebars are com-
    bined to form a bicycle, this entity *possesses* the power to facilitate trans-
    portation. This power endures even if the bicycle remains locked in a
    garden shed.
b   A person may *exercise* the power by bringing the bicycle out of the shed
    and mounting it – i.e. a person triggers the power. However, due (say)
    to excessive alcohol consumption, strong head winds or steep gradients,
    the effect may not be the transportation of a cyclist from A to B. In this
    situation, the bicycle's exercised power is being deflected or counteracted
    by interference from other exercised powers.
c   A person may *actualise* the (exercised) power and successfully cycle from A
    to B. The bicycle's power is not being counteracted by any other powers
    such as alcohol, strong head winds or steep gradients.

With this understanding of structures and powers, let us move on to the
related issue of mechanisms. According to Lawson (1997: 21):

> A *mechanism* is basically the way of acting or working of a structured thing
> . . . Mechanisms then exist as the causal powers of things. Structured
> things . . . possess causal powers which, when triggered or released, act
> as generative mechanisms to determine the actual phenomena of the
> world.

The key to understanding the critical realist conception of a mechanism
(and eventually tendency) lies not with the notions of a power *possessed* or
actualised, but with the notion of a power *exercised*. A possessed power is (relatively) uninteresting because it generates no effects.[4] An *actualised* power is
(relatively) uninteresting because it is only in special circumstances that an
exercised power is not interfered with. A power exercised, however, is one
that has been triggered, is generating effects, is acting transfactually and, as
will become clear in a moment, is involved in generating tendencies. Being
triggered is, typically, a complex process requiring that the entity enters
into a web of relations with other relevant entities. A bicycle exists in
relations to a shed wall, a road, sky, grass, wind, hills, gravity, cyclists
(drunken and sober) and so on. If the bicycle enters into appropriate

relations (e.g. with a sober cyclist), its power is triggered, and becomes an exercised power.

It appears that the term mechanism[5] is a label we apply to the *ensemble* of structures, powers and relations. Once a specific set of intrinsic structures combine to form an entity with a power, and this entity enters into appropriate relations with other entities, the power is triggered and becomes an exercised power, whereupon a tendency is generated. When we write that *a mechanism* has a tendency to x, this is, strictly speaking, inaccurate: it is the *ensemble* that has a tendency to x, and we should write that the *ensemble* of structures, powers and relations has a tendency to x. Re-working Reuten's (1997: 157) terminology we might say that the tendency 'belongs' or is 'attached' to the ensemble – not merely to the mechanism, or to the power.

Now, to write that an ensemble has a tendency to x, does not mean that it *will* x. In an open system, ensembles do not, typically, exist in isolation from one other, rather there are a multiplicity of ensembles, each with their own tendencies and these tendencies converge in some space-time location. The actual outcome of this confluence of tendencies is impossible to predict *a priori*. The tendency for bicycles to facilitate transportation, for example, depends upon the existence or absence in the same space-time location of other tendencies such as the tendency for alcohol in the bloodstream to cause dizziness; the tendency for steep slopes or strong head winds to reduce forward momentum and so on. This is why a tendency acts transfactually.

A tendency then, metaphorically speaking, is akin to a force. When we think of a force we think of terms like: drive, propel, push, thrust, pressure and so on. The term 'tendency' relates not to any *results, consequences, or outcomes* of some acting force, such as a regularity or pattern in the resulting flux of events. *The term 'tendency' refers to the force itself.*

Now, I frequently encounter Marxists who opine that they too operate with tendencies and not laws: moreover, they do so without any help from critical realism. When the conversation gets a little deeper, however, it soon becomes clear that they are operating with a notion of tendency along the lines of some kind of loosely operating (Humean) law. From the critical realist perspective, the interpretation of tendency as some kind of loosely operating (Humean) law is, arguably, mistaken. Explaining the origin of this mistake is made easier by considering several commonly held (mis) interpretations of the term 'tendency'.[6]

- A tendency can be interpreted as a statistical trend such as: profits tend to fall over time. One might style this as 'Whenever event x (i.e. *passage of time*), then event y'.
- A tendency can be interpreted as a high relative frequency of a given subset of a class of possible events, such as: if the organic composition of capital increases, there is some probability that the rate of profit will decline.

We might style this as: 'whenever event x, then event y *under some well defined probability condition*'.

- A tendency can be interpreted as a counterfactual claim about what would come about under certain closure conditions such as: if the organic composition of capital increases, the rate of profit will decline *ceteris paribus*. We might style this as 'whenever event x, then event y *under conditions z*'.

- A tendency can be interpreted as a constant conjunction of events that holds with some unspecified regularity: a kind of loosely operating Humean law. MacBride (above) refers to tendencies as 'high level generalisations' (1977: 59). We might style this as 'whenever event x, then *most of the time* event y'.

- A tendency can be interpreted as an expression, outcome or result of some phenomenon such as: 'the capitalist mode of production (CMP) inherently produces an increasing social productivity of labour (prodtt) and this gets expressed in a tendential fall in the rate of profit (r)' (Reuten, 1997: 160). We might style this as 'whenever events x_1 (CMP) and x_2 (prodtt) then event y (r) as a "stylised fact"'.[7]

These interpretations are mistaken because they share a (possibly inadvertent) lapse into an empiricist, or more accurately, empirical realist mode of thinking.[8] These interpretations treat a tendency as a *result, consequence, or outcome*. The term 'tendency' is conceived of as some kind of empirically identifiable, and systematic, pattern in the flux of events. The pattern might be one of: perfect regularity, imperfect regularity, statistical regularity or 'stylised regularity'. The important point to note here is that, contra to critical realism, none of these interpretations identify a tendency with the *force itself*. There is, however, no longer a reason for Marxists to operate with one foot tied to empirical realism. Adopting critical realism as a philosophy of science compatible with Marxism has allowed us to place the notion of tendency on a more secure footing. This is an example of how critical realism has added to Marxism without taking anything away.

Marxism does not require the services of critical realism (John Michael Roberts)

Steve Fleetwood (SF) presents a highly sophisticated defence for the use of critical realism in developing a Marxist scientific theory (see also his chapter 4 in this volume). In this short reply I want to question some of his observations concerning the incorporation of critical realism within Marxist theory. I do this, first, by making some comments on the argument presented above and then, second, by briefly outlining some of the underlying differences between Marxism and critical realism as I see them. This will enable me to suggest that a more suitable way for Marxist theory to proceed is to develop categories in line with the fundamentals of historical materialism.

Critical realism: augmenting Marxism?

SF starts by quite rightly observing that there are a number of Marxisms. Specifically, he divides Marxism into political practice, theory and philosophy. Rightly he suggests that there is no one-to-one relationship between all three. Critical realism thus presents us with a useful set of theoretical tools with which to 'assist in formulating the *kinds* of theories deemed appropriate by Marxists'. I certainly believe that critical realism has helped Marxism to think more carefully about issues of 'depth', 'causality', 'powers', 'interconnections', and so on. I also agree that a level of contingency exists between Marxist political practice, theory and philosophy. Thus Marxism does need an overarching guiding hand to connect these various factors. However, the important question here is whether critical realism can give Marxism this guiding hand.

To begin my part of the discussion I would like first to air some caution about how we go about analysing the level of contingency between Marxist political practice, theory and philosophy. For it is still the case that there *must* be a *limit* to disagreement amongst Marxists about these three factors. Otherwise any debate which ensues could easily pass beyond Marxism into a standpoint that is decidedly non-Marxist. The argument about the incorporation of other methodological, theoretical and philosophical approaches into Marxism would therefore seem to rest upon the extent to which such an incorporation alters substantially the fundamentals upon which Marxism rests. I come back momentarily to what these fundamentals might be.

SF claims that Marxism requires a 'full-blown Marxist philosophy of science'. This is important for him because (i) there has been little work within Marxism to develop a full-blown philosophy of science and (ii) such a philosophy could be 'used to place Marxist theories and political practices on a secure footing'. Apart from the curious fact that he fails to mention Engels' attempt to provide such a philosophy, I think SF indicates a level of urgency about the need for such a philosophy within Marxism which is somewhat overstated. Whilst it is indeed true that a Marxist philosophy of science could aid Marxist theory and practice, it should also be remembered that Marxists have been involved in debates over a diverse range of practical issues *without* ever seeing the need to preface such debates by developing a full-blown philosophy of science. Indeed, we could take this point further. The quantitative examples wherein critical realism could be of some assistance to Marxism, namely the transformation problem, the (mis)use of rational choice models and the (mis)use of econometrics to test particular hypotheses, have already been heavily discussed, debated and criticised by Marxists without resort to critical realism. This fact alone surely begs the question of why we need critical realism to provide a critique of quantitative approaches if it has already been achieved by 'qualitative' versions of Marxism.

But I think there is a more fundamental weakness at the heart of SF's argument in that it rests on contradictory foundations. On the one hand he claims that a *Marxist* philosophy of science needs to be established. On the other hand he claims that critical realism can establish a Marxist *philosophy of science*. The first claim suggests that a Marxist philosophy of science should be developed within the remit of Marxism. The second claim suggests that a Marxist philosophy of science should be developed outside of the remit of Marxism. Obviously if Marxism is to expand its horizons then it is legitimate to use the ideas of other theories and philosophies. However, there is a crucial difference between incorporating these ideas within Marxism, but changing their form and content in line with Marxism (a *Marxist* philosophy of science), and developing a full-blown theoretical paradigm and then assessing the extent to which Marxism is compatible with that paradigm (a Marxist *philosophy of science*).

Yet SF asserts that he is merely 'adding to' Marxism. But this line of defence is inconsistent with his attempt to assess quantitative social theories against the qualitative paradigm of critical realism. This is because there is a tension between his assertion that he wishes to develop Marxism and his continual (sometimes implicit) fallback upon critical realism rather than Marxism to illustrate his arguments. In his chapter, for example, SF first sets out critical realist arguments *and then* fits Marx into those arguments. To flag up one illustration, in SF's chapter, he presents an argument for the transformational model of social action (TMSA) (the critical realist argument concerning structure and agency), and then shows how Marx's ideas fit with the TMSA. But notice here that he does not begin by first exploring the fundamentals of Marxism itself. This neglect means that he does not consider the extent to which Marx's own insights are defective. Nor does he consider, first, the extent to which Marx's *own* categories may be extended and developed to take account of other social forms of life beyond the strictly 'economic' *without* the need for a full-blown *critical realist* philosophy of science. Yet some of the most fruitful developments of Marxism have attempted this. The work of the Marxist linguist, V. N. Voloshinov, is one notable example, as is the work of the Marxist legal theorist, E. V. Pashukanis. In both cases Marx's discussion of historical materialism and his critique of capitalist social relations are taken as the starting point for deriving the social form of language and law respectively.

In the discussion so far I have already hinted at what I consider to be the fundamentals of Marxism, but it would be useful at this stage if I spelt out these fundamentals in a little more detail. It would seem to me that any development of Marxist theory would need to be compatible with at least two fundamentals of Marxist theory: (i) historical materialism; (ii) the application of historical materialism to the critique of political economy as outlined by Marx in the three volumes of *Capital*. I will briefly say a few words about both.

Historical materialism is premised, at the simplest level, upon the idea that societies progress through distinctive modes of production. A mode of production is characterised by the unity of forces of production (those instruments through which concrete, everyday human labour produces useful products) with the relations of production (the form which labour takes for it to engender surplus extraction within historical periods). When *class* societies are the object of analytical attention then the relationship between forces and relations of production assumes a *contradictory* unity because this relationship is defined primarily through opposing class forces that encapsulate a form of *exploitation* (see my chapter 12 for a fuller explanation). Methodologically speaking, Marx suggests in the *Grundrisse* that the relationship between forces and relations of production is a useful starting point with which to understand the systematic and contradictory connections within the concrete totality of a mode of production.

Marx extends these theoretical and methodological insights into his critique of capitalism by locating the contradictory unity of the forces and relations of production within simple capitalist production. Here Marx discovers a contradiction as that obtaining between use-value of commodities and the exchange value of commodities. Simply stated, Marx wishes to understand how different commodities come to be exchanged. Marx suggests that exchange transpires in simple capitalist production through the contradictory relationship between concrete labour and abstract labour. Marx's point here is that the social form of labour under capitalism is not merely socially productive activity – 'concrete labour' – but is also a form of objectified social relations – 'abstract labour'. Under capitalism labour not only produces social products in which social labour is itself objectified, labour also produces objective social relations themselves. The commodity, representing concrete and abstract labour, both reveals and conceals these social relations by acting as a social mediation in its own right. These abstract social relations are alienating because they invoke a social compulsion, a compulsion whose ideological form Marx terms 'commodity fetishism', which is at the same time impersonal, objective and natural (cf. Postone 1993). This social form is specific only for capitalism. It is also a social form which can be systematically unfolded into the contradictory totality of capitalist social relations. I explore this point in more detail in the next section.

Although these fundamentals are not exhaustive, they do present us with a comparative base from which to assess the incorporation of critical realism within Marxism. They also suggest that we need to revise SF's justification for the incorporation of other theoretical frameworks within Marxism. Rather than ask after the deficiencies of different forms of Marxisms and then proceed to construct an alternative paradigm with which to remedy these deficiencies, it would be more productive to start with these fundamentals and then develop them in a manner that does not violently abstract from their basis. Obviously such a reorientation in perspective does not imply that philosophy is no longer required to guide us in understanding the world. Indeed, I agree with critical realists that philosophy is a crucial factor in clarifying existing and new concepts and categories. To show this, and to extend the critical observations of critical realism made so far, I turn to the respective philosophical legacies of critical realism and Marxism. Following this discussion I return briefly to some of SF's arguments about the incorporation of critical realism to Marxism.

Philosophical legacies

It can be said with some justification that critical realism is strongly influenced by a Kantian legacy. As is well known, Kant believed that reason was the crucial instrument through which we gained knowledge about the world. This seemingly simple and common sense idea in fact challenged many of the prevailing philosophical ideas of the day. Before Kant outlined his ideas, empiricist philosophies had been widely accepted as presenting a correct standpoint about how we gain knowledge. Empiricists such as Hume and Locke had argued that we only ever gain knowledge of how the world directly appears to us. Such appearances generate ideas about the world through our experience of them. On this understanding the mind simply registers experience and passively records images of the world through the senses. Kant disputed this rather static picture of our mind. In his essay, 'What is Enlightenment?' (1784/1991), Kant defends the point that reason is a necessary prerequisite for 'man's emergence from his self-imposed immaturity' (Kant 1784/1991: 54). According to Kant, the development of reason pulled individuals out of a quagmire of dogma and set them on the royal road to transcendental critical judgement.

At a minimum, therefore, Kant argued that reason is an active and creative capacity of human beings. As a result Kant also insisted, contra empiricists, that reason imposes order and unity upon the diverse and random features of the world. Even at an intuitive level we know that we daily make connections between discrete phenomena and impose necessary and universal laws upon the world. Thus for Kant reason must have an organising capacity which goes beyond mere experience. These *a priori* faculties were necessary features of the mind (see also Sayers (1985) who provides a superbly clear discussion of Kant). From these faculties Kant constructed a philosophical system that demonstrated how we could critically comprehend the world. For example, Kant (1983) developed his transcendental position to argue for the universal properties of 'free and open discussion'. These properties rest upon three maxims: the ability to think for yourself; the ability to think from the standpoint of everyone else; and the ability to think consistently. Kant therefore developed transcendental moral laws from his construction of the *a priori* faculties of human understanding.

There are a number of reasons why critical realism can be situated within a Kantian legacy. In the first instance, critical realism is a *transcendental* social theory. At its simplest, transcendental realism aims to identify the underlying 'causal powers' of objects. This is achieved through a method of abstraction termed 'retroduction'. This type of abstraction is primarily concerned to isolate the necessary and internal properties of an object, namely its 'causal powers'. Once identified, the diverse but contingently combined determination of these properties can be examined at a more concrete level. This move is particularly important because only then will we be able to identify the outcome of the transfactually acting causal mechanism. An example might be the internal relationship between landlord and tenant, a relationship which assumes many guises in different contexts. In this way a precise definition of the object can be arrived at so that when a move is made back to the concrete one can gain a more accurate understanding of the object's interaction with a diverse range of elements. The finished product is the movement: concrete → abstract, abstract → concrete (see Sayer 1994: 87).

Critical realists claim that abstraction can be carried out by building a model of the generative mechanism via the already existing stock of cognitive resources that we have about the phenomenon. Information is collected about the generative mechanism which, if it were to exist, would account for the phenomenon in question (Bhaskar 1989: 19–20). A three-phase scheme emerges:

> science identifies a phenomenon (or a range of phenomena), constructs explanations for it and empirically tests its explanations, leading to the identification of the generative mechanism at work, which then becomes the phenomenon to be explained; and so on.
>
> (Bhaskar 1989: 20)

Correspondingly the *intransitive* realm (the real entities and structures of the natural world) can only be explored through the *transitive* realm (models and concepts of the natural world) (Bhaskar 1978: 21–4). However, in 'normal' conditions closed experimental systems do not exist. Indeed the social sciences, whose object of investigation revolves around unpredictable human behaviour, do not have the luxury of experimental closed systems. Mechanisms and causal powers cannot survive in a vacuum but only within open systems.

Critical realists thereby break from previous Kantian theories of the philosophy of science by showing that under some conditions models about the world can explore a deeper aspect of reality (Archer *et al.* 1998: xi). Yet it is also the case that critical realism still contains residues of a form of Kantianism. This can be seen in the chosen use of the retroductive method of abstraction. Retroduction clearly stresses the necessity of thought to discover underlying realities. In particular it wishes to go beyond how the world appears because such appearances tend to conceal and to distort reality. In a manner reminiscent of Kant, it is believed that only thought at some distance from the distorting influence of appearances can explore reality. In this way a type of dualism is theoretically reimposed whereby reality is taken to be hidden behind appearances. Thought can grasp the nature of this reality, but it can only do so through the rational subject. Those causal powers eventually retroduced do not therefore share an internal relationship to the real world through either appearances or experience (Sayers 1985: 29–31).

The problems here for critical realism can be appreciated in greater depth if we momentarily pause to consider the main philosophical legacy of Marxism. Here the leading thinker is, of course, Hegel. In *The Science of Logic*, Hegel suggests that the essence of an object must *necessarily* appear to consciousness. As Hegel says when describing an object: 'It is the manifesting of its essence in such a manner that this essence consists simply and solely in being that which manifests itself' (Hegel 1812–1816/1969: 528). But even though essence reveals itself through appearance, appearance is not exactly the same as essence. This implies that even the illusions we may hold about an object are still aspects of an essence. 'Essence *appears*, so that it is now *real illusory being*, since the moments of illusory being have Existence' (Hegel 1812–1816/1969: 499–500). Correspondingly our subjective experience of an object is based upon a necessary connection with the object in question. There can be no absolute separation of the objective world and our subjective experiences of it, even if those subjective experiences only reveal partial aspects of the world. Our experience of an object and the categories we develop to explain the object are informed by the reality of the object in one way or another. Knowledge *reflects* the object-in-itself to various degrees (see also my chapter 12).

This is an important point to the extent that it suggests that how we think about the world is necessarily confined within the determining limits of the world. Even so, gaining such knowledge is an evolving process wherein our initial methodological starting point is increasingly complexified as new knowledge is gained. When we therefore return to our starting point it too has become complexified as we now understand more thoroughly some of the interconnecting relationships bound up with our initial starting point within the same determining limits.

An example of Hegel's thinking here is provided by Marx. In the *Grundrisse* Marx (1858/1973) suggests that the concept 'population' presupposes an understanding of the determinative social relationships bound up within the concepts 'wage labour', 'capital', etc. These determinative social relations themselves presuppose 'thinner abstractions'. Once we have worked our way back to the most abstract and simple determinations (the thinnest abstractions, if you like) of a specific set of social relations we can then comprehend how these social relations are reflected and refracted within the concept 'population'. Only now the concept 'population' can be understood as inhering within a specific determining totality. Thus the concept 'population' is not the *beginning* of the analysis but its *result*. That is to say, the diverse determination(s) embedded within the concept 'population' can only be fully derived *after* it has been placed within the more determinate concepts comprising a systematic totality. Thus abstraction moves 'forwards', as progression ('population' is placed within a systematic closed totality), and 'backwards', as a retrogression ('population' is complexified and concretised as a moment, or social form, of the diverse forms of that totality). What we create, therefore, is a circular movement in method (Arthur 1998).

We can now see why the critical realist method of retroduction is incompatible with the Hegelian–Marxist methodological position. This can be seen more clearly through the manner in which the relationship of 'simple' and 'complex' is understood. For example, critical realists insist that we first isolate the simple and abstract structure of a causal power and then take the analysis down further levels of abstraction in order to explore its more complex and concrete manifestations. Method is characterised by a move in thought of a simple model to a more complex model. The element connecting this movement is 'thought' or the *transitive* realm. This movement, however, conflates 'thinking' with 'reality' for it is believed that thinking about simple aspects of the world actually reflect simple realities whilst complex concepts reflect complex realities. In addition, it is believed that complexity is linked in some way or another to the contingent, open and indeterminate real, while simplicity is related to thought. Thought only becomes complex when it seeks to apprehend the complex structuring of reality. But, as Shamsavari (1991: 42) notes, 'this movement . . . is the form in which the fixed opposition between simple and complex is reproduced rather than solved'. If this is the case then critical realists reinstate a *linear* movement of simple to complex corresponding to a movement from abstract to concrete. In other words, retroduction moves forward, but does not create the accompanying circular move of going backwards (see also Roberts 2001).

SF himself provides us with an example to illustrate the problem here. In his chapter he unintentionally presents a linear account of the underlying structures, mechanisms, relations and powers that are necessary 'to sustain a system whereby the relations between people (as producing units) appear in the form of a relation between things (commodities)'. He wishes to explain this phenomenon through the use of 'contrastive explanation'.

> I will *not* ask: why does labouring activity under capitalist conditions appear in the value form? Rather I will ask: why does labouring activity under capitalist conditions appear in the value form when labouring activity under non capitalist conditions does not require this form?
>
> (p. 78)

SF's justification for the use of contrastive explanation is to pinpoint 'what is essential to capitalism'. But this seems a strange methodological route for a Marxist to take. For it is surely the case that Marx takes the opposite methodological route. In order to understand the specificity of capitalism

Marx *begins* his analysis with capitalism. Hence his reason for starting with simple capitalist production via the commodity. From what we now know of Marx's debt to Hegel this should not surprise us. Marx was interested in comprehending the dynamics of the systematic totality of capitalism. And when exploring this totality it made perfect sense to start an analysis from *within* that totality.

SF's debt to critical realism, however, prompts him to start at a much higher trans-historical level of abstraction, namely at the level of the material basis of human life, and then work progressively down levels of abstraction until he finally reaches capitalism. Such a route invites a logical-historical reading of human progress whereby successive models of human development are seen to naturally evolve from one to another (cf. Arthur 1998). Indeed, the absence of the category 'contradiction' encourages this interpretation of SF's analysis because it is difficult to see why one mode of production will necessarily be transformed into another mode of production. Instead we have a linear progression from one model to another.

This linear presentation and its corresponding complexity is shadowed by the increasing complexity of thought constructing successive complex models. Hence the move from the model of non-capitalist societies to the model of capitalist society which SF makes in his chapter. But this type of model-building also nourishes a non-historical analysis of the world in two respects. First, the specific social relations of non-capitalist societies such as Stalinism and feudalism are collapsed into one model, 'a highly abstract, stylised non-capitalist system'. Yet there is a world of difference between Stalinist and feudal societies. Second, the exploration of models instead of systems also encourages a non-historical analysis of the internal relations associated with a specific mode of production. For example, SF suggests that capitalism can be defined as 'a system whereby the relations between people (as producing units) appear in the form of a relations between things (commodities)' (p. 81). However, this abstraction appears to misinterpret Marx's abstraction of the *social form* of capitalism. As I have already suggested above, commodity production under capitalism is defined through the dominance of *abstract* labour over concrete producers. This is an abstraction produced everyday by labour itself. SF's abstraction, by contrast, draws attention to the dominance of concrete commodities over individuals. But this is a dominance which has been prevalent in many non-capitalist societies. Thus we have still as yet to discover the social form of commodity production under capitalism through this abstraction.

As a result of this underlying theoretical difference, it must be doubted whether critical realism can act as a philosophical underlabourer for Marxism. A more suitable position to take would be one that sought to develop the theoretical categories of historical materialism themselves rather than incorporate concepts and categories incompatible with historical materialism.

What contemporary Marxism can learn from critical realism (Andrew Brown)

I articulate below a view which adopts some of the respective arguments made by SF and JR, whilst disagreeing with others. SF's case for a 'full-blown' philosophy of science will be endorsed and amplified. Had SF's 'opponent' been an 'open Marxist' critic such as Gunn (1989) then the very need for Marxist philosophy would have been put into question. In this context, it will be argued, against JR, that the task of articulating such a philosophy is indeed as urgent, for contemporary Marxism, as SF suggests. Furthermore, the success of critical realism across a broad range of traditional disciplinary fields suggests that contemporary Marxism has much to learn from critical realism, not only as regards the flagging of the need for philosophy, but also as regards the content of any such philosophy. There are simply too many genuine Marxist adherents to, or sympathisers with, critical realism for the extreme rejections of critical realism recommended by some of its detractors to be wholly accepted. Structural causality, the notion of tendencies, the key distinction between thought and object, the notion of emergence, etc. must, as critical realist Marxists argue, be upheld together in a unified Marxist philosophy. But these lessons do not extend, I will argue, to the need for contemporary Marxism to embrace the *specifically critical realist* (or dialectical critical realist) articulation of structural causality, emergence, and so on. My chapter 9 argues that E. V. Ilyenkov's Marxist philosophy provides, preserves and transcends the crucial critical realist concepts. Here I briefly note the historical and theoretic context that informed Ilyenkov's philosophy.

Critical realism and the need for Marxist philosophy

The content of critical realism and the diverse disciplinary backgrounds of critical realist sympathisers, provide a salient lesson to Marxism. Critical realism has attracted followers from a very broad range of disciplines in the social sciences, humanities and beyond. One explanation for this broad appeal must lie in a general dissatisfaction with the respective traditional materials taught in philosophy of science and methodology courses aimed at social scientists, and at other practitioners. It is useful, in order to comprehend critical realism's success, to distinguish two broad types of such courses. First, there are courses in the philosophy of science. Second, there are diverse 'methodology' courses where specific methods prevalent in a particular discipline are taught.

Take, first, the 'philosophy of science'. Whilst there have been many diverse developments within the philosophy of science discipline itself, it remains the case that the names of Popper, Kuhn, Lakatos and Feyerabend are likely to be the first that social scientists will invoke as exemplifying the 'philosophy of science'. The debate amongst these philosophers regarding both the correct description of, and the correct prescription for, scientific progress is by no means irrelevant to social researchers. The debate sensitises the researcher to issues surrounding 'falsifiability' and to the social context of science. However, the relevance might well be described as limited. Critical realism correctly stresses that the debate does not contain much explicit reference to the nature of the mind-independent real world, even though some such world is a presupposition of the debate. It is, in other words, a largely epistemological debate, leaving the researcher without purchase on the mind-independent world that is the object of research. The impression that can be left is that any 'abstract' discourse must inherently lack such 'real world' content, and hence be inherently lacking in practical salience.

Turning to the diverse 'methodology' courses, here two broad strands can usefully (if, again rather sweepingly) be picked out. On the one hand there are 'quantitative' courses concentrating, for example, on the theory and practice of statistical inference. On the other hand there are 'qualitative' courses considering, for example, the theory and practice of questionnaire design. Both quantitative and qualitative courses and methods can, if used well, be very useful, of course. But they are *difficult* to use in practice, i.e. in the context of a real world object. And, by their very nature, such courses must focus on the *method* rather than on the *object*. The impression, once again, is left that a high level of generality necessarily implies abstraction from explicit consideration of mind-independent reality (i.e. a neglect of ontology).

The critical realist argument demonstrates that philosophy in general, and ontology in particular, need not be a mere side issue, of little practical relevance. Critical realism articulates what practitioners often already feel implicitly to be the case. There are many statements at the level of generality of philosophy that refer to the real, mind-independent world. Through such reference, these concepts are practically important. First, there is the basic fact of science itself. Through the *hard practical effort* of science, knowledge of the mind-independent real world is obtained. Astonishingly, this fact is not made explicit in the debate between Popper, Kuhn and Lakatos. It may be implicitly recognised, but the failure to make it explicit leads to an unwarranted divorce of philosophy from reality. For example, the concept of 'paradigm' or its Lakatosian counterpart, 'scientific research program', refers to the realm of knowledge rather than to the object of that knowledge, the real world: to epistemology rather than ontology. Critical realism demonstrates that the Kuhnian/Lakatosian perspective must have a real world analogue in *ontological* 'emergence'. The recognition that reality is layered in successive emergent strata is in turn able to explain the development of new 'paradigms' noted by Kuhn and Lakatos. The development of a new paradigm may simply correspond to the uncovering of a hitherto unknown stratum. More generally, the notion of emergence is tied to the critical realist notions of structures, mechanisms, tendencies and, for the social realm, the notions of social structure and of the emergence of mind and hence of human agency. All these notions referring to the real world, are practically useful and are located at the level of generality of philosophy. They are entwined philosophical concepts, articulated by critical realism, yet absent from the philosophy and methodology that is most familiar to practitioners and students in the human (and indeed natural) sciences.

The intuitive appeal of the critical realist ontology, coupled with the absence of ontological considerations from the philosophy and methodology traditionally encountered by social scientific practitioners, goes some way towards explaining the breadth of the appeal of critical realism. Critical realism thematises salient and general features that practitioners actually encounter in research, salient features of the real world. Thereby critical realism demonstrates that concepts at such a high level of generality (the trans-historical level) need not be lifeless, sterile or without practical import. Armed with the critical realist ontology it is possible to critique both the 'traditional' philosophy of science and the varied quantitative and qualitative 'methodologies', encountered by researchers. Critical realism foregrounds the need to adapt the research methodology to the object and not vice versa. Quantitative and qualitative methods of statistical inference can be assessed in terms of their applicability to the object. The object itself can be grasped as a natural or social structure with attendant mechanisms. As a result the most prevalent *theories* within disciplines can be interrogated on methodological grounds. For example, many theories existing under the rubric of poststructuralism, postmodernism and social constructionism stand revealed as one-sided: such theories recognise the conceptual aspect but not the objective aspect of science. The converse trend towards greater and greater mathematical sophistication within economics can likewise be recognised as one-sided. Here the problem arises from recognition of the quantitative but not the crucial qualitative characteristics of the economy and human agency.

The lesson Marxism can learn from critical realism, then, is the need to articulate Marxist and hence real-world concepts at the level of generality of philosophy, i.e. at the trans-historical level. Moreover, Marxism can recognise within the critical realist concepts, a glimpse of just what Marxist philosophy should, and, I would argue, Marx and Engel's philosophy does in fact, embrace: the concepts of structural causality, the distinction between thought and mind-independent object, the notion of tendencies, a conception of social structure and agency, the notion of emergence, the practical side of knowledge, and so on.

To illustrate the point, it is useful to consider two well-known 'alternatives' to critical realism, both explicitly Marxist philosophies. First, there is the case of Althusserianism. The initial promise and subsequent demise of Althusserian Marxism fostered attacks on the very notion of Marxist philosophy (e.g. E. P. Thompson, Open Marxism). Ultimately Althusserian Marxism failed to uphold successfully a mind-independent reality, fallibly knowable by human agents endowed with free will. Critical realism attempts to uphold that promise, and thus is argued by some proponents (Collier 1989) to fill the specifically *philosophical* gap left by the demise of Althusserianism.

Second, there is the case of the many and varied strands of Hegelian influenced Marxism, as, for example, represented by JR's contribution to this book. The recent revival of such strands has prompted the coining of a new phrase, 'new dialectics' (Arthur 1993). New dialectics, in all its variety, does not *stress*, in the strident fashion of critical realism, a set of philosophical concepts explicitly and clearly referring to a mind-independent reality. As a rough approximation, it is possible to characterise the varied strands of new dialectics as united by a rejection of Marx's own philosophical remarks to the effect that Hegel is an idealist. This contrasts sharply with the strident critical realist (and dialectical critical realist) critique of Hegel. To be sure, it is possible that the philosophical content of some strands of new dialectics is very close to that of critical realism, despite the outward differences of emphasis. Thus Arthur's chapter in this book draws upon dialectical critical realism. But for the majority of new dialecticians, the clear different outward emphasis does suggest significant philosophical differences with critical realism. Certainly, it is critical realism, and not new dialectics, that articulates explicitly the key notions of structural causality, etc.

Why Marxism should not be 'augmented' by critical realism

Why, given the lessons that can be learnt from critical realism, should Marxism not embrace critical realism with open arms? There are two related aspects to my answer. First, and as JR has pointed out, it is important to recognise that there may be more than one philosophy that stresses a mind-independent reality, emergence, human agency and practice and so on. That is to say, SF's case for a 'full-blown' philosophy of science, containing key critical realist notions, a case that I have tried to amplify and extend above, does not establish the need for the *specifically critical realist* attempt to sustain such a philosophy, even where key concepts such as structural causality are endorsed. Second, there *are* alternative Marxist philosophical positions, able to embrace and transcend critical realism. Of course, I cannot defend this latter claim here, and the reader is referred to my chapter below but it may be useful to indicate briefly the historical and theoretical location of my preferred philosophy, *viz.* 'materialist dialectics'. Bakhurst (1991) has demonstrated in detail that the history of Russian philosophy in the twentieth century does not display the sterility that many in the West had assumed, given the Stalinist regime. Rather, a vibrant philosophical tradition existed in defiance of the authorities. It was in this context that E. V. Ilyenkov (1977) gained prominence through his articulation of a materialist dialectics, drawing upon Marx and Engels, and upon the rich vein of philosophical debate within Russia. In this way it can be argued that

Ilyenkov was able to develop a 'full-blown' Marxist philosophy from *within* the Marxist tradition, in the way that JR endorses above.

Notes

1 I opt to leave a discussion of political practice out of this chapter partly for brevity, but also because, as noted above, there is no one-to-one mapping between a particular political practice, a particular theory and a particular philosophy anyway.
2 Clearly, the debate between critical realists and Marxists covers more than philosophy of science, as many of the contributions to this collection show – especially those contributions from Brown, Collier, Creaven, Ehrbar, and Roberts.
3 'Asides' *vis-à-vis* laws as tendencies are to be found, e.g. in Fine and Harris (1979); MacBride (1977); Meikle (1985); Ollman (1993); Reuten and Williams (1989); Ruben (1979); Sayer (1983); Wilson (1991) and Zeleny (1980). One of the more detailed discussions of tendencies is Cutler *et al.* (1977; part II, especially chapter 4), although even here one is left wanting more discussion. Certain other places where one would expect to find at least an 'aside' we find no mention at all of laws as tendencies – e.g. Farr and Ball (1984) and Murray (1988).
4 This might not be strictly accurate because, to stay with the example, even the activated power of a bicycle locked in a garden shed might effect the owner's decision about using the car to travel to work. Examples like these are highly context dependent and must be treated so.
5 A mechanism, typically, comprises of a set of sub-mechanisms and sub-sub-mechanisms and so on. A bicycle is a mechanism, but it comprises of sub-mechanisms such as wheels, which themselves comprise of sub-sub-mechanisms such as spokes and so on. See Jessop's notion of tendencies as being 'doubly tendential' in this volume.
6 This section draws heavily on Lawson 1997. Hausman (1992, section 8.1) also provides a useful discussion of tendencies.
7 My necessarily brief comments here do not do justice to the sophistication of Reuten's work. He is well aware of the notion of tendency used by critical realists which he refers to as a 'power notion of tendency' (1997: 157). His claim is that, despite considerable ambiguity even in Marx's work, Marx probably does not operate with tendency as power, but with tendency as result. If Reuten is correct, and Marx does operate with tendency as result, then (in my humble opinion) Marx is mistaken.
8 This is a typical example of how the vacuum created by the absence of a full-blown Marxist philosophy of science is often filled by Marxists borrowing topics from non-Marxist philosophies of science – with damaging consequences for Marxism.

Bibliography

Archer, M., Bhaskar, R., Collier, A., Lawson, T. and Norrie, A. (1998) 'General Introduction', in M. Archer, R. Bhaskar, A. Collier, T. Lawson and A. Norrie (eds) *Critical Realism: Essential Readings*, London: Routledge.

Arthur, C. (1993) 'Review of Ali Shamsavari's *Dialectics and Social Theory: The Logic of Capital*', *Capital and Class* 50: 175–80.

—— (1998) 'Systematic Dialectics', *Science and Society* 62 (3): 447–59.

Bakhurst, D. (1991) *Consciousness and Revolution in Soviet Philosophy: From the Bolsheviks to Evald Ilyenkov*, Cambridge: Cambridge University Press.

Bhaskar, R. (1978) *A Realist Theory of Science*, 2nd edition, London: Verso.
—— (1989) *Reclaiming Reality*, London: Verso.
Collier, A. (1989) *Scientific Realism and Socialist Thought*, Hemel Hempstead: Harvester Wheatsheaf.
Cutler, A., Hindess, B., Hirst, P. and Hussain, A. (1977) *Marx's Capital and Capitalism Today*, London: Routledge & Kegan Paul.
Farr, J. and Ball, T. (eds) (1984) *After Marx*, Cambridge: Cambridge University Press.
Fine, B. and Harris, L. (1979) *Rereading Capital*, London: Macmillan.
Gunn, R. (1989) 'Marxism and Philosophy: A Critique of Critical Realism', *Capital and Class* 37: 86–116.
Hausman, D. (1992) *The Inexact and Separate Science of Economics*, Cambridge: Cambridge University Press.
Hegel, G. W. F. (1812–1816/1969) *Science of Logic*, translated by A.V. Miller, London: Allen & Unwin.
Ilyenkov, E.V. (1977) *Dialectical Logic: Essays on its Theory and History*, translated by H. Campbell Creighton, Moscow: Progress.
Kant, I. (1784/1991) 'An Answer to the Question: What is the Enlightenment?' in H. Reiss (ed.) *Kant's Political Writings*, Cambridge: Cambridge University Press.
—— (1983) *Critique of Pure Reason*, translated by N. Kemp-Smith, London: Macmillan.
Lawson, T. (1997) *Economics and Reality*, London: Routledge.
Lipton, P. (1993) *Inference to the Best Explanation*, London: Routledge.
MacBride, W. (1977) *The Philosophy of Marx*, London: Hutchinson.
Marx, K. (1858/1973) *Grundrisse*, London: Pelican.
—— (1984) *Capital*, vol. III, London: Lawrence & Wishart.
Meikle, S. (1985) *Essentialism in the Thought of Karl Marx*, Gloucester: Duckworth.
Murray, P. (1988) *Marx's Theory of Scientific Knowledge*, Atlantic Highlands: Humanities Academic Press.
Ollman, B. (1993) *Dialectical Investigations*, London: Routledge.
Postone, M. (1993) *Time, Labor and Social Domination: A Reinterpretation of Marx's Critical Social Theory*, Cambridge: Cambridge University Press.
Reuten, G. (1997) 'The Notion of Tendency in Marx's 1894 Law of Profit', in F. Mosely and M. Campbell (eds) *New Investigations of Marx's Method*, New Jersey: Humanities Press.
Reuten, G. and Williams, M. (1989) *Value-Form and the State: The Tendencies of Accumulation and the Determination of Economic Policy in Capitalist Society*, London: Routledge.
Roberts, J. M. (2001 forthcoming) 'Realistic Spatial Abstraction? Marxist Observations of a Claim within Critical Realist Geography'. *Progress in Human Geography*.
Ruben, D-H. (1979) *Marxism and Materialism: A Study in Marxist Theory of Knowledge*, Sussex: Harvester Wheatsheaf.
Sayer, A. (1994) *Method in Social Science: A Realist Approach*, 2nd edition, London: Routledge.
Sayer, D. (1983) *Marx's Method: Ideology, Science and Critique in 'Capital'*, London: Macmillan.
Sayers, S. (1985) *Reality and Reason*, Oxford: Basil Blackwell.
Shamsavari, A. (1991) *Dialectics and Social Theory: The Logic of Capital*, Devon: Merlin Books.
Wilson, H. (1991) *Marx's Critical Dialectical Procedure*, London: Routledge.
Zeleny, J. (1980) *The Logic of Marx*, Oxford: Basil Blackwell.

2 Five ways in which critical realism can help Marxism[1]

Jonathan Joseph

Introduction

The claim that Marxism is in something of a crisis has been fashionable for many years. However, beyond questions of theoretical consistency, we are confronted with the real problem of Marxism's place in the world. Perry Anderson famously linked the development of Western Marxism – and its turn away from politics and class struggle, its emphasis on philosophy and culture and its pessimistic outlook – to the real world triumphs of fascism, Stalinism and later the effects of post-war capitalist society (Anderson 1979). Since then the Marxist Left has suffered further decline. The collapse of 'Communism' has had a bad effect, further discrediting Marxism in the eyes of the working class and giving renewed impetus to the ideological offensive of the ruling class. Marxist theory, meanwhile, undergoes a further process of mutation as its most dogmatic and intransigent aspects are used to justify a process of 're-thinking', leading to an array of 'new realist' and 'post-Marxist' alternatives.

In this context, critical realism can provide some fresh hope for those who wish to retain the essence of Marxism while remaining critical of some Marxist approaches. Below we shall outline the critical realist approach alongside an exploration of the weakness of Marxist theory. The aim, however, is not to replace Marxist theory but to correct it. Critical realist philosophy can help us engage in a process of re-thinking Marxism without having to re-think it in a post-Marxist way. The benefit of critical realism as opposed to more overtly Marxist philosophies is that:

1 Critical realism comes to Marxism 'from outside' in the sense that it is not intrinsically Marxist, but approaches Marxism in a scientific way. By distancing itself from Marxism (by presenting itself as a conceptual analysis) critical realism is better placed to provide a genuinely critical appraisal.
2 It insists on a degree of precision and rigour missing from much of the pseudo-theorising of 'Marxist philosophy'. It provides a new framework for the conceptualisation of social relations.

3   Against the dominant trend of inter-subjective, praxis-oriented philoso-
     phising, critical realism advocates an ontological approach that moves
     beyond questions of knowledge and action to ask what the world itself
     must be like for these to be the case.

However, it is necessary to begin by stating affiliations and attachments.
A commitment to Marxism is taken as given, the question is whether critical
realism can help Marxism in any way. In answering this positively, the
article draws almost exclusively on the earlier works of critical realism. This
is not to say that *Dialectic* and other more recent works have nothing to offer
Marxism. But they are regarded as the beginning of a different kind of
approach, a much more ambitious project which moves away from the idea
that critical realism can work alongside Marxism. This is not the place to go
into a full-scale critique of (transcendental) dialectical critical realism, but
it is necessary to state that this article is informed by the belief that the
systematic philosophising of Roy Bhaskar's latest work is incompatible with
and undermines a Marxist study of society. Basic Marxist concepts like
class, mode of production and structural determination are pushed aside by
Bhaskar's ubiquitous master–slave relations, his non-specific dialectic of
freedom, the transcendental notion of ethics and the primacy given to non-
being over being. If what follows seems like a re-statement of old ideas, it is
because these old ideas are the best ideas. Against the ambitious claims of
Bhaskar Mark II, not to mention the re-incarnated Bhaskar of *From East to
West*, it is necessary to re-stake our ground. By establishing this ground, an
alternative project to the current one can be developed. It is not yet time to
sound the charge of the left Bhaskarians, but it is time at least to prepare our
battle tent!

Critical realist underlabouring

Perhaps the first and most important question is: what is Marxist philosophy?
It is the very difficulty of this question that makes philosophy necessary.

  In contrast to other attempts at social theory, Marxism maintains that
it alone can provide an adequate degree of scientificity, and that other
theories – like classical economics, functionalist sociology or behaviourist
psychology – are inadequate, partial, misleading, false or in some other way
'ideological'. But how do we measure Marxism against something that is
not strictly 'scientific' – namely philosophy? And if philosophy is distinct
from science, can there be a Marxist 'philosophy', either as something distin-
guishable from Marxist science or as a critical part of it? Our contention
here will be that philosophy is indeed distinct from science and that this distinction must be maintained if we want to preserve the possibility of a critical
appraisal of science. However, this very distinction also means that there is
no 'Marxist' philosophy as such, for Marxism will be defined as a theory
that studies society and develops a scientific ontology, while philosophy, it

is maintained, is not a study of society in this direct sense, but is a study of science and other cognitive practices, including theories of society (Marxism). Of course science and Marxism are themselves social practices and in this sense philosophy does study a part of society. But the wider claims about the nature of society must go through such a social practice, they cannot be made directly. In Bhaskar's view the:

> syncategorematic (or, as it were, only proxy-referential) character of the nevertheless irreducible discourse of philosophy . . . has to be contrasted with the directly referential character of social scientific discourse.
>
> (Bhaskar 1989a: 50)

Thus Marxism and philosophy are distinct in the sense that they are concerned with different types of knowledge. While Marxism produces first-order knowledge of society, philosophy is second-order knowledge in that it is knowledge of this knowledge of society (just as it may also reflect on the knowledge of natural science without itself becoming a natural science). The fact that Marxism directly studies society while philosophy studies the study of society (Marxism) means that philosophy cannot be Marxism even if philosophy must operate *through* Marxism. But in commenting on Marxism's findings, claims, theories and methods, critical realism does set itself up against other attempts at philosophy. In this sense, critical realism is a complement to Marxism but a rival to 'Marxist philosophy'. In particular, it is necessary to critique those attempts to blend Marxism and philosophy together such as might be found in the 'praxis' Marxism of Lukács (1971): Korsch (1970): Gramsci (1971) and Sartre (1976). Although praxis Marxism sees itself as rebelling against the mechanical viewpoint of 'orthodox Marxism' more often than not it imposes its own teleological schema where history becomes the process of confirmation of subjective knowledge or class consciousness. In other words, the praxis Marxists confront objectivist teleology with their own subjectivist teleology (I will return to this issue later). Whether Marxist theory adopts the mechanical, positivistic and determinist evolutionism of orthodox dialectical materialism or whether we accept Korsch's view that the 'emergence of Marxist theory is, in Hegelian–Marxist terms, only the "other side" of the emergence of the real proletarian movement' (Korsch 1970: 42), it seems that the common error is to *impose* a philosophical framework onto historical materialism thereby pre-judging and undermining an actual scientific investigation of real historical relations.

We need a more humble philosophical project that sees its role as clarifying Marxism rather than orchestrating it. In his early work Bhaskar sets out his conception of critical realist philosophy as an underlabourer to the sciences, producing second order knowledge and clarifying questions of methodology (e.g. Bhaskar 1997: 10, 1989a: 8). Although this may seem a modest task, it is one that is crucially important and potentially explosive. For while it may be science that attempts to show us how the world is, philosophy can help clarify the method of this science in order for us to see more clearly.

In social science this is all the more important given a) the close relationship between social theory and society (theory attempts to explain society while also being the product of it), and b) the debates and confusions which exist within social science and Marxist theory. Therefore, even if philosophy does not *directly* analyse society, it certainly analyses social scientific theories about the social world. To simplify, we might say that a) the philosophy of social science analyses the practice of social science while b) social science itself analyses the social world. Philosophy's relation to the social world (as object of analysis) is as an indirect or second order critique.

The importance of critical realism and its superiority over the various attempts at 'Marxist philosophy' lies in the fact that it is necessarily 'outside' Marxism. It is true that the nature of the social and its conceptual aspect means that critical realism and social analysis do get entwined. However, critical realism conceives of philosophy in a more general sense as related to a range of sciences. This is important because when we do start to sort through the confusions within Marxist theory, we need a tool that is intimately connected, but not reducible, to the scientific practice itself. If we abandon the distinction between Marxism and philosophy, then we abandon any hope of critical scrutiny of Marxism's method.

Critical realism, conceived of as a philosophy, therefore plays this underlabouring role. And if Marxism is conceived of as the main element of social science, then in this field, critical realism's task is to act as an underlabourer to Marxism, commenting on its method, practice and claims. As Andrew Collier points out, although it does not yield new knowledge, philosophy is a *cognitive* practice. The knowledge it draws upon comes from the sciences including Marxist social science (Collier 1989: 120).

According to our theory, therefore, Marxism should be seen as a scientific analysis of society. But in order to fulfil this role it needs to draw on an explicitly critical realist philosophy capable of sustaining an ontological account of the world and maintaining careful scrutiny of the scientific method employed. If we conceive of critical realism as an underlabourer then we see it working alongside Marxism. This relationship must be kept in careful balance. Philosophy should not intrude on Marxism and impose its own schema on our understanding of the world. Only Marxism itself can provide the analysis of the specific features of the social world for this is the task of science rather than philosophy. However, philosophy can assess the nature of these claims and insist on a scientific framework that is consistent with a critical realist ontology. This then is the first way in which critical realism can help Marxism. This is also the most general way in which critical realism helps Marxism since the underlabouring role is embodied in the four other ways that follow.

Ontological primacy and the intransitive dimension

The chief errors of both sides of the objective–subjective debate are the imposition of a philosophical schema on reality and the conflation of our knowledge of reality with the real world itself. On the side of objectivist mechanical materialism we find writers like Plekhanov who draws his philosophical schema from the evolutionary theories of Darwin, torn from their specific (natural) context and reapplied to the social domain in a non-emergent way that fails to do justice to the specificity of the social as a level with its own emergent laws, properties and dynamics. Plekhanov combines this with an objectified version of the philosophies of Hegel and Feuerbach drawing heavily on the empirical generalisations of Engels' philosophical work and the most schematic and mechanical interpretation of Marx's view of historical development:

> Thus, the properties of the geographical environment determine the development of the productive forces, which in its turn determines the development of the economic forces, and therefore all other social relations.
>
> (Plekhanov 1920: 49)

It is not surprising that most of the mechanical determinists of the Second International became renegades who abandoned revolutionary practice. The development of the productive forces became the new historical *Geist* that would ensure a socialist future, allowing the Second International to get on with the day-to-day business of reformism. As Kautsky argued: 'Our task is not to organise the revolution, but to organise ourselves *for* the revolution; it is not to *make* the revolution, but *to take advantage of it*' (quoted in Salvadori 1990: 21). It is understandable why, in opposing the politics of these figures, and in opposition to vulgar Stalinism, theorists like Lukács, Gramsci, Korsch and Sartre should emphasise the concept of praxis. But while Korsch, for example, is correct to link revisionism to the development of reformist trade unions and political parties, and while he is correct to suggest that the abstract nature of 'vulgar Marxism' reflects the need to separate it from actual struggles, by claiming that 'the Marxist system is the theoretical expression of the revolutionary movement of the proletariat' (Korsch 1970: 42), he is *reducing* Marxism to the philosophical viewpoint or world-outlook of a subject, the chief error of 'historicism'.

Following Bhaskar, we can say that these theorists embrace a historicism that reduces Marxism to the theoretical expression of the working class, that rubbishes other forms of knowledge (including, often natural science) as bourgeois ideology, and that sees Marxism as a self-sufficient, comprehensive and totalising standpoint (Bhaskar 1991: 172). This is perfectly expressed in Lukács' view that 'self-knowledge coincides with knowledge of the whole so that the proletariat is at one and the same time the subject and object of its knowledge' (Lukács 1971: 20). Instead of being a science, Marxism becomes a perspective, or world-view. This immediately poses the danger of relativism as Marxism is no longer defined in relation to knowledge of the real world. In order to avoid the conclusion that there is no objective truth and that one group's view of the world is as good as another's, the praxis philosophers seek to give certain groups a prominent historical place and purpose and so they adopt a teleology. This focuses on a key subject such as the party or the proletariat whose viewpoint is to be confirmed by history.

Ironically then, it is philosophy that must return to rescue Marxism from philosophy for, in its underlabouring capacity, critical realism argues that we must insist on the separateness of the world and the knowledge we have of the world. Just because the world is revealed to us through knowledge and action, this does not mean that this is all there is to it. Critical realism takes an unashamedly *ontological* standpoint that focuses on the independently existing reality that knowledge and action try to comprehend or change. This independently existing reality is described by Bhaskar as an *intransitive* realm. It is contrasted with the *transitive* knowledge that tries to comprehend or explain it. Indeed, the one reinforces the other for a transitive realm of knowledge would be incomprehensible without an independently existing reality to which it refers. Therefore, the intransitive is a condition for the intelligibility of the transitive; reality must exist independently of our knowledge of it if scientific development and debate are to have any relevance.

The fact that science is an organised human practice that takes place in a social context and relies on pre-existing, socially produced knowledge means that philosophy has an important role to play in examining its methods. It must try to render explicit what is already implicitly assumed. It must indeed, as the praxis theorists emphasise, take account of the particular class standpoint of the agents involved. But in taking an ontological stance it must ask what theory implies about the nature of the world itself. By insisting on the separateness of transitive and intransitive it rejects the stance that sees thought as a direct reflection of reality. The separateness of the two realms means that there is no direct 'correspondence' between thought and its object.

This necessarily leads us to embrace some form of epistemic relativism whereby we recognise that there is no *direct* correspondence between knowledge and its object. This does not mean that we bring in a judgmental relativism as the post-structuralists and post-Marxists would wish, only that we recognise the necessarily social character of knowledge. While insisting on the separate realms of transitive knowledge and intransitive object, critical realism does recognise the specific nature of social science, in particular, the relational aspect that social sciences are part of their own field of enquiry and that they are a product of the same society that they seek to explain. Against the rationalism of the Althusserian school, it must be stressed that social theory cannot stand above society in a haughty scientific manner. It is already necessarily 'contaminated' by social, historical and ideological elements. Nevertheless, Marxist explanation should aim at being 'scientific' in attempting to provide the best possible explanation of the way that the world is. In doing this it should attempt to show that the social world is more than just a bundle of meanings, actions and understandings but is comprised of real, intransitive social structures.

Structure, strata and social transformation

Critical realism argues that the intelligibility of knowledge of society presupposes that society itself has some kind of structure that is relatively enduring and consistent and which is therefore open to investigation. It recognises that the social world differs from the natural world in a number of important ways, in particular that social structures are bound up with the activities of the agents that they govern and that, therefore, society has a conceptual aspect. But against the praxis Marxists and those, like Habermas, who are influenced by the hermeneutic tradition, critical realism maintains that society is not exhausted by its conceptual or praxis aspects and that we should study objective social structures.

But the Marxist notion of social structure has been given a bad name by the most mechanical interpretations of Marx's work, not only by the wooden dialectical materialists of the Second International but also by those who sought to maintain 'classical Marxism' – the Leninists and Trotskyists. They have tended to ignore the more sophisticated socio-economic analysis of *Capital* in favour of the five pages of historical generalisations contained in Marx's Preface to *A Contribution to the Critique of Political Economy* which links the famous base–superstructure metaphor to the historical development of society:

> The totality of these relations of production constitutes the economic structure of society, the real foundation, on which arises a legal and political superstructure and to which correspond definite forms of social consciousness . . . At a certain stage of development, the material productive forces of society come into conflict with the existing relations of production . . . From the forms of development of the productive forces these relations turn into their fetters. Then begins an era of social revolution.
>
> (Marx 1975: 425–6)

According to this view the economic structure of society becomes the prime driving force of history. While this is not necessarily wrong, the mechanical and deterministic emphasis arises from the fact that the historical process is reduced to a single mechanism. Problems arise once we start to examine the bold claims of this statement. What is the economic structure of society? Does the production process not contain a whole range of social relations like education, training and the family that cannot be simply reduced to the economic? Can the economic base be separated from 'superstructural' factors? Legal relations, for example, would seem to be both superstructural and economic (property based). Can the productive forces be separated from relations of production? This gives the false impression that the productive forces have some kind of autonomy outside their social forms. And when does the certain stage of development occur? How do we decide when society becomes a 'fetter' on the supposedly autonomous development of production? After Trotsky claimed that '[t]he economic prerequisite for the proletarian revolution has already in general achieved the highest point of fruition that can be reached under capitalism', his followers proceeded to describe the phenomenal growth of the post-war period by means of Trotsky's claim that 'Mankind's productive forces stagnate' (Trotsky 1977: 111). Above all, they ignored the important influence of 'non-internal' factors such as state intervention and regulation, the development of a consumer society, welfare and education reforms, corporatism and the integrated role of social democracy and the trade unions and a new system of world relations based on the domination of the United States.

Althusser attempted to overcome the problem of economic reductionism by stressing that society is made up of a number of different structures or layers, each enjoying relative autonomy, although they are determined by the economy 'in the last instance' (Althusser 1979: 112–13). However, the problem remains, when does the last instance arrive? Without the last instance, there is a danger that each layer of the social formation remains autonomous, a position that conflicts with Althusser's notion of overdetermination – or the interactions, contradictions and uneven developments of the social whole. This latter notion fits better with critical realism's emphasis on a stratified and overlapping social totality where the different layers interact and co-determine each other. In this sense the notion of determination 'in the last instance' should be rejected in favour of the view that 'economic' determination takes place in *every* instance. But against economic reductionism it should be stressed that this determination has varying degrees of influence and that many other powerful generative mechanisms exist alongside economic ones.

Althusser is right to reject reductionist models of social determination. This exists not only in the form of the mechanical interpretations of Marx's base–superstructure metaphor but also in the humanist and praxis Marxist alternatives which maintain the Hegelian notion of a mono-linear causality although this time it is based on the historical confirmation of a subject rather than the mechanical development of an object. While the 'vulgar Marxist' model reduces the social whole to the question of the economic base and the stage of development of the productive forces, the Lukácsian or Sartrean alternative is based on the idea of an 'expressive totality', where each moment contains the whole and 'the whole method can be unravelled from every single aspect' (Lukács 1971: 170). This again represents a crude simplification of social complexities.

Critical realism argues that the social world, like the natural world is comprised of a series of structures and generative mechanisms combined with a number of organised human practices and understandings. In contrast to mechanical materialism, it argues that these structures form a stratified and differentiated totality. Different layers overlap, mutually co-determine and complement or contradict one another. Some structures are emergent out of others; that is they are based in lower order structures, but develop their own irreducible properties and powers. In these cases, some structures may be said to be constitutive of others – more often or not they are likely to be internally rather than externally related, or at least they may share certain features – for example the legal framework links property relations to a patriarchal family structure. Although this model is non-contemporaneous and pluralistic rather than mono-linear and mono-causal, it should still be possible to argue that there exists a hierarchy of social structures and that economic structures – or the various structures that make up the mode of production – are the most powerful social mechanisms. But by insisting on stratification and emergence it must be maintained that these structures relate to each other in a non-reductive way.

The school of praxis Marxism tends to ignore the question of social structure and focuses instead on human actions and divisions within class consciousness. Humanist Marxism, such as the historiography of E. P. Thompson, also concentrates on 'human relations' at the expense of 'objective' social structures:

> If we stop history at a given point, then there are no classes but simply a multitude of individuals with a multitude of experiences. But if we watch these men over an adequate period of social change, we observe patterns in their relationships, their ideas, and their institutions.
>
> (Thompson 1968: 11)

However, surely the fact that these human actions and relations are intelligible and enduring over time presupposes that this structured context is more than simply what people do at certain points in history? A critical realist position insists that just because the social world, unlike the natural world, is dependent on practical activity and human conceptions, it is not reducible to concepts and practice but rather, these necessarily entail a pre-existing structured context.

Thompson launches a fierce attack on Althusser whose structuralism is accused of stasis and a failure to explain social change; his categories are accused of being de-socialised and de-historicised; we hear nothing of values or consciousness (Thompson 1978: 95). To an extent Thompson's criticism is correct; Althusser does illustrate the dangers of a de-socialised, de-historicised, structural schematism, particularly in the much quoted passage: 'the structure of the relations of production determines the *places* and *functions* occupied and adopted by the agents of production, who are never anything more than the occupants of these places, insofar as they are the 'supports' (*Träger*) of these functions' (Althusser and Balibar 1979: 180). Here the problem seems to be that Althusser is rejecting the determinism of mechanical Marxism by rightly shifting emphasis away from the forces of production onto social relations, but he does this by claiming that these relations, and not people, are the true subjects of history. Thompson, as well as many others from the 'Western Marxist' and 'classical Marxist' traditions, rightly insists on bringing back the human subject, but he does so at the expense of social relations.

Critical realism combines structure and agency in its transformational model of social activity (TMSA). According to the TMSA, the arguments for which are well represented elsewhere (Bhaskar 1989a: 34–5, Collier 1994: 141–51; Joseph 2000: 185–90; Joseph and Kennedy 2000), social structures are both the necessary conditions for and the reproduced outcomes of human action. Structures pre-exist and hence shape and determine human action, but at the same time, the continued existence of these structures depends upon the activities of the agents they govern. While structures tend to predominate over agents, the very 'placement' and 'functioning' of agents that Althusser mentions means that people have the *potential*, albeit within these strict limits, to alter or transform these structures and the wider social ensembles that they make up.

It is still important that the structural aspect is allowed to predominate. Structures do depend on actions for their reproduction, but these are largely unconscious acts. At least, agents do act on intentions, but these have wider, unintentional consequences. When someone sells their labour power their intention is to earn a wage. The unintentional consequences of millions of workers doing the same thing is the reproduction of the structures of capitalist exploitation. Hence the properties of social structures cannot be reduced to the actions, intentions or consciousness of their agents. To do so would be to engage in the 'flat ontologising' of humanist Marxism and inter-subjective praxis ontology. Against this, critical realism argues that the activities of agents are set within a pre-defined structural context and that the effects of their actions are stratified across a range of social structures and generative mechanisms. Here lies a slight criticism of Bhaskar's TMSA model – its level of generality and its notion of the 'duality of structure and agency' which gives the impression that structure and agent stand in a one-to-one relationship. However, the notion of social stratification on which critical realism rightly insists means that the activities of agents relate to not just one particular structure, but a range of other inter-related structures, practices and generative mechanisms. Agents often believe that they are operating within a limited context, but social stratification and overdetermination gives rise to unintentional consequences. The TMSA must take into account the fact that it is not the relations between structures and individual agents that are important, but the relations between structures and collective agents. Along with the effects of stratification this also gives primacy to structures over agents, for to transform a set of structures requires collective rather than individual activity, something that depends on a complex process of strategic organisation and mediation.

This again undermines the Lukácsian view which bases itself on the unity of the proletariat. Like social structures, social agents are stratified too. The proletariat is not a homogenous grouping, it has a stratified, differentiated character based on its relation to different social structures. Overcoming this objective situation does not depend on self-realisation, but on concrete relations with the specific structures and generative mechanisms in question. Transformative activity is not based on overcoming divisions within consciousness, it is about overcoming the stratification of real structures and agents.

The method of abstraction

Critical realism argues that the world has a structured and stratified character and that science attempts to develop an analysis of the various processes and mechanisms that operate in this structured context. In the natural sciences these tendencies and mechanisms are usually isolated through the conduct of experiments that are carried out, usually in the laboratory, under conditions of artificial closure. The generation of phenomena and events then needs to be explained by the postulation of underlying structures and causal mechanisms.

Social science does not have the option of using experiments or imposing conditions of artificial closure. However, the Marxist method still proceeds by means of hypothesising certain structures and causal mechanisms and attempting to study their operation, initially in isolation, then in combination. Instead of conducting experiments in the laboratory, social science must proceed to isolate causal mechanisms in theory by means of a process of abstraction. In Marx's famous explanation of his method, it can be seen how he emphasises the need to abstract from the concrete starting point in order to understand the workings in theory which in turn allows us to understand the workings in the concrete which, it turns out, does not have the simplicity of the starting point, but represents the 'concentration of many determinations'.

> The concrete is concrete because it is the concentration of many determinations, hence the unity of the diverse. It appears in the process of thinking, therefore, as a process of concentration, as a result, not as a point of departure in reality, even though it is the point of departure in reality and hence also the point of departure for observation and conception.
>
> (Marx 1973: 101)

The method by which Marx studies the workings of the economy can be compared to critical realism's retroduction. Beginning with the concrete social form of the commodity, Marx postulates the process by which the phenomenal or concrete form is generated. The isolation of social forms like exchange value is accompanied by a retroductive analysis of their conditions (the labour theory of value). However, isolation and retroduction must be followed by a return to the concrete. The postulated mechanism must be recontextualised in an open situation.

The complexities of this process can be illustrated by the transformation problem. Considering the commodity form, in abstraction from other forms, as a premise, Marx develops the labour theory of value to explain the basis of this form (that the value produced is equivalent to the labour time expended in its production). In the complex capitalist economy, this has to be posed as socially necessary abstract labour (SNAL).

However, the labour theory of value represents the isolation of only one – albeit a fundamental – economic mechanism. Marx's explanation is based on the isolation of this process in order to explain the creation of value. But Marx develops the category of prices of production in recognition of the need to move once more from the postulated entities to their operation in an open context where other mechanisms and tendencies will be in operation.

Thus price (the amount of money needed to buy a commodity) can diverge from value (the amount of SNAL embodied in the commodity) because of the effect of other processes – such as the competition of capitals, the redistribution of the total surplus value among different sectors of production and the dislocation of supply and demand. This does not invalidate the labour theory of value but reveals different levels of analytical abstraction. The labour theory of value is based on isolating the determination of value from the competition between capitals and is based on capital as a whole. The analysis of prices of production then re-examines this in the context of competing capitals and other social processes. These theoretical complexities are very troublesome, but they reflect the dialectical complexity of the real world where competing structures and mechanisms operate side by side.

In highlighting the transformation problem we have drawn attention to some fundamental necessities of social analysis. As a process these can be listed as isolation, abstraction and hypothesisation, recontextualisation and the consequent development of a stratified social theory in keeping with the stratified object of its analysis. The variations within a social context might also be dealt with by employing Tony Lawson's notion of contrastive explanation (Lawson 1997: 204–9) where, in contrasting two similar situations, something stands out or causes surprise, thereby calling attention to some other possible tendency or mechanism in operation.

Abstraction necessarily entails a critical stance towards concrete forms as they appear in their immediacy – e.g. the commodity form or the wage form. Marx's analysis reveals that behind their immediate form lies a social relation. It also reveals how various relations entail other relations and how social mechanisms and structures work in a contradictory co-determination. By revealing the complexity of concrete social forms, such an analysis entails a critique of their immediate appearance, or more precisely, a critique of the ideology of their appearance. It can also show how a belief in these forms (e.g. commodity fetishism) is actually a necessary part of the reproduction of the capitalist mode of production. Developing an analysis of these forms inevitably leads to a negative evaluation of them. This can be described as an explanatory critique. As Bhaskar argues, this involves a critique of both:

> (1) conceptual and conceptualised entities (economic theories and categories; phenomenal forms) and of (2) the objects (systems of structured relations) which necessitate or otherwise explain them. At the first level, the entities are shown to be false *simpliciter* (e.g. the wage form), fetishised (e.g. the value form) or otherwise defective. At the second level, Marx's explanations logically entail *ceteris paribus* a negative evaluation of the objects generating such entities and a commitment to their practical transformation.
>
> (Bhaskar 1991: 166–7)

This contrasts with classical political economy which ultimately succumbs to these forms and re-enforces them through its theoretical analysis. Thus classical political economy embraces an empirical ontology which ahistorically naturalises capitalist class relations. Classical political economy has to conceive of social relations as natural relations, unable as it is to deal with the radical consequences of seeing capitalist relations in their historically relative form. For to pose the question of the historicity of capitalist social relations is to imply the possibility of their transformation.

Unfortunately, however, classical Marxism also succumbs to these errors when it predicts the impending economic collapse of society. It often focuses on the question of the tendency of the rate of profit to fall without recognising that this mechanism is a *tendency* precisely because there may be other, counteracting tendencies that may, albeit temporarily, arrest this process. For critical realism the falling rate of profit is a real tendency, but it is one that may or may not be realised depending on concrete conditions. Likewise, the Trotskyist notion that the productive forces tend to stagnate may not be absolutely wrong, but it is held up in isolation as if it were the only real tendency within the social process. Marx argues, however, that the capitalist system is dynamic precisely because it attempts to find ways to overcome such tendencies and to continually revolutionise the means of production. The idea of the stagnation of the productive forces and the crude theory that explains history in terms of the conflict between forces and relations of production are, like classical political economy, ahistorical accounts which study abstract mechanisms in isolation. The concrete, social history of capitalism is somewhat different to this – not the abstract development of iron laws, but the concrete relations between capital and labour, between competing capitals, between different countries, between states and markets and so on. Economic tendencies cannot be left in isolation, they have to be seen in their actual social context.

Explanatory critiques and philosophical partisanship

Critical realism insists on the distinction between the intransitive character of the world and the transitive knowledge we have of it. It is the relatively enduring and structured character of the intransitive world that makes knowledge both possible and intelligible. However, our knowledge of the world is determined, not only by the nature of the intransitive object (and it can be argued that its very intransitivity makes perfect knowledge impossible), but also by the inescapably social character of the transitive. Scientific development must be understood not only on the basis of theory's relation to its object but also according to the social production of (transitive) knowledge as an ongoing practice within wider social conditions. As Bhaskar writes:

> Recognition of the transitive dimension implies that scientific beliefs can no longer be distinguished by their content. For experiences and the facts they generate must now be viewed as socially produced and what is socially produced is socially changeable.
>
> (Bhaskar 1997: 189)

The social and historical specificity of knowledge is often disguised by the 'fact form' just as the 'value form' disguises the social character of labour. The natural, atomistic facts of classical political economy are perfect companions to the alienated form of labour. An explanatory critique posits real interests, needs and motives and a conception of common nature. Bhaskar writes that the subject matter of social science comprises both social objects (including beliefs) and beliefs about those objects. The connection between social ideas and the social objects that produce these ideas is a fundamental aspect of a critical realist critique. These connections are often ignored – by empiricists who objectivise beliefs, undermining their epistemic significance, and by idealists who bracket off the historical context (Bhaskar 1986: 176).

Science has an inter-discursively critical aspect so that acceptance of one explanation requires a negative evaluation of competing or incompatible theories. In order to critically assess these theories, it is necessary to make some claims about the social objects they are attempting to describe and to look at why other theories were unable to develop such a conception. Therefore:

the critical role of the human sciences in human history is not an optional extra: it is *intrinsic* to their explanatory function – for this depends indispensably on the identification and description, and proceeds naturally to the explanation, of ideas.

(Bhaskar 1986: 193)

Good social science represents an explanatory critique. It has to criticise the inadequacies of other theories and explain why the inadequacies occur. It is necessary to examine whether there is a connection between particular social objects and false descriptions of them. If certain views of the world predominate, it is necessary to explain why this should be the case. And if these ideas are false or inadequate, it is necessary to produce a better explanation. If a connection can be established between false ideas about social objects and the social objects themselves, then a critique of these social objects follows. An alternative is posed, not just at the level of theory but also in terms of how the world could or should be.

If we accept that social theory and social reality are causally interdependent – i.e. social theory is practically conditioned by and has potentially practical consequences in society (Bhaskar 1989b: 5) – then neutrality in social theory, however desirable, is impossible. In this context, the practice of philosophy, in assessing social scientific theory, is also inescapably political. To deny this is, in fact, to take a political stance – a conservative stance that defends the status quo, either of social reality, or of the methods used to study it, or more probably, both. Critical realism does not shy away from this problem, but embraces its political role. It does this through emphasising such things as openness, diversity and historicity and exposing those theories that deny them.

Critical realism's stance, in relation to a study of the social world, is to emphasise its structure and complexity. To examine structure poses the question of whether this structure, or ensemble of structures, is hierarchical. If this is so, it is necessary to investigate which structures are dominant or have causal primacy. Likewise, to examine the complexity of society is to examine its overdetermined and contradictory character. A recognition of the historicity of social relations also requires an investigation of the necessary conditions for the reproduction of the social formation. Critical realism argues that social structures have a relatively enduring character. However, the requirements for reproducing this enduring character need to be assessed. Thus it seems legitimate for critical realism to move from the question of the structure of society to the question of its maintenance. By pointing to unconscious reproduction, and possible exploitation as a consequence – as in the case of the extraction of surplus value – critical realism points to the need for an explanatory critique which can assess the *real* nature of such processes and explain the gap between individual intentions and the actual reproduced outcome of human practices.

Critical realism also argues that social structures generate and distribute upon agents certain causal powers, social identities and interests. It points to the need to examine these interests in their structural context and to assess the possibilities and limitations that these structures present for human action. In posing the question of their reproduction, critical realism highlights the *possibility* of their transformation. The next step is to examine the location of the various collectives of social agents and the transformative capacities that they might have. The act of transformation is the job of the agents themselves, while the description of social transformation is the job of the political analyst and requires an examination of the specific historical circumstances of such action. Critical realism should content itself showing the importance of explanatory critique by posing the question of the possibility of transformation and in highlighting the need to study the specific structural and historical conditions.

The radicality of critical realism flows, not from what it prescribes as a political solution to social ills, but through raising questions about society and scientific practice. Critical realism does not provide the political solutions itself, but helps provide the basis for assessing such solutions. Various political conclusions flow from a critical realist analysis just as surely as critical realism can show that political conclusions flow from rival social theories. In assessing social science, critical realism takes a partisan stance. But this is done through criticising the assumptions of social theories and highlighting the connection between the errors of social theory and the contradictions at the level of social reality that these ideas in some way reflect.

Critical realism questions not only social ideas, but also the social processes that generate such ideas. To put it crudely, and without succumbing completely to praxis Marxism, 'bourgeois' ideas about society reflect the state of that society and its dominant social structures and practices. Historically, the social analysis of bourgeois theories is marked by an ahistorical, fetishised world view. By contrast, the exploited and oppressed have an interest in knowledge which the exploiters not only lack, but may have an interest in suppressing. Developing a critique both of the wrong ideas and the practices producing them is part of what Bhaskar calls hegemonic/hermeneutic struggles, isolating, for example, theory/practice inconsistencies (Bhaskar 1994: 94). But these scientific positions must be developed through a careful study of society. Just because the working class has an interest in explanatory knowledge, this does not mean that it flows naturally from their class consciousness.

Our advocacy of partisanship also reminds us of Althusser's understanding of the role of philosophy. It will be remembered that Althusser abandoned his 'scientistic' view that philosophy is the 'theory of theoretical practice' in favour of the view that philosophy represents 'the class struggle in theory'. The problem with this new conception is that it loses its connection to the practice of science and is conceived of purely as an ideological battle. This embraces Lenin and Gramsci's conception of ideology as a positive, motivating force which can be used by the working class movement (Larrain 1983). What critical realism advocates is a more *negative* conception of ideology in the context of social theories being the product of social conditions. Wrong social theories represent an inability to explain real structures, processes and contradictions. If bourgeois ideas are wrong, a 'proletarian' alternative will only be right if it can explain the connection between false ideas and their origin in social reality. Opposition to bourgeois ideas is no good in and of itself. However, the interest that the oppressed have in opposing the ideological products of an exploitative society means, as Roy Edgley argues, that:

> The materialist involvement of ideas in the practical social and political context, specifically the conscious participation of social science in the working class struggle, far from undermining scientificity, is a positive condition of it. It is not that Marx's science, being ideological, is none the worse for that. On the contrary, being proletarian ideology it is scientifically all the better for that.
>
> (Edgley 1983: 287)

Conclusion

The main errors of Marxist theory tend to flow from the attempt to impose a philosophical schema onto its analysis. This occurs in both mechanical dialectical materialism, and the attempts to overcome this – whether this be praxis-based Western Marxism or the more activist oriented 'classical Marxism' of the post-war period. Against this, critical realism tries to distinguish between philosophy and Marxist social science in order to emphasise the scientificity of Marxism while allowing for a critical assessment of its arguments and methods. Strictly speaking, philosophy, as second order knowledge, cannot tell us about the workings of the world itself and the possible actions that might flow from our knowledge of these workings. However, philosophy can comment on our *knowledge* of the world and the various theories and ideologies that attempt to explain it. If it is science and not philosophy that gives us first order knowledge of the world, then philosophy's task is to give us first order knowledge of that knowledge, or second order knowledge of the world. Such a task is an important one. It can help us clarify aspects of social theory and help us to decide what is important and what is ideological, rendering explicit any implicit ontology. This underlabouring role can lead to a breakthrough; by clarifying questions of scientific method it can revolutionise scientific practice and help us achieve a better understanding of the world.

However, this outline of the distinction between philosophy and social science is still problematic. For whilst it looks neat and clear on paper, the reality is somewhat different. Both social science and the philosophy of social science are embodied in the social world they seek to explain. They are both critiques and products of the society they study. Moreover, if philosophy is a conceptual practice, social philosophy has to deal with social theory which has a considerable conceptual component and deals in turn with a reality which is pre-interpreted. It is therefore inevitable that the claims of social philosophy and social science are going to overlap somewhat and that social claims and judgements are going to follow on from philosophical underlabouring. No amount of 'good philosophising' will get around this, it is something intrinsic to the relationship between philosophy, social science and society.

This may seem to undermine the idea of critical realism as an under-labourer, but in fact this connection between philosophy and social science reinforces the importance of this role. Of course it is impossible to prevent social science from affecting the role of the underlabourer. But then it is also impossible to get away from the social character of knowledge more gener-ally. We still strive for knowledge and we still strive for scientificity even if we know that these will be imperfect and inadequate. Likewise, Marxist theory insists on the importance of the totality, and it attempts to achieve this knowledge even though the 'totality' can never be fully known. In these cases, what is important is the process of striving. In the case of philosophy as an underlabourer, we must recognise that this role cannot be carried out adequately and that philosophy and social science are inevitably going to get entwined. Nevertheless (and basing itself on this recognition) critical realism must *strive* to be an underlabourer to Marxism, it must strive to remain distinct in order to remain explanatory. Our understanding of the role of underlabourer must be dialecticised so that we recognise both the necessity and the impossibility of this distinction.

Instead of trying to escape these difficulties, critical realism's first role is to point them out. A critical scrutiny of the underlabouring role might be the first task of the underlabourer. A next step might be to make explicit the social and political claims that infect philosophical and social theory. Critical realism must assess the relation of these claims to society and whether they play a critical or subservient role. While Althusser is wrong to say that philo-sophy is *simply* the class struggle in theory, certainly the class structure of society plays a crucial role in the development of all social theories, philoso-phies and discourses. This flows from the transitive nature of knowledge. Attempts at genuinely explanatory social theory must be able to break from the dominant bourgeois theories about bourgeois society.

To return to Perry Anderson, he famously linked the philosophical atti-tude of 'Western' Marxism to its separation from practice while, writing from a broadly Trotskyist standpoint, he saw the superiority of 'classical' Marxism as guaranteed by its unity with the struggles of the working class. This, he later realised, was an error. It represented a reduction of epistemo-logical issues to the unity of theory and practice, an attempt to shield classical Marxism from critical scrutiny (Anderson 1979: 112). The problem that

Anderson begins to formulate is this; if we reject the various errors of Western Marxism – such things as Lukács's views on reification and class consciousness, or Sartre's constitution of the totality through scarcity and praxis, or Habermas's Kantian separation of system and lifeworld, or Althusser's scientism – if we reject these views; what have we left to fall back on? Does the 'classical' Marxism of the post-war period have the necessary degree of scientificity and explanatory power, or is it also infested with schematic posturing? The problem seems to be that since the beginning of the last century, all the alternatives to Stalinism and reformism have been categorised as either 'Western' Marxist or 'classical' Marxist. Perhaps the answer to this Andersonian problem is to take up critical realism and, through its underlabouring, rid ourselves of the unnecessaries so that we can get back to being just plain Marxists.

Notes

1 I would like to thank Mervyn Hartwig, Steve Fleetwood and, in particular, Andy Brown for their critical comments on this paper. An earlier version of this article was presented at the 2000 Critical Realism conference at Lancaster University and I would like to thank those who commented on the paper at the conference and also the Open University for providing financial assistance.

Bibliography

Althusser, L. (1979) *For Marx*, London: Verso.

Althusser, L. and Balibar, E. (1979) *Reading Capital*, London: Verso.

Anderson, P. (1979) *Considerations on Western Marxism*, London: Verso.

Bhaskar, R. (1986) *Socialist Realism and Human Emancipation*, London: Verso.

—— (1989a) *The Possibility of Naturalism*, Hemel Hempstead, UK: Harvester Wheatsheaf.

—— (1989b) *Reclaiming Reality*, London: Verso.

—— (1991) *Philosophy and the Idea of Freedom*, Oxford: Blackwell.

—— (1994) *Plato Etc.*, London: Verso.

—— (1997) *A Realist Theory of Science* (2nd edition), London: Verso.

Collier, A. (1989) *Scientific Realism and Socialist Thought*, Hemel Hempstead, UK: Harvester Wheatsheaf.

—— (1994) *Critical Realism*, London: Verso.

Edgley, R. (1983) 'Philosophy', in D. McLellan (ed.) *Marx: the First Hundred Years*, Glasgow: Fontana.

Gramsci, A. (1971) *Selections from the Prison Notebooks*, London: Lawrence & Wishart.

Joseph, J. (2000) 'A Realist Theory of Hegemony', *Journal for the Theory of Social Behaviour* 30, 2: 179–202.

Joseph, J. and Kennedy, S. (2000) 'The Structure of the Social', *Philosophy of the Social Sciences*, 30, 4: 508–27.

Korsch, K. (1970) *Marxism and Philosophy*, London: New Left Books.

Larrain, J. (1983) *Marxism and Ideology*, London: Macmillan.

Lawson, T. (1997) *Economics and Reality*, London and New York: Routledge.

Lukács, G. (1971) *History and Class Consciousness*, London: Merlin.

Marx, K. (1973) *Grundrisse*, Harmondsworth, UK: Penguin.

—— (1975) Preface to 'A Contribution to the Critique of Political Economy' in K. Marx, *Early Writings*, Harmondsworth, UK: Penguin.

Plekhanov, G. (1920) *Fundamental Problems of Marxism*, Moscow: Foreign Languages Press.

Salvadori, M. (1990) *Karl Kautsky and the Socialist Revolution 1880–1938*, London: Verso.

Sartre, J-P. (1976) *Critique of Dialectical Reason*, vol. 1, London: Verso.

Thompson, E.P. (1968) *The Making of the English Working Class*, Harmondsworth, UK: Penguin.

—— (1978) *The Poverty of Philosophy*, London: Merlin.

Trotsky, L. (1977) *The Transitional Programme for Socialist Revolution*, New York: Pathfinder.

3   Critical realist arguments in Marx's *Capital*

Hans G. Ehrbar

From Hegel to Bhaskar

In *Capital*, Marx uses Hegelian concepts and terminology extensively. For instance, shortly after the beginning of the first chapter, Marx concludes that the exchange value of commodities must be the 'form of appearance' of some 'substance', called 'value', which is different from exchange value itself. The subsequent discussion seems more akin to literary criticism than to political economy. Marx interprets the *meaning* of certain familiar kinds of market transactions, in order to come to the conclusion that value consists of congealed abstract labour. Later on, a long section of the first chapter derives various 'forms of value' as surface *expressions* of this congealed abstract labour. These expressions have 'defects' which lead, in a dialectical development, to more satisfactory forms.

Some Marx scholars try to ignore these Hegelianisms, others consider them an important part of Marx's argument. Lenin belonged to the latter camp; he wrote in his Philosophical Notebooks:

> Aphorism: It is impossible to completely understand Marx's *Capital*, and especially its first chapter, without having thoroughly studied and understood the *whole* of Hegel's *Logic*. Consequently, half a century later none of the Marxists understood Marx!
>
> (Lenin 1961: 180)

Eighty years after Lenin it is doubtful whether even an extensive knowledge of Hegel can make it possible to 'completely' understand Marx's *Capital*. Those Marx and Hegel scholars who went this route have not achieved the hoped-for breakthroughs.

Hegel's system was presumably the best framework available at Marx's time to represent the structure of modern society. But it is not a perfect fit for the purposes for which Marx put it to work. Many arguments which Marx makes in the Hegelian paradigm are metaphorical (Marsden 1998: 304), others are implicit, only indicated by Marx's choice of words (often lost in the translations), and certain other arguments are simply never made at all (Althusser and Balibar 1970: 86). As a consequence, to understand Marx has become a secret science, open only to the 'initiated', those who know long passages of Marx's writings by heart, so that they can hum a melody along in a tonal system which they are not quite sure about.

Fortunately, in the last quarter century, a cleaner and more persuasive framework for social sciences has been developed than Hegel's philosophy. I am speaking here of Bhaskar's 'critical realism', as it is laid out in Bhaskar (1997), Bhaskar (1989a), Bhaskar (1993) and other works. Bhaskar gives, in the framework of the modern critique of positivism, a systematic and coherent formulation of the philosophical outlook to which Marx himself became more and more committed (Bhaskar 1989b: 126). This essay tries to reproduce Marx's arguments in the early parts of *Capital I* in a critical realist rather than a Hegelian framework. It can be considered a test of a conjecture formulated by Bhaskar:

> What accounts for Marx's (and Engels's subsequent) recourse to dialectics? My conjecture is that it took the place of critical realism as the missing methodological fulcrum of Marx's work.
>
> (Bhaskar 1989a: 178)

If Marx was indeed a critical realist 'avant la lettre', it should be possible and beneficial to translate Marx's Hegelian arguments in *Capital* into critical realist terms.

This essay attempts such a translation. It gives a summary of Marx's argument which tries to stay as close as possible to Marx's own, but in which critical realist categories take the place of Marx's Hegelianisms. My summary will differ from Marx's own development only because those steps which are hidden in the Hegelian terminology have been made explicit, using categories informed by dialectical critical realism (DCR). Of course, a different paradigm makes things visible from a slightly different angle, therefore the arguments will also get a different flavour. Perhaps the reader of this summary will not even recognise them. Those interested are invited to download from the web the preliminary version of my extensive sentence-by-sentence interpretation of Marx's micro-logic, called *Annotations to Karl Marx's 'Capital'* (Ehrbar 2000). There they will find detailed textual evidence for the summary that follows.

Marx's opening moves

Since society cannot be reduced to the individual, Marx does not begin *Capital* with the individual. His entry point into the social structure of capitalism is the *commodity*. This is a plausible starting point, since almost everything produced in capitalism is produced for sale, i.e., takes commodity form.

The first thing that needs to be said about the commodity is that it has two factors, use value and exchange value. Marx discusses use value only briefly and then goes over to exchange value. Here he observes that our day-to-day experiences with exchange value are contradictory. Part of these experiences seem to indicate that exchange value is intrinsic in the commodities (if you drop a commodity and break it then its exchange value disappears too), and others seem to indicate that exchange value is relative and only depends on the circumstances of the exchange (the same good is sold at different prices in different stores or at different times).

Marx takes this as evidence that a deeper level of reality must be involved. This is one of several places in *Capital* where Marx identifies a contradiction, and then, often with the words 'let us look at the matter more closely', expands the 'discursive domain' (Bhaskar 1993: 57) in order to arrive at a more comprehensive explanation. Bhaskar recommends this procedure:

> A logical (or other) contradiction is not something to fear and/or to seek to disguise, cover up or isolate. Rather it should be taken as a sign that the existing conceptual field is incomplete in some relevant respect.
>
> (Bhaskar 1993: 378–9)

In the present situation, Marx comes to the conclusion that exchange value is the 'form of appearance' in which some deeper attribute of commodities, which he calls 'value', 'expresses' itself.

Surface and core of the economy

In order to follow Marx's argument we need to know what the words 'form of appearance' and 'expression' mean. I will therefore interrupt my summary here in order to explain these terms.

When we observe the commodity producers trading their goods in the market, we are witnessing the second act of a two-act drama, which can only be understood if we also know the first act. The first act is the production of these goods.

Although commodities are produced on private initiative, their production is a thoroughly social process. The capitalists take it for granted that they will be able to find the inputs for production and labour power waiting for them to be purchased, that their money will be accepted, that their employees in turn can buy their subsistence means with their wages, that their own and their workers' skills enable them to produce a competitive product, etc. The seemingly autonomous activity of the capitalist competitors would not be possible without a high degree of co-ordination in the economy as a whole.

How is this co-ordination achieved? Interestingly it is a mere side effect of the market activity of producers and consumers. In response to market signals, consumers adjust what they consume, and producers adjust their production schedules and technologies, in ways which facilitate the functioning and reproduction of the economy as a whole. But they do not do it out of concern about the overall economy but out of self-interest. Their intent is to reach the best possible outcome for themselves in the framework of the market, and they employ many different techniques to achieve this. Despite these myopic motives, their interactions generally have the unintended side effect of keeping production on track.

If there is not enough of something, productive resources are directed into producing it, not because of a concern for the consumers or responsibility towards the economy, but because production of the scarce article is rewarded with high prices. The producers' self-interest also induces them to introduce innovations quickly, to maintain the continuity of the production process, and to pay attention to costs and the consumers. This does not exactly lead to the most efficient use of resources, and does not make the consumer 'king' either. On the contrary, it ravages the earth's natural resources most irresponsibly while at the same time keeping the majority of the earth's population in abject poverty. But obviously the system itself has remained intact for a long time under this regime.

Commodity exchange and private property – relations which are located on what Marx calls the 'surface' of society – are the institutions which induce the producers to take actions that enable the continued functioning of the economy. If the market provides the social interactions which keep production on track, one might think that the structure of the market determines the character of production. This is a fallacy. Production, in any society, is a much more fundamental activity than the market. If social production were not structured in such a way that a market is needed, there would be no market. People go to market to exchange their products only because of the specific character of the relations which bind them together (and at the same time keep them apart) in the social production process.

Causality goes therefore from production to the market, not vice versa. Market interactions induce the economic agents to take actions that uphold the systemic structure of social production, but this structure itself is logically prior to the market. Marx does not have a consistent terminology for the structure which lies beneath the surface of market activity; I will introduce such a terminology here and call it the 'core' of the economy.

Marx uses Hegel's form–content paradigm for the indirect and asymmetric link between surface and core: the surface relations among the economic agents are the *forms of appearance* of the principles which govern social production in the core of the economy. In Hegel's system, there is a close link between content and form:

> On the question of the relation between content and form, Marx took the standpoint of Hegel and not of Kant. Kant treated form as something external in relation to the content, and as something which adds itself to the content from the outside. From the standpoint of Hegel's philosophy, the content itself, through its development, generates that form which

was already latently contained in the content. Form necessarily grows from the content itself.

(Rubin 1972: 117)

The form–content paradigm is therefore in many respects appropriate for the situation at hand. It connotes that the market affects production in an indirect manner. It also connotes that the principles co-ordinating production in a commodity society are not *generated* by the market. Although they *manifest* themselves in and are *mediated* through the market, they invisibly already exist in the production process itself and can be defined without reference to the market.

Nevertheless, I will not use these Hegelian terms in my summary of Marx's arguments, but look at the links between core and surface explicitly. The core–surface distinction can be located in the intersection of critical realism and historical materialism. A critical realist knows that society is stratified. Bhaskar speaks of the 'hiatus' between the level of social structure and the level of the individual: neither level is reducible to the other. Historical materialism explores the inner structure and historical development of the social stratum, distinguishing between base and superstructure, and between various modes of production. The core–surface distinction captures the specifics of the social–individual interaction in capitalism. In capitalism, the economic base of society consists of two layers, core and surface. The interactions of the individuals which sustain the economic and wider social structure take place against the backdrop of the surface relations, whereas the all-important relations of production are submerged in the core. The core is a hidden skeleton which holds everything in place but which the practical agents do not address directly. Interpersonal interactions are two steps removed from the co-ordination of production: they generate market outcomes (surface) which in turn have repercussions for production itself (core).

The dislocation of the co-ordination of production from the sphere of production itself (the core) to the market (the surface) requires that two opposite channels of communication exist between core and surface:

1   The core sends information about itself to the surface.
2   The economic agents, who interact within the framework of the surface relations, respond to this information by actions which, as an unintended side effect, maintain and reproduce the core structure.

From the fact that capitalism does indeed function can be inferred that these two channels of communication between core and surface must be operative. Whenever Marx uses the word 'expression' he refers to channel 1, and whenever he uses the word 'form' he refers to channel 2.

A metaphor may be useful to illustrate these two channels. Say the core of the economy is your computer, and the surface is you. In order to run the computer you need a monitor, which tells you what state the computer is in (channel 1), and a keyboard, through which you give the computer instructions (channel 2).

At the beginning of *Capital*, Marx takes a round trip through these two channels. In section one of the first chapter, Marx begins on the surface and follows channel 2, asking how the core must be structured if the market interactions of the economic agents are what mediates this structure. In Hegelian terms this is the inference from the form to the content, a deciphering of the 'meaning' of the form. In our computer illustration, this is the attempt to infer the structure of a computer program by the keyboard input. Section two verifies that the core structures postulated by this retroductive argument do indeed exist. Here the computer illustration does not fit very well; perhaps one can say that this step verifies that what we assume the computer program does can really be done on the basis of the inputs. In section three, Marx follows the opposite channel (channel 1) and asks how the information in the core is transmitted to the surface, i.e., in Hegelian terms, how the content 'expresses' itself in the form. This is the question of how the state of the computer is displayed on the monitor. The second chapter verifies that this expression of the core principles developed in section three of the first chapter indeed creates tools on the surface which allow the economic agents to pursue their immediate interests. In the computer illustration this verifies whether this display is something the user can understand and respond to in human language. One notices that in none of these steps is the computer opened or is its program analysed directly – since in the case of social structures there is no box to open; social structures only exist in their effects.

From surface to core

I will now describe each of these four steps in more detail. After coming to the conclusion that there must be something deeper underlying the exchange value, Marx explores what this deeper thing is. For this, he looks at the instructions (keyboard inputs) which the market interactions on the surface send down to the core of the economy. Here our computer analogy again has its limits. The economic agents do not deliberately generate instructions for the economy. Instead, they interact with each other in specific ways referring to concrete situations. The instructions which the core receives from these surface interactions are not based on these specifics, they are, in critical realist terms, transfactual. One might view them as the resultant force from the sum total of innumerable interactions, or their general footprint.

Since each exchange equates one commodity with another in certain quantitative proportions, the transfactual impact of the multitude of exchanges criss-crossing the economy is that all goods have the same quality and differ only quantitatively. This common same quality in the commodities cannot have anything to do with the bodily properties of the goods, since it is exactly the purpose of the exchanges to replace different use values with each other, i.e., the use values are too transitory to have an impact on the core.

The instructions which the surface sends to the core must be compatible with the core structure itself, otherwise the economy would not function. If the instructions which the core receives treat all goods as equal, as long as they are available in the fitting proportions, then the core structure of the economy must be such that all goods indeed count as smaller or bigger quantities of one and the same thing. What is this one and the same thing, this common substance of all products? Marx starts with the plausible, and at his time still uncontroversial, assumption that it must be the labour in the commodities. But since the difference of the use values is not visible to the core, the different kinds of useful labour cannot be visible either. The labour which serves as a measuring stick for all goods in the core must therefore be 'labour in the abstract', i.e., labour which is indifferent towards the form in which it is expended. And the commodities, as seen from the core, must be congelations of abstract human labour.

The double character of labour

Section two of the first chapter verifies that abstract human labour is not just a fiction but that it really exists, i.e., that there is really something that is common to all labour processes. Every labour process has two aspects. On the one hand it is the skilful handling of the object, and on the other it is the expenditure of human brain, muscle, etc. Under this second aspect, all labour is very much alike, otherwise it would not be possible that the same humans can use their brains, muscles, etc. to perform a multitude of different kinds of labour. Labour is not completely alike, i.e., not all kinds of labour can be performed by everybody, but most labours can be performed by most members of society, and this is what matters. Usually, the workers need training before they can perform specific labour processes, but if one pro-rates the training time over the labour time performed, one ends up with quantitative, not qualitative differences of abstract labour.

One often hears the argument that abstract human labour is the product of capitalism, i.e., that there is no abstract labour outside capitalism. This is not my reading of Marx. Every labour process is the expenditure of human brain, muscle, sense organs, etc. In other words, abstract human labour is an aspect of every labour process. The fact that the same word 'labour' is used for many different activities shows that this abstraction can be made. What is special about capitalism is that this aspect of the labour process is the criterion by which social production is directed. The core only sees the abstract labour, i.e., only through abstract labour is the labour process socially connected. This special role of abstract labour leads to the *split* of the labour process into two parts, concrete labour creating use values and abstract labour creating values.

From core to surface

Section three of the first chapter explains how information from the core of the economy is transmitted to the surface, i.e., how the computer represents its inner state on the monitor. Marx shows that already the simplest exchange relation, for instance '20 yards of linen = 1 coat', contains expressions of the values of the commodities involved; i.e., the two parties agreeing to such an exchange import information about the values of their products from the core into the surface.

Look for instance at the linen weaver. She knows how much labour and expenses are contained in the 20 yards of linen she just produced. She does not have the same information about the coat, but she knows that it is a product of labour, i.e., that she has to give up part of her own labour to get it, and she knows the use value of the coat. By agreeing to exchange her linen for the coat she tells the market that to her the coat is a worthwhile reward for having produced the linen; i.e., she expresses the value of her linen in the use value of the coat.

Marx observes that here the linen is active and the coat is passive. The linen weaver has spent labour producing the linen, labour which is wasted if she cannot exchange the linen against something she needs. She will not rest until she has made this exchange.

This expression of value is only an individual act, although value itself is a social relation binding every social production process together. In the remainder of section three, Marx explains how this expression develops through its own inner dialectic into the institution of money.

The linen weaver needs not only a coat but many other things. The activity of the linen creates, therefore, not only one but many expressions of the value of linen: besides in coats, it is also expressed in tea, coffee, wheat, gold, iron, etc. This so-called expanded form of value is no longer purely individual but reaches out into society. The very arbitrariness of the individual expression has given rise to a social totality of expressions. But these expressions do not yet induce a surface behaviour that can leave a transfactual impact on the core, because the expressions are not homogeneous and simple enough. What Marx calls 'defects' are those features of the expressions of value which prevent them from functioning as conduits through which the surface agents pass instructions down to the core.

Therefore, a second transformation becomes necessary, and again this transformation is already implicitly given. Since linen expresses its value in coats, tea, coffee, wheat, gold, iron, etc., all those other commodities also express their values in linen. Now a deliberate social act is necessary, namely, the consensus to set linen aside as the commodity in which all other commodities express their values. This leads to the General form of value, the first form of value in which the expressions of value resonate with each other to yield a social consensus which can 'be heard' in the core.

This is not yet the end of it. The Money form of value differs from the General form of value in only one seemingly innocuous detail: now it is known *a priori* that gold is everywhere and always the General equivalent. Since there can only be one General equivalent, this is an obvious further step, but we will see that this welding together of a social form of value with one particular use value has far-reaching implications. But before taking this up, Marx discusses a different issue.

The fetish-like character of commodities

Section four of the first chapter is not part of our round trip, although channels 1 and 2 play a role in it too. Immediately after the detailed analysis of the commodity, Marx surprises the reader with the assertion that the commodity is 'mysterious'. By this he means that a society in which individuals deal with each other through commodities does not allow them to control their own social relations. Marx asks two questions, which correspond to the two channels:

- Where is the mysterious character of the commodity located, i.e., what are the mechanisms through which social control is lost? (This corresponds to channel 2, from surface to core).
- What is the origin of this mysterious character, i.e., since the surface is a reflection of the production process (channel 1, from core to surface), what aspect of the production process is responsible for that 'mysterious' character of the surface relations?

The answer to the first question lies in the discrepancy between those aspects of the social production process which are regulated by the surface inter-actions of the agents, and the forms in which these interactions are experienced by the agents. The equality of all human labour is enforced by the exchangeability of all commodities, and social labour time is allocated and accounted by the quantitative market relations between goods. In other words, the social connections between the producers' labours are not perceived and acted upon by the producers as such, but take the form of properties of things.

People try to take advantage of these social properties of their things, but they are often frustrated in their efforts, because the social properties change in the exact moment when people react to them:

> The magnitudes of value vary continually, independently of the will, foreknowledge and actions of the exchangers. Their own social movement has for them the form of a movement of things – things which, far from being under their control, in fact control them.

(Marx 1976: 167–8)

Critical realism can clarify this argument. For this let us turn to Bhaskar's primordial retroductive argument, which infers general properties of the world (stratification, homogeneity, openness, etc.) from the fact that science is possible. Our world might be such that science is impossible, but in fact it is possible to learn about the world through science, and this tells us something about the world.

Bhaskar registers the abstract possibility of the impossibility of science, but does not give any examples of areas in which science is indeed impossible. Marx, in the commodity fetishism section, gives such an example: the market is an area in which science and rational activity is not possible for the market participants. This is why Marx calls the commodity 'magical'. With respect to the social properties of the commodities, there is no separation between the transitive and intransitive dimensions, because that which the agents investigate and act upon is already the secret by-product of their own activity. This is a framework in which rationality and ingenuity does not allow the economic agents to impose their will on the world, but on the contrary, they become the pawns in a bigger game which they do not control. Marx uses the metaphor of a 'phantasmagoria', translated as 'fantastic' in Marx (1976: 165), an optical illusion created with the help of a magic lantern. In more modern terms, the market participants live in a virtual reality, which gives them the illusion that they are able to act in their own interest, but which channels them towards a predetermined outcome.

The second question is as follows: is there anything in the production process itself which paves the ground for this lack of social control? Marx points out that already during production the producers consider not only the natural properties of the labour process, but they take a peek at the elusive social properties of their products as well.

Unfortunately Marx does not elaborate on the significance of this. Therefore I will try to supply my own explanation. To Marx, the relations in the production process proper, where human individuals interact with nature, are central to the fabric of the whole society. This is the point where no illusions are allowed, where actions must be most rational, where mankind has to be most awake. Nature does not yield to pious wishes but only to scientifically guided purposeful activity. Now if the man-made market properties of goods are given consideration in this domain of direct production, this introduces irrealism precisely at that point where relations should most strongly be directed towards reality. The lack of control is the spread of this irrealism.

The exchange process

In the second chapter, Marx investigates how the expressions of value discussed in section three of the first chapter serve the practical needs of the commodity traders on the surface of the economy. While section two of the first chapter confirmed that the core is real, the second chapter confirms that the surface is functional.

A simple commodity producer who goes to market in order to barter his products pursues two opposite goals in the same transaction. On the one hand, he wants to get the use value in this exchange that best suits his needs, and on the other, he wants to realise the value of his commodity which he is giving in exchange.

These two goals are so much at odds with each other, that Marx presents them metaphorically as the goals of two different agents, of the commodity producer himself on the one hand, and his commodity on the other. The commodity is single-mindedly interested in realising its *value*, while the commodity producer is the procrastinator restraining the commodity until he has found a *use value* that suits him. The commodity, which represents the social context in which the commodity producer stands, is depicted as having its own will, because the market relations between the commodities are beyond the control of the traders. Marx's metaphorical conflict between the commodity and its owner is an apt characterisation of the juggling act, by which people fit their individual goals and desires into the invisible but inescapable social framework in which they find themselves.

The contradiction between the two goals can be seen as follows: as soon as the commodity producer has set his mind on a specific use value, he is limited in offering his commodity only to the producers of this article, and therefore cannot get the same fair equivalent which he would be able to get if he offered his commodity to everyone.

This contradiction can be 'solved' by splitting the barter into two transactions: a sale which has the purpose of realising the value of the commodity, and a purchase which has the purpose of selecting the use value desired by the individual. For this, money is necessary. But Marx emphasises that this money does not have to be introduced now as an instrument to facilitate the exchange, since it already exists as the most appropriate social expression of value.

In other words, the origin of money lies in the core, not the surface. This is an important insight. Whether something is a good money or not is not decided by how well it facilitates the exchange, but by how well it induces the economic agents to treat their products as values, i.e., to equalise their labours, and encourages them to make profits by production instead of speculation. In today's global economy, money does not need to be commodity money, but these criteria for a good money still apply.

The curse of money

The second chapter shows therefore that the expressions of value developed in section three of the first chapter are functional for the exchange process, which in turn co-ordinates production in such a way that abstract labour is the main organising principle. The system is consistent, channels 1 and 2 fit together. But the third chapter shows that the best expression of value on the surface also generates surface behaviours which send messages down to the core that go beyond the needs of a social production process based on abstract labour.

This novelty appears at first in the function of money as a hoard. After the social form of General equivalent has once and for all been attached to a specific use value, say gold, new behaviours arise. Now it becomes practically desirable to accumulate gold, to hold on to wealth in its abstract form. The desire to accumulate money is *insatiable* because:

> according to its concept, money is the quintessence of all use values; but, since it is always only a given amount of money (here, capital), its quantitative limitation stands in contradiction to its quality. The constant drive beyond its own limitation is therefore inherent in its nature.
>
> (Marx 1973: 270 and Marx 1986: 200, translation adjusted)

This quote is from *Grundrisse*, but it is obvious that Marx was employing the same argument in *Capital*.

Let me restate: Qualitatively, money gives access to all use values, i.e., qualitatively it is universal. This qualitative universality comes into conflict with its quantitative boundedness, since money always only exists as a limited sum of money. This conflict is felt by everyone dealing with money, and an obvious resolution is to try to get more money. The drive for quantitative expansion belongs therefore to the nature of money. It is what I call the 'curse' of money. Now money is no longer servant but king.

The tendency of money to multiply itself is therefore as old as money itself. It does not come from human greed but from the money form. If there is one key which unlocks all doors, it seems very rational to get hold of that key. Not only the greedy capitalist, but also the worker who willingly agrees to overtime, the consumers who purchase shiny toys so that they do not have to feel their social isolation (i.e., the modern version of Marx's 'spendthrift') are victims of the curse of money.

The curse of money has its origin in circulation. But it finds its rational kernel, its alethia, not in the withdrawal of money from circulation, but in the production of surplus value, which necessarily encompasses both production and circulation, as Marx shows in the fifth chapter; i.e., not the miser but the capitalist is its 'rational' agent.

Capitalist business can only be an exception as long as the mechanisms to multiply values are not in place in the core of the economy. For a long time, capital existed therefore only at the periphery of the economy, as merchant capital or usury capital siphoning surplus value out of circulation. Early examples, mentioned by Marx in the tenth chapter (Marx 1976: 345), in which the motive to make more and more money was directly tied into production, are the gold and silver mines in antiquity – these were at the same time among the few places where slaves were systematically worked to death.

Only with the creation of a modern proletariat, i.e., with the wholesale exclusion of the direct producers from their means of production, could the principle of self-valorisation be elevated to the main principle governing production. In the formal subsumption of labour under capital, the capital relation still in part hovers on the surface, in the changed property relations, while the character of the production process is unchanged. Only with the real subsumption of labour under capital, i.e., with the development of machinery which controls the labourer, speeds the labourer up, and at the same time sucks the skills out of the labour process, has the capital relation become fully centred in the core of the economy, and has the expropriation of the worker been completed.

Does critical realism make a difference?

I will break off my summary here. Although this summary is deeply informed by critical realism, it does not have Bhaskarianisms sticking out of it everywhere comparable to the Hegelianisms in Marx's own text. This is a sign that dialectical critical realism fits Marx better than Hegel's philosophy and blends in with the flow of Marx's argument. Dialectical critical realism comes in through the stratification of the economy into core and surface, the reality of generative mechanisms, the use of retroductive arguments and of dialectics, the conscious use of irreducibility and emergence, the recognition of contradictions and their use as signposts pointing toward hidden layers, the recognition of situations where science is not possible, etc. Nevertheless, even someone unfamiliar with these general concepts should find this narrative understandable. The framework proposed here is more systematic and more easily accessible than Marx's original argument – but it is also narrower, since something is always lost in such translations.

The interpretations of Marx given in this essay are a summary of my *Annotations* (Ehrbar 2000), a work which is still incomplete at the time of this writing. Some of the interpretations given here may have to be revised, but I hope that:

- any errors in the above translation of Marx's arguments can be corrected within the DCR framework or will lead to a remedy of those shortcomings that may exist in DCR or Marxism itself;
- Marx's easier accessibility will take him out of the hands of the 'cranks' and open him to a wider scientific community;
- the gap between Marxism and modern emancipatory social sciences will be narrowed, and that this will make it easier to refute irrealist apologies of capitalism.

The main stumbling block however is not the theoretical power of academic emancipatory social sciences, which is steadily increasing, but its theory-practice inconsistency. Again, besides Marxism there is only one branch of the modern social sciences which addresses this: dialectical critical realism.

Bibliography

Althusser, L. and Balibar, E. (1970) *Reading Capital*, translated by B. Brewster, London: New Left Books.

Bhaskar, R. (1989a) *The Possibility of Naturalism: A Philosophical Critique of Contemporary Human Sciences*, 2nd edition, London and New York: Harvester Wheatsheaf.

—— (1989b) *Reclaiming Reality: A Critical Introduction to Contemporary Philosophy*, London and New York: Verso.

—— (1993) *Dialectic: The Pulse of Freedom*, London and New York: Verso.

—— (1997) *A Realist Theory of Science*, London and New York: Verso. Reprint of the 1977 2nd edition.

Ehrbar, H.G. (2000) *Annotations to Karl Marx's 'Capital'*, draft version under development. Online – available at http://www.econ.utah.edu/ehrbar/akmc.htm

Lenin, V.I. (1961) *Philosophical Notebooks*, *Lenin Collected Works 38*, Moscow: Foreign Languages Publishing House.

Marsden, R. (1998) 'The unknown masterpiece: Marx's model of capital', *Cambridge Journal of Economics* 22, 3: 297–324.

Marx, K. (1973) *Grundrisse*, translated by M. Nicolaus, New York: Vintage.

—— (1976) *Capital*, vol. I, translated by B. Fowkes, New York: Vintage (Random House).

—— (1986) *Economic Works 1857–61*, *Marx-Engels Collected Works 28*, New York: International Publishers. Contains the beginning of the economic manuscripts of 1857–8 (the first version of *Capital*), known as *Grundrisse*.

Rubin, I. (1972) *Essays on Marx's Theory of Value*, Detroit: Black and Red. Originally appeared in Moscow in 1928.

4 What kind of *theory* is Marx's labour *theory* of value?

A critical realist inquiry

Steve Fleetwood

Introduction[1]

Whilst much ink has been spilled discussing the nature of 'labour' and 'value' in Marx's labour theory of value, the nature of 'theory' has often been neglected.[2] Methodological questions such as 'What *kind* of theory should the labour theory of value be?' are hardly ever asked. This is a serious omission. If, as seems likely, substantive theory can be *positively* influenced by being rooted in an appropriate method or mode of theorisation then it can be *negatively* influenced by being rooted in an inappropriate mode. As a substantive theory, the labour theory of value (LTV) is no different. Rooting the LTV in an inappropriate (*deductivist*) mode of theorisation has a negative influence in the sense that it encourages the formulation of (*quantitative*) versions of the LTV that (a) have severe problems and (b) lack explanatory power. Rooting the LTV in an appropriate (*causal-explanatory*) mode, by contrast, has a positive influence in the sense that it encourages the formulation of (*qualitative*) versions of the LTV that (a) lack such problems and (b) have explanatory power. The mode of theorisation one employs, therefore, has a strong influence upon the version of the LTV one ends up with.

Now, given the fact that there are not only numerous versions of the LTV, but also numerous methodological approaches, I employ two generalising devices. First, I use Sweezy's distinction between *quantitative* and *qualitative* versions of the LTV, placing all versions in one or other of these categories. Second, I use the *critical realist* argument that, basically, there are only two modes of theorisation, namely the deductivist and what I call the causal-explanatory, placing all modes of theorisation in one or other of these categories. The combinations of theories and modes of theorising can be schematised as in Figure 4.1.

This chapter was first published as an article in the journal *Capital & Class* 73(2001): 41–77.

		Version of the LTV encouraged by the mode of theorisation	
		Qualitative	Quantitative
Mode of theorisation	Deductivist	no	yes
	Causal-explanatory	yes	no

Figure 4.1 Version of the LTV and corresponding modes of theorisation

Format

The chapter consists of two distinct parts. Part 1 focuses on methodology. It opens with an introduction to the deductivist mode of theorisation before turning to critical realism to (a) establish a critique of this mode and (b) elaborate upon the alternative encouraged by critical realism, namely the causal-explanatory mode of theorisation. Part 2 applies the conclusions from the discussion of methodology to value theory. It opens with an exposition of the quantitative versions of the LTV and explains why they can be conceived of as rooted in the deductivist mode of theorising. It then turns to critical realism to (a) establish a critique of these quantitative versions of the LTV and (b) elaborate upon the alternative qualitative versions of the LTV encouraged by the causal-explanatory mode of theorisation. In this way, methodological arguments emanating from the critical realist perspective, generate both the critique of, and the alternative to, quantitative versions of the LTV, and facilitate an answer to the question: 'What kind of theory should the LTV be?'

PART 1: METHODOLOGY

Deductivist mode of theorising

Critical realists like Lawson (1997) argue that the dominant mode of explanation in economics is the *deductivist* mode,[3] wherein to 'explain' something is to deduce a statement about that something from a set of initial conditions, assumptions, axioms, and a law, and/or some other form of constant conjunction of events. Advocates usually claim that the deductivist mode offers more than just explanation. *Amongst* their claims (justified or not) are the following:

- Deductivism allows consistent behaviour to be deduced or predicted from antecedents. Some, but not all, advocate the empirical testing of hypotheses via predictive power.

- Deductivism allows our thoughts to be presented systematically, with clarity and with the (spurious?) precision of mathematics.
- Deductivism, because it presents an idealised version of reality, allows the relationships between certain important variables to be expressed simply and free from the 'clutter' of other, less important variables.
- Deductivism allows one to understand pathological states (i.e. disequilibrium) by comparing them to hypothetical non-pathological states (i.e. equilibrium).
- Proving the existence of a unique solution or an equilibrium, under simplified conditions, gives economists a reason to believe that they are 'on the right track' as Hausman (1992: 100–1) puts it (cf. Lawson 1997: ch. 8).

Generally speaking, then, and for reasons that are almost never spelled out, economists appear to believe they have demonstrated something important about the real world when they can consistently deduce a set of conclusions from a set of initial premises.[4] In virtue of the slightly wider nature of these claims I refer to this mode as the deductivist mode of *theorising*, rather than mode of *explanation*.

Now, whilst the deductivist mode of theorising derives what intellectual support and justification it does from positivism, its employment *in economics* is often extended way beyond any empirical level that most positivists would wish to sanction. Simply put, deductivism often generates purely algebraic or 'toy' models (Pencavel 1991: 84) which are neither derived from, nor tested against, sense experience or empirical data. Because Marxist economic theory is replete with such models, a little elaboration will pay dividends.

Broadly speaking, there are two (incorrect) approaches to 'doing' economic theory. The first approach, econometric modelling, is clearly rooted in sense data and hence empiricism. The economist constructs a model which hypothesises a relationship between certain variables (i.e. a constant conjunction of events), then confronts the model with data. The model is deemed 'adequate' if the hypothesised relationship is consistent with the data. In the second approach, 'toy' modelling, the economist constructs a purely algebraic model and makes no attempt to confront it with data. These models are often acknowledged by their advocates to be unrealistic, and are legitimised in various ways – as noted above.

Now, 'toy' models appear not to be rooted in empiricism; appear not to involve the events of sense experience; and appear not to involve constant conjunctions of events. This has led some to argue that whilst these models are not immune from criticism, they are immune from the particular criticism offered by critical realists which turns on a critique of constant conjunctions – elaborated upon in section 1.2 below.[5] This argument is, I think, incorrect. In 'toy' models, scientific knowledge is generated by constant conjunctions of events, but because the latter are implicitly built into the model as an *a priori* premise, they do not manifest themselves explicitly as in the case of the empirical relationships of econometric models. This is why some have concluded (incorrectly) that scientific knowledge is being generated by something other than constant conjunctions of events.

To explain how constant conjunctions of events are implicitly built into a model as an *a priori* premise, consider the following example.[6] In their classic paper on efficiency wage theory Shapiro and Stiglitz (1990: 48) attempt to predict when a worker will choose not to shirk. They write: 'if and only if $V^s/_e$ is greater than or equal to $V^n/_e$ the worker will choose to shirk'.[7] In what follows, I briefly sketch four reasons why constant conjunctions of events are implicitly built into this 'toy' model as an *a priori* premise.

i   Another way of expressing this situation is to write whenever event x $(V^s/_e \geq V^n/_e)$, then event y (shirking behaviour). True, Shapiro and Stiglitz did not arrive at this conclusion via sense experience, rather it is spun out of the axioms, assumptions and theorems of mainstream economics. The presumption, however, must be that, under certain conditions, the hypothesised constant conjunctions of events have a counterpart in reality and could even, perhaps, be observed. If this is not presumed, then the relevance of the model is undermined: why should anyone bother modelling something that does not, however remote, express some feature of reality.

ii   The whole analysis takes place *at the level of events*. If one event is observed or hypothesised, one can only seek its cause in terms of another observed or hypothesised event. If causality is implied (and if it is not then the whole point of the model is in doubt) then so too are *constantly* conjoined events – causality is elaborated upon in the following section.

iii Epistemology presupposes ontology. Ideas about how knowledge of reality is gained from a 'toy' model, are intelligible only via the presumption that the socio-economic world is a certain kind of place – i.e. a place where, under certain conditions, whenever $V^s/_e \geq V^n/_e$, then shirking behaviour will follow. *If* the socio-economic world is (presupposedly) characterised by constant conjunctions of events, then building a model that expresses such regular behaviour is a consistent way to obtain knowledge of it.

iv   The centrality of the built-in event constancy can be seen by considering how useless a model would be if statements couched in terms of events were allowed, but event constancy was not present. Consider how useless the following statement would be: 'if and only if $V^s/_e$ is greater than or equal to $V^n/_e$, the worker will, *on some occasions* choose to shirk, and *other occasions* choose not to shirk'. If constant conjunctions of events are *not* implicitly built into 'toy' models as an *a priori* premise, then nothing can be deduced from the antecedents: the model is useless on its own terms.

Once one understands that constant conjunctions of events are implicitly built into 'toy' models, one can see constancy appearing in the following two general guises.

i Constant conjunctions can form part of a 'toy' model (e.g.) $y = f(x)$ *ceteris paribus*. Here the constant conjunctions of events that constitute this functional relation have been spun out of the basic axioms, assumptions and theorems, and will not be tested against observed events. The implication, however, (*on pain of irrelevance*) is that the constant conjunctions of events that are built into the 'toy' model have a counterpart in reality.

ii The constant conjunctions can form part of an econometric model (e.g.) $y = a + \beta_1 x_1, + \beta_2 x_2 + \beta_n x_n, + v$. Here the constant conjunctions of events may have been spun out of the basic axioms, assumptions and theorems; may have been derived from the observation and recording of events; or may have been simply hypothesised.

The difference between (i) and (ii) is that in the latter, the alleged constancy will be tested against observed events. What is significant for our purposes, however, is that in both of these cases the mode of theorisation turns, fundamentally, upon the alleged existence and ubiquity of constant conjunctions of events. Without event constancy, the deductivist mode of theorisation does not get off the ground.[8]

1.2 Critical realist critique of the deductivist mode

From the perspective of critical realism, the deductive mode of theorisation is inappropriate for two reasons. First, because the need to engineer *closed systems* generates a set of problematic and counterintuitive implications; and second, the deductive mode of theorisation lacks explanatory power. Significantly, the root cause of these difficulties lies in the impoverished ontology presupposed by this mode. These will now be considered in turn.

Closed systems

Now whilst constant conjunctions of events are clearly fundamental to deductivism, they are exceptionally rare phenomena. There appear to be very few spontaneously occurring systems wherein constant conjunctions of events occur in the natural world, and virtually none in the social world. That is not to deny the possibility that constant conjunctions may occur accidentally, or over some restricted spatio-temporal region, or be trivial. But virtually all of the constant conjunctions of interest to science (including economics) occur only in experimental situations. The point of experiment is to *close the system* by creating a particular set of conditions that will isolate the one interesting mechanism. This mechanism is then allowed to operate unimpeded and the results, the constant conjunctions, recorded. For economists, constant conjunctions of events appear to be found only in the 'conceptual experiments' (Pencavel 1994, p.15) that constitute closed systems. Herein constant conjunctions are engineered by satisfying (minimally) four *closure conditions*.[9]

i Intrinsic closure conditions (ICC)

The *internal state* of the individuals that constitute the system must be engineered in such a way that when acted upon by causal factors $x_1, x_2 \ldots x_n$, the relevant individual *always* responds in the same *a priori* predictable way, by initiating action y. Most economic analysis is specified in terms of individual entities (e.g. human beings, or collectivities such as firms) with an intrinsic state. How an individual responds to a causal influence, depends, in part, upon this intrinsic state. For example, the response by a workforce, *vis-à-vis* levels of output, to the introduction of performance related pay is likely to depend upon factors like *expectations*. The ICC is satisfied when the individual is specified *atomistically*. The atomistic individual is 'inert' in the sense that when acted upon by a causal influence, it will initiate one, predictable and constant course of action.

ii The extrinsic closure condition (ECC)

The ECC ensures that the system is completely isolated from any *external* influences. This occurs when: (i) all relevant causal factors are internalised within the system, or, if there remain relevant influences extrinsic to the system, either (ii) these factors are specified such that they exercise a perpetually constant influence, or (iii) the elements within the system are isolated from their effects. There are numerous context specific ways to satisfy these conditions.

iii The aggregational closure condition (ACC)

Even if the ECC and ICC are satisfied, there is still no guarantee that when faced with relevant causal factors the entity will initiate one predictable, unique and constant course of action. This is because economic analysis often has to deal with individual entities combined into groups. The whole point of the union, for example, is to initiate a course of action that one individual acting alone would be unlikely to take. The response of the workforce to causal factors $x_1, x_2 \ldots x_n$, will vary depending upon the characteristics, and distribution, of individuals or sub-group of individuals that constitute that workforce. Internal constancy must be maintained over an aggregate of individuals. One way of doing this is to focus upon the objectives of some appropriate sub-group – e.g. the trade union as a collectivity is specified to behave as the leadership does.

iv The reducibility closure (sub) condition (RCsC)

Finally, a sub-condition needs to be appended to the ICC, ECC and ACC to ensure that the number of potential courses of action an individual might initiate is *reduced* to one and hence is unique. Deducing a unique solution requires that the system is fully specified via a series of auxiliary assumptions, or assumptions of *tractability*. These are merely technical assumptions whose sole purpose is to ensure the relevant functions are well behaved, thereby preventing perverse outcomes.

Whilst closed systems are necessary to generate the constant conjunctions of events, they create, as unintended consequences, a series of problematic and counterintuitive implications:

i   Outside closed systems, where constant conjunctions of events are not usually found (i.e. reality), one would have to conclude that there are no laws. This would be tantamount to saying that nothing governs the non-constant flux of events in open systems; science (including economics) would, then, become a fruitless endeavour.

ii   It is often the case in natural science that conclusions derived from experimental situations (i.e. in closed systems) are successfully applied outside experimental situations (i.e. in open systems). This occurs *not* because the scientist has discovered a constant conjunction of events, but because the causal mechanism at work has been uncovered and understood, and can, therefore, be used even in situations where it does not generate constant conjunctions of events. Because of (i) above, this state of affairs would have no valid explanation.

iii Deducing statements about the action of agents operating in a closed system, and transferring them to the action of agents in the open system, commits the fallacy called *ignoratio elenchi*. This entails assuming that one has demonstrated something to be true of X when the argument or evidence really applies to Y which is not the same as X in some respect (Gordon 1991: 108). What is 'not the same' is the existence and ubiquity of constant conjunctions of events. The various claims made by advocates of the deductive mode of theorisation in support of this mode (some of which were mentioned in section 1.1 seem to commit this fallacy.[10]

Explanation

Following Lipton (1993: 33) I argue that to 'explain a phenomenon is to give information on the phenomenon's causal history', and on this basis, I offer three reasons why the deductivist mode of theorising lacks explanatory power.

i Explanation is not merely event regularity

The 'causal history of a phenomenon' is not merely (if at all) one couched in terms of the event that happens to precede the phenomenon, but in terms of the underlying, transfactually operating, causal mechanisms, structures, powers and relations. One does not, for example, adequately explain (the event of) my office light becoming illuminated simply by pointing to the (event of) flicking of the switch that preceded it. Yet this form of 'explanation' is all that is available in the deductivist mode. The need to engineer closed systems means that the model has to remove, theoretically of course, all potential causal factors that might violate the closure conditions. It is crucially important to grasp that *once removed from the model, relevant causal factors cannot subsequently be recalled and offered as part of the causal explanation. Relevant causal factors are either included in the model, in which case they contribute to the causal explanation, or they are excluded, in which case they cannot make such a contribution.*

ii Explanation is not prediction

Prediction does not constitute explanation. The conflation of prediction and explanation is referred to as the 'symmetry thesis'. Here the only real difference between explanation and prediction relates to the direction of time (Caldwell 1991: 54). Explanation entails the deduction of an event after it has (or is known to have) occurred. Prediction entails the deduction of an event prior to (knowledge of) its occurrence. One can, however, predict *without explaining anything at all.* One can predict the onset of measles following the emergence of Koplic spots, but the latter does not explain measles.[11]

iii Explanation does not allow known falsehoods

If, as part of this causal story, one opts to include a *known* falsehood, or, which amounts to the same thing, leaves out important causal factors that one *knows* are important (falsehood by omission) then any claim to have provided an explanation can immediately be rejected by pointing to the falsehood(s). One only has to reflect upon this for a moment to see this conclusion is self-evidently correct: if known fictions were allowed into explanations all manner of bizarre explanations could be advanced.

In sum, then, the deductivist mode of theorisation suffers from two major flaws. First, a series of problems arise when analysis is couched in terms of closed systems where constant conjunctions of events are allegedly ubiquitous, when socio-economic reality is an open system where such conjunctions are not found. The lack of constant conjunctions means, of course, that the main objective of positivist versions of 'science', namely predictive power, is redundant. Second, lacking explanatory power, the deductivist mode has no alternative but to *substitute* prediction, deduction solution, determination and calculation as the objective of science. The lack of explanatory power combined with the redundancy of predictive power, however, seriously damages deductivism: the objective it pursues is invalid, whilst the only remaining objective is out of its grasp.[12]

The impoverished ontology of deductivism

The problems afflicting the deductivist mode of theorising can, ultimately, be traced back to ontology. Every time one makes a theoretical or meta-theoretical statement, one has already made explicit or implicit claims about the way the world is thought to be; one has made ontological commitments or presuppositions; one has an ontology. And it is these ontological presuppositions that render theoretical and meta-theoretical statements intelligible. For example, a theory couched in terms of individuals is rendered intelligible by the presupposition of an ontology of atomism: such a theory would be rendered *un*intelligible by the presupposition of an ontology of holism.

In what follows, the central features of the deductivist mode of theorisation are clearly stated so that, step by step, the ontology that renders these features intelligible is identified. Once identified, the inappropriateness of this ontology can be ascertained and, furthermore, the way is prepared (in section 1.3) for an elaboration of the alternative, and by contrast, appropriate ontology that roots the causal-explanatory mode of theorisation.

- Central to the way the deductivist mode of theorising is operationalised are functional relations, generalised as $y = f(x)$. These can also be expressed as laws and styled *'whenever event x then event y'*.

- If functional relations and laws are to have economic meaning (as opposed to 'mere' mathematical meaning) then they *must* imply causality. Causality renders them intelligible. The clear implication, for example, of writing, $q = f(p)$ is that the quantity (demanded or supplied) varies with, and is caused to vary by, price.

- Functional relations and laws are not, however, rendered intelligible by just any account of causality, but by one based upon constant conjunctions of events, and deriving from Hume.[13] The use of this notion of causality might arise from a conscious decision, or it might arise by default, because other notions of causality that involve, for example, transfactually acting mechanisms and powers (see section 1.3) would render functional relations and laws unintelligible. Laws as constant conjunctions of events are, thereby, referred to as 'Humean'.

- If one were to discover a constant conjunction of events in the form of a Humean law or functional relation, one might claim to have *scientific* knowledge. This is because it is the constant conjunction of events that makes possible the deduction or prediction of some event(s) from antecedents. Crucially, then, *constant conjunctions of events drive the nomological machinery of the deductivist mode of theorising.*

- Scientific knowledge in the form of constant conjunctions of events is only intelligible on the presumption that *particular* knowledge is derived via experiencing, and subsequently recording unique, individual, or atomistic events. These events cannot be other than atomistic, since any connection or relation between them would be impervious to sense experience, otherwise the nature of the connections would require prior explanation, thus undermining the explanatory power of sense experience. The ontology, implicit or explicit, is, therefore, one of *atomistic* events.

• Ontology is confined to that which is experienced[14] and is, therefore, of the atomistic events of sense experience.[15] Because these objects are confined to experience the ontology is *empirical*; and because these objects are thought to exist independently of one's identification of them, it is *realist;* the ontology can, thereby, be labeled *empirical realist.*

The deductivist mode of theorising, and the functional relations and laws that operationalise it, are rendered intelligible, therefore, by the consistent presupposition of causality as constant event conjunctions and an empirical realist ontology.[16] Table 4.1 illustrates that this empirical realist ontology consists of two *fused* domains referred to as the empirical and the actual.

Table 4.1 Empirical realist or 'flat' ontology

Domain	Entity
Empirical	Experiences, perceptions
Actual	Events and actions

What *is*, is presumed co-existent with what is (or what could, under certain conditions be) *perceived*. Causality as constant event conjunctions means that if some event is perceived, one can only seek its cause in terms of another perceived event. *There is nowhere else to seek a cause* because any other domain in this ontological spectrum is ruled out. The result is not only an impoverished ontology, one restricted to the domains of the empirical and the actual, but also a set of implicit (ontological) claims about the world that are, in fact, *at odds with the way the world really is*. The world does not consist merely of events and their experiences: nor does it consist merely of constant conjunctions of these events. This is a serious state of affairs because it means the very building blocks out of which theories are constructed fail to express reality.

1.3 Critical realist alternative: the causal-explanatory mode

Being fully cognisant of the problems that can arise from a lack of ontological reflection, critical realism takes ontology seriously. The following sections demonstrate how critical realism can generate an alternative ontology, an alternative mode of theorising, and, ultimately, an alternative version of the LTV.

Firmly rejecting constant conjunctions of events as most unlikely features of social reality and, thereby, abandoning the notion of causality as mere

Table 4.2 A structured ontology

Domain	Entity
Empirical	Experiences, perceptions
Actual	Events and actions
'Deep'	Structures, mechanisms, powers, relations

regularity, the critical realist is free to seek the cause of an event elsewhere in the ontological spectrum. Attention turns away from the flux of events (constant or otherwise) and towards the *causal mechanisms, social structures, powers and relations* that govern them. Rather than the ontology being restricted to the fused domains of the actual and empirical, the critical realist adds another domain, namely the (metaphoric) 'deep'. Table 4.2 illustrates this *stratified* ontology.

In an *open* system, these domains are, typically, out of phase with one another meaning, one cannot map (say) the effect of a power or causal mechanism to its manifestation at the level of events and perceptions. This is because powers and causal mechanisms act *transfactually*: once set in motion, they continue to have an influence, even if other countervailing powers and mechanisms prevent this influence manifesting itself. An aeroplane has the power to fly even when it remains locked in a hanger: this power acts transfactually. In Marxist economics transfactuality underpins Marx's notion of tendencies. The causal mechanisms and powers that combine to generate the tendency of the rate of profit to decline act transfactually. These mechanisms and powers are always in operation even when empirically the rate of profit is rising. They are transfactual due to the operation of other causal mechanisms such as technological advances acting in a countervailing manner (for an elaboration of tendencies, see Fleetwood 2001b).

Now, not only is the ontology adopted by critical realism stratified, it is also *transformational*. Bhaskar establishes the possibility of a transformational ontology from an investigation into the nature of society.[17] Whilst traditionally most commentators recognise that society consists (in some sense) of agents and structures, the debate centres upon the way they interact. With the Transformational Model of Social Action (TMSA), Bhaskar enjoins this debate. Nothing happens out of nothing. Agents do not create or produce structures *ab initio,* rather they *re*create, *re*produce and/or *transform* a set of pre-existing structures. Society continues to exist only because agents reproduce and/or transform those structures that they encounter in their social actions. Every action performed requires the pre-existence of some social structures which agents draw upon in order to initiate that action, and in doing so reproduce and/or transform them. For example, communicating requires a medium (e.g. language), and the operation of the market requires the rules of private property. This ensemble of social structures, according to Bhaskar, simply *is* society. As Bhaskar observes:

> people do not create society. For it always pre-exists them and is a necessary condition for their activity. Rather society must be regarded as an ensemble of structures, practices and conventions which individuals reproduce and transform, but which would not exist unless they did so. Society does not exist independently of human activity (the error of reification). But it is not the product of it (the error of voluntarism).
>
> (Bhaskar 1989: 36, see also 1987: 129)

The transformational principle, then, centres upon the *causal mechanisms, structures, powers and relations* that are the *ever-present condition, and the continually reproduced and/or transformed outcome, of* human agency. Agents, acting purposefully or consciously, unconsciously draw upon, and thereby reproduce, the mechanisms, structures, powers and relations which govern their actions in daily life.

Switch in the mode of theorising

Operating with a stratified and transformational ontology, the emphasis of investigation necessarily switches from the domains of the empirical and actual and the ensuing event patterns observed (or hypothesised) to the domain of the deep and the mechanisms that govern these events. Investigation switches from the *consequences*, that is, from the *outcomes or results* (in the form of events and their patterns) of some particular human action, to the conditions that make that action possible. As Bhaskar puts matters:

> Looked at in this way [TMSA] . . . the task of the various social sciences [is] to lay out the structural conditions for various conscious human actions – for example, what economic processes must take place for Christmas shopping to be possible – but they do not describe the latter.
>
> (Bhaskar 1989: 36)

Because of the openness of socio-economic systems and the transfactual nature of the causal mechanisms, consequences or outcomes *cannot* be deduced or predicted. The causal mechanisms that govern this human action *can*, however, be uncovered and explained. Explanation is *substituted* for deduction, prediction, solution, determination and calculation as the objectives of science.

It is worth saying a little more here about explanation. The causal-explanatory mode of reasoning makes significant use of a particular kind of explanation, namely *contrastive explanation*. Lipton (1993: 35) describes this with exceptional clarity:

What gets explained is not simply 'Why this?', but 'Why this rather than that?' . . . We may not explain why the leaves turn yellow in November, but only, for example, why they turn yellow in November rather than in January, or why they turn yellow in November rather than turning blue.

Whilst contrastive explanation will be employed in section 2.3, note two points. First, the nature of explanation is far richer than that utilised in the deductive mode of theorisation where explanation reduces to efficient causality, prediction/deduction, and often requires the introduction of falsehoods. Second, one can now understand the reason for calling the mode of reasoning 'causal-explanatory'. In this mode, to *explain* a phenomenon is to give information about relevant *causes*. This information is, typically, about the underlying, transfactually operating, causal mechanisms, social structures and powers.[18] It also expresses the main objective of science, namely, explanatory power.

PART 2: VALUE THEORY

As noted in the introduction, the existence of not only numerous versions of the LTV, but also numerous methodological approaches, requires the employment of two generalising devices. First, I differentiate between *quantitative* and *qualitative* versions of the LTV, placing all versions in one or other of these categories. Second, I argue that, basically, there are only two modes of theorisation, namely deductivist and causal-explanatory, placing all modes of theorisation in one or other of these categories.

2.1 Quantitative versions of the LTV

As the name implies, quantitative versions of the LTV deal explicitly with the (alleged) quantitative relationship between the expenditure of a quantity of labour power and the resultant commodity value, price of production, market value or market price.[19] The term 'quantitative', as used here, applies equally to both econometric and 'toy' models. Models are quantitative in the sense that when definite magnitudes are attached to concepts like labour, value and price, they are transformed into variables whereupon they can be dealt with in terms of functional relations and/or laws.

Although a little dated, Meek's work has the merit of succinctly elaborating the conventional wisdom underlying quantitative versions of the LTV, namely the (alleged) existence of 'an important *functional relationship* between embodied labour and individual equilibrium prices, which may be expressed in the following symbolic form:

$$\text{Price of a commodity} = c + v + \frac{c + v}{\sum(c + v)}(\textstyle\sum s) \tag{1}$$

He then adds:

> Since all the items on the right hand side of the formula are expressible in terms of quantities of embodied labour, it can plausibly be maintained that there still is a *causal connection*, however indirect and circuitous between . . . 'values' and . . . 'prices of production'.
>
> (Meek 1967: 104, all emphases added)

Put simply, quantitative versions of the LTV allege the existence of a *causal connection* between quantities of labour and prices. This connection is also evident in more recent forms of expression. Consider a fairly typical price of production model.

$$\mathbf{p} = [\mathbf{pA} + w\mathbf{l}](1 + r) \tag{2}$$

where **p** is a vector of production prices, *r* is the (equalised) rate of profit; *w* is the wage rate; **A**, the technology matrix, is an expression for the means of production set in motion by **l,** the vector of labour hours used. This equation suggests, once again, that a causal connection exists between labour input and prices. As noted above, causal connections like these can be expressed as functional relations such as $\mathbf{p} = f(\mathbf{l})$ *ceteris paribus*; 'whenever event **l** (change in labour input), then event **p** (change in price)', or more generally, *'whenever event x then event y'.*

Models like these are clear examples of the kind of 'toy' models discussed above and exemplified by Shapiro and Stiglitz's model of shirking behaviour. Model (2) effectively says: 'if *r*, *w* and **A** remain unchanged, a change in **l** *always* causes a change in **p**'. I will neither repeat the four reasons why constant conjunctions of events are built into this model of the LTV, nor the reasons why constant conjunctions can be expressed in terms of 'toy' and/or econometric models, because the arguments are exactly the same as those used to illustrate the shirking model in section 1.1.

What is significant for our purposes, however, is the crucial role played by constant conjunctions of events. Without constant conjunctions of events, quantitative versions of the LTV, rooted as they are in the deductivist mode of theorisation, simply do not get off the ground because they lack causal connections.

2.2 Critical realist critique of deductivist versions of the LTV

Part 1 established that the deductivist mode of theorisation suffers from two major flaws. First, a series of problems arise when analysis is couched in terms of closed systems. Second, lacking explanatory power, the deductivist

mode falls back on deduction, prediction, solution, determination and calculation as objectives of theorisation. In what follows, I demonstrate that
exactly the same flaws afflict quantitative versions of the LTV, using the
example of model (2).

Closed systems

The aim of the following four sub-sections is to show how model (2) has to be
specified to maintain the closure conditions. It also reveals the extensive use
of falsehoods which will be picked up again in section 2.4.

i Intrinsic closure conditions (ICC)

The ICC is satisfied when the individual is specified *atomistically*, which is
another way of saying they are specified as *homo-economicus*. One might, however, object that no individuals are specified in model (2), in which case
they cannot be specified atomistically, and hence the ICC is irrelevant in
this context. This objection fails to see that although no individuals are
explicitly specified, they are *implicitly* presupposed. Presupposed individuals
include labourers, capitalists, productive systems, firms, unions, consumers
and so on.

Consider the case of expectations. Expectations are especially important
for the more recent versions of the LTV because they are keen to emphasise
how real or chronological time matters. An agent specified non-atomistically
has the power to formulate expectations, whereas if specified atomistically,
this property is removed by assumption. Belofiore (1989: 13–15) alerts us to
the way expectations on the part of workers and capitalists play a role in
forming prices when expected prices are/are not translated into actual
prices. Model (2) assumes total income is sufficient to purchase the total
output in order to ensure reproduction. But expectations, when frustrated,
can prevent reproduction. Some capitalists will make errors of judgement
and will be forced into bankruptcy leaving creditors unpaid and workers
made redundant – with various knock-on effects for expectation. In order
to ensure reproduction, however, the model either assumes these agents are
not included, or that all expectations are fulfilled. Either way this is tantamount to (falsely) assuming that agents are atomistic, or there are no
expectations.

ii The extrinsic closure condition (ECC)

The ECC ensures that the system is completely isolated from any *external*
influences. Model (2) (falsely) ignores a range of external influences such as:
supply and demand, technological innovation, recession, government
policy, political ideology, and so on. To be sure, advocates of these models
are well aware of the role played by these factors, and some have been

captured within the formation of socially necessary labour, but others simply have to be ignored because including them would make the system unstable.

iii   The aggregational closure condition (ACC)

The ACC ensures that when individual entities combine into groups, the behaviour of the group remains as predictable as the individuals that constitute it. Consider the labour input. The vector of labour hours used l, does not specify anything about the composition of those who supply these labour hours. However, it must implicitly assume (falsely) that no matter how many or how few labourers are buried within the vector l, the effect on output remains constant. The ACC is maintained by implicit assumption.

iv   The reducibility closure (sub) condition (RCsC)

Deducing a unique solution requires assumptions of *tractability*. These are merely technical assumptions whose sole purpose is to ensure the relevant functions are well behaved, thereby preventing perverse outcomes. In model (2) the matrix A expresses the technology or machinery that is activated via labour. In the matrix A, a_{ij} represents the quantity of ith input used to produce a unit of output j. The relation between inputs and outputs from the machinery operating in conjunction with labour, is assumed never to falter, and to be known *a priori*. As the powerful (Marxist) *labour process theory* reveals, this is an unreasonable (false) assumption. The point is that it (and/or assumptions like it) must be made solely for purposes of mathematical tractability.

Points i to iv demonstrate that model (2) is an example of a closed system. As such, it reproduces the problematic and counterintuitive implications noted in section 1.2 and, thereby, immediately falls foul of the critical realist critique.

Moreover, the need to maintain closure makes it necessary to proceed by assuming that there are no expectations; assuming that no matter how many labourers are buried within the vector l, the effect on output remains constant; assuming the relation between inputs and outputs is assumed never to falter; and/or ignoring a range of external influences such as supply and demand, technological innovation, recession, government policy, political ideology and so on. Allow me to make two observations here to prevent any misunderstanding.

First, I am sure advocates of qualitative versions of the LTV are well aware of the range of causal influences that are important for considerations of value. The problem is they have no choice but to leave them out of the model. For example, quantitative versions of the LTV can be augmented to encompass things like the technological change resulting in workplace closures and restructuring, unemployment, state intervention and regulation, declining profit rates and crisis. But this augmentation cannot be accomplished via the deductive mode of reasoning, nor on the basis of closed systems, because these factors do not manifest themselves as constant conjunctions of events. The actual level of unemployment is multi-causal and cannot be deduced or predicted from (say) a change in technology: it is just not empirically true to say that some technological change (x) causes a reduction in unemployment (y). Hence, one cannot (meaningfully) 'bolt' a chain of theoretical pronouncements about things like technology and unemployment onto quantitative models like (2). Furthermore, the above (by no means exhaustive) range of assumptions illustrates the use of known falsehoods and/or falsehood by omission. The significance of such falsehoods will be discussed in a moment.

Second, model (2) contains a vector for labour (**1**). What kind of labour is this? Whilst models of this kind almost never spell it out, it does appear to be the kind of labour that could be observed interacting with the technology (**A**), and receiving a wage (w) – i.e. it is individual and concrete labour. Yet for Marx, the 'substance' of value is socially necessary and abstract labour. Whilst, to put matters very simply, the mechanism(s) that constitute the market are also those that facilitate the doubling of individual and concrete labour into itself and socially necessary abstract labour. At worst, the market is simply ignored in quantitative models, and at best, whatever the market does, it is presumed to have already done it. How this individual and concrete labour doubles into a unity of itself and socially necessary abstract labour is a mystery that no deductivist model could even begin to explain because they do not have the intellectual apparatus to deal with such qualitative issues. Should any such explanation be given, it would be an 'add on' to the model. Whatever the merits of the model then, the explanatory power would lie elsewhere. It is time to discuss explanation more fully.

Explanation

When considering models like (2) I am often minded to ask; do they actually *explain* anything? In a recent (and I must add extremely interesting) paper, Saad-Filho offers a clue, writing:

> This equation expresses the definition of price of production and it can, theoretically, be used to *calculate the price vector*. However *the equation does not explain* the logical determination of price nor the relation between price and value.
>
> (Saad-Filho 1997: 473, emphasis added)

If the model '*does not explain* the (logical) determination of price nor the relation between price and value' what does it explain? Arguably, models like this, rooted as they are in the deductivist mode of theorisation, offer no explanation whatsoever. The reasons are as follows.

Explanation is not merely efficient causality

The explanation of a phenomenon is irreducible to a statement of the event that happens to precede it. Unfortunately for models rooted in the deductivist mode of theorisation, this is precisely all that they have to offer. *All* model (2) states, therefore, is that if *r*, *w* and **A** remain unchanged then a change in **p** can be deduced from a change in **l**. If one asks what explains this change in **p** the only 'explanation' on offer is the change in **l** that preceded it.

Explanation is not prediction

As an example of a 'toy' model, model 2 does not make empirical predictions. Whilst it could be specified econometrically for this purpose, it would still not constitute an explanation because, prediction does not constitute explanation. All model (2) allows us to do is to calculate the price vector, that is, deduce the vector of prices consistent with the data on a highly restricted number of variables, namely interest rates, wages and technology.

In both of the above cases, the need to engineer closed systems requires the removal, theoretically of course, of all potential causal factors such as transfactually operating causal mechanisms, structures and powers, because these would almost certainly violate the closure conditions. Once removed from the model these factors cannot subsequently be recalled and offered as part of the causal explanation.

Explanation does not allow known falsehoods

If, as part of this causal story, one opts to include a *known* falsehood, or, opts for falsehood by omission, then the explanation can always be objected to simply by pointing to this falsehood. As noted above, model (2) is replete with falsehoods. Moreover, the further one delves into models like (2), the more one uncovers implicitly and explicitly false assumptions. To show how this can be done, consider the following.

In the deductive mode of theorisation the constant conjunctions of events often drives the inferential machinery by providing the covering law. Whilst the covering law in use here is the law of value, *it is understood in thoroughly Humean terms*. That is, the law of value is treated as a constant conjunction of events. Recall above that model (2) can be conceived of in terms of a functional relation $p = f(l)$. This implies that a change in the magnitude of labour input, causes a change in the magnitude of price *ceteris paribus*. As we saw, this can be generalised using the Humean formula 'whenever event x then event y'. The problem with this (Humean) way of interpreting the law of value is that it is empirically false. It is, I suggest, self-evidently true that there is no such constancy between an increase in the amount of labour and an increase in the value, production price, market value or market price of the commodity. After all, this is why Marx introduces the term 'socially necessary labour'.

There are, however, counter-arguments that are often deployed to legitimise the use of known falsehoods. The first is a retreat to spurious accounts of abstraction; the second turns on the method of successive approximation or isolation. Since they are common objections, it is important to show that they cannot carry the weight of the counter-argument.

The retreat to spurious abstraction

The first counter-argument runs as follows: 'all theory has to leave out the inessential, has to abstract from reality, has to make unrealistic assumptions, so all theory is inevitably false in the strict sense of the word'. Now whilst the process of abstraction is complex and cannot be elaborated upon here, I simply put the following point to the reader. Models like (2) are replete with fictions and to suggest they are really abstractions is merely a neat piece of footwork to try and avoid having to discuss methodology. Furthermore, whilst mainstream economists can, in a sense, be forgiven for this retreat to a spurious account of abstraction because their canon has never discussed abstraction, Marxist economists have no such excuse. As Marx himself put matters: 'In the analysis of economic forms neither microscopes nor chemical reagents are of use. The force of abstraction must replace both' (1983: 19). Whilst Marx never really elaborated upon the notion of abstraction, others have, and the need to take abstraction seriously is widely recognised in Marxist circles – it is just ignored when the deductive mode of theorisation is employed to formulate quantitative versions of the LTV.

Method of successive approximation or successive isolation

The second counter-argument runs as follows. 'Models like (2) are very simple and, necessarily, make many unrealistic assumptions. This, however, is an initial stage of theorisation. Explanatory power can be added via the progressive relaxing of these unrealistic assumptions.' The method being employed, then, is the 'method of successive approximation' (Sweezy 1968: 11) or the 'method of isolation' (Maki 1992).

Whilst a thoroughgoing critique of this defence cannot be undertaken here, the following brief comments can be made. First, the method of successive approximation or isolation would be appropriate in two situations that almost never arise in the socio-economic world.

i When the factors considered in isolation express reality and are not falsehoods. When the earlier analytical stages involve the use of falsehoods like 'no frustrated expectations', then the succession is one of falsehood built upon falsehood.

ii   When the successive analytical steps merely involve the *mechanical* adding
     in of factors that were previously excluded, and the overall outcome is a
     resultant. This mechanical addition is, however, not appropriate for sys-
     tems where the elements possess emergent properties. When, for example:
     new technology is introduced to a workplace; a new management
     regime is installed; the workforce grows to a particular size; or the work-
     force becomes unionised, its behaviour evolves so that previous accounts
     of its behaviour are obsolete. Any theoretical propositions that were
     deduced on the basis of the previous account are immediately invalidated
     and provide no basis for the mechanical addition of a new set of
     behaviour.[20]

Second, none of this overcomes the objection that the model is still rooted
in a closed system approach. All that has happened is that one closed system
has been added to another (slightly broader) closed system. A bundle of
sequentially closed systems do not, however, add up to an open system. One
cannot for example, start with a model that assumes price is reducible to
dated inputs of individual and concrete labour (and deduce a set of conclusions from this), then relax this assumption and assume that price is governed
by socially necessary abstract labour, because if the latter is true, then the
former is false and so the conclusions derived from it are also false. The
method of successive approximations, or successive closures might, therefore,
be more accurately termed the 'method of successive falsehoods' or the
'method of successive closed systems'.

   It appears that quantitative versions of the LTV, rooted as they are in the
deductivist mode of theorisation and its emaciated ontology reproduce the
two major flaws afflicting this mode in general. First, they engender a series
of problems arising from analysis couched in terms of closed systems when
socio-economic reality is an open system. Second, lacking explanatory
power, quantitative versions of the LTV *substitute* prediction, deduction,
solution, determination and calculation as the objectives of science. Devoid
of explanatory power, the only thing left to do, and so the whole point of constructing quantitative versions of the LTV, is 'to calculate the price vector'.
And that really is that. This state of affairs makes quantitative versions of the
LTV not so much 'wrong' as *irrelevant*. Performing formal operations such as
calculating the price vector in a model that has no connection to reality is as
(ir)relevant as calculating the speed of a pig flying between London and
New York.

2.3 Qualitative versions of the LTV as causal-explanatory

This final section argues not only that Marx appears to have employed something like the causal-explanatory mode but, more importantly, that this

mode encourages the formulation of qualitative versions of the LTV that possess explanatory power.

Marx starts from the 'stylised fact' that under capitalism, in contrast to all other modes of production, human labouring activity appears in an estranged or alienated form. It appears in the form of the products this labouring activity produces, namely commodities as values.

> The wealth of those societies in which the capitalist mode of production prevails, presents itself as an immense accumulation of commodities, its unit being a single commodity. Our investigation must therefore begin with the analysis of the commodity.
>
> (Marx 1983: 43)

This starting point appears to be motivated by something like the following transcendental question: what economic, social, political, ideological relations (mechanism, structures, powers and so on) would explain how and why human labouring activity appears in the value form? Marx retroduces to a set of underlying relations (deep structures) and connects them to *their* observable forms.[21] Although Marx does not, of course, explain his *modus operandi* in these terms, it appears to be a perfectly acceptable, although not a well known, interpretation. According to Sayer:

> Marx's object is the social forms assumed by economic phenomena . . . His 'analytic' consists of an excavation of the conditions that must be supposed for the phenomena to assume such forms, that is, of the essential relations that must exist if the world as experienced is to be possible. Marx's reasoning is thus eminently transcendental, although pace Kant, his is a transcendental realism.
>
> (Sayer 1979: 37)

Not only is Marx's ontology stratified, it is also *transformational*. According to the Marxian TMSA presented here, society is the ensemble of material-technical and socio-economic relations. These relations are, however, not thrown together in a heap, there is a principle of organisation, and that principle is transformation. The relations are treated as the ever-present condition, and the continually reproduced outcome of, human agency. As Marx, pre-empting critical realist terminology puts matters:

> The conditions . . . of the direct production process . . . are themselves equally moments of it, and its only subjects are the individuals, but individuals in mutual relationships, which they equally reproduce and produce anew. The constant processes of their own movement, in which they renew themselves even as they renew the world of the wealth they create.
>
> (Marx 1974: 712)

Table 4.3 Marx's stratified (and fetishised) socio-economic ontology

Domain	Entity
Empirical	Exchange of money for commodities
Actual	Co-ordination of the labouring activity of millions of atomistic producing units
'Deep'	Material-technical and socio-economic relations; private property, alienated labour, the state and so on

Whilst Marx appears to make use of something like the stratified and transformational ontology set out above, he adds another element: the ontology is also fetishised. To say things are fetishised, means that there is a rather special relation between the way things are and the way they appear. It is not just that things appear in a distorted form, but (a) the distortion is systematic and (b) this systematically distorted form is the only way these things can appear.

Table 4.3 not only summarises the stratified, transformational and fetishised ontology presupposed by the LTV, but also illustrates how this can be interpreted along critical realist lines.[22]

From critical realism to Marx

The causal-explanatory mode of theorising, and the socio-economic ontology in which it is rooted, generates an entirely different problematic to that generated by the deductivist mode of theorisation underlying quantitative versions of the LTV. The causal-explanatory mode encourages an enquiry into the nature of (alienated) labouring activity and its form of appearance, whereas the deductivist mode enquires solely into the magnitude of value. Without the intellectual apparatus with which to carry out an enquiry into qualitative phenomena such as these, deductivism is capable of doing no more than dealing with quantitative phenomena such as value magnitudes.

Using the causal-explanatory mode of theorisation, and explicitly recognising this structured, transformational and fetishised socio-economic ontology, one is encouraged to interpret the problematic of Marx's LTV as follows. What 'deep' structures, mechanisms, relations and powers are necessary to sustain a system whereby the relations between people (as producing units) appear in the form of a relation between things (commodities)?

In addressing this problematic, I will make use of contrastive explanation. I will *not* ask: why does labouring activity under capitalist conditions appear in the value form? Rather I will ask: why does labouring activity under capitalist conditions appear in the value form when labouring activity under non-capitalist conditions does not require this form? Framing the explanation in terms of this contrast pinpoints what is essential to capitalism. As it happens, this is exactly how Rubin (1990: chapter 2) proceeds – although he does not mention the mode of reasoning he uses. I will follow Rubin by comparing relations under a stylised non-capitalist system to relations under a stylised capitalist system in order to bring out the specifics of the latter.

Let us begin, however, by reflecting upon the centrality of labouring activity and reminding ourselves that, as Elson (1979) puts it, the labour theory of value is primarily about labour and the form (of value) it takes: it ought to be described as the *value theory of labour*.[23]

At the basis of all human life is a material-technical transformation brought about by labouring activity whereby matter is transformed from one state to another, more useful, state. This *material-technical* process is characterised by the following points:

- It is spatio-temporally universal.
- It results in the production of a good or service, and relates therefore to the domain of use value.
- It requires material-technical co-ordination. That is, raw materials and machinery must be spatially and temporally co-ordinated.
- This co-ordination is ensured if, when, and to the extent, material-technical relations are established. This is what Marx has in mind when he refers to the *material relations between things*.

If this material-technical transformation is to occur, however, millions of isolated, atomised producers must enter into relations to co-ordinate and regulate their labouring activities. And this entails a *socio-economic* process characterised by the following points:

- Material transformation occurs by humans co-ordinating and regulating their socio-economic activities. Thus, material-technical relations necessarily imply socio-economic relations.
- Not only are various material entities produced and reproduced, so too are the relations into which people have entered.
- The socio-economic process captures social relations between people as opposed to material relations between things. This is what Marx has in mind when he refers to the *social relations between people*.
- Socio-economic relations are spatio-temporally specific, in that the mode of co-ordination of humans differs fundamentally in space and between epochs.[24]

Although human labouring activity is spatio-temporally universal, the form in which it appears is spatio-temporally specific. Whilst our concern is with the form under which labouring activity occurs under capitalism, one way of actually grasping the specifics of this form is to contrast it with stylised non-capitalist forms.

Stylised non-capitalist system

Consider a highly abstract, stylised, non-capitalist system such as a slave society, feudal society, Stalinist planned economy or even a capitalist enterprise consisting of spatially differentiated production sites. Production takes place on isolated, unconnected production sites and requires the existence of a conscious agency (i.e. a slave owner, feudal lord, central planner or manager) to design and oversee a production plan. Although the actual administration of the plan might be very difficult, the principle upon which it works (however badly) is quite straightforward. This conscious agency, possessing knowledge of material-technical properties of things and production sites, ensures that labour, semi-finished objects and raw materials are spatio-temporally distributed in accordance with the technical requirements of the various stages of the productive processes.

Things flow from production site A to B to C (etc.) because the conscious agency, knowing a range of material-technical properties, knows that each subsequent site has the technical ability to transform the thing into some other thing that is more useful. By issuing instructions based only upon material technical properties, relations are established between the sites. The relations that ensure the uninterrupted co-ordination of things are *permanent*, *direct* and *social*.

- They are *permanent* because once they are established by the conscious agency, they endure until removed or altered.
- They are *direct* because they are established without the intervention of any other vehicle. The connection is directly between plant and plant at the behest of the conscious agency.
- They are *social* because the central agency has already 'socially sanctioned' the products and thereby the human labour expended upon them. Sanctioning occurs, typically, in the interests of the central agency.

Under this stylised non-capitalist system, then, things move between productive stages because some conscious, central agency, possessing knowledge of material-technical properties of things and production sites, is able to establish a set of permanent, and directly social relations to co-ordinate production. The things themselves are, however, unimportant for the establishment of the relations which co-ordinate the processes that produce them – the importance of this will become clear in a moment.

Stylised capitalist system

A capitalist socio-economic system, one where labouring activity is carried out by millions of atomised, isolated, individual producing units – ranging from the self-employed to trans-national corporations. These producers never meet to discuss the co-ordination of their labouring activities, nor are their activities co-ordinated by a central agency. Yet clearly their labouring activity is co-ordinated (however badly) or the socio-economic system would grind to a halt. Labouring activities are indirectly co-ordinated via the systematic exchange of the products of these very activities, commodities. And the systematic exchange of commodities involves the systematic evaluation of these commodities, that is, the assignment of appropriate value or, more concretely, (money) price tags.

In this stylised capitalist system, the three production sites mentioned above are now owned by completely different firms. Things still circulate between independent production sites, but now for different reasons. Things pass from A to B, not *because* of any technical ability possessed by B to transform that object into something useful (although this is an obvious presupposition) but because a sum of money passes from B to A. Firm A is no longer interested in firm B's material-technical ability to transform things, they are no longer merely given away, but are now sold.

Things now cease to be mere things and become, in addition, *commodities* produced solely for exchange on the market. They cease to be mere use values and become, in addition, exchange values. There are no *permanent* production relations between A and B initiated at the behest of a conscious agency. Production relations are now only established through the successful exchange of commodities. The relations that ensure the uninterrupted co-ordination of things are *indirect, social and transient*.

- The relations are established not directly via a conscious agency, but *indirectly* via the commodity successfully entering into an exchange for money.
- The relations, whilst now indirect, remain *social*, but two important changes have occurred. (a) The temporal location where the 'social sanctioning' takes place has changed *vis-à-vis* the production process, from *a priori* to *a posteriori*. It is now *not* in production but exchange that the labour embodied[25] in the commodity is recognised as socially necessary – or not. (b) The person(s) who do the sanctioning have changed from the conscious agency to consumers – of capital in this example.
- The now indirectly social relations only endure as long as commodity exchange endures, hence the relations are *transient* and in need of continual renewal or re-production.

If and only if, the commodity finds a buyer on the market can the socio-economic relations and, therefore, the material-technical relations be established. Failure to sell, results in the failure to establish relations of production and therefore the failure of production and reproduction. The things themselves, the commodities, are now crucially important for the establishment and maintenance of the relations, and therefore for the co-ordination of the very process which produces them. Unlike non-commodity production, commodity production is based upon a curious system whereby it is the very existence of the product as a *bona fide* commodity that creates the conditions for the reproduction of that commodity.

And in all this the market is crucial.[26] It is only via the market that the physiological, concrete, individual labour expended in the production of a commodity doubles into a unity of itself and abstract, and recognised as socially necessary. In other words, it is *essentially* via the market that one isolated producer comes to obtain implicit knowledge about the productive conditions of the multiplicity of other producers, and can, therefore, attempt to co-ordinate his/her labouring activities with these others. How well or how badly the market actually does this is irrelevant for the purposes of this chapter; the point is merely that under capitalism, the market *is* the process by which this co-ordination occurs.

It appears that this qualitative version of the LTV is explanatorily powerful and relevant. It explains how relations between people (as producing units) appear in the (value) form of a relation between things (commodities) by invoking the 'deep' causal mechanisms that facilitate production and exchange under capitalism.[27]

So, what kind of theory should the LTV be?

At this point, the question that motivated this chapter, namely: 'What *kind* of theory should the LTV be?' can finally be answered – negatively and positively. The LTV *should not* be the kind of theory that is quantitative in nature and rooted in the deductivist mode of theorisation because, lacking explanatory power, this kind of theory leads, ultimately to irrelevance. The LTV *should*, by contrast, be the kind of theory that is qualitative in nature and rooted in the causal-explanatory mode of theorisation because, unencumbered by pursuing inappropriate objectives, and possessing explanatory power, this kind of theory leads, ultimately, to relevance. Moreover, by elaborating upon the conditions necessary for the reproduction of key socio-economic relations, the quantitative version of the LTV presented here can be thought of, in critical realist terminology, as a *Transformational Theory of Socio-Economic Order*.

Conclusion

None of the foregoing argument requires the abandonment of the basic premise of Marx's value analysis, namely, that the reason commodities are valuable at all is because they involve human labouring activity, and the value form is the form in which this activity manifests itself under capitalism. What must be abandoned, however, is the 'untenable claim to complete exactness' encouraged by the deductive mode of theorisation. I find myself in agreement with the following comment from Joan Robinson because, in it, she seems to put her finger on exactly what should and should not be abandoned in Marx's LTV.

by and large, the main determinant of difference in prices, say between a packet of pins and a motor car, is obviously differences in labour cost . . . Moreover, the movement through time of relative prices is predominantly influenced by changes in labour costs . . . By giving up the *untenable claim to complete exactness*, the labour theory can establish the right to be considered broadly true and highly important.

(Robinson 1964: 50, emphasis added)

Wedded to the deductivist mode of theorising, however, one cannot give up the 'untenable claim to complete exactness' because from this perspective, there is nothing else.

Notes

1 I would like to thank Hans Erbar, Guilio Garofala, Peter Kennedy, Clive and Tony Lawson, Brian Pinkstone, Steve Pratten and Andrew Sayer for their constructive comments on an earlier draft of this paper.

2 The fact that Marx himself never refers to the 'labour theory of value' makes no difference for this paper because the concept has a long history within Marxist economics, although as we will see, the meaning is less than clear.

3 The deductive mode of theorising (or simply 'deductivism' as I will occasionally call it) is also variously known as: the covering law model; Popper–Hempel theory of explanation; the deductive-nomological or D-N model (*nomos* being Greek for law); and where the law is statistical the D-N model becomes the I-P model ('inductive probabilistic'). Hausman (1992: 288–9) also sees the D-N model as the 'dominant view' amongst economists.

4 Sraffian or neo Ricardian economists are advocates of the deductivist mode of theorising and the quantitative versions of the LTV – although they do not use this terminology. They at least offer a defence of their method by claiming it can be used to represent the functional relations that constitute the 'core' of the economy; relations outside the 'core' require a different mode of theorisation. Pratten's (1999) critical realist critique of neo-Ricardian economics is equally applicable to Marxist economists who also advocate the deductive mode of theorising and quantitative versions of the LTV.

5 Parsons (1996: 421) and Hands (1999: 174–8) make arguments similar to this and Lawson (1999) replies.

6 I specifically do not use an example drawn from Marxist economic theory here (part 1 of this paper), to avoid giving the impression that my critique is located at the level of theory: it is located at the level of methodology and subsequently (in part 2) motivates a critique at the level of theory. Furthermore, the use of an example drawn from mainstream economics has the following advantage. Once (in part 2) some quantitative versions of the LTV are also shown to be 'toy' models, it is easy to see that some Marxist economics and mainstream economics are identical *vis-à-vis* method.

7 Where V_e^n denotes the expected lifetime utility of an employed non-shirker; and V_e^s denotes the expected lifetime utility of an employed shirker.

8 To avoid any misunderstanding, here, please note the following. The distinction between 'toy' and econometric models is not the same as that between deductivist and causal-explanatory modes. Both 'toy' and econometric models are rooted in deductivism. Even if one starts with a 'toy' model, and proceeds to estimate it

(which many economists do not) one is still operating within a deductivist framework.

9 One does not avoid using closed systems simply by introducing some notion of probability. A stochastically closed system, as opposed to a deterministic system, is still a closed system. The alleged constant conjunctions, now assumed to hold under some probability condition, are still generated by a confluence of causal mechanisms, and should anything in this array of causal mechanisms alter, the probabilities would alter. The initial specification of the relationship between the events in the system would no longer be as initially described, meaning, in effect, it was a different system. See note 18.

10 Although the argument is developed from the practice of natural science, it is applicable to social science in general, and mainstream economics in particular, for two reasons. (i) Mainstream economists quite readily admit they are using the methods of the natural sciences. (ii) If human agency is real, then (a) human agents could always have acted otherwise, and (b) human action must make a difference to the social world. If (a) and (b) are accepted, the social world cannot be a closed system.

11 Even supposing an econometric model successfully predicted some economic event, the regression might be grounded in no economic theory whatsoever, or, as is more likely, grounded in a theory that contains fictional claims. Successful prediction does not amount to explanation.

12 On the role of explanatory power as criteria for evaluating theories see Boylan and O'Gorman (1995), and Fleetwood (2001a).

13 For Hume's work on causality see Hume (1888/1978: 73–94: 155–72) and for a critical discussion see Bhaskar (1978, chapters 1, 2 and appendix); Meikle (1985, especially chapters 1 and 7); and Cartwright (1995).

14 Notice the transposition of ontology into epistemology, a move Bhaskar (1978: 36) refers to as the 'epistemic fallacy'. Realists do not argue that positivists are committed to the claim that events in sense experience are all that exist. Realists do argue that positivists transpose questions of ontology into questions of epistemology so that in effect, they are committed to the claim that all that exists *vis-à-vis* scientific enquiry are events in sense experience – i.e. they cannot countenance unobservable entities such as powers.

15 One might object that the use of 'toy' models appears not to require an ontology of sense experience. Whilst it is true that writing $y = f(x)$ does not require that episodes of y and x were experienced, the clear implication (on pain of irrelevance) is that they could, under certain conditions, be experienced.

16 Deductivism cannot, consistently, be rooted in anything other than empirical realist ontology; and conversely, empirical realist ontology cannot, consistently, engender anything other than deductivism, or at least something similar – it cannot, for example engender a causal-explanatory mode. Inconsistency can, of course, lead to any combinations of ontology, causality and modes of reasoning.

17 Bhaskar (1987: 104–36 and 1989: ch. 2); Lawson (1997: ch. 12).

18 Notice that our ability to explain why leaves turn yellow in November is not merely an extrapolation from past inductions, but due to our knowledge of causal mechanisms and powers. Anyway, in some circumstances leaves may fall off before November. Whilst this would disallow statements about laws and constant conjunction between colour and month (i.e. the system is not closed), it does not disallow statements about the tendencies generated by causal mechanisms and powers that are transfactually at work. See Runde (1998) for an elaboration of critical realist views on causal explanations.

19 For ease of exposition I couch the discussion simply in terms of (undefined) labour and (undefined) price. For the purposes of this paper, nothing is lost in using this

terminology. It is used to avoid distractions like the distinction between concrete (physiological) and abstract labour, the transformation problem, the role of money in expressing price and so on. I will, however, make comments where absolutely necessary.

20 For a fuller discussion of this, see Lawson (1997: 127–33). See also note 5 above.

21 On Marx's use of retroduction see Wilson (1991: ch. 6).

22 Note that, *contra* Roberts (1999) there is nothing in the critical realist approach that means the domains of the deep, actual and empirical cannot be related – although such a relation can be contingent. In this context, however, social relations between people, necessarily take the fetishised form of relations between commodities. Furthermore, as will become clear in a moment, and again *contra* Roberts, there is nothing in the critical realist approach that prevents a historical analysis. The relevant causal mechanisms, social structures and relations are temporally located. To avoid any misunderstanding note that whilst one can observe labouring activity, one is observing concrete and individual labour and not abstract and social and/or socially necessary labour. Furthermore, whilst one can observe the exchange of labouring activity for a wage, one cannot observe the co-ordination that is going on between the labouring activities of millions of atomised producers.

23 This section draws heavily on Rubin's (1990) and Elson's (1979) interpretation of Marx; and on Marx (1982: 42–8).

24 Whilst the human race would obviously perish without this labouring activity, this is not the reason why Marx treats labouring activity as central to human society. Rather, in labouring activity humans reproduce themselves as a species that consciously thinks and acts (production) upon the natural world, and reflects upon this thinking and acting. As Marx puts it: [L]ife activity, productive life itself appears to man only as . . . the need to preserve physical existence. But productive life is species life . . . The object of labour is therefore the objectification of the species life of man' (1975: 328–9).

25 I hesitate to use this (fraught) term but stick with it for the sake of simplicity.

26 I would look to the very kind of processes Saad-Filho (1997: 457–77) sketches out as part of the way forward. I would also consider more sophisticated versions of the market process, such as those that I have tried to develop in my own work on Hayek (Fleetwood 1995, 1996).

27 A full exposition of these 'deep' structures, mechanisms, relations and powers would amount to nothing less than an exposition of how the various components of the capitalist system articulate with one another, and would involve a gradual transition from the abstract to the concrete – which is clearly beyond the scope of one paper.

Bibliography

Belofiore, R. (1989) 'A Monetary Labour Theory of Value', *Review of Radical Political Economics*, vol. 21: 21–40.

Bhaskar, R. (1978) *A Realist Theory of Science*, Hemel Hempstead, UK: Harvester Wheatsheaf.

—— (1987) *Scientific Realism and Human Emancipation*, London: Verso.

—— (1989) *The Possibility of Naturalism*, Hemel Hempstead, UK: Harvester Wheatsheaf.

Boylan, T. and O'Gorman, P. (1995) *Beyond Rhetoric and Realism: Towards a Reformulation of Economic Methodology*, London: Routledge.

Caldwell, B. (1991) *Beyond Positivism: Economic Methodology in the Twentieth Century*, London: Unwin Hyman.

Cartwright, N. (1995) 'Ceteris Paribus Laws and Socio Economic Machines', *The Monist*, vol. 78, no. 3: 276–94.

Elson, D. (1979) 'The Value Theory of Labour', in D. Elson (ed.) *Value: The Representation of Labour in Capitalism*, Brighton, UK: CSE Books.

Fleetwood, S. (1995) *Hayek's Political Economy: The Socio-Economics of Order*, London: Routledge.

—— (1996) 'Order Without Equilibrium: A Critical Realist Interpretation of Hayek's Notion of Spontaneous Order', *Cambridge Journal of Economics*, vol. 20, no. 6: 729–47.

—— (2001a) 'Boylan and O'Gorman's Causal Holism: a Critical Realist Evaluation', *Cambridge Journal of Economics*.

—— (2001b) 'Causal Laws, Functional Relations and *Tendencies*', *Review of Political Economy*, vol. 13, no. 2: 202–20.

Gordon, S. (1991) *The History and Philosophy of Social Science*, London: Routledge.

Hands, W. (1999) 'Empirical Realism as Meta-Method: Tony Lawson on Neoclassical Economics', in S. Fleetwood (ed.) *Critical Realism in Economics: Development and Debate*, London: Routledge.

Hausman, D. (1992) *The Inexact and Separate Science of Economics*, Cambridge: Cambridge University Press.

Howard, M. and King, J. (1985) *The Political Economy of Marx*, London: Longman.

Hume, D. (1888/1978) *A Treatise of Human Nature*, Oxford: Clarendon Press.

Lawson, T. (1997) *Economics and Reality*, London: Routledge.

—— (1999) 'Critical Issues in Economics as Realist Social Theory', in S. Fleetwood (ed.) *Critical Realism in Economics: Development and Debate*, London: Routledge.

Lipton, P. (1993) *Inference to the Best Explanation*, London: Routledge.

Maki, U. (1992) 'On the Method of Isolation in Economics', in C. Dilworth (ed.) *Intelligibility in Science IV*, Amsterdam: Rodophi.

Marx, K. (1974) *Grundrisse*, Harmondsworth, UK: Penguin.

—— (1975) *Economic and Philosophical Manuscripts*, in *Karl Marx, Early Writings*, Harmondsworth, UK: Penguin.

—— (1982) *The German Ideology*, London: Lawrence & Wishart.

—— (1983) *Capital*, vol. I, London: Lawrence & Wishart.

Meek, R. (1967) *Essays on Ideology and Other Essays*, London: Chapman Hall.

Meikle, S. (1985) *Essentialism in the Thought of Karl Marx*, Gloucester, UK: Duckworth.

Parsons, S. (1996) 'Post Keynesianism, Realism and Keynes' General Theory', *Journal of Post Keynesian Economics*, vol. 18, no. 3: 419–41.

Pencavel, J. (1991) 'Prospects for Economics', *Economic Journal*, 101: 81–7.

—— (1994) *Labour Markets under Trade Unionism: Employment, Wages and Hours*, Oxford: Blackwell.

Pratten, S. (1999) 'The "Closure" Assumption as a First Step', in S. Fleetwood (ed.) *Critical Realism in Economics: Development and Debate*, London: Routledge.

Roberts, J. (1999) 'Marxism and Critical Realism', *Capital and Class*, no. 68: 21–49.

Robinson, J. (1964) *Collected Papers*, vol. 2, Oxford: Blackwell.

Rubin, I. (1990) *Essays on Marx's Theory of Value*, Montreal: Black Rose Books.

Runde, J. (1998) 'Assessing Causal Economic Explanations', *Oxford Economic Papers* no. 50: 151–72.

Saad-Fihlo, A. (1997) 'Concrete and Abstract Labour in Marx's Theory of Value', *Review of Radical Political Economics*, vol. 9, no. 4: 457–77.

Sayer, D. (1979) 'Science as Critique' Issues in J. Mepham and D. Hillel-Ruben *Marxist Philosophy Vol III: Epistemology, Science, Ideology*, Sussex: Harvester Press.

Shapiro, C. and Stiglitz, J. (1990) 'Equilibrium Unemployment as a Worker Discipline Device', in A. Akerlof and J. Yellen (eds) *Efficiency Wage Models of the Labour Market*, Cambridge: Cambridge University Press.

Sweezy, P. (1968) *Theory of Capitalist Development*, New York: Monthly Review Press.

Wilson, H. (1991) *Marx's Critical Dialectical Procedure*, London: Routledge.

5 Capitalism, the regulation approach, and critical realism[1]

Bob Jessop

Committed critical realist commentators on the economics discipline have not discussed, as far as I am aware, the regulation approach as an exemplar of critical realism (e.g., Baert 1996; Lawson 1989, 1995, 1997; Pratten 1993; Fleetwood 1999; Nielsen 2000). In some cases this neglect is due to a concern to develop a meta-theoretical critique of orthodox economics and/or to uncover critical realist aspects of heterodox economic theorising. In other cases it is due to a concern to show that Marx's own work at its best already illustrates critical realism (Bhaskar 1991: 143; Marsden 1998, 1999)[2] or can be re-interpreted in critical realist terms (Pratten 1993; Ehrbar 1998, 2000; Kanth 1999). Where critical realists have shown interest in Marxism, their neglect of regulationism may reflect a judgement that regulationism can be safely ignored as just another current within a critical realist Marxism. Alternatively, and more probably, the regulation approach, whether or not regarded as critical realist, simply does not appear within the horizon of those critical realists interested in economics.

This chapter responds to this neglect in five ways: first, it introduces the regulation approach (hereafter RA) to readers interested in critical realism; second, it identifies four of its distinctive features as a specific current in heterodox economics; third, it reveals the critical realist assumptions that inform early regulationist work and suggests that it has engaged in middle-range retroductive inference to explain the specificities of Atlantic Fordism as an object of scientific investigation; fourth, it argues that this work has also developed some insights that are useful for critical realist purposes more generally – notably in regard to the doubly tendential nature of tendencies and counter-tendencies, the co-constitution of objects and modes of regulation, the articulation of the economic and extra-economic, and issues of structure and agency; and, fifth, it offers some new retroductive arguments from a regulationist perspective about spatio-temporal fixes and contemporary capitalism. In addressing the first three themes, I focus on early contributions to the RA (especially by two Parisian regulationists, Aglietta and Lipietz) and also suggest how their initial arguments can be developed. This emphasis might seem odd given that the RA emerged over 25 years ago, that it comprises many different schools and currents, and that recent studies are much more complex and detailed. However, as regulationist concepts have become common academic currency and regulationists have become increasingly concerned with more middle-range issues in comparative institutionalism, the original methodological concerns of the pioneer regulationists tend to be forgotten. Yet it is these pioneer texts that most clearly state the key onto-logical, epistemological, and methodological assumptions underpinning the RA – and neglect of which explains some of the weaknesses of current regula-tionism despite strengths in other respects.[3] Scientific progress often depends on forgetting pioneering work but this does not always hold: classic texts may have a continuing relevance. This latter claim informs my discussion of the fifth set of issues.

What is the regulation approach?

The regulation approach is a still evolving research programme[4] that offers a very interesting and fruitful way to analyse the interconnections between the institutional forms and dynamic regularities of capitalist economies (for a comprehensive anthology of regulationist work, see Jessop 2001). In con-trast with orthodox economics but in line with Marx's own work, the RA does not aim to provide a general, trans-historical account of economic con-duct or economic performance. Nor does it seek to naturalise capitalism by treating its continued reproduction as an essentially unproblematic expres-sion of rational economic behaviour. Instead it aims to develop concepts and models that correspond to the historically specific features of capitalism (regarding both its *differentia specifica* relative to pre- or non-capitalist modes of organisation and the distinctive stages of capitalist development itself) and to enable its adherents to explain why capital accumulation, although it is inherently improbable in the light of these features, can nonetheless con-tinue for relatively extended periods without witnessing major crises. These concerns are linked to interest in the generic crisis-tendencies of capitalism, the specific forms of these crisis-tendencies in specific accumulation regimes, and the major ruptures and structural shifts that occur as accumulation and its regulation develop in and through class struggle. In this context it treats economic activities and institutions as socially embedded and emphasises that it is impossible to secure continued accumulation purely through economic mechanisms – the analysis of which, taking its lead from Marx's abstract reproduction schemas, it treats under the rubric of 'reproduction'. Accordingly, the RA provides a retroductive account of the changing com-binations of economic and extra-economic institutions, norms, and practices that help to secure, if only temporarily and always in specific economic spaces, a certain stability and predictability in economic conduct and accu-mulation – despite the fundamental contradictions and conflicts inherent in capitalism. Regulation is the overall category that the eponymous RA deploys to summarise (and, as appropriate, to synthesise) the various

processes and practices involved in this always relative stabilisation of the
capital relation.

The regulationist research programme has four principal features. Two of
these are methodological and two substantive. All four are rooted in the
Marxist heritage of early regulationism – something that has become less
evident with time but that still links the main regulationist schools. This
shared inheritance derives primarily from Marx's 'scientific' studies (notably
the 1857 *Introduction*, the *Grundrisse*, and, above all, *Capital*) rather than his
political, utopian, or eschatological writings. It is also reflected in the regulationists' concern to develop institutionally sensitive comparative and
historical analyses of capitalism rather than to look beyond capitalism(s) in
order to propose alternative, post-capitalist modes of production and/or
regulation. Indeed, this basic concern with the generative mechanisms, crisis
tendencies, and recurrent stabilisation of capitalism has provoked from
some quarters fierce – but mistaken – criticism of the RA's alleged confirmation of capitalism's inevitability and its role in belittling class struggles
aimed at overthrowing it (see Bonefeld and Holloway 1991; Bonefeld 1994;
Gambino 1996; for responses, see Jessop 1997a; Hay 1994).

The first feature of the regulationist research programme to be explored
here is that the RA typically works with an *implicitly* critical realist scientific
ontology and epistemology. These are implicit in the sense that, whilst the
RA adopts critical realist assumptions and procedures in practice, it does
not present them as critical realist. This is largely because it is examining
capitalism as a specific object of inquiry with specific structures and mechanisms rather than presenting an underlabouring philosophical argument for
the validity of critical realism in general.[5] Second, its broad substantive
theoretical concerns derive from the general Marxist tradition of historical
materialism with its interest in developing a critical political economy of
capitalism and anatomy of bourgeois civil society. Taking Marx's own more
abstract–simple arguments in the *Grundrisse* and *Capital* for granted, however,
the RA explores these themes at more concrete–complex levels of analysis.
Third, more specifically, it explores the changing forms and mechanisms –
extra-economic as well as economic – through which the expanded reproduction of capital relation is at least provisionally secured despite its inherent
structural contradictions and emergent conflictual properties. And, fourth,
in line with this implicit critical realism and its substantive concerns, the
RA rejects both the essentialist method of 'subsumption' and the reductionist
method of 'logical derivation' in developing its concepts and analysis.[6]
Instead, emphasising the contingent actualisation of natural necessities, it
adopts a method of 'articulation' in building accounts of regulation. This
can be seen in its progressive elaboration of its key categories at different
levels of abstraction–concretisation and simplicity–complexity (immediacy–
mediation) as it approaches specific conjunctures. I will now elaborate on
some of these features.

Critical realist aspects of the regulation approach

Ontologically, the RA's implicit critical realism derives initially from Marx but was then elaborated via a critique of Althusserian structuralism (Althusser 1969; Althusser and Balibar 1970; on Althusserian structuralism, see, for example, Benton 1984; Elliott 1994; Resch 1992; and, for a regulationist critique, Lipietz 1993). Althusser identified an alleged 'epistemological break' occurring around 1847 that enabled Marx to develop a scientific analysis of capitalism and, like critical realists in Britain, this French philosopher discussed the distinctive features and conditions of the possibility of science as a theoretical practice. In this context he distinguished between 'dialectical materialism' and 'historical materialism'. Whereas the former designates the general ontology and epistemology of Marxist scientific inquiry, the latter refers to the particular ontology and epistemology appropriate to studying modes of production and their transformation in and through class struggle.[7] Developing these ideas, Althusser rejected Hegelian readings of Marx on the grounds that they erroneously reproduce an Hegelian unitary, 'expressive totality'[8] rather than recognising that Marx's ontology and epistemology both involved a dialectical, 'overdetermined totality'. Accordingly he introduced the concept of 'structural causality' to designate what critical realists would call the hidden inner structure of capitalism as the generative mechanism of its phenomenal forms and surface movement. In his approach to these issues he affirmed Marx's insight that 'all science would be superfluous if the outward appearances and essences of things directly coincided' (Marx 1971: 817). Thus Althusser's 'symptomatic reading' of *Capital* sought – not wholly satisfactorily – to identify the categories and mechanisms through which Marx explained how surface appearances are related to the underlying realities of capital as a social relation. He and his collaborators also sought retroductively to show how surface phenomena are often distorted, inverted, or misrecognised effects of these mechanisms (Althusser and Balibar 1970). These themes were taken up by Aglietta and Lipietz, the pioneer Parisian regulationists. But they also argued that Althusser paid insufficient attention to the transformative potential of social action (notably class struggle) in shaping the dynamic of individual modes of production and transitions between them (see Lipietz 1993 explicitly, Aglietta 1979 implicitly).

Marx's work is actually far better described in critical realist than structural Marxist terms even though both involve notions of ontological depth and commitments to retroduction. By breaking with the more structuralist elements of Althusserianism whilst embracing its account of the specificity of the Marxian dialectic, Aglietta and Lipietz were able to develop a better retroductive analysis of capitalism than that provided by Althusser and his collaborators. Thus they sought to identify the 'naturally necessary' properties and laws of motion of capital as a social relation, i.e., properties and laws that are inherent in the relation between capital and labour and/or between individual capitals. Moreover, although certainly strongly interested in the categories of money and capital, the RA was also particularly concerned with the nature of the wage relation (*rapport salarial*). In this sense their work can be interpreted as an attempt to correct the 'one-sidedness of *Capital*' (Lebowitz 1982) by providing the 'missing book of *Capital*' (Lebowitz 1991). The starting points for such regulationist analyses are the basic contradictions of the commodity and/or value as the most basic 'structural forms' (or modes of existence)[9] of the capitalist mode of production, the implications of the generalisation of the commodity form to labour-power (even though it remains a fictitious commodity, i.e., one that is not produced in formally rational, profit-oriented capitalist enterprises), the historically specific nature of capitalism as a mode of production (or 'mode of organisation of social labour', Aglietta 1979: 37) that is based on the capital–labour relation and capitalist competition, and the centrality of the wage relation and the variant forms of capitalism, both historically and geographically.

With the continued development of the RA, however, these relatively abstract–simple starting points are increasingly taken for granted and regulationists now focus on more middle-range (concrete–complex) aspects of capitalism that are also rooted in the centrality of the commodity form. This is linked to a second round of retroduction and theorisation of more concrete properties and 'laws' of capitalism. For, just as Marx could not elaborate his abstract 'laws of motion' (such as the law of value or the law of the tendency of the rate of profit to fall) without considering the inherent structural properties of capitalism as a mode of production, the RA had to retroduce intermediate categories of analysis to address more specific periods and/or variant forms of capitalism. Thus Aglietta writes that, '[i]n order to achieve a precise analysis of the forms of regulation under capitalism, it is necessary first to define an intermediate concept, less abstract than the principle of accumulation so far introduced. This is the concept of the regime of accumulation' (Aglietta 1979: 68). Having defined this, he later introduces the related concept of 'mode of regulation'. Likewise, Lipietz writes that:

> it [sc. capitalism] works . . . except, of course, when there is a crisis. In order to understand how it works we have to produce new concepts. A number of French research workers have proposed the concepts of *'regime of accumulation'* and *mode of regulation*.
>
> (1987: 14)

In this sense the RA builds on concepts and arguments from *Capital*[10] and re-specifies them so that they can be deployed at more concrete, complex levels of analysis. Five such concepts are of particular importance for the Parisian regulation approach.

The most general of these concepts, taken for granted in the preceding quotation from Aglietta, is, of course, 'régulation' as a complement to 'reproduction'. This was initially introduced, as a pre-theoretical intuition, in Aglietta's doctoral thesis (1974); it has since been grounded theoretically in the Marxist critique of political economy by later regulationist work (beginning with Aglietta 1979). The other four are 'industrial paradigm', 'accumulation regime', 'mode of regulation', and 'model of development'. Together these enable the RA to identify the internal structures associated with more concrete–complex features of specific periods of capitalist development and/or specific national variants of capitalism. I will now briefly define these latter concepts and show how they are related.

First, an *industrial paradigm* is a model governing the technical and social division of labour. One such paradigm is mass production. This concept is primarily micro-economic. Second, an *accumulation regime* is a complementary pattern of production and consumption that is reproducible over a long period. Accumulation regimes are sometimes analysed abstractly in terms of their typical reproduction requirements; but, specified as national modes of growth, they can be related to the international division of labour. This concept is broadly macro-economic. Third, a *mode of regulation* is an emergent ensemble of norms, institutions, organisational forms, social networks, and patterns of conduct that can stabilise an accumulation regime. This is a more meso-level concept embracing both economic and extra-economic factors. It is generally analysed in terms of five dimensions: the wage relation (labour markets and wage-effort bargaining, individual and social wages, life styles); the enterprise form (its internal organisation, the source of profits, forms of competition, ties among enterprises, links to banking capital); the nature of money (its dominant form and its emission, the banking and credit system, the allocation of money capital to production);[11] the state (the institutionalised compromise between capital and labour, forms of state intervention); and international regimes (the trade, investment, monetary settlements, and political arrangements that link national economies, nation states, and the world system). And, fourth, according to Lipietz, when an industrial paradigm, an accumulation regime, and a mode of regulation complement each other sufficiently to secure for a time the conditions for a long wave[12] of capitalist expansion, the resulting complex is often analysed more inclusively and comprehensively as a *model of development*. This is a holistic concept that attempts to depict the economy in its most inclusive or integral sense. It could also be described as a meta-economic concept (cf. Ruigrok and van Tulder 1995: 33; Messner 1997) but, whether or not one accepts this designation, it is clearly the most concrete–complex of the new concepts introduced by the pioneer regulationists. All of these are typically defined to take account of the conflictual and antagonistic nature of capitalism. This explains why four complementary concepts are used, why the Parisian regulation school insists on the provisional, unstable, and contradictory character of capitalism, and, of course, why the very concept of *régulation* was developed in the first place to modify and complement that of *reproduction*.

Such retroductively inferred objects are introduced for two main reasons. The first is to explain in relatively abstract–simple terms the general mechanism that compensates for the posited inability of purely economic mechanisms (i.e., in this context, market forces) to secure the expanded reproduction of capitalism. The second is to re-specify this general mechanism in more concrete–complex terms to explain the historically specific dynamics of different periods and/or variants of capitalism, including the distinctive forms of appearance of their crisis-tendencies. In particular, the RA originated in the attempt to explain the relative stability of Atlantic Fordism and its distinctive crisis-tendencies – especially the apparently anomalous phenomenon of stagflation (for a detailed commentary on regulationist analyses of Fordism and post-Fordism, see Jessop 1992). The categories it has developed to analyse these problems would have belonged in the three unfinished books of Marx's projected critique of political economy but they are no less potentially valid for being more relevant to these later theoretical stages in a Marxist appropriation of the 'real-concrete' as a 'concrete-in-thought'.

Indeed, far from being inconsistent with Marx's project, the RA could help to realise it. For Marx could not present the full complexity of the social embeddedness and social regulation of the circuit of capital nor the complex reciprocal relationship between the so-called 'base' and 'superstructure' at more abstract, simple levels of analysis. This is amply indicated in the many and varied similes, metaphors, and circumlocutions that Marx had to deploy in dealing with the complexities of capitalist social formations in order to avoid simple functionalist or economic reductionist arguments. Once concepts and arguments are introduced on more concrete and complex levels of analysis, however, both reductionism and figurative language can be expected to disappear (cf. Woodiwiss 1990). Instead attention can turn to the structural coupling and co-evolution of different structural forms, social practices, and discursive systems in the overall reproduction–regulation of the economy. Delivering such analyses is one of the promises of the regulationist research programme.

Epistemologically, both the RA and critical realism imply the inadequacy of attempts to develop scientific knowledge on the basis of constant conjunctions or other empirical regularities. Instead they pose retroductive questions about the necessary and/or sufficient conditions of a given explanendum and thus to develop knowledge of real causal powers or mechanisms. It also implies that an explanation is only adequate relative to a given definition of the explanendum. This requires a movement from abstract to concrete, i.e., the increasing concretisation of a given phenomenon (e.g., from commodities in general to labour-power as a fictitious commodity to the wage relation on to the determination of the nominal money wage to the real wage, and so on). It also requires a movement from simple to complex, i.e., introducing further dimensions of a given phenomenon (e.g., state, capitalist state, patriarchal capitalist state, multicultural patriarchal capitalist state, etc.).

Elsewhere I have described the methodology of this dual movement from abstract to concrete and from simple to complex as that of 'articulation' (Jessop 1982: 213–20).

Implications of the regulation approach for critical realism

Having established important affinities between the RA and critical realism, I now address three general theoretical issues: (a) the ontological assumptions that typically underpin the RA; (b) the complex movement involved in theory construction and explanation; and (c) the order of presentation appropriate to studies of regulation. The main ideas here were already present in the classic Marxian texts and then outlined more systematically in early regulationist texts. Thus it is surprising that more recent commentaries on the RA rarely critically examine its methodological foundations. This might be explained through the increasing identification of the RA with the analysis of Fordism and post-Fordism, topics that could be understood in purely 'middle-range' terms and integrated into a wide range of analyses. This has led to the weakening or abandonment of the early RA's distinctive methodological assumptions. But only by re-examining the RA's methodological assumptions can we understand both its key contributions and its limitations for an analysis of capitalism.

Hans Ehrbar has recently proposed that:

> Although Hegel's system was probably the best framework available at Marx's time to represent the structure of modern society, it still does not fit well enough for the purposes for which Marx put it to work. . . . As a consequence, the understanding of Marx could not progress past the stage of a secret science, open only to the 'initiated' . . . critical realism would have given a better framework than Hegel for Marx's arguments.
> (Ehrbar 2000: 3, 4; cf. Ehrbar 1998; contrast Brown 1999: 12–14)

The RA is an interesting example of a Marxist account of capital as a social relation that, inspired by structural Marxism, rejects a Hegelian reading of Marx and instead develops an alternative, albeit implicit, critical realist account.[13] Indeed, both the realist ontology implicit in *Capital* and its associated epistemology, outlined in the 1857 *Introduction* and elsewhere, were affirmed and adopted by the early Parisian regulationists. For Marx the causal powers and liabilities in the domain of capital as a social relation were typically analysed in terms of tendencies and counter-tendencies that together constitute its 'laws of motion'. These 'laws' operate as tendential causal mechanisms whose outcome depends on specific initial conditions as well as on the contingent interaction among tendencies and counter-tendencies; thus, in addition to real mechanisms, Marx also described their actual results in specific conjunctures and sometimes gave empirical indicators for these results. Labour-power is the most obvious example of a real power; but, as Marx emphasised, its actualisation depends on the outcome of the struggle between capital and labour in specific conjunctures. The tendency of the rate of profit to fall and its counter-tendencies are the best known (and certainly the most contentious) of these real mechanisms: whether or not the profit rate actually falls or not (and by how much) depends on the conditions in which the tendency and counter-tendencies operate. In turn this realist ontology implies that the social world comprises a complex synthesis of multiple determinations.

Given these ontological assumptions, Marx concluded that the ultimate task of theory is to appropriate the 'real concrete' as a 'concrete in thought'. Modern epistemologists might well argue, however, that, as it really exists beyond thought, the 'real concrete' can never be fully apprehended. For, although realists presuppose the existence of the real world and make this belief into a crucial 'regulative idea' in their critique of rationalist and pragmatist accounts of science, they do not make any strong epistemological claims about having direct access to this reality. Indeed, as Aglietta notes, the empirical is not external to theoretical construction itself:

> facts are not atoms of reality to be classified, linked and assembled. Facts must rather be treated as units in a process, or articulations between relations in motion, which interfere and fuse with one another. They can only be grasped by the collaboration of different modes of investigation, and this is why the concrete can be reached in thought only at the end of a globalising procedure in which deductive and critical moments interact.
>
> (Aglietta 1979: 66)

Our knowledge of the real world is never theoretically innocent. This implies that the starting point for any enquiry is discursively constituted: one cannot move from a theory-free 'real-concrete' to a theory-laden 'concrete in thought' (cf. Althusser and Balibar 1970; Aglietta 1979: 15). In this sense the movement from 'real-concrete' to 'concrete in thought' is a movement from a simple and superficial category to an account which is complex (synthesising multiple determinations) and also has ontological depth (identifying the underlying real mechanisms and connecting them to the actual and empirical aspects of the real-concrete). Thus, as Marx begins to move from the analysis of money to that of capital in the *Grundrisse*, he notes that, '[i]f we speak here of capital, this is still merely a word' (1973b: 262). He then proceeds to show that '[c]apital is not a simple relation, but a *process*, in whose various moments it is always capital' (1973b: 258). Likewise, in his 1857 *Introduction*, he suggests that scientific inquiry would begin with simple categories, 'chaotic conceptions', such as population, but would then decompose them into their elements and reconstruct them again as a complex of diverse determinations (1973a: 100–1).

As the spiral of scientific enquiry continues, the elements of the 'real-concrete' are defined with increasing complexity and concreteness. This means that 'concepts are never introduced once and for all at a single level of abstraction but are continually redefined in the movement from abstract to concrete – acquiring new forms and transcending the limits of their previous formulations' (Aglietta 1979: 15–16). In this sense 'the objective is the development of concepts and not the "verification" of a finished theory' (Aglietta 1979: 66, cf. 15). Lipietz likewise argues that realist theorists have 'always to strive for greater precision in the concepts and thus always be producing more concepts that must then be articulated (1987: 5–6). And Norton criticises the American radical economists who work on 'social structures of accumulation' for failing to rethink and transform their initially-posited causal mechanisms as they develop their argument more concretely and consider additional processes and relationships. Instead, in contrast with Aglietta's approach, he argues, they treat these mechanisms as fixed, once established at an abstract level (Norton 1988: 203, 220–2).

This is not to deny the key role of empirical evidence in theory construction and evaluation. Indeed, as Beamish notes:

> a major dimension to Marx's method is located within the actual concrete processes of inquiry, elaboration, and intellectual reconstruction. No attempt to comprehend his method will be satisfactory unless it deals with the fundamental, dialectical relationship between abstract and concrete in Marx's intellectual labor process – that is, the dialectic between Marx's conceptions (the abstract) and his interaction with a variety of textual materials, plus the practical activities involved in the writing and indexing of his texts (the concrete).
>
> (Beamish 1992: 4)

A similar point is made by Marsden, who writes:

> Regarded less grandly and more prosaically than is customary, Marx's method of critique-retroduction is a serendipitous process of writing, editing, revising and rewriting – sitting up into the middle of the night scrutinising the logical structure of other people's work and writing, revising and rewriting his own. It is a process of conceptual writing or modelling, an *a posteriori* mode of concept formation, the ultimate aim of which is to orient empirical work by indicating where investigations 'must enter in' (Marx 1858, p. 460).
>
> (Marsden 1998: 309)

Aglietta likewise argues that '(p)recise conclusions can be reached only after assembling, classifying and interpreting a vast number of data' and also describes how his own work results from 'an interchange between conceptual elaboration and historical analysis of the economy of the United

States' (1979: 22). And Lipietz adds that regulationists must 'study *each national social formation in its own right,* using the weapons of history, statistics and even econometrics to identify its successive regimes of accumulation and modes of regulation' (1987: 20).

If Marxist epistemology can be described as involving the appropriation of the 'real-concrete' as a 'concrete in thought', appropriation must refer to the qualitative transformation of our understanding of the 'real world'. This would involve a complex and spiral process in which theoretical statements and evidential statements are confronted and modify each other (cf., on the natural sciences, Bhaskar 1989: 12). Thus the essence of science for critical realism is a continuing, spiral movement from knowledge of manifest (empirical) phenomena to knowledge of the underlying structures and causal mechanisms that generate them. This spiral movement is not purely theoretical – it also involves careful consideration of empirical studies of actual tendencies (cf. Marx on 'the working up of observation and conception into concepts', 1973a: 101; also Beamish 1992; Marsden 1999). Or, as Aglietta put it,

> the progression of thought cannot just consist in exposition of conclusions already implicitly contained in an axiomatic system; instead it should move between hypothetico-deductive and experimental phases so that there is a continual, dialectical transformation of concepts. Indeed it is the dialectical phases that are most important for scientific development and make theory something other than the exposition of conclusions already implicitly contained in an axiomatic system.
>
> (Aglietta 1979:15–16; see also Lipietz 1987: 5, 20, 26–7)

Hence, theory is an open process, not a final product.

This argument does not fundamentally challenge Marx's methodology. For this comprises a dialectical interplay of abstract and concrete: an interplay which involves a spiral movement because the introduction of lower order concepts entails modifications in higher order concepts (cf. Benassy *et al.* 1977; Gerstein 1989). Likewise explanation would remain the same: an explanation would be adequate if, at the level of abstraction and the degree of complexity in terms of which a problem is defined, it establishes a set of conditions that are together necessary and/or sufficient to produce the effects specified in the explanendum. Indeed, if concepts are transformed 'by an experimental procedure, a concatenation of concepts can become a representation of a historical movement' (Aglietta 1979: 16).

This suggests two strategies for explanation. Either an explanation must recognise its indeterminacy *vis-à-vis* lower levels of abstraction and leave certain issues unresolved at its chosen level of operation; or it must make certain assumptions which permit a determinate explanation without pre-empting subsequent concretisation. The former strategy can be seen in the argument that the formal possibilities of capitalist crisis do not mean that a crisis will actually occur and/or must take a given form; the latter can be seen in the postulation of an average rate of profit or the assumption that individual capitals act simply as 'bearers' (*Träger*) of the capital relation. This criterion also implies that explanations adequate to one plane of analysis should be commensurable with those adequate to the explanation of other planes. In the case of incommensurability, however, any rules for preferring one of these explanations to others must be conventional. There are no formal rules that could guarantee a correct choice as to which explanation should be retained and which rejected. In addition, of course, any substantive rules will depend on the specific theoretical framework(s) within which investigators work.

Third, whatever the specific methods of discovery, Marx's methodology requires that the theory itself be presented as a movement from abstract to concrete. This holds both for a systematic presentation of the basic theoretical framework as well as for specific explanations of historical events and/or processes. However, in focusing mainly on the economic region in the capitalist mode of production (with its characteristic institutional separation and relative autonomy of different societal spheres), Marx tended to overlook the fact that there are actually two types of movement in any realist analysis: abstract–concrete and simple–complex. The first involves the position a given concept should occupy in the spiral movement from abstract to concrete along one plane of analysis. The second type of movement concerns the combination of different planes of analysis. The greater the number of planes of analysis which are articulated, the more complex is the analysis. This second movement is particularly relevant for understanding the overdetermination of events, processes, and conjunctures through the interaction of several regions. Although Marx himself did not explicate this distinction between types of theoretical movement, it is certainly implicit in his well-known statement that one should aim to reproduce the 'real-concrete' as a 'concrete-in-thought', i.e., as the concrete synthesis of multiple determinations and relations (Marx 1973a: 100).

The regulation approach is more explicit about this movement from the immediate to the mediate as well as from the abstract to the concrete. For it denies that there can be a 'pure economy'. Thus Aglietta argues that the concept of the economy is

> solely a methodological demarcation within the domain of social relations, one perpetually probed and shifted by the development of theoretical analysis itself. The study of capitalist regulation, therefore, cannot be the investigation of abstract economic laws. It is the study of the transformation of social relations as it creates new forms that are both economic and non-economic, that are organised in structures and themselves reproduce a determinate structure, the mode of production.
> (Aglietta 1979: 16)

In short, the RA is specifically concerned with the extra-economic as well as economic conditions of accumulation. It argues, for example, that the state is always already present in the constitution of capitalist social relations and that norms of production and consumption are essential to the institutionalisation of an accumulation regime.

To these arguments Lipietz has added another. He suggests that the original Marxian method involved not only a movement from abstract to concrete to analyse the natural necessities (laws, tendencies) entailed in the internal articulation of objective social relations but also a movement from the 'esoteric' to the 'exoteric' to analyse the connections between these objective relations and the fetishised world of lived experience and the impact that this enchanted world has on the overall movement of capital (1986: 11–12; cf. Marx 1978: 269–72, 290–2). According to Lipietz, this exoteric, enchanted world comprises all those representations created by economic agents in connection with their own behaviour and the circumstances they face. Even though their conduct and circumstances are rooted in the esoteric world, men live their lives through these representations. Ignoring these external forms would therefore prevent any significant understanding of a large part of reality (Lipietz 1986: 12–13). For Lipietz, the key category for deciphering the enchanted world of lived experience is 'fetishism', with particular forms of fetishism associated with each of the three main contradictory relations in capitalism as well as a number of secondary forms (Lipietz 1986: 18–31, 45–52). He also argues that crisis is rooted as much in the exoteric as the esoteric world. Thus different connections between the esoteric world of values and the exoteric world of prices obtain in the competitive and monopoly modes of regulation and this entails different forms of crisis (Lipietz 1986: 102–3).

One final point should be made about this methodology: its open character. Thus Aglietta stated in his doctoral thesis:

> regulation theory would not be a closed theory describing the functioning of an economic model; this is the theory of equilibrated growth in its many forms. It must be open, i.e., susceptible to continued elaboration; which means not only additions and refinements, but ruptures in the theory which must be made possible by the problematic adopted.
>
> (1974: VI)

'Theory, for its part, is never final and complete; it is always in the process of development. The progression of thought does not consist simply of hypothetico-deductive phases; these rather alternate with dialectical phases. It is the dialectical phases that are most important, and make theory seem something other than the exposition of conclusions already implicitly contained in an axiomatic system' (Aglietta 1979: 15–16). It is in this sense too, as well as in the 'family resemblance' among different approaches to regulation, that we can see regulation studies as moments in a continuing research programme.

Regulationist challenges to critical realism

In this section I consider some aspects of the early regulation approach that provide important challenges to critical realism; the next section in turn develops some newer regulationist arguments with a similar significance. The first question to be posed here is why does capitalism need regulating? The answer suggested in the pioneer works in the RA (notably of Aglietta and Lipietz) is the indeterminate but antagonistic nature of capital as a social relation. Indeed Lipietz goes so far as to claim that 'the existence of concrete capitalisms is more improbable than necessary' (1987: 16). Since this claim was largely taken for granted in the early texts, however, I will suggest an explanation that is faithful both to Marx and the RA. This has three key aspects, listed here in increasing order of concreteness and complexity:

a   the constitutive incompleteness of the capital relation in the real world such that a pure (capitalist) economy is impossible and its reproduction depends, in an unstable and contradictory way, on changing extra-economic conditions;
b   the various structural contradictions and strategic dilemmas inherent in the capital relation and their forms of appearance in different accumulation regimes, modes of regulation, and conjunctures; and
c   conflicts over the regularisation and/or governance of these contradictions and dilemmas as they are expressed both in the circuit of capital and the wider social formation.

First, the constitutive incompleteness of capital refers to the inherent incapacity of capitalism as a mode of production to achieve self-closure, i.e., to reproduce itself wholly through the value form. This incompleteness is a defining (i.e., naturally necessary), feature of capitalism. For, even at the most abstract level of analysis, let alone in actually existing capitalism(s), accumulation depends on maintaining an unstable balance between its economic supports in the various expressions of the value forms and its extra-economic supports beyond the value form. This rules out the eventual commodification of everything and, *a fortiori*, a pure capitalist economy. In other words, capitalism does not (and cannot) secure the tendential self-closure implied in the self-expanding logic of commodification. This is rendered impossible by the dependence of capital accumulation on fictitious commodities and extra-economic supports (see especially Aglietta 1979: 32; Lipietz 1987: 30–2). Instead we find uneven waves of commodification, de-commodification, and re-commodification as the struggle to extend the exchange-value moments of the capital relation encounters real

structural limits and/or increasing resistance and seeks new ways to overcome them. This is also associated with uneven waves of territorialisation,
de-territorialisation, and re-territorialisation (Brenner 1998).

Second, the various structural contradictions and strategic dilemmas
inherent in the capital relation are all expressions of the basic contradiction
between exchange- and use-value in the commodity form. There are different
forms of this contradiction. The commodity is both an exchange-value and
a use-value; productive capital is both abstract value in motion (notably in
the form of realised profits available for re-investment) and a concrete stock
of time- and place-specific assets in the course of being valorised; the worker
is both an abstract unit of labour-power substitutable by other such units
(or, indeed, other factors of production) and a concrete individual with specific skills, knowledge, and creativity; the wage is both a cost of production
and a source of demand; money functions both as an international currency
exchangeable against other currencies (ideally in stateless space) and as
national money[14] circulating within national societies and subject to state
control; land functions both as a form of property (based on the private
appropriation of nature) deployed in terms of expected rents and as a natural
resource (modified by past actions) that is more or less renewable and recycl-
able. Likewise, the state is not only responsible for securing certain key conditions for the valorisation of capital and the social reproduction of labour
power as a fictitious commodity but also has overall political responsibility
for maintaining social cohesion in a socially divided, pluralistic social formation. In turn, taxes are both an unproductive deduction from private
revenues (profits of enterprise, wages, interest, rents) and a means of finan-
cing collective investment and consumption to compensate for so-called
'market failures'.

Such structural contradictions and associated strategic dilemmas are
permanent features of the capital relation but assume different forms and pri-
macies in different contexts. They are typically expressed in the opposition
between different agents, institutions, and systems as the prime bearers of
one or other aspect of a given contradiction or dilemma. They can also
prove more or less manageable depending on the specific 'spatio-temporal
fixes' and the institutionalised class compromises with which they are from
time to time associated. According to the early Parisian regulation theorists,
this spatio-temporal fix was organised around the primacy of the national
state, which was seen to have a key role in securing the mode of regulation
(Aglietta 1979: 28–9, 32, 69, 70–1; Lipietz 1987: 19–20). However, insofar
as these compromises marginalise forces that act as bearers of functions or
operations essential to long-run accumulation, the emergence of significant
imbalances, disproportionalities, or disunity in the circuit of capital will
tend to strengthen these marginalised forces and enable them to disrupt the
institutionalised compromises associated with a particular accumulation
regime, mode of regulation, state form, and spatio-temporal fix (cf. Clarke
1977). Such crises typically act as a steering mechanism for the always

provisional, partial, and unstable re-equilibration of capital accumulation (cf. Lindner 1973; Hirsch 1997).

Third, modes of regulation and governance vary widely. This follows from the constitutive incompleteness of the capital relation and the various forms of appearance of capitalism, accumulation regimes, and modes of regulation, the relative weight of different contradictions, etc. For there are different ways to seek the closure of the circuit of capital and to compensate for its lack of closure. Which of these comes to dominate depends on the specific social and spatio-temporal frameworks within which these attempts occur. Indeed, notwithstanding the tendency for capital accumulation to expand until a single world market is achieved, there are important counter-tendencies and other limits to complete globalisation. Hence specific accumulation regimes and modes of regulation are typically constructed within specific social spaces and spatio-temporal matrices. It is this tendency that justifies the analysis of comparative capitalisms and of their embedding in specific institutional and spatio-temporal complexes. It also justifies exploration of the path-dependent linkages between different economic trajectories and broader social developments.

These arguments have important implications for modes of regulation. The key ontological and methodological question here is whether its objects pre-exist regulation. The regulationists' answer is 'yes and no'! For they both pre-exist regulation and are constituted in and through it. The incompleteness of the capital relation implies that the various aspects of the value form exist as relatively underdetermined 'elements' but, once subject to regularisation, they are transformed into so many 'moments' within a mode of regulation characterised by relative 'structured coherence'. In Marxian terms, capital as a social relation becomes a 'definite' object of regulation. Moreover, pursuing this line of analysis, the same elements have points of articulation with alternative modes of regulation and can never be fully fixed within any one mode of regulation. Thus regulation is always partial and unstable and the balance between fixity and fluidity (or, in terms more familiar to regulation theorists, rigidity and flexibility) is complex and changing. Accordingly we must explain how regulatory procedures emerge, interact, and combine to produce particular objects of regulation rather than others and, once produced, what follows for the crisis-tendencies of capitalism. One could perhaps re-interpret the work of Aglietta and Brender (1984) along these lines. For they argue that regulation depends on a network of routines and institutions which fix practices in ways compatible with accumulation. And crises occur when these routines and conventions lose their meaning and create periods of radical uncertainty until new patterns emerge.

A second issue raised by the RA with significant implications for critical realism is the doubly tendential character of capitalism. For it suggests that the tendencies and counter-tendencies of capitalism are doubly tendential. This idea can already be discerned at the level of categories for economic analysis (such as commodity, value, capital, or wage) in Marx's critique of Proudhon, who, according to Marx, has not seen that '[e]conomic categories are only the theoretical expressions, the abstractions of the social relations of production. Thus these ideas, these categories, are as little eternal as the relations they express. They are *historical and transitory products*' (Marx 1976: 165–6, italics in original). Likewise, referring to what critical realists would term the intransitive dimension of the social relations of production, Aglietta notes that the inherent properties of the capital–labour and capital–capital relations are reproduced insofar as the capital relation itself is reproduced (1979: 24–5). Let us explore this doubly tendential nature of the inherent properties and laws of motion of capitalism. First, they are tendential because the real causal mechanisms that produce them are only actualised in specific conditions that both activate the tendencies and limit the effects of any counter-tendencies. Second, they are tendential in a deeper sense: for their underlying causal mechanisms are themselves tendential, provisional, and unstable. If we accept that social phenomena are discursively constituted and that they never achieve complete closure, it follows that any natural necessities entailed in the internal relations of a given social phenomenon are themselves tendential. They would only be fully realised if the phenomena themselves were fully constituted and continually reproduced through recursive social practices entailed in such phenomena. Yet capitalist relations always exist in articulation with other relations of production and, at most, they occupy a position of relative dominance in the overall economic formation or productive system. Thus their laws of motion are always liable to disruption through the intrusion of other social relations which undermine the formal and/or the substantive unity of the capital relation. This can be established even at the most abstract levels of analysis since the reproduction of the capital relation itself always depends on the contradictory articulation of commodity and non-commodity forms (cf. Jessop 1983; 1997a; 1997b; 2000). In turn this implies that capital accumulation is never automatic but depends on a continuing struggle to prevent the disarticulation of the capital relation and a resulting loss of formal and/or substantive unity. Moreover, as we have already indicated, this is always and inevitably a struggle to maintain definite capitalist relations rather than capitalism in general. How this is achieved has been the RA's principal theoretical concern.

This also implies that the distinction between internal and external relations is at best relative rather than absolute (Lipietz 1987: 22–3). For, whatever the typical case in the natural world, real social objects are not fully constituted with clear and unambiguous boundaries within which definite internal relations could then generate natural necessities. On the contrary, real objects in the social world exist only tendentially and, *a fortiori*, as we have argued above, their 'laws of motion' are doubly tendential. This suggests in turn that well entrenched and stable modes of regulation could be seen as having their own natural necessities and laws of motion – which would, of course, be doubly tendential in the same way as the tendencies and counter-tendencies of the capitalist mode of production. Thus one could examine the logic of Fordism as an accumulation regime and/or mode of regulation in exactly the same way as one might explore the dynamic of the capitalist mode of production. Indeed, since neither capitalist production in general nor general capitalist production actually exist but only particular capitalist production and capitalist production as a whole and since the two last are always overdetermined by specific modes of regulation, there cannot be a radical break in the spiral movement of analysis as one proceeds from the abstract and simple to the concrete and complex – with natural necessities on one side, contingent events on the other. For any natural necessities of capitalism must be recursively and tendentially reproduced through social practices which are always (and inevitably) definite social practices, articulated more or less closely as moments in specific modes of regulation. In this sense these natural necessities are rational abstractions: there is no logic of capital but a series of logics with a family resemblance, corresponding to different modes of regulation and accumulation strategies. In turn this means that Fordism could have its own laws of motion (which would modify the abstract tendencies of capitalism) constituted in and through the stable articulation between the invariant elements of capitalism and the variant elements of Fordism: the invariant elements are nonetheless transformed as they become 'moments' within Fordism. On a more concrete level still, we could distinguish the laws of motion of US Fordism from those of West German 'flexi-Fordism' or British 'flawed Fordism' in terms of the stable tendencies and counter-tendencies of the three different concrete forms of Fordism (cf. Jessop 1988). Here the focus would be on how the invariant elements of Fordism in general are overdetermined through their articulation with elements specific to each social and economic formation. In short the distinctions between invariant and variant elements, natural necessities and contingent circumstances, and reproduction and regulation, would, in each case, be relative to the particular stage in the movement from the abstract and simple to the concrete and complex.

Another area where the RA has a potential contribution to make to the RA is in its analysis of the relationship between 'structure and agency'. Baert has criticised the transformational model of social agency developed by Bhaskar for being unable to explain social change. Conversely, 'relying upon a recursive model of social action (in which structures are both medium and output of social action) the TMSA is well-placed to explain the reproduction of structures, not their transformation' (Baert 1996: 521; cf. Archer's critique of Giddens's structuration theory, Archer 1995: 93–134). In contrast, the RA starts out, not from a general ontology of social action, but from a specific account of the conflictual and antagonistic nature of the capital relation; and it insists, as we have seen, on the inherent improbability of continuing, stable capital accumulation. In this context, regulationists refuse to study regulation in terms of a structuralist model of reproduction or a voluntarist model of intentional action. For the reproduction of capitalist societies is neither a fateful necessity nor a wilful contingency. Thus Aglietta (1982) and Lipietz (1987) regard the emergence of modes of regulation as improbable; and Lipietz described them as chance discoveries (1986, 1987). Many other accounts stress how accumulation regimes and/or modes of regulation emerge in a contingent, non-intentional manner. Where strategic conduct is involved it could well be more concerned to impose some coherence and direction on an already emergent structure in order to bring it into existence. But such efforts will co-exist with others seeking to impose different forms of coherence and other trajectories. Thus any accumulation regime and mode of regulation always represents an unstable institutionalised compromise. In this sense, any regime has many, often unacknowledged and/or uncontrollable, conditions of existence and emerges from the clash of multiple strategies. It has only a relative unity and, in this sense, is better described as a structural ensemble than as a simple structure. Moreover, within such an ensemble, there are typically many irrelevant, residual, marginal, secondary, and even potentially contradictory elements; and even the unity of the more central elements typically involves gaps, redundancies, tensions, and contradictions. This explains why some regulationists insist that accumulation regimes, modes of growth, and modes of regulation are 'discovered' rather than planned. There is no global subject to plan accumulation strategies, regulatory mechanisms, or hegemonic projects and to guarantee their successful implementation. Instead we find only different subjects whose activities are more or less co-ordinated, whose activities meet more or less resistance from other forces, and whose strategies are pursued within a structural context which is both constraining and facilitating. And this in turn creates many opportunities for agents to intervene, intentionally or otherwise, to disrupt the expanded reproduction of a given regime. Failure to recognise these issues can lead to just that *Begriffsrealismus* (reification of concepts) which Lipietz condemned in theories of imperialism and also claimed to discern in some recent regulation theories (Lipietz 1987: 11, 27). Moreover, given the contradictions at the heart of the capital relation, its inner structure generates crisis-tendencies and conflicts that continually threaten the relative stability of the accumulation regime and its mode of regulation.

Rethinking regulation and the role of spatio-temporal fixes

Marx argues in the 1857 *Introduction* that there is no production in general or general production, only particular production and the totality of production. This implies that there can be no regulation in general nor general regulation. Instead, following Marx, we can expect 'a definite regulation' oriented to 'a definite consumption, distribution, and exchange as well as *definite relations between these different moments*' (Marx 1973a: 99). The RA emphasises not only the labour process and accumulation regimes but also the mode of regulation (including the wage relation, forms of competition, money, the state, and international regimes) and the broader social consequences of the dominance of capital accumulation. It extends the scope of reproduction–régulation well beyond the capitalist economy in its narrow sense (profit-oriented production, market-mediated exchange) to include the direct and indirect extra-economic conditions of accumulation as well as the handling of the various repercussions of commodification and accumulation on the wider society.

Building on these arguments, I infer retroductively that reproducing and regularising capitalism involves a 'social fix' that partially compensates for the incompleteness of the pure capital relation and gives it a specific dynamic through the articulation of its economic and extra-economic elements. This helps to secure a relatively durable pattern of structural coherence in the handling of the contradictions and dilemmas inherent in the capital relation. One necessary aspect of this social fix is the imposition of a 'spatio-temporal fix' on these economic and extra-economic elements. It achieves this by establishing spatial and temporal boundaries within which the relative structural coherence is secured and by externalising certain costs of securing this coherence beyond these boundaries. Even within these boundaries we typically find that some classes, class fractions, social categories, or other social forces located within these spatio-temporal boundaries are marginalised, excluded, or subject to coercion.

Spatio-temporal fixes have both strategic and structural dimensions. Strategically, since the contradictions and dilemmas are insoluble in the abstract, they can only be resolved – partially and provisionally at best – through the formulation-realisation of specific accumulation strategies in specific spatio-temporal contexts. These strategies seek to resolve conflicts between the needs of 'capital in general' and particular capitals by constructing an imagined 'general interest' that will necessarily marginalise some capitalist interests. Interests are not only relational but also relative, i.e., one has interests in relation to others and relative to different spatial and temporal horizons. The general interest thus delimits the identities and relations relative to which calculation of interests occurs; and it confines the spatial and temporal horizons within which this occurs. It involves specific notions about which identities and interests can be synthesised within a general interest, about the intertemporal articulation of different time horizons (short-, medium-, and long-term, business cycle, electoral cycle, long wave, etc.), and about the relative importance of different spatial and/or scalar horizons (local, regional, national, supranational, etc.). Thus a conception of the general interest privileges some identities, interests, and spatio-temporal horizons and marginalises or sanctions others. It also refers to what is needed to secure an institutionalised class compromise and to address wider problems of social cohesion. Such success is often secured only through a trial-and-error search that reveals the requirements of 'capital in general' more through repeated failure than sustained success (Clarke 1977; Jessop 1983, 1999). In establishing this general interest and institutionalised compromise, however, accumulation strategies and hegemonic projects typically displace and defer their material and social costs beyond the social, spatial, and temporal boundaries of that compromise. This can involve super-exploitation of internal or external spaces outside the compromise, super-exploitation of nature or inherited social resources, deferral of problems into an indefinite future, and, of course, the exploitation and/or oppression of specific classes or other social categories.

Different scales of action and different temporal horizons may be used in a given spatio-temporal fix to handle different aspects of capital's structural contradictions and/or horns of resulting strategic dilemmas. For example, in Atlantic Fordism, the national state set the macro-economic framework, the local state acted as its relay, and intergovernmental co-operation maintained the conditions for national economic growth. Likewise, in contemporary neo-liberal accumulation regimes, the neo-liberal state's relative neglect of substantive (as opposed to formal) supply-side conditions at the international and national levels is partly compensated by more interventionist policies at the regional, urban, and local levels (Gough and Eisenschitz 1996; Brenner 1998). In addition, the withdrawal of the state is compensated by capital's increasing resort on all levels to networking and other forms of public–private partnership to secure its reproduction requirements. Another illustration of spatial-scalar divisions of labour is the tendential dissolution of the distinction between foreign and domestic relations. State organisation is premised on a distinction between nation states; and, in this context, some parts of the state apparatus specialise in external relations, some in internal relations. However, with the growing impact of globalisation and new forms of competitiveness, inherited divisions of state labour have changed. Not only is the distinction between domestic and foreign policy becoming blurred but we also find sub-national governments engaging in foreign (economic) policy through cross-border co-operation, international localisation, etc.

There can also be temporal divisions of labour with different institutions, apparatuses, or agencies responding to contradictions, dilemmas, and para-doxes over different time horizons. For example, whereas finance ministries deal with annual budgets, industry ministries would assume responsibility for longer-term restructuring. Similarly, corporatist arrangements have often been introduced to address long-term economic and social issues where complex, reciprocal interdependence requires long-term co-operation – thereby taking the relevant policy areas outside the short-term time horizons of electoral cycles and parliamentary in-fighting. In both cases there is also scope for meta-steering to re-balance the relations among these institutions, apparatuses, or agencies through a differential allocation of resources; allowing them to compete for legitimacy in changing circumstances, etc.

Concluding remarks

This chapter has addressed the role of realist assumptions and arguments in the regulation approach and describes some of its implications for critical realism more generally. It has argued that the RA's import is as much methodological as substantive and that its research potential depends critically on how fully and explicitly the core methodological presuppositions are integrated into future studies (for an argument that it has failed to transcend a middle-range analysis in this regard and has turned from an initial mild structuralism to an equally mild post-structuralism and post-modernism, see Mavroudeas 1999). Thus I identified four distinctive features of the RA. It works with a realist ontology and epistemology; adopts the method of 'articulation' in theory construction; operates within the general Marxist tradition of historical materialism with its interest in the political economy of capitalism and the anatomy of bourgeois society; and is especially concerned with the changing economic *and extra-economic* forms and mechanisms (institutions, networks, procedures, modes of calculation, and norms) in and through which the expanded reproduction of capital as a social relation is secured. Nonetheless there are important differences within and across the various regulation schools and currents which provide a continuing stimulus to further theoretical work.

In this light I think the following remarks on the RA's critical realism and on critical realism more generally are justified. First, if we take Bhaskar's approach to realism as a reference point, the regulation approach works (whether implicitly or explicitly) with a critical realist ontology and epistemology. It clearly rests on the distinction between real mechanisms, actual events, and empirical observations. Obviously, while the transcendental approach can justify a 'critical realist ontology and epistemology in general', it cannot validate a 'critical realist ontology and epistemology in particular'. The latter depends on specific analyses of a specific object and its associated self-movement of a contradictory essence rather than on a simplistic and generic application of the critical realist approach (Roberts 2000: *passim*; cf. Lawson 1997: 60, 326; and Burkett 2000: 384–8). There are various distinctive features in the RA's critical realism that can be attributed to its Marxist assumptions and antecedents and that deserve more extended treatment than they have received here. In particular I want to stress that the regulationist approach is, in important respects, 'strategic-relational'. It treats capital as a social relation and analyses it as a complex system of relations among relations; and, in this context, it regards these relations as produced in and through meaningful social action. Thus an adequate account of regulation must not only consider the material preconditions of, and constraints upon, reproduction (e.g., as revealed in the reproduction schemas and their significance for the quantitative constraints on capital accumulation) but must also take account of the different modes of calculation and the orientations of the various social forces involved in economic and social regulation. An important theoretical development in this context would be a more explicit concern with the 'spatio-temporal fixes' within which capitalist reproduction and regularisation occur.[15]

Second, building on the RA, I hope to have shown that the real mechanisms are doubly tendential: not only do these mechanisms themselves operate in terms of tendencies which may or may not be actualised, they are themselves only tendential. This can be seen as an alternative way of thinking about Bhaskar's claim that, whereas real causal mechanisms in the natural sciences exist independently of their actualisation, in the social sciences they cannot exist apart from their reproduction in and through social action and are short-lived and contingent compared to tendencies in the natural world. The concept of spatio-temporal fix helps us here by identifying the specific social contexts within which these specific mechanisms, tendencies, and counter-tendencies are tendentially reproduced and regularised.

Third, the regulationists' insistence that their work is concerned with regulation rather than with simple (or even expanded) reproduction indicates that they work with a transformational analysis of social relations. Regulation theorists treat the reproduction of the capital relation as a process that is secured in and through the actions of social agents: but they do not create this relation, they transform or reproduce it (cf. Bhaskar 1989: 76). Moreover, as I have argued elsewhere (e.g. Jessop 1983, 1990, 1996), their actions in reproducing the capital relation have a strategic dimension. For the dominance of the value form (including its various moments – the forms involved in the commodity, money, capital, wage, tax, legal, state, etc.) involve only a formal unity; any substantive unity depends additionally on the dominance and consistency of specific accumulation strategies. Here, too, we find one of Bhaskar's theses confirmed: that,

> because social structures exist only in virtue of the activities they govern, they do not exist independently of the conceptions that the agents possess of what they are doing in their activity; that is, of some theory of these activities.
>
> (Bhaskar 1989: 78)

But the regulation approach can take this argument and its associated transformational model of social action further insofar as it is concerned not with a general ontology of social structuration but with the ontology of a specific object of analysis (capitalism in its inclusive sense) that is inherently self-contradictory and therefore generates pressures and opportunities for more or less radical transformation.

Finally, my proposed revisions to the RA imply a critique of the hegemonic Parisian regulation school. In particular, I have re-specified the object, modes, contradictions, dilemmas, and limits of regulation. In doing so, I have proceeded more consistently than do most Parisian regulationists today from the Marxian premise that capital involves inherently antagonistic and contradictory social relations. Thus my approach stresses the inherent limits to the regulation (or, better, regularisation) of capital accumulation and seeks to avoid a 'premature harmonisation of contradictions' in analysing capitalist social formations. Nonetheless, in contrast to the tendency for non-Parisian theorists to turn the regulation approach into soft economic sociology, I share the Parisians' hard political economy emphasis on the central role of economic mechanisms in capital accumulation. Only thus can we develop a critical realist analysis of the reproduction and regulation of capitalism.

Notes

1 This chapter has benefited from discussions with Andrew Brown, Steve Fleetwood, Jonathan Joseph, Tony Lawson, Peter Nielsen, and Andrew Sayer and from some excellent written comments by John Roberts supplemented by his recent article (Roberts 2000). The usual disclaimers apply.
2 These are quite recent texts. It could be argued that Sayer anticipated the critical realist interpretation of Marx in his *Marx's Method* (1979, especially 75–150).
3 For example, some recent work has been shaped by trends in orthodox economics and in conventions analysis among economists (for a review, see Jessop 1997b).
4 Cf. Bhaskar's claim that 'it is vital to explicitly conceptualise historical materialism as an ongoing research programme . . . committed to a scientific realist ontology' (Bhaskar 1986: 145, n. 51).
5 Cf. in relation to Marx rather than the RA, Marsden's justifiable complaint that '(w)ith few exceptions . . . realists use Marx to illustrate and legitimise the philosophy, rather than use the philosophy to rethink and further the work Marx began' (1998: 298).
6 On subsumption and derivation as methods, see Jessop 1982.
7 This explains the occasional references to dialectical materialism in early RA work: it is not to be confused with the essentialist Stalinist versions of 'diamat' but should be read in a structuralist manner (see Althusser 1969).
8 Bhaskar (1993) also seeks to overcome an Hegelian account of the dialectic.
9 This reflects Marx's own approach in starting with the commodity as 'the simplest economic concretum', 'the concrete social form of the labour-product', the 'simplest social form in which the labour-product is presented in contemporary society' (see Carver 1975: 169). On form as 'the mode(s) of existence of the contradictory movement in which social existence consists', see Bonefeld *et al.* (1992: xv ff.).
10 The three volumes of *Capital* correspond essentially to the proposed books on capital, landed property, and, albeit only in part, that on wage-labour. See: Oakley 1983, 105–13; and Rosdolsky 1977: 40–62.
11 The best regulationist work on the money form is, of course, Aglietta's. See Aglietta 1986, Aglietta and Orléan (1982, 1998); and, for a commentary, Grahl (2000).
12 As a long wave (rather than a long cycle) account of capitalist dynamics, the RA treats the succession of stages as discontinuous, creatively destructive, and mediated through class conflict and institutional change. Long wave and long cycle theories can be distinguished as follows. Whilst both identify long waves of economic expansion and contraction, the former do not seek to identify a single causal mechanism which explains both the dynamic of individual long waves and the transition between them; the latter do regard the transition between periods

as having a single causal mechanism (or set of mechanisms) which remains the same across succeeding cycles. Thus long wave theories emphasise the ruptural, discontinuous form of economic reproduction–regulation and search for the conditions leading to each long wave in chance historical discoveries.

13 In contrast, Marsden (1998, 1999) argues that Marx's critical realism is quite definitely Hegelian in inspiration; Brown (1999) prefers, in turn, to see Marx's scientific breakthrough as indebted more to a skilful reappropriation of Hegelian dialectics than to any implicit critical realism. More generally, on 'systematic dialectics' as a new approach to the Hegel–Marx connection, see Smith (1990) and Mosely (1993).

14 Plurinational monetary blocs organised by states could also be included here.

15 It should be noted here that Bhaskar has acknowledged that 'critical realism' abstracts from time and space, even though these issues are essential to understand transformation, and suggests that his reformulated 'dialectical critical realism' can reincorporate them (Bhaskar 1993: 8). Nonetheless this move is subject to the same criticism that it provides a general account rather than one that reflects the specificities of a particular object of investigation.

16 Lipietz is the principal current exception here; see Lipietz (1986, 1987, 1993).

17 This phrase was introduced by Ernst Bloch to describe the function of utopian thought in maintaining social cohesion (1959: 178).

Bibliography

Aglietta, M. (1974) *Accumulation et régulation du capitalisme en longue période. Exemple des Etats-Unis (1870–1970)*, Paris: INSEE.

—— (1979) *A Theory of Capitalist Regulation: the U.S. Experience*, London: NLB (first published in French 1976).

—— (1982) 'Avant-propos à la deuxième édition', *Régulation et crises du capitalisme: l'expérience des Etats-Unis*, Paris: Calmann-Lévy.

—— (1986) *La Fin de devises clés*, Paris: la Découverte.

Aglietta, M. and Brender, A. (1984) *Les Métamorphoses de la société salariale: La France en projet*, Paris: Calmann-Lévy.

Aglietta, M. and Orléan, A. (1982) *La Violence de la monnaie*, Paris: Presses Universitaires de France.

—— (eds) (1998) *La Monnaie souveraine*, Paris: Odile Jacob.

Althusser, L. (1969) *For Marx*, London: Allen Lane.

Althusser, L. and Balibar, E. (1970) *Reading Capital*, London: New Left Books.

Archer, M.S. (1995) *Realist Social Theory: the Morphogenetic Approach*, Cambridge: Cambridge University Press.

Baert, P. (1996) 'Realist Philosophy of the Social Sciences and Economics: A Critique', *Cambridge Journal of Economics* 20 (5): 513–22.

Beamish, R. (1992) *Marx, Method, and the Division of Labour*, Urbana, IL: University of Illinois Press.

Benassy J.P. *et al.* (1977) *Approches de l'inflation: L'Example français, rapport au CORDES*, Paris: CEPREMAP, mimeo.

Benton, T. (1984) *The Rise and Fall of Structural Marxism: Althusser and his Influence*, Basingstoke, UK: Macmillan.

Bhaskar, R. (1986) *Scientific Realism and Human Emancipation*, London: Verso.

—— (1989) *The Possibility of Naturalism*, 2nd edition, London: Verso.

—— (1991) *Philosophy and the Idea of Freedom*, Oxford: Blackwell.

—— (1993) *Dialectic. The Pulse of Freedom*, London: Verso.

Bloch, E. (1959) *Das Prinzip Hoffnung, Kapitel 1–37*, Frankfurt: Suhrkamp.

Bonefeld, W. (1994) 'Aglietta in England: Bob Jessop's Contribution to the Regulation Approach', *Futur Antérieur*, special issue: 299–330.

Bonefeld, W. and Holloway, J. (eds) (1991) *Post-Fordism and Social Form*, Basingstoke, UK: Macmillan.

Bonefeld, W., Gunn, R. and Psychopedis, K. (1992) 'Introduction', in W. Bonefeld, R. Gunn and K. Psychopedis (eds) *Open Marxism: Theory and Practice*, London: Pluto Press, xi–xviii.

Brenner, N. (1998) 'Global Cities, Glocal States: Global City Formation and State Territorial Restructuring in Contemporary Europe', *Review of International Political Economy* 5 (1): 1–38.

Brown, A. (1999) 'Developing Realistic Methodology: How New Dialectics Surpasses the Critical Realist Method for Social Sciences', Middlesex University Business School Discussion Paper, March.

Burkett, J.P. (2000) 'Marx's Concept of an Economic Law of Motion', *History of Political Economy* 32 (2): 381–94.

Carver, T. (1975) *Texts on Method*, Oxford: Blackwell.

Clarke, S. (1977) 'Marxism, Sociology, and Poulantzas's Theory of the Capitalist State', *Capital and Class* 2: 1–31.

Ehrbar, H. (1998) 'Marxism and Critical Realism', Presentation for the Heterodox Economics Students Association, 25 September 1998 (downloadable from http://www.econ.utah.edu/ehrbar/marxre.pdf (accessed 2 December 2000)).

—— (2000) Critical Realist Arguments in Marx's *Capital* (downloadable from http://www.econ.utah.edu/ehrbar/argument.pdf (accessed 2 December 2000)).

Elliott, G. (ed.) (1994) *Althusser: A Critical Reader*, Oxford: Blackwell.

Fleetwood, S. (ed.) (1999) *Critical Realism in Economics: Development and Debate*, London: Routledge.

Gambino, F. (1996) 'A Critique of the Fordism of the Regulation School', *Common Sense* 19: 42–63.

Gerstein, I. (1989) '(Re)structuring Structural Marxism', *Rethinking MARXISM* 2 (1): 103–33.

Gough, J. and Eisenschitz, A. (1996) 'The Modernization of Britain and Local Economic Policy: Promise and Contradictions', *Local Government Studies* 14 (2): 203–19.

Grahl, J. (2000) 'Money as Sovereignty: the Economics of Michel Aglietta', *New Political Economy* 5 (2): 291–316.

Hay, C. (1994) 'Werner in *Wunderland* or Notes on a Marxism beyond Pessimism and False Optimism', *Futur Antérieur*, special issue: 331–62.

Hirsch, J. (1997) 'Kapitalreproduktion, Klassenauseinandersetzungen und Widersprüche im Staatsapparat', in V. Brandes, J. Hoffmann, U. Jürgens and W. Semmler (eds) *Handbuch 5 (Staat)*, Frankfurt: EVA, 161–81.

Jessop, B. (1982) *The Capitalist State*, Oxford: Martin Robertson.

—— (1983) 'Accumulation Strategies, State Forms, and Hegemonic Projects', *Kapitalistate* 10/11: 89–112.

—— (1988) 'Neo-Conservative Regimes and the Transition to Post-Fordism', in M. Gottdiener and N. Komninos (eds) *Capitalist Development and Crisis Theory Accumulation, Regulation, and Spatial Restructuring*, Basingstoke, UK: Macmillan, 261–99.

—— (1990) 'Regulation Theories in Retrospect and Prospect', *Economy and Society* 19 (2): 153–216.

—— (1992) 'Fordism and Post-Fordism: a Critical Reformulation', in A. J. Scott and M. J. Storper (eds) *Pathways to Regionalism and Industrial Development*, London: Routledge, 43–65.

—— (1996) 'Interpretive Sociology and the Dialectic of Structure and Agency: Reflections on Holmwood and Stewart's "Explanation and Social Theory"', *Theory, Culture, and Society* 13 (1): 119–28.

—— (1997a) 'Twenty Years of the Regulation Approach: the Paradox of Success and Failure at Home and Abroad', *New Political Economy* 2 (3): 499–522.

—— (1997b) 'Capitalism and its Future: Remarks on Regulation, Government, and Governance', *Review of International Political Economy* 4 (3): 435–55.

—— (1999) 'Narrating the Future of the National Economy and the National State? Remarks on Re-mapping Regulation and Re-inventing Governance', in G. Steinmetz (ed.) *State/Culture: State Formation after the Cultural Turn*, Ithaca, NY: Cornell University Press, 378–405.

—— (2000) 'The Crisis of the National Spatio-Temporal Fix and the Ecological Dominance of Globalizing Capitalism', *International Journal of Urban and Regional Studies* 24 (2): 273–310.

—— (ed.) (2001) *Regulation Theory and the Crisis of Capitalism*, Aldershot, UK: Edward Elgar, 5 volumes.

Kanth, R. (1999) 'Against Eurocentred Epistemologies', in S. Fleetwood (ed.) *Critical Realism in Economics*, London: Routledge, 187–208.

Lawson, T. (1989) 'Abstraction, Tendencies and Stylized Facts: A Realist Approach to Economic Analysis', *Cambridge Journal of Economics*, 13 (1): 59–78.

—— (1995) 'A Realist Perspective on Contemporary "Economic Theory"', *Journal of Economic Issues* 29 (1): 1–32.

—— (1997) *Economics and Reality*, London: Routledge.

Lebowitz, M. (1982) 'The One-Sidedness of *Capital*', *Review of Radical Political Economics* 14 (4): 40–51.

—— (1991) 'The Significance of Marx's Missing Book on Wage-Labor', *Rethinking MARXISM* 4 (2): 105–18.

Lindner, G. (1973) 'Die Krise als Steuerungsmittel', *Leviathan* 3 (4): 342–82.

Lipietz, A. (1986) *The Enchanted World: Inflation, Credit, and the World Crisis*, London: New Left Books.

—— (1987) *Mirages and Miracles*, London: New Left Books.

—— (1993) 'From Althusserianism to "Regulation Theory"', in E. A. Kaplan and M. Sprinker (eds) *The Althusserian Legacy*, London: Verso.

Marsden, R. (1998) 'The Unknown Masterpiece: Marx's Model of Capital', *Cambridge Journal of Economics* 22 (3): 297–324.

—— (1999) *The Nature of Capital: Marx after Foucault*, London: Routledge.

Marx, K. (1971) *Capital*, vol. III, London: Lawrence & Wishart.

—— (1973a) 'Introduction', in K. Marx, *Grundrisse*, Harmondsworth, UK: Penguin, 81–111 [this text is usually known as the *1857 Introduction*].

—— (1973b) *Grundrisse*, Harmondsworth, UK: Penguin.

—— (1976) 'The Poverty of Philosophy', in *Karl Marx and Friedrich Engels, Collected Works*, London: Lawrence & Wishart, vol. 6, 215–312.

—— (1978) *Capital*, vol. II, Harmondsworth, UK: Penguin.

Mavroudeas, S. (1999) 'Regulation Theory: the Road from Creative Marxism to Postmodern Disintegration', *Science & Society* 63 (3): 310–37.

Messner, D. (1997) *The Network Society*, London: Cass.

Mosely, F. (ed.) (1993) *Marx's Method in 'Capital'*, Atlantic Highlands, NJ: Humanities Press.

Nielsen, P. (2000) 'Critical Realism in Economics: Heterodoxy and Common Ground', Roskilde: Department of Economics, Roskilde University, unpublished paper.

Norton, B. (1988) 'Epochs and Essences: a Review of Marxist Long-wave and Stagnation Theories', *Cambridge Journal of Economics* 12 (2): 203–24.

Oakley, A. (1983) *The Making of Marx's Critical Theory: A Bibliographical Analysis*, London: Routledge & Kegan Paul.

Pratten, S. (1993) 'Structure and Agency and Marx's Analysis of the Labour Process', *Review of Political Economy* 5 (4): 403–26.

Resch, R.P. (1992) *Althusser and the Renewal of Marxist Social Theory*, Berkeley, CA: University of California Press.

Roberts, J.M. (2000) 'Abstraction, Method and System: A Tale of Two Dialectics', Paper presented at the International Association of Critical Realism Annual Conference, Lancaster University 18–20 August.

Rosdolsky, R. (1977) *The Making of Marx's Capital*, London: Pluto Press.

Ruigrok, W. and van Tulder, R. (1995) *The Logic of International Restructuring*, London: Routledge.

Sayer, D. (1979) *Marx's Method: Ideology, Science, and Critique in 'Capital'*, Hassocks, UK: Harvester.

Smith, T. (1990) *The Logic of Marx's 'Capital'. Replies to Hegelian Criticisms*, Albany, NY: State University of New York Press.

Woodiwiss, A. (1990) *Social Theory After Postmodernism: Rethinking Production, Law And Class*, London: Pluto Press.

6 Critical realism

Beyond the Marxism/post-Marxism divide

Neil Curry

The Philosophers have only interpreted the world, in various ways: the point is to change it.

(Marx 1992: 423)

Introduction

Roy Bhaskar and Ernesto Laclau met recently at the University of Essex in order to debate their respective approaches, critical realism and discourse theory. A second meeting is also planned on the political consequences of both approaches in the near future. I take this to indicate their relation to the continuing developments in contemporary Marxist theorising.

I will consider the debate by locating the arguments into five sections. In the first section I will consider the conceptual overhaul both Bhaskar and Laclau have undertaken. In the second section I will outline Bhaskar's critical realism (notwithstanding the fact that there are many other influential voices writing under its general schemata); in the third section I will consider what I deem to be the main contribution of the work of Ernesto Laclau (including the sizeable contribution of his collaborative work carried out with Chantal Mouffe); in the fourth section I will develop the major points of philosophical contention between the two, that is Laclau's distinction between existence and being and Bhaskar's distinction between the intransitive and transitive dimensions. I will then consider their subsequent political differences. My concluding remarks will concentrate on the relation between Marxism and critical realism suggesting that in fact critical realism makes a better bed partner for a certain form of post-Marxism than orthodox Marxism (Isaac 1990: 21). I will substantiate this claim by dispelling the usual myth that post-Marxism signals the end of Marxism, or more accurately, Marxism(s). In this way I will pose the question: can critical realism bridge the Marxism/post-Marxism divide and if so what are the political implications for the Left, especially with regard to the issue of class?

Revolution(s)

Marx was deeply influenced by the events centred round the French Revolution, and drew inspiration from subsequent interpretations which rendered these events a transfer of power from the aristocracy to the bourgeoisie, a class-based movement. However controversial this thesis remains amongst historians, the French Revolution had an enormous impact on Marx, especially in terms of his development of the notion of 'permanent revolution'. If the central reference point for what we might call orthodox Marxism is the October Revolution, then the focus for both Bhaskar and Laclau is firmly rooted in a Copernican Revolution. Perhaps it is time to rethink this notion of revolution, and re-route it through the political. Today the crucial question both Bhaskar and Laclau need to consider concerns what kind of concrete political project their work endorses. The political should emerge as part of this conceptual overhaul without ever exhausting it. Yet, at the same time, should be attentive to the contingency and variability of struggle, for classes are what are formed in struggle, not what pre-exist struggle (Smith 1993: 103). It is time for clarification in order to avoid merely dreaming the revolution: 'taking the fast excursion to Ambrosia' (Waterhouse 1959: 15).

What were Left academics up to when Thatcherism, after reaching its most destructive moments in the mid-1980s was beginning to unravel itself at the end of the decade? Two of the most renowned figures of Left politics Roy Bhaskar and Ernesto Laclau were in their different ways busy forging Copernican Revolutions in their respective fields. Copernican Revolutions continue to be espoused by anyone who is anybody in their respective subjects; it is, however, the very notion of revolution as proposed by Copernicus that places in question the centrality usually given to the French and/or October Revolution (Balibar 1995: 8).

Bhaskar's Copernican Revolution is rooted firmly in the work of Rom Harre's anti-deductivism and the attack upon Humean causality. Building upon this approach Bhaskar 'stood the world back on its feet again, critiqued the epistemic fallacy and situated epistemology constellationally within ontology' (Bhaskar 1993: 299). This involved a switch within ontology, moving away from events and states of affairs to the underlying generative mechanisms that bring them about, and this, in turn, following this retroductive argument, ushered in a switch within philosophy from epistemology to ontology based around the transcendental realist assertion of the independent existence and the transfactual efficacy of structures and efficacious things. For, 'it does not follow from the fact that we can only know in knowledge that we can only know knowledge' (Bhaskar 1989: 188). Thus Bhaskar describes his philosophy as Copernican, for 'reclaiming reality' is to deanthropomorphise it, so that any conception of reality is contingent, partial and locally humanised. Yet this reality is in no way exhausted by our conceptions of it, or reducible to them, and thereby places us in a limited and precarious position in the world. Bhaskar's target is the anthropic fallacy which is based around the confusion arising from the exchange between the ontic and epistemic fallacies. The anthropic fallacy is the analysis of being in terms of human being, a reductivist position stemming from the ontic fallacy which involves the reduction of knowledge to being, which usually operates along an axis of misunderstanding with the epistemic fallacy, the reduction of being to knowledge about being.

Laclau's Copernican Revolution involves the development of the concept of hegemony beyond the scope Gramsci envisaged for it, to include the proliferation of new antagonisms to emerge in advanced capitalism. It is based around the possibility of the absence of a centre and the even more radical suggestion that man, even as the subject of knowledge, is not the central reference point of what he knows (Laplanche 1999). So that the very centre of human being was no longer to be found at the place assigned to it by a whole humanist tradition (Lacan 1997: 114). Laclau and Mouffe state their position better than I could, when they write:

> We have now arrived at the heart of the Copernican Revolution which we mentioned earlier. This consists in leading through to its conclusion the break with economism that was initiated by Lenin and developed by Gramsci and Togliatti, and in breaking decisively with the essentialist metaphysic of the 'guarantees of history' and the forms of a scientificity that declares itself the 'absolute truth' of a historical process, claiming to be able to predict its necessary course. We have rather to conceive society as a complex field, crossed by a diversity of political struggles, in which multiplicity of subjects must be recognised and accepted if we are one day to achieve a truly liberated and self managed society.
>
> (Laclau and Mouffe 1981: 22)

The achievements of Copernicus were deemed to be revolutionary because although his work was associated with methods and assumptions that had been familiar for centuries, the wider implications for the relations between humankind and the universe at large were to be far reaching. The question as to whether critical realism or discourse theory achieve this is something prone to disputation. For both Bhaskar and Laclau would agree on the refusal to naturalise knowledge (the ontic fallacy); however, for Bhaskar, this is not enough, for in making this statement one must attempt to avoid falling into the reduction of ontology into epistemology (the epistemic fallacy), which merely reintroduces a different form of anthropocentrism. The key point of disagreement would not therefore be on epistemological grounds, but rather concerning questions surrounding ontology. Laclau wants to enclose being within knowledge, whereas Bhaskar wishes to encircle knowledge within being (not merely human being) and thereby relativise epistemology without ontological relativity: 'Everything is contained (constellationally) within ontology (including epistemology and ethics)' (Bhaskar

1997: 142). Laclau on the other hand wishes to relativise both ontology and epistemology so that there is nothing left to be discovered, only different discursive configurations constantly emerging. This is due to the fact that for Laclau ontology is about human beings, whereas for Bhaskar it entails and even prioritises non-being. So there is obviously a problem of commensurability between the starting points of these two approaches before one gets into the broader consequences of their work.

Roy Bhaskar: critical realism

The work of Roy Bhaskar is generally taken to be co-existent with the Marxist tradition. Bhaskar's work was most aptly summarised some years ago by Outhwaite as 'ontologically bold and epistemologically cautious' (Outhwaite 1987: 34). There is however no mention of Marx in Bhaskar's first book *A Realist Theory of Science*. He emerges in *The Possibility of Naturalism*. Yet in his first work *A Realist Theory of Science*, it is widely acknowledged that Althusser had a decisive influence (Callinicos 1994: 8). Bhaskar himself acknowledges that 'Louis Althusser made a contribution of decisive importance. The Althusserian legacy demands nothing less than the most thorough-going critical reappropriation' (Bhaskar 1991: 183). Bhaskar locates the single most important Althusserian contribution as his attempt within the concept of overdetermination to capture the multiple determination of events and phenomena generally in what are open systems (Bhaskar 1989: 187–8).

Bhaskar's name is synonymous with critical realism and yet as the project of critical realism has developed (especially through the annual conferences) so that divergences have emerged between the key protagonists. This is not the place however, nor do I have the space available to lay down the ongoing disputes between critical realists. In this paper I will concentrate on Bhaskar, who is 'the most original and influential' critical realist philosopher (Collier 1995: ix). Bhaskar's *oeuvre* has developed through a number of stages to the point where it can now be defined as dialectical critical realism (Bhaskar 1993: ch. 3). Critical realism involves four themes; these are, transcendental realism, critical naturalism, explanatory critique and the dialectical moment. Within each of these four themes we may indicate a number of key moments.

Transcendental realism involves the assertion that any theory of knowledge presupposes what the world must be like for knowledge to be possible. This is the transcendental aspect which Bhaskar marries onto the claim that this always entails some statement about being, rather than just knowledge of being, because the objects under investigation exist independently of human activity and thought. This leads to the assertion of the independent existence and transfactual efficacy of structures and efficacious things. It employs retroductive arguments which involve a movement in investigation from domains of the empirical and actual to the domain of deep structures which bring about these events. The ontological consequences of this are that monovalence is rejected in favour of a multi-layered and emergent ontology. This has important consequences, which I will consider for the next element of dialectical critical realism.

Critical naturalism, born out of the transcendental realist arguments previously rehearsed, involves the rejection of both individualistic/voluntaristic and collectivist/reificationist tendencies in social theory. It attempts to overcome the dichotomous disputes between hyper-naturalists (positivism) and the anti-naturalists (hermeneutics). Bhaskar poses the transcendental question: 'What properties do societies possess that might make them possible objects of knowledge for us?' (Bhaskar 1979: 31). The transformational model of social activity proffers a relational theory which has a close affinity with a dialectical model but differs in the crucial respect of the irreducibility of social structures to the agents who work upon them.

> Society provides the means, media, rules and resources for everything we do . . . Society then is the ensemble of positioned practices and networked interrelationships which individuals never create but in their practical activity always presuppose, and in doing so everywhere reproduce or transform.
>
> (Bhaskar 1989: 4)

Here Bhaskar's argument resonates with the Althusserian concept of structural causality, whereby social structures are irreducible to but present only in its effects (Callinicos 1994: 8). The key move that becomes apparent is that people do not create societies, but rather because society is pre-existent, they recreate it. Social structures exist by virtue of the activities of people, yet are not reducible to them. These structures are relatively enduring and not mere properties of people's activities. They attain some kind of entitative status themselves and as a result of this processual pre-existing status, structures both make possible and constrain human agency. Bhaskar's critical naturalism has been the subject of wide-ranging critique and also seems closely akin to Giddens's theory of structuration (a refutation of this can be found in Archer 1995). This comes to fruition in the social cube in which, according to Bhaskar:

> social life qua totality is constituted by four dialectically interdependent planes: of material transactions with nature, inter-personal action, social relations and intra-subjectivity. The social cube must be conceived in terms of depth and stratification and the elements of each plane are subject to multiple and conflicting determinations and mediations in a totalising conception which dialecticises existing realist ideas such as the transformational model of social agency and the position-practice system.
>
> (Bhaskar and Norrie 1998: 570)

Explanatory critique makes up the third aspect of the Bhaskarian model. It emerges and derives from the previous assertions and vindicates a modified form of a substantive ethical naturalism based around the notion that the objects of the social sciences, unlike the natural sciences, includes beliefs about themselves which entail judgements of value and action. The normative moment is implicit and therefore the gap between facts and values maintained by Hume is bridgeable. For any rational value judgement must have factual grounding, otherwise it must be seen as radically incomplete.

Bhaskar's dialectical move came later, culminating in the publication of *Dialectic: The Pulse of Freedom*. Bhaskar states, 'I want to show that it is possible to think and act dialectically without necessarily being a Hegelian' (Bhaskar 1993: 3). He outdoes Hegel by typically encompassing four moments into his dialectic which will be 'diffracted and retotalised': non-identity, negativity, totality and transformative agency (Bhaskar 1993: 37). Central to the dialectic is the concept of absence stemming from Bhaskar's critique of ontological monovalence, which encompasses the reduction of the real to the actual. This places absence at the heart of positivity so that non-being is the condition of the possibility of being and dialectic is the process of absenting absence. 'Importantly, if absence (negativity) is one pole of the positive, then the positive cannot be successfully positivised . . . Dialectic becomes the "great loosener", permitting empirical "open texture" . . . and structural fluidity and interconnectedness' (Bhaskar and Norrie 1998: 564). Critical realism involves definite ontological commitments with specific epistemological concerns and, according to Joseph, it acts as a 'philosophical underlabourer whose job it is to clarify the conceptual aspects of Marxism's work' (Joseph 1998: 102).

Ernesto Laclau: discourse theory

Discourse theory as espoused by Ernesto Laclau, and subsequently post-Marxism, is a very different response and is somewhat philosophically distant to critical realism. Any direct comparison is difficult because they tend to operate in and emerge out of vastly different fields of enquiry – these being political philosophy and the philosophy of science respectively. However, Laclau was also deeply influenced, one might even say embedded, in Althusserian Marxism in a similar fashion to Bhaskar. Whereas Bhaskar has argued that Althusser effectively neutralised the intransitive dimension. (A more detailed discussion of the relationship between Althusser and Bhaskar can be found in Sprinker 1992: 122–4.) Laclau, reacted against the apparent rigidities of structural Marxism and took on board the post-structuralist strategy of decentring, exemplified by Derrida as:

> The moment when language invaded the universal problematic, the moment when, in the absence of a centre or origin, everything became discourse – provided we can agree on this word – that is to say, a system

in which the central signified, the original or transcendental signified, is never absolutely present outside a system of differences. The absence of the transcendental signified extends the domain and the play of signification infinitely.

(Derrida 1978: 280)

Laclau applies a deconstructive logic usually associated with Jacques Derrida (though not exclusively) to the realm of politics. More precisely, Laclau, with Chantal Mouffe, attempts to deconstruct the categories of Marxist thought, through a privileging of the political moment over the moment of structural determinism, in order to recast Marxism as a movement that is responsive to the central issues of contemporary politics. They are carrying out the task inaugurated by Gramsci in his deployment of the concept of hegemony, which opened up the categories of Marxism to the possibility of contingency and rearticulation, but which he never fully followed through. However, while a direct tracing of the concept of hegemony, and the decisive influence of Gramsci on Laclau and Mouffe is correct, Althusser also played a decisive role. Of course, this is not to suggest that there is no link between Althusser and Gramsci. Laclau however, points to what he deems to be a 'lingering essentialism' in Gramsci which is also apparent in Althusser's 'lonely hour of the last instance', something he vehemently rejects. But Laclau sees in Gramsci something indiscernible in Althusser, a way out of the limitations imposed by Structural Marxism. This is the crucial distinction between Marxism and post-Marxism and marks out the terrain of possible articulation for a variety of Marxism(s). Before going on to explore this relationship, however, I will offer some introductory remarks concerned with discourse theory following the remarks made by Laclau in the debate.

For Laclau, the notion of discourse as developed in much contemporary thought has distant roots in the transcendental turn in modern philosophy, with an emphasis not primarily on facts but rather on their conditions of possibility (Laclau 1993: 431). However, the sustained critique of language put forward by a variety of approaches has led to a movement away from this classical transcendental approach, so that today discourse means something radically different. This is because 'contemporary discourse theories are eminently historical and try to study discursive fields which experience temporal variations in spite of their transcendental role' and take on board fully the changes undergone in relation to the notion of structure (Laclau 1993: 431). According to Laclau, the crucial elements to discourse theory are: first, that a basic grammar exists within which possible objects are constituted and this mediates any contact with reality, based around the 'increasing realisation that "discourse" did not refer to a particular set of objects, but to a view point from which it was possible to redescribe the totality of social life' (Laclau 1993: 433); second, that discourse is not merely speech and writing, and therefore not reducible to the linguistic, but is always a combination of words and actions. Following Wittgenstein, Laclau's notion of a language game always encompasses both the linguistic and non-linguistic and this takes place within a meaningful totality which cannot therefore be either linguistic or extra-linguistic and must then be prior to this distinction; the performative dimension is intrinsic to any linguistic operation. Action is therefore inherent to any linguistic operation, something entirely constitutive of discourse; finally, the main approach that discourse theory opposes is Idealism. Arguing on two fronts discourse theory maintains the irreducibility of the real to thought and also questions the notion of a unified subject or unity of the mind. Laclau makes the case for this by insisting on the distinction between the being of an object, which is historical and changing, and its entity, which is not.

Philosophy: being and existence

> Most people would agree that transcendentalism, in its classic formulations, is totally unsustainable, but there is also a generalised agreement that some kind of weak transcendentalism is unavoidable.
>
> (Laclau 1997: 17)

For Laclau, the point is that the being of things cannot be fixed once and for all. To do so would be to commit one of two common mistakes, the essentialisation of the object and the reduction of the subject to a passive recipient of an already constituted meaning, or the essentialisation of the subject and thus the reduction of the object to an object of thought. For Laclau, the discursive is coterminous with the being of every object, and it is this horizon which constitutes the being of every object, therefore, the conditions of possibility of the being of discourse is meaningless:

> if the process of naming of objects amounts to the very act of their constitution, then their descriptive features will be fundamentally unstable and open to all kinds of hegemonic rearticulations. The essentially performative character of naming is the precondition for all hegemony and politics.
>
> (Laclau 1989: xiv)

This, as we have seen, does not lead to idealism, because the irreducibility of the world to our conceptions of it is still maintained, even if it has become an impossibility. However, whilst this may be true, the notion of the real that we are left with is little better than an idealist reduction. It may be a non-idealist constructivism but by the same token it is also a recalcitrant realism that we are left with. This has also been called an empty realism (Jessop 1990). For Laclau, that something which guarantees the identity of an object in all counterfactual situations is merely the retroactive process of naming itself. The excess in the object which stays the same in all possible worlds has no positive consistency because it is just the positivation of a void, the filling of a space (for a critique of Laclau's notion of space see Massey 1993). It is the impossibility of filling this space indefinitely which makes the political construction of this space possible.

> The traditional debate as to the relationship between agent and structure thus appears fundamentally displaced: the issue is no longer a problem of autonomy, of determinism versus free will, in which two entities fully constituted as objectivities mutually limit each other. On the contrary, the subject emerges as a result of the failure of substance in the process of its self-constitution.
>
> (Laclau 1989: xv)

Laclau is not arguing that an external world does not exist independent of our accounts of it, but instead seems to be saying that in order to have any meaning at all it must be constitutive of a discursive configuration. The outcome of this may be summarised as follows: that the object has no being in and of itself but only attains this in a discursive field, so that it does not make sense to speak of an object *a priori* of discourse, because it is only through discourse that an object gets meaning (Laclau 1990: 109–12). The object and discourse are therefore coterminous with one another and the moment at which the object has any sort of meaning resides within discursivity, such that what we think is external is actually internal. The 'limit' between the external and the internal is never fixed for all time but is inherent to the object and discursive configuration. The moment where meaning is formed is not after the object is complete (descriptivism/anti-descriptivism) it actually constitutes the object and is prior to the descriptivist/anti-descriptivist dispute. Because the limit of objectivity is not fixed, and the limit is precisely the point at which fixity breaks down, it is negotiable and this is what Laclau means when he says that politics is an instituting moment rather than that which is relegated as a secondary moment emerging out of society. This is Laclau's crucial intervention and instantiates the radical democratic project. This challenges the claims made by orthodox Marxists of the economic with its own interiority, but which is able to determine outside this interiority other realms exterior to one another. It is precisely this paradox which Laclau is attempting to circumvent on behalf of socialism.

The problem here for a more nuanced realism is that Laclau seems to rule out even a minimal causal account. This is because he considers causality in Humean terms as a constant conjuncture of events rather than 'structures, generative mechanisms and the like (forming the real basis of causal laws), which are normally out of phase with them' (Bhaskar 1989: 16). Laclau seems to be suggesting that in order for causation to take place there must exist fully-formed entities. Yet, even if we agree with Laclau on the distinction between the being of an object and the entity of an object, this would seem at least to leave open the possibility that that which is absent, or left over, may in some way limit or impinge upon the discursive constitution of an object. This would indicate that Laclau is arguing that the object is not prior to discourse but that in order to mean anything it is already discursively constituted, hence there can be no meaning outside of our discursive actions. This is something that would be problematic for Bhaskar who has constantly argued against the reduction of being to human being, and asserts that causal processes go on independent of human cognition of these processes. For Bhaskar, even in change some things stay the same. This can be expressed in terms of social life being both symbolic and causal, whereas for Laclau social life is just symbolic.

Laclau (with Chantal Mouffe) in *Hegemony and Socialist Strategy* (1985) and in their subsequent disagreement with Geras (Geras 1987; Laclau and Mouffe 1981; Mouzelis 1988; Geras 1988) initiated the move from Marxism into the realm of post-Marxism, in the understanding of course that this was never a rejection but more a radical questioning. Laclau argues that the categories of Marxism are neither 'removed nor reabsorbed by a higher rationality but shown in their contingency and historicity' (Laclau 1990: 96). In order to substantiate his move into discursive configurations he made the crucial distinction between the being of an object and its existence. This dispute is crucial for Laclau to maintain his anti-essentialist stance, based around the Heideggerian premise that 'Being cannot be explained through entities' (Heidegger 1967: 251). Laclau would endorse this Heideggerian motif, yet he cannot say, unless he is an idealist (which he apparently is not), that objects stay the same for all time in their existential qualities (pure absence), but instead of considering this outside he speaks only of what can be known inside. If, however, objects are always discursively articulated and if a discourse cannot exhaust the whole meaning of an object because the object is never fully substantiated, just as any discourse is never fully closed, then this possibility of excess meaning (the left over) in objects always has the potential to impinge on that discourse. To put this in Derridean terms, the point that marks any limit is an opening onto something irreducible to that which it marks. Therefore, how can we ever be sure that that which exists, if not prior then external to the discursive, is exhausted into the discursive. The only way to be sure would be to reduce the external and any existential traces to the purely internal or discursive. And this is precisely what Laclau does. This form of constructivism would seem to usher in a form of irrealism based around the reduction of the real to the physical qualities entities possess, ignoring potentiality and reducing the real to the material, or as we have already stated an 'empty realism'- a real out there in the Kantian sense without any relationship to what is inside. Slavoj Žižek has recently pointed out Laclau's implicit Kantianism when he writes that, for Laclau, the very impossibility is represented in a positive element, inherent impossibility is changed into an external obstacle (Butler *et al.* 2000: 107). I have hopefully demonstrated why I think Laclau has prematurely ruled out the idea that when a discourse runs up against its limits it may be possible that there is more than just another discourse affecting it. This is because of the limited notion of the object he adopts. The production of knowledge constructs objects, but in doing so it by no means exhausts the objects into its construction. Yet it is also at the same moment also reconstructed by its encounter with the object. This processural encounter never takes place outside the objects but is a constitutive moment in the ongoing formation of these objects, so one could say that the objects are never given in any unmediated sense, but always in a process of being constantly reconstructed and never exhausted in the encounter. However, this also poses serious problems for Bhaskar, especially with regard to maintaining the distinction he develops between the transitive and intransitive dimensions. It is precisely on this matter that Bhaskar has made an important contribution, which I will now consider.

Philosophy: transitive/intransitive dimensions

> The intransitive dimension is initially the domain of the objects of scientific knowledge: but the concept can be extended to take in anything existentially intransitive, whether known, knowable or not. The transfactuality of laws and socialisation into science imply the distinction between the intransitive or ontological and the transitive or epistemological dimensions of science. This latter must logically be extended to include the whole material and cultural infrastructure of society.
>
> (Bhaskar 1993: 399–400)

Bhaskar detects a residual Kantianism in the work of Laclau when he states 'you've got rid of the unified subject, but you still want the unified object, you still want this non-existent stone out there. Why can't we disaggregate the notion of the object' (Bhaskar and Laclau 1998: 17).

His conceptualisation of the object marks a crucial departure, containing within it innate voids and absences, something like absence within presence. The notion of the intransitive dimension enables one to say that people socially construct their world, but this is always a construction of something. What is the status of this something? The dilemma would seem to be that the intransitive dimension by definition exceeds what we know about it (which is transitive), yet in order to say something (if not how much) about the intransitive dimension then the transitive/intransitive distinction must be at least partially breachable, and therefore open to reconfiguration. Perhaps it can be said then that the intransitive dimension, that which stays the same, is itself only relatively enduring and always partially transitive. This multi-dimensional openness, it could be argued, is therefore open to negotiation and itself somehow prone to change. Bhaskar is no foundationalist, making certaintist claims about the world out there. He argues that all knowledge is fallible, subject to contestation and transformation. But the crucial question is whether the limitations to our transitive statements are located within another discourse (as for Laclau) or in the realm of the extra-discursive, which itself is only relatively enduring. It is at this point that the logic of the both/and appears rather than the logic of either/or. But since all our statements are transitively situated, and the transitive dimension is constellationally situated within the intransitive dimension, then this would seem at least to open up the possibility that the deep structures identified behind manifest phenomena are capable of being reconstructed in the encounter, and are not therefore as intransitive as previously thought. What is left of the intransitive dimension if the emphasis is placed on 'the transitive apprehension of entities and processes posited as intransitive (which) are positioned within linguistic and cultural economies' (Castree 1995: 40). This would focus on the realm of political action as the means of social transformation, but not reduce everything to the political. That which is out-side (intransitivity) is never fully out there, and at the same time that which is in here (transitivity) is never purely in here, therefore they are constel-lationally contained within one another (yet irreducible) and hence open to being transformed in their relation to one another. But this relation between the two becomes less permanent than previously envisaged and open to disputation.

Politics: whatever happened to class?

> Everything which touches on politics may be fatal to philosophy, for philosophy lives on politics.
>
> (Althusser 1990: 173)

Both Bhaskar and Laclau have attempted to develop their own projects from inside and outside the Marxist tradition. Both have attempted to undermine 'essentialism' in its crudest form. Yet neither has ever claimed to have trans-cended Marxism or rejected it in its entirety. In different ways both have attempted to reformulate Marxism and continue to draw on the tradition.

Post-Marxism ushered in a Copernican revolution within Marxism whereby class was radically decentred and consequently no longer occupies the central position as the motor of history and social change. However, rather than a mere displacement, class seems to have disappeared from the political agenda altogether. At best it seems to be presented in an apologetic fashion. Does this removal of class struggle as the primary mover in social transformation not afford the opportunity for rethinking class and enlarging its role in a 'collective resistance to capitalist dominance' (Kaplan 2000: 10). How does one begin to bring class back into play, to reinvigorate a concept, to think class as still crucially important in Late Capitalism? And would the work of Laclau or Bhaskar endorse such a manoeuvre?

According to Bhaskar, Marx 'remains fixated on the wage-labour/capital relation at the expense of the totality of master–slave relations (most obviously those of nationality, ethnicity, gender, religious affiliation, sexual orientation, age, health and bodily disabilities generally)' (Bhaskar 1993: 333). Critical realism would therefore seem to want to extend the scope beyond Marxism and class relations to include other oppressions, that take place within capitalism but which also exceed it.

However, Laclau has recently commented on this formulation as setting in motion something which is radically incompatible with the Marxist theory of class. For Laclau, the Marxist notion of 'class' cannot be incorporated into an enumerative chain of identities, simply because it is supposed to be the articulating core around which all identity is constituted. The term 'class', by becoming part of an enumerative chain has lost its articulating role without acquiring any new precise meaning. We are dealing with something approaching the status of a 'floating signifier'.

So, it is precisely because class fails to constitute itself as a full presence beyond all exclusions, that it exists at all. This impossibility at once cancels out both pure difference and equivalence at the same time. That which prevents class from ever being fully positivised (its limits, the beyond) is also that which makes it possible. Its conditions of impossibility are at the same time the conditions of possibility. An empty signifier is a signifier which announces itself through the 'logic in which differences collapse into equivalential chains' (Laclau 1996: 39).

According to Laclau, when a class discourse reaches its limit, this can only ever be another discourse competing to fill this empty space, or displace the dominant hegemonic discourse. Whilst Bhaskar does not concern himself directly with the issue of class, it would seem that it is possible that there is more than this going on. For class is constituted by both a discursive (transitive dimension) and something which exceeds this transitive dimension (the intransitive dimension). For Bhaskar, class as well as other modes of oppression are both discursive and causal at the same time. This operates in a similar manner (yet deeper) to Laclau's notion of the logic of equivalence, which prevents pure difference. For Bhaskar, a discourse is always a construction of something and it is this something that both facilitates and constrains a discourse and prevents it from closure.

How have Marxists more recently attempted to retheorise class? According to David Harvey, 'a preparatory step is to broaden somewhat the conventional Marxian definition of "class" (or more exactly of "class relation") under capitalism to mean positionality in relation to capital circulation and accumulation' (Harvey 2000: 102). In a similar formulation, Neil Smith comments that 'the increasing intellectual influence of Marxism and the resulting focus on class in the 1970s and early 1980s found itself increasingly at odds with a wider political context' (Smith 2000: 1018). It is for this reason that one should avoid positing class as a given entity. According to Smith, Marx's privileging of class and particularly the working class was politically motivated rather than based upon moral or philosophical reasons. As for the contemporary situation Smith writes: 'That the renewed importance of class discourse is not at all inconsistent with an evolving politics of race, gender, and sexuality . . . there seems to be no alternative. "Back to Class" in any narrow sense is its own self-defeating *cul-de-sac*.'

The problem with Laclau's version of post-Marxism is that it levels political struggle to the point where no justification can be given for any one project over another. Bhaskar and critical realism however, whilst embracing epistemic relativity refuse 'judgmental relativism, into which non-foundationalist irrealism tends to fall' (Bhaskar 1993: 403). There seems to be no reason to choose between new social movements and class politics. Capitalism and class still constitute the major forms of oppression and domination, albeit intertwined with non-capitalist relations. These issues are inextricably linked so perhaps we can all agree with Slavoj Žižek when he suggests that when given the choice class politics or postmodernism the most radical gesture is to resist this opposition as a false alternative!

Bibliography

Althusser, L. (1990) *Philosophy and the Spontaneous Philosophy of the Scientists and other Essays*, translated by B. Brewster, London: Verso.

Archer, M. (1995) *Realist Social Theory: The Morphogenetic Approach*, Cambridge: Cambridge University Press.

Balibar, E. (1995) *The Philosophy of Marx*, translated by C. Turner, London: Verso.

Bhaskar, R. (1979) *The Possibility of Naturalism*, Brighton, UK: Harvester.

—— (1989) *Reclaiming Reality*, London: Verso.

—— (1991) *Philosophy and the Idea of Freedom*, Oxford: Blackwell.

—— (1993) *Dialectic: The Pulse of Freedom*, London: Verso.

—— (1997) 'On the ontological status of ideas', *Journal for the Theory of Social Behaviour* 27, 2/3: 139–47.

Bhaskar, R. and Laclau, E. (1998) 'Critical realism vs discourse theory', *Alethia* 1, 2: 9–14.

Bhaskar, R. and Norrie, A. (1998) 'Introduction', in M. Archer, R. Bhaskar, A. Collier, T. Lawson and A. Norrie (eds) *Critical Realism: Essential Readings*, London: Routledge.

Butler, J., Laclau, E. and Žižek, S. (2000) *Contingency, Hegemony, Universality: Contemporary Dialogues on the Left*, London: Verso.

Callinicos, A. (1994) 'Critical realism and beyond: Roy Bhaskar's dialectic', Department of Politics Working Paper, University of York.

Castree, N. (1995) 'The nature of produced nature: materiality and knowledge construction in Marxism', *Antipode* 27, 1: 12–48.

Collier, A. (1995) *Critical Realism*, London: Verso.

Derrida, J. (1978) 'Structure, sign and play in the discourse of the human sciences', in *Writing and Difference* translated by A. Bass, London: Routledge.

Geras, N. (1987) 'Post-Marxism?', *New Left Review* 163: 40–82.

—— (1988) 'Ex-Marxism without substance: being a real reply to Laclau and Mouffe', *New Left Review* 169: 34–61.

Harvey, D. (2000) *Spaces of Hope*, Edinburgh: Edinburgh University Press.

Heidegger, M. (1967) *Being and Time*, Oxford: Blackwell.

Isaac, J. (1990) 'Realism and reality: some realistic reconsideration's', *Journal for the Theory of Social Behaviour* 20, 1: 1–31.

Jessop, B. (1990) *State Theory: Putting the Capitalist State in its Place*, Cambridge: Polity.

Joseph, J. (1998) 'In defence of critical realism', *Capital and Class* 65: 73–106.

Kaplan, C. (2000) 'Millennium class', *Proceedings of the Modern Language Association of America (PMLA)* 115: 9–19.

Lacan, J. (1997) *Ecrits: A Selection*, London: Routledge.

Laclau, E. (1989) 'Preface', in S. Žižek, *The Sublime Object of Ideology*, London: Verso.

—— (1990) *New Reflections on the Revolution of Our Time*, London: Verso.

—— (1993) 'Discourse', in R. Goodin and P. Pettit (eds) *The Blackwell Companion to Contemporary Political Philosophy*, Oxford: Blackwell.

—— (1996) *Emancipation(s)*, London: Verso.

—— (1997) 'Converging on an open quest', *Diacritics* 27, 1:17–19.

Laclau, E. and Mouffe, C. (1981) 'Socialist strategy: where next?', *Marxism Today*, January: 17–22.

—— (1985) *Hegemony and Socialist Strategy*, London: Verso.

Laplanche, J. (1999) *Essays on Otherness*, London: Routledge.

Marx, K. (1992) *The Early Writings*, Harmondsworth, UK: Penguin.

Massey, D. (1993) 'Politics and space/time', *New Left Review* 196: 65–84.

Mouzelis, N. (1988) 'Marxism or post-Marxism?', *New Left Review* 107: 123.

Outhwaite, W. (1987) *New Philosophies of Social Science*, London: Macmillan.

Smith, N. (2000) 'Whatever happened to class?', *Environment and Planning A* 32: 1011–32.

Smith, P. (1993) 'A memory of Marxism', *Polygraph* 6/7: 98–105.

Sprinker, M. (1992) 'The royal road: Marxism and the philosophy of science', *New Left Review* 191: 122–44.

Waterhouse, K. (1959) *Billy Liar*, Harmondsworth, UK: Penguin.

7 Materialism, realism and dialectics

Sean Creaven

Introduction

The purpose of this essay is to demonstrate how critical realism allied to materialist dialectics is capable of resolving two central weaknesses of western philosophy and social science. These are: the fallacy of reductionism, whether of systems to their parts (e.g. atomism), or of parts to their system (e.g. holism); and the unresolved conflict between materialism and idealism, and pluralist or 'dualist' compromises between the two. Now I wish to argue here two basic points. First, that critical realism articulates a defensible onto-logical alternative to reductionism in philosophy and the human sciences. Second, that the materialist dialectics of the classical Marxist tradition, though enriched by the ontological insights of critical realism, is nonetheless indispensable to critical realism. This is because materialist dialectics is precisely a *historicisation* of emergence, and because, unlike critical realism, offers a viable alternative to the abstract polarities of idealism, mechanical materialism and dualism.

I will organise the work on the basis of an exposition and defence of an ontological approach I shall entitle 'dialectical emergentialist Marxism'. This will entail the following procedure. First, I will defend Bhaskar's 'depth realism', showing how it transcends reductionism. Then I will intro-duce the 'materialist dialectic' of Marx and Engels, analysing its core concepts, and identifying its points of contact with critical realism.[1] Here I will also briefly address the vexed question of the relationship between the Hegelian and Marxian dialectic, showing how Marx 'inverts' Hegel, and why this 'inversion' is necessary. Finally, I will demonstrate how depth realism is enormously enriched by engaging with Engels' 'dialectical materialism'.

Critical realism

Roy Bhaskar defines critical realism as a 'tradition' in the philosophy of science which:

regards the objects of knowledge as the structures and mechanisms that generate phenomena; and the knowledge as produced in the social activity of science. These objects are neither phenomena (empiricism) nor human constructs imposed upon the phenomena (idealism), but real structures, which endure and operate independently of our knowledge, our experience and the conditions which allow us access to them. Against empiricism, the objects of knowledge are structures, not events; against idealism, they are intransitive. According to this view, both knowledge and the world are structured, both are differentiated and changing; the latter exists independently of the former (though not our knowledge of this fact); and experiences and the things and causal laws to which it affords us access are normally out of phase with one another. On this view, science is not an epiphenomenon of nature, nor is nature a product of man.

(Bhaskar 1998: 19)

An important function of Bhaskar's philosophy is to establish the case for endorsing a 'depth model' of reality in opposition to the claims of classical empiricism (the view that only 'impressions' or 'sense data' can be said to comprise the real) and 'empirical realism' or 'actualism' (the view that the real is comprised of both 'impressions' and 'events', the former being experiences of the latter). Bhaskar establishes that the basic problem with classical empiricism, which reduces reality to sense impressions, is that it leaves the 'experiences' of which sense data is composed unexplained. This approach also rides roughshod over the obvious fact that not all events are the subject of experience (Bhaskar 1998: 23–4). For these reasons most empiricists are prepared to endorse actualism. Actualists introduce a second level or dimension into their explanatory models. This is, of course, the level of 'events', which experiences are about, and which may often occur unexperienced, but whose reality can nonetheless be established by observing their empirical effects (i.e. the 'happenings' which are caused by other 'happenings').

Now whereas Bhaskar's argument disposes of the warranty of classical empiricism (in its Berkeleian and Humean forms), by demonstrating that experience presupposes the intransitivity of the object world, it is not by itself sufficient to refute actualism. In order to achieve this purpose, Bhaskar has to be able to show that the objects of science are not only intransitive but also 'structured'. In other words, if depth realism is to be defensible, Bhaskar has to find some means of demonstrating that real-world events are comprehensible in terms of underlying structures and attendant generative mechanisms, and not simply in terms of 'other events'.

Bhaskar goes about this task by considering the question of what the actuality of experimental science tells us about the nature of its objects. 'The intelligibility of experimental activity presupposes not just the intransitivity but the structured character of the objects investigated under experimental conditions' (Bhaskar 1998: 25). Bhaskar points out that the practice of experimental science involves setting up an 'artificial closure' under laboratory conditions in order to establish the existence of those real structures responsible for the causal mechanisms which account for observable events. By means of experimental closure, the scientist triggers or activates a 'single kind of mechanism or process in relative isolation, free from the interfering flux of the open world, so as to observe its detailed workings or record its characteristic mode of effect and/or test some hypothesis about them' (Bhaskar 1986: 35). In this way, the scientist identifies the specificity of causal mechanisms pertaining to particular structures, and the kinds of events or effects which (in closed systems) must necessarily follow from their activation.

But if causal laws are simply 'constant conjunctures' between events in the realm of the actual (which they must be if underlying mechanisms do not explain events), this kind of painstaking scientific endeavour must be both pointless and impossible. Pointless because one does not need experimental closure to observe sequences of events at the level of the actual, since closure would already exist in this unidimensional world, of which 'constant conjunctures' would be the inevitable expression. Pointless because 'experimental activity can only be given a satisfactory rationale if the causal law it enables us to identify is held to prevail outside the contexts under which the sequence of events is generated', this suggesting 'there must be an ontological distinction' between causal laws and sequences of events (Bhaskar 1998: 25). Pointless because if experimental science is simply about engineering events so as to bring about other events, it must be a process which 'constructs' causal laws, not one which discovers pre-existing laws (by activating them in isolation from other variables), and is thus scientifically uninteresting. Impossible because one can establish a closed system by means of scientific procedure (in which a generative mechanism, the events it governs, and the observation of these processes by a knowing subject are brought into correspondence) only on the assumption that nature is an open system, comprised of a plurality of causal mechanisms, each of which can be rationally apprehended only by means of experimental closure (Collier 1994: 34–8).

Bhaskar's transcendental realism therefore provides a philosophical rationale for holding to a conception of reality as 'ontological depth'. But does his approach allow us to take the further step of grasping nature as stratified? My belief is that it does succeed in doing this, though it is not the only acceptable way of doing so.[2] Bhaskar bases his argument for the stratification of nature on the explanatory logic of scientific inquiry itself. He makes the legitimate point that science proceeds by uncovering specific generative mechanisms, before then going on to seek out a causal explanation of these mechanisms in terms of others, which are necessarily more 'basic' or 'fundamental' (such as the explanation of psychological mechanisms in terms of biological mechanisms).

Now one important feature of this process of scientific work is that, having established a 'tree' of sciences, each relating to real aspects of the world, it has been unable to establish the redundancy of the higher in favour of the lower. For example, despite the best efforts of many generations of practising philosophers of social science to argue the case for treating the 'real objects' of sociology (i.e. social structures) as epiphenomena of the 'real objects' of cognitive psychology and/or human biology, no practical results have been forthcoming, and nor are they expected. But this stratification of the sciences, which has proven highly resistant to attempts by 'greedy reductionism' (Dennett 1996: 81–3) to dissolve, is precisely good evidence of the 'relative autonomy' and 'hierarchical layering' of their respective objects of knowledge in the real world, that is, of the 'stratification of nature'.

Stratification and emergence in critical realism

Bhaskar's philosophical ontology identifies a hierarchically ordered world of distinct strata and attendant generative mechanisms governed by causal relations of vertical determination. Such a worldview need not rest upon Bhaskar's philosophical arguments, however. In fact, it can instead be legitimately derived from the *results* of the sciences, from the development of scientific knowledge itself. From this it appears reasonable to draw two conclusions. First, that a materialistic view of nature (including human nature) is altogether appropriate, on the grounds that:

> the material universe existed before there was organic life, and . . . living organisms can only exist as composed of and surrounded by matter. In this sense, matter may be said to be more 'basic' than life; life in turn may be said to be more basic than rationality (in the sense that we are rational animals), and hence than human society and its history. This suggests that the sciences that explain a more basic layer may have some explanatory primacy over those explaining a less basic layer. Laws of physics and chemistry may *in some sense* explain the laws of biology.
>
> (Collier 1994: 46)

Second, that a 'naturalistic' approach to the human and social sciences, which stress a fundamental methodological unity between these and the natural sciences, is at least possible, for the simple reason that it is now philosophically defensible to view the world:

> historically, as a complex of processes of development . . . in which there are no sharp distinctions, on the one hand, between the various domains of the physical world . . . and, on the other hand, between the physical world as a whole and the human, social world.
>
> (Callinicos 1996: 107)

In this sense, Bhaskar's philosophy of nature is entirely consistent with that form of ontological materialism (defended by Marx and Engels) which postulates the unilateral existential dependence of the objects of knowledge of the human and social sciences upon those of the natural sciences, and the historical development of the former out of the latter. From this point of view, the stratification of nature must be grasped from the 'bottom up' (so to speak), as running from the physico-chemical to the human and socio-cultural, via the intermediary of the biological. This is for the simple reason that it is impossible to conceive of social or cultural mechanisms existing in the absence of biological ones, or of biological mechanisms existing in the absence of physico-chemical ones, but perfectly possible to conceive of the converse arrangements.

Nonetheless it is important to be clear that this vertical explanation of higher mechanisms by lower ones does not 'explain away' the latter. The higher are as real as the lower by virtue of the distinct causal powers and properties that pertain uniquely to them. Chemical structures explain biological structures, for example, in the sense that the latter arise from the former and could not exist without them, the reverse never being the case. But the generative mechanisms of organic structures are nonetheless 'irreducible' to those of chemical structures, since nothing about the organisational and behavioural properties of the first will tell us anything about those of the second. Zoological laws, not the laws of chemistry and physics, explain the development, capacities and behaviours of organisms, though not of course the micro-elements from which organisms are composed.

Yet this 'stratification model' of nature in no way implies that more basic mechanisms or strata pack a greater causal punch than higher level ones in accounting for the constitution of 'objects' or 'entities'. This point is well made by Steven Rose.

> A living organism – a human, say – is an assemblage of subatomic particles, an assemblage of atoms, an assemblage of molecules, an assemblage of tissues and organs. But it is not first a set of atoms, then molecules, then cells; it is all of these things at the same time.
>
> (Rose *et al.* 1984: 277–8)

Nor does Bhaskar's ontology commit us to the peculiar idea that more basic strata or mechanisms have explanatory priority over higher level ones in shaping the pattern of events in the phenomenal world.

> Being a more basic stratum does not necessarily mean being a stratum whose effects are more widespread. For though animals are *governed* by zoological laws while inanimate things are not, anything and everything may be *effected* by zoological laws, since animals have effects on the inanimate world.
>
> (Collier 1994: 109)

Clearly, there is a necessary distinction being made here between relations of vertical determination between strata and relations of horizontal causality between mechanisms and events/or objects. Events and things are determined conjointly by the plurality of mechanisms operative at different levels of reality. So, for instance, zoological laws presuppose chemical laws, which in turn presuppose physical laws, living creatures being a combinatory of physico-chemical and organic structures. This means that relations of vertical causality between strata, aside from being relations of 'ontological presupposition', are also often 'one-way relations of inclusion of the various strata' (Bhaskar 1978: 119). Thus organic entities (such as animals) will be necessarily subject to a broader range of causal mechanisms than inorganic entities (such as rocks), just as cultural entities (e.g. individual speakers) will necessarily be subject to a wider range of causal mechanisms (those of society, mind, biology, chemistry and physics) than biological entities (to which only the last three apply).

But how is it that higher order mechanisms and structures are explainable but yet irreducible to lower order ones? Bhaskar's solution to this problem is to grasp the interface between the two in terms of 'rootedness' and 'emergence': higher order strata are rooted in and emergent from lower order strata. 'Rootedness' simply denotes the elementary fact that 'the more complex aspects of reality (e.g. life, mind) presuppose the less complex (e.g. matter)' (Collier 1994: 110). The idea here is 'of some lower-order or microscopic domain providing a *basis* for the existence of some higher-order property or power; as for example the neuro-physiological organisation of human beings may be said to provide a basis for their power of speech' (Bhaskar 1978: 115).

'Emergence' is a more difficult idea to grasp, not least because it has a complicated intellectual history. For realists, however, it has two basic meanings and functions. First, as simply another way of *articulating* and *defending* their thesis of the irreducibility of the constituent levels of reality:

> We would not try to explain the power of people to think by reference to the cells that constitute them, as if cells possessed this power too. Nor would we explain the power of water to extinguish fire by deriving it from the powers of its constituents, for oxygen and hydrogen are highly inflammable. In such cases objects are said to have 'emergent powers', that is, powers or liabilities which cannot be reduced to those of their constituents.
>
> (Sayer 1992:119)

Second, as an explanatory thesis which locates the emergence of a higher-order stratum in a specific interaction or combination of generative mechanisms internal to those objects or mechanisms that exist at the stratum immediately 'basic' to it. In this sense, 'emergent properties' are a function of internally related objects or structures, because the relations which define or comprise them as such grant their constituents powers and capacities they would not possess apart from their interaction or combination as parts of a whole:

> The nature or constitution of an object and its causal powers are internally or necessarily related: a plane can fly by virtue of its aerodynamic form, engines, etc.; gunpowder can explode by virtue of its unstable chemical structure; multinational firms can sell their products dear and buy their labour power cheap by virtue of operating in several different countries with different levels of development; people can change their behaviour by virtue of their ability to monitor their own monitorings, and so on.
>
> (Sayer 1992: 119)

Biological reality, for instance, is 'emergent' from a specific combination of generative mechanisms internal to the chemical level, just as socio-cultural reality is 'emergent' from a specific interaction of causal powers internal to the biological level.

Emergent properties are also to be found *within* particular domains of reality. Thus the 'physical', the 'chemical', the 'biological', and the 'human-social' level each give rise to higher and lower strata. For example, totally novel powers arise within the socio-cultural domain as a result of social interaction. 'Even though social structures exist only where people reproduce them, they have powers irreducible to those of individuals (you can't pay rent to yourself)' (Sayer 1992: 105). In this situation, individuals obtain novel characteristics by virtue of their insertion within *specific kinds* of social relations, not simply by pooling their individual capacities or powers. Because such properties and powers of individuals are not merely 'aggregative' products of their interaction, they must instead be recognised as 'emergent properties' of the 'societal organisation' in which their interactions are situated. Such is what renders meaningful the idea that society is more than the sum of its parts, and that its 'parts' (i.e. people and their interpersonal relations) are transformed by being parts of the social whole.

The dialectic in classical Marxism

What is the relationship between Hegel's dialectic and the dialectic as understood by classical Marxism? It is a commonplace that Marx himself never found the time 'to make accessible to the ordinary human intelligence, in two or three printers sheets, what is rational in the method which Hegel discovered but at the same time enveloped in mysticism' (Marx and Engels 1965: 100). Instead we are left with his suggestive assertion that Hegel's dialectic 'is standing on its head' and requires 'inverting' in order 'to discover the rational kernel within the mystical shell' (Marx 1976: 103).

Now I would argue that an adequate understanding of the dialectic, developed by Marx and Engels, including especially its point of contact and departure from Hegel, can be apprehended from a close textual reading of their core theoretical writings. On this basis, what seems uncontentious is that the 'rational core' of Hegel's dialectic, for them, is precisely the fundamental principles of 'totality', 'mediation', 'change' and 'contradiction', which constitute the theoretical foundations of the Hegelian system.[3] Certainly, these can be seen at work in the methodological framework that informs all of Marx and Engels' theoretical positions and specific explanatory hypotheses.

A single example will, unfortunately, have to suffice.[4] Consider Marx and Engels' 'dialectic of labour'. The basic theoretical structure of Hegel's dialectic is clearly visible here. On the one hand, Marx argues that the relationship between human beings and their sensuous physical environment has to be grasped as a contradictory totality, a unity of opposites. The unity is derived from the fact that nature is the 'inorganic body' of human thought and action, with which human beings 'must remain in continual interchange' if they 'are not to die', humanity being 'a part of nature' (Marx 1959: 67). The opposition is derived from the fact that, although human consciousness is a product of nature, it is nonetheless a qualitatively distinct part of nature, by virtue of its power to reflect upon and transform nature in the service of human needs, and because it must still encounter the world as an objective power, as a set of circumstances which confront and constrain thought and action from without (Creaven 2000: 71–9). On the other hand, this contradictory totality, which constitutes the relationship between human subjects and objective conditions, is a dynamic one, in continual interaction and development. This is because collaborative labour on the material world, in the service of human needs and interests, mediates the two poles, bringing thought into closer correspondence with its objects, combining materiality and consciousness as conscious *practice*, thereby transcending, without harmonising, the abstract polarities represented by both sides of this existential contradiction.

Now Hegel identified 'three laws' of the dialectic – the 'unity of opposites', the 'transformation of quantity into quality', and the 'negation of the negation'. For Hegel, these are ways of specifying how dialectical processes unfold, though these concepts are not the only acceptable way of doing so, because not every dialectical process will fit the pattern they outline. Now there can be little doubt that Marx and Engels adopt these basic analytical tools of Hegel's dialectic, though again without assuming these capture or exhaust every dialectical process at work in the world.[5] But it is important to understand that they do so, not as a mechanical or deterministic formula adopted prior to research, into which real world processes have to be fitted, as tended to be the case with Hegel, but rather as elements of an explanatory framework, based on the findings or knowledge of empirical science, which is also of practical efficacy in interpreting and organising research data (Rees 1998: 114–18). As Engels puts it:

> there is no question of building the laws of dialectics into nature . . . in every field of science, in natural as well as in historical science, one must proceed from the given facts . . . the interconnections are not to be built into the facts but to be discovered from them, and when discovered to be verified as far as possible by experiment.
>
> (Marx and Engels 1987: 12–13, 342–3)

This is one sense in which the Marxist dialectic can be legitimately said to invert the Hegelian. Because Hegel's dialectic is a conceptual dialectic, in which contradictions arise from the limitations of human consciousness as it struggles to apprehend the world, and in which contradictions are eventually dissolved as thought finally appropriates the world as its own mirror, as identical to itself, as simply the 'other side' of Absolute Spirit or Reason, it is unsurprising that his dialectical concepts are emancipated from the disciplines of empirical testing and the possibility of refutation by scientific knowledge.[6] Instead, Hegel's dialectic unfolds at the height of philosophical abstraction, presenting properties or objects of the material world as more or less developed forms of the general abstract concepts that are applied to them.

Thus Hegel's dialectic does reveal the contradictions that exist in categories and conceptual thought; for example the false consciousness of the servant of his own relationship to his master, articulated in Hegel's famous 'master–slave dialectic' (Hegel 1977). But these conceptual contradictions are never related to contradictions built into the structures of material and social reality, nor seen as expressions of these real world contradictions. The latter have no real autonomy from thought. There is, in other words, a simple *identity* of thought and reality in Hegel. It will be recalled that Hegel's 'master–slave dialectic' is resolved when the servant understands that his master is dependent on him, rather than vice versa (because the servant produces both his own and his master's existence, his master living only through the servant's labour), thereby 'overcoming' his alienation. In this understanding, material reality (in this case the labour of the servant to produce his own and his master's subsistence) exists only as the middle term of the dialectic, which mediates between two different states of consciousness, lower alienated consciousness and higher unalienated consciousness. The objective social relationship between master and servant is unchanged at the end of the process (the master is still parasitic on the labour of the servant), but now the servant understands that his master is dependent on him and not vice versa, and has thus freed himself from servile thinking. Thought is reconciled with reality; reality itself isn't reshaped.

In contrast to this idealist method, Marx and Engels insist that their 'point of departure' is the material world, the object and instrument of human labour, from which all forms of consciousness are derived. Concepts are the product of real conditions, shaped by existential contradictions, even if they have to be abstracted from their objects, and subjected to rational procedures of scientific testing, then reapplied to their objects in the form of more sophisticated concepts, if they are to apprehend the nature of real world processes or structures. Further, because contradictions exist outside consciousness, indeed often account for the contradictions in consciousness, existing in their own right in the structures of society and nature, it follows that these cannot be dissolved in thought. There is a *unity* between subjective and objective dialectics, not a simple identity.[7] Contradictions in nature unfold independently of thought via the struggle of real material oppositions, whereas contradictions in society unfold through the struggles of real social forces, not simply or primarily through the clash of ideas. For Marx and Engels, then, consciousness is not the first and last term of the dialectic, but its mediating middle term. And this middle term is understood not as abstract Reason, but as conscious collaborative labour in the sensuous world, in the service of human needs and wants (Rees 1998: 69–74).

This understanding allows us to grasp the manner in which Marx and Engels apply Hegel's 'three laws' of the dialectic. In Hegel these unfold in a deterministic fashion, as a simple concept inevitably begets a more refined concept, which contains and transcends the simpler one, and so on, until the Idea is evolved into self-consciousness of the Absolute (the common rational structure of thought and the material world which Hegel understands as Absolute Spirit). In Hegel, furthermore, the historical process by which Spirit discovers or even constructs the world as its own creation is essentially teleological, since the self-reconciliation of Spirit at the final stage of the dialectic is immanent in its beginning, the goal to which history inevitably gravitates, since this unfolds by virtue of logical necessity, as would a sequence of self-generating concepts. For classical Marxism, by contrast, neither the transformation of quantity into quality, nor the negation of the negation, can be interpreted as teleological laws of necessity, of absolute determinism, whether in social or natural systems.

This interpretation of the dialectic follows from its 'inversion', its transformation from an idealist to a *materialist* dialectic. For change is now grasped as the collision of social or physical oppositions, without the certainty that a specific resultant or fixed end-state must follow from initial causes or conditions, in advance of the developmental process itself, as would the conclusion of a problem in logic from its initial premises. This is equally true of physical and social systems. In both cases, the process of the transformation of quantity into quality, i.e. the development of structural forms by means of internal and external contradictions, does not inevitably resolve itself in the negation of the negation (the successive transcendence of lower by higher systems which nonetheless preserve in a modified form elements or properties of the lower).[8]

In society, on the one hand, thoroughgoing change occurs only when subordinate social classes decisively defeat entrenched elites in open class warfare and remodel social relations in their own image. Social crises are inevitable, because structural and social malintegration is inevitable, given the dialectical nature of class societies, but not the outcome of the class struggle itself, not least because subjective factors (leadership, ideology, consciousness, organisation) are as indispensable to change as objective factors, even if the weight of these objective factors (recurring organic social crises, etc.) renders radical change a probable outcome in the longer run. For these reasons Engels argues against using the 'negation of the negation' concept as 'a mere proof producing statement', as a substitute for empirical study, and hence as a statement of the inevitability of capitalist collapse and socialist reconstruction (Marx and Engels 1987: 124).

In nature, on the other hand, although the evolutionary development of matter is a law-governed process, even here the laws are not mechanical, and nor is the determinism absolute. Again, Engels argues against this kind of absolutist and teleological determinism in natural or physical systems, and he is right to do so (Engels 1982: 499). In recent years, of course, important developments in the 'sciences of complexity' (quantum mechanics, thermodynamics and chaos theory) have struck a blow against determinism. For these have revealed the existence of *probalistic*, not deterministic, laws of nature (at the sub-atomic level), of random or unpredictable behaviour in physical systems under certain circumstances (within determinate limits) at certain scales of nature, and of the co-existence of and continuous transmission between orderly, deterministic behaviour and chaotic or probalistic behaviour at different strata of reality.[9] Overall, it now seems that a determinate *range* of outcomes and pathways and behaviours are often possible for a physical system from the same initial boundary conditions, even if some pathways and outcomes are radically more probable or necessary than others.

Ontological materialism and dialectics

I have asserted that critical realism would be substantially enriched by engaging with, and learning from, the basic concepts of dialectical materialism, as understood by classical Marxism. It is now time to add a little substance to this argument. Clearly, I do not mean that Marx and Engels are alone in possession of the 'master key' (i.e. the 'materialist dialectic') to unlock the secrets of existence. My purpose is not to rehabilitate Stalinist dogmatics. Nor am I arguing that Marxism has nothing to learn from other philosophical traditions, including and especially Bhaskar's realism. This should be clear enough from what I have said here already. My contention in the foregoing has been that the core concepts of Bhaskar's philosophical realism (i.e. stratification, rootedness and emergence) are *indispensable* to the articulation of a defensible anti-reductive materialist ontology of being. Thus, what I am proposing is not that dialectical materialism supplant depth realism, or obviously that depth realism supplant dialectical material- ism, but rather that the best elements of each be combined in a new synthesis.

This synthesis is necessary because, despite its strengths, critical realism is by itself insufficient to 'under-labour' the human sciences. This is for the simple reason that 'realism' as such is non-committal in relation to the funda- mental question of which strata of reality are basic to or emergent from which, and this applies as much to the stratification of nature as to that of society. Instead this becomes a matter for individuals to decide on other grounds, specifically on the basis of whether they are materialists or idealists, or have conceived some kind of uneasy or unstable compromise between these unmixables, such as that articulated by dualism.

After all, it can scarcely be doubted that many philosophers, social theorists and even natural scientists, who would endorse a strong realist view of the world (as enmattered, independent of human consciousness, differentiated, even stratified), might as easily insist that the universe is the product of a spiritual 'first cause' than nothing but cause and consequence of the movement of matter through ascending levels of complexity. Indeed, it is far from uncommon for working scientists to accept that, say, physical structures explain chemical structures, or that biological structures explain psychological structures, or whatever, yet still make their appeal to some kind of cosmic super-subject (i.e. God) to furnish the 'basic constituents' of nature and the laws governing their interaction. In this case, of course, the theorist or analyst remains a materialist in his or her *science* but an idealist in his or her *philosophy*.

This is a case of what Engels once described as 'shamefaced materialism' (Marx and Engels 1977: 295–8). For it is the *practical undermining* of idealism during the history of scientific advance and investigation, in the sense that God has been shown to be superfluous to a rational and empirically testable knowledge of natural laws, which has forced its allegiants to make their appeal to a 'final instance' of undetermined causation beyond current knowl- edge, and therefore outside the reach of rational criticism. Now one should always be suspicious of 'final instances', which base their authority not on firm scientific knowledge (albeit provisional), but on its *uncertainty* or even *absence*. The possibility that physical scientists may never develop a satis- factory theory of the 'origins' of the universe should not be allowed to give comfort to those idealists whose own belief in a spiritualist 'first cause' of nature is entirely speculative and intuitive. But it is important to be clear that the realist emphasis on stratification and emergence, and the externality of the world to the knowing subject, provides no redoubt against this kind of manoeuvre. For it is 'equally possible' that materialist or idealist philosophy be either emergentist or conflationist in terms of ontology, either reductive or anti-reductive in terms of methodology.

This being the case, the belief of some realists that 'realism' is preferable to 'materialism' in ontological matters, is doubtless based on their assumption that scientific knowledge can neither establish the unreality of God,[10] nor 'rule out' the possibility that such an 'ultimatum' is responsible for the 'micro constituents' of the material universe, and the laws of their inter-action, from which a hierarchy of material strata and their immaterial emergents have developed historically. In this case, the theorist claims to be 'open-minded' on the materialism versus idealism debate, ruling out neither standpoint as impossible. On this view, 'ontological realism' is more appropriate than 'ontological materialism', because all we can say for certain is that both 'mind' and 'matter' are real and efficacious, that human consciousness exists only in association with a particular organisation of organic matter, and that nature is stratified. Philosophers and scientists can then plumb either for idealism or materialism, on the 'ultimate question', secure in the knowledge that a scientifically informed ontology can never settle the matter.

If such a view is implicit in the 'agnostic attitude' of many realist scientists and philosophers, it is an unsatisfactory one. For 'realist agnosticism' is no more reasonable than idealist speculative appeals to a 'first cause' of nature. Like idealism, this too is based on the necessarily provisional nature of scientific knowledge, meaning that its warranty (like idealism) is also a 'negative', ignorance, rather than a 'positive', the knowledge empirical science has given us about the universe. To claim the contrary is precisely to provide legitimation for the characteristic attitude of religionists, that in order to explain something which is understood not very well (the 'origin' of the universe), it is necessary to attribute its causation or essence to something else (God), which is understood not at all. But ignorance is no more an argument for 'open-mindedness', on the question of the 'ultimate' of nature, than it is for the existence of God. Further, the agnostic attitude, because it fails to confront the idea of God, fails also to confront the barrier erected by ontological idealism to the acquisition of rational knowledge about the cosmos, since it is insensitive to the fact that if 'we explain what is at the moment unknown by reference to God, we are blocking the way to new discoveries' (Siegel 1986: 36).

This means that the fundamental problem with 'realism' as ontology is that it is over-plastic or over-permissive. This renders it attractive to all comers (excepting those idealists who insist that the materiality of the world is an illusion of cognition or simply formless until structure is foisted on it by human consciousness). Indeed, this compatibility of realism with agnosticism (or 'shamefaced idealism') doubtless explains why for some it is preferable to the term 'materialism', or is somehow seen to 'transcend' the terms of the old idealism–materialism debate in the philosophy of science. But, although realist agnosticism appears to be a model of liberal 'open-mindedness', in reality it merely fudges the real issue. For under the guise of the unavoidable imperfection of science, it arbitrarily withholds ontological significance from those findings of the sciences that *unambiguously* show that the highest strata of nature – mind, rationality, self-consciousness, etc. – are historically emergent from the lower-order structures of materiality. Yet, if to the best of our scientific knowledge, material strata are basic to ideational strata, there is no sense in denying this knowledge ontological signification. Failing this, ontology becomes an imposition on the facts, rather than a generalisation from the (provisional and inexact) facts. This means that the failure of philosophical realism to identify itself as 'emergentialist materialism' is an unnecessary concession to ontological idealism.

But perhaps another important reason which explains this preference for the term 'realism' over 'materialism' in the contemporary philosophy of science is that the latter has traditionally been associated with reductive-mechanical outlooks in both the physical and human-social sciences, and obviously critical realists do not wish to be found guilty of the same errors by terminological association. Yet an 'emergentialist' materialism, such as that endorsed *in practice* by certain realists, is not in the least bit vulnerable to a micro-regress of higher order strata and attendant sciences to lower order ones. Indeed, identifying critical realism as 'emergentialist materialism' has the positive advantage of undermining the rational basis of both vulgar materialism (the view that the objects of the human and social sciences are 'translatable' into the objects of the biological and physico-chemical sciences) and 'shamefaced' idealism (the postulation of a spiritualist 'cause' in accounting for the universe). This is one of the great virtues of dialectical materialism. From its inception in the work of Engels, this has been an ontological approach, which has explicitly acknowledged the falsity of these abstract dualisms. Thus dialectical materialism is important, because it is precisely a form of anti-reductive materialism, and as such suffers from none of the ambiguities associated with philosophical realism.

But perhaps those allegiants of philosophical realism who accept that their approach is indeed 'materialistic' might object to my critique on other grounds. One obvious candidate springs to mind. This is that dialectical materialism is not an emergentialist ontology at all, or at least not a successful one, hamstrung as it is by concepts which are vague, misleading or plain wrong. From this point of view, critical realism has no need of any kind of dialogue or encounter with dialectical materialism, only of a change of title to something less neutral and more appropriate.

Now my response to this (hypothetical) argument is to suggest that certain of the basic concepts of dialectical Marxist philosophy are neither misleading nor false, though some of them are difficult by necessity because they are designed to capture a reality which is ambiguous because dialectical and fluid rather than functional and static. On the contrary, these concepts remain valid and necessary, for three basic reasons. First, dialectical concepts are in fact explicit *descriptions* of the reality of stratification and emergence, though expressed in a different philosophical vocabulary to that of contemporary critical realists. As Ted Benton rightly points out:

> Engels proposes a hierarchy of 'forms of motion' with transitions one to the other. . . . The different domains of the universe are constituted by levels in the hierarchy of complexity of laws of motion.
>
> (Benton 1979: 122)

This stratification of the world ensures that the sciences must also be arranged hierarchically and treated as mutually irreducible. This is for the simple reason that at each level of organisation or interaction of matter, those laws operative at lower levels are 'subsumed' or 'pushed into the background by other, higher laws', which themselves constitute 'a leap, a decisive change':

> If I term physics the mechanics of molecules, chemistry the physics of atoms, and furthermore biology the chemistry of albumens, I wish thereby to express the passing of any of these sciences into one of the others, hence both the connection, the continuity, and the distinction, the discrete separation.
>
> (Engels 1969: 442)

But it was Engels' utilisation of dialectical-materialist concepts that allowed him to obtain this insight nearly one hundred years ahead of his time.

Second, and more importantly, such concepts are as reasonable a way as any of capturing in the most general terms the reality of the world as a 'differentiated unity':[11]

> What is involved here is a kind of natural scientific ontology of nature as a unified, though internally structured and differentiated whole, which Engels regards as preferable to the ontology implicit in mechanical reductionism. . . . Engels' ontology is the product of philosophical reflection on what is presupposed by the recent development of the sciences. The convergence, the realignment of whole fields of theory which had previously developed separately (organic/inorganic chemistry, mechanics/theory of heat, etc.) is unintelligible, as is the replacement of one theory by another within the same specialism, unless these different fields of theoretical discourse are apprehended as so many attempts at knowledge of a unitary, though internally differentiated, natural universe. This unity of nature is an essential precondition for convergence of the sciences, for the repeated discovery of 'interconnections', whilst the differentiation of nature is implied by the discreteness and uneven historical development of the different sciences.
>
> (Benton 1979: 121, 125)

Benton thus notes the 'points of contact' between Engels' ontology of nature and Bhaskar's transcendental realism. But he makes the further point that the latter legitimately transcends the former in one important respect:

> Bhaskar's transcendental realism argues for the philosophical legitimacy of arguments from the character of rational procedures in science (for example experimentation) to conclusions of a very general kind about the nature of the world as presupposed in the rationality of those procedures. . . . Engels' scientific metaphysics includes arguments and conclusions of this general type, but it goes beyond this to represent in a unified and more-or-less coherent form a detailed ontology based on current substantive knowledge in the different sciences. Engels is here doing no more than generalising from procedures employed by scientists themselves in bringing to bear discoveries in one discipline upon controversies in an adjacent one, but this generalisation of the procedure results in a quite distinct type of theoretical structure (a 'world-view') and discourse.
>
> (Benton 1979: 121, 125, 126)

Finally, and most importantly of all, Engels' dialectical concepts are *successful* in historicising stratification and emergence. That is, they allow us to grasp the dynamics or processes through which higher-order levels of the material world develop out of lower-order levels, not as 'radical contingencies', but as integral aspects of a continually evolving totality of interrelated systems:

> The great basic thought is that the world is not to be comprehended as a complex of ready-made things, but as a complex of processes, in which the things apparently stable . . . go through an uninterrupted process of becoming and passing away. . . . For dialectical philosophy nothing is final, absolute, sacred. It reveals the transitory nature of everything and in everything; nothing can endure before it except the uninterrupted process of becoming and passing away, of endless ascendancy from the lower to the higher. . . . The motion of matter is not merely crude mechanical motion, mere change of place, it is heat and light, electric and magnetic tension, chemical combination and dissociation, life, and finally, consciousness.
>
> (Marx and Engels 1973: 339, 362–3)

This is the most controversial aspect of Engels' 'dialectics of nature'. For he is often taxed with endorsing an evolutionary teleology, according to which lower forms inevitably give rise to higher forms in a linear fashion, governed by a universal 'dialectical law', uniformly operative at all levels of reality. This, for example, seems to be Benton's view, notwithstanding his acknowledgement of and high praise for Engels' 'first approximation' to 'a concept

of emergent qualities and laws'. He accuses Engels of mixing with his legitimate 'attempt to confront the problem of the emergence of new forms and
structures as a specifically historical problem . . . a dubious . . . notion of
historicity as progressive development'. The reader will be unsurprised that
Engels' 'external' and 'inessential' use of Hegelian categories is held by
Benton to be responsible for the alleged 'tendency' of his philosophy to veer
towards teleological determinism.

> That Engels suggests, by his indifferent application of the dialectical laws
> of the transition of quantity into quality, and negation of the negation,
> to all of these histories, that they. . . . share a 'common' historicity is, to
> say the least, unfortunate . . . the indifferent application of categories of
> the 'dialectic' to different domains in nature can give the impression
> that human history and the history of . . . nature can be understood
> through identical philosophical . . . categories.
>
> (Benton 1979: 122, 124, 128)

But such an interpretation fails on a number of counts. First, Benton provides no solid evidence that Engels does in fact hold that development in
nature and society share a simple identity, following a uniform evolutionary
process, governed by a universal dialectical law, or that this development is
inevitably linear, and has generated absolutely certain results. Benton's only
substantive argument against Engels' use of dialectical concepts is that he
does not always apply these appropriately or successfully when dealing with
emergent properties and laws, which is hardly proof of any dalliance on his
part with the Hegelian notion of an 'identity' of development in nature and
society. Indeed, Benton admits that 'surprisingly enough, Engels does recognise that nature and human society do not share a common historicity, the
looseness of his appropriation of the dialectic notwithstanding' (Benton
1979: 125).

Second, Benton appears to believe that a historical account of nature is
teleological, or 'quasi-teleological' (whatever that means), simply by virtue
of the fact it postulates a certain 'directionality' or evolutionary movement
from the simple to the complex in structural forms. Not only is such a conception manifestly non-teleological (by any reasonable definition of the
term),[12] it is also far from being indefensible. Such a pattern of development
is certainly discernible at the biological level (the 'ratchet' of natural
selection generating cumulative organismic specialisation and enhanced
survival-value). It is also discernible at the societal level: the cumulative
development of the productive forces, under the stimulus of meeting and
developing human needs. So too at the physico-chemical level, since the
view of many physical scientists today is one of 'the inevitability and probable
universality of life', on the grounds that 'life is a logical consequence of
known chemical principles operating on the atomic composition of the
universe' (Melvin Calvin, in Siegel 1986: 11).

That this latter argument is overstated (given the existence of chaotic or random behaviour and of probabilistic laws of tendency rather than absolute necessity in certain physical systems) is beside the point. At certain levels or scales of physical reality, more deterministic behaviour certainly prevails (as is the case for the objects of macro physics, for example), even if this is not the universal pattern. Thus it might be true that the evolution of organic life is an 'algorithmic process',[13] even if this is not true of the emergence of other strata (for example, the emergence of consciousness and of different forms of human social relations). Nonetheless Engels is right to suggest that the differentiated elements of nature (physico-chemical, biological, human-social, etc.) have a common historicity in a certain sense. For all are 'phases' in the development of matter through ascending levels of complexity, all are composed of those 'basic' elements that ontologically and historically pre-suppose their existence, and it is always the evolution of the lower which generate their own negation in the higher. Yet it is important to be clear that there is nothing in this conception that implies that this 'common historicity' of nature is an undifferentiated one, postulating the identity rather than unity of the structures of matter, or that the evolutionary emergence of higher from lower domains of nature was always absolutely necessary.

Finally, Benton's 'surprise' at not discovering simply a materialist restate-ment of Hegel's monistic logic in Engels' writings, is a function of his own arbitrary imposition of the unreconstructed Hegelian 'system' upon Engels' philosophy. He simply assumes that Engels' dialectical concepts must logically commit him to a monistic and teleological view of the universe, on the grounds that these are borrowed from Hegel's teleological and monistic logic. Benton does not appear to see that the content of concepts is deter-mined by their function within a theoretical discourse. Transposed into a different theoretical system, their meaning can be and often is transformed. This is clear enough if we consider what Engels has to say about his own application of the dialectical method to the different domains of society and nature. For a start, I have pointed out that Engels insists that dialectics is no ready-made formula into which the real world has to be fitted, but must instead be discovered by means of empirical-scientific investigation into the different facets of the world. Of equal importance, Engels also recognises that dialectical processes function differently for each distinct stratum of reality. Contrary to Benton, Engels does not see an identity of subjective and objective dialectics. 'Every kind of thing . . . has a peculiar way of being negated in such a way that it gives rise to development, and it is just the same with every kind of conception or idea' (Marx and Engels 1987: 132). Engels is grappling here with the idea that 'the structure of the dialectic in society is different to that in nature – the former must take account of the development of consciousness in a way that the latter need not' (Rees 1998: 286).

I have suggested that dialectical concepts are appropriate and indispens-able to the analysis of nature, for the simple reason that natural evolution is governed by dialectical interaction. Now there is a considerable and growing body of research evidence, derived from the findings of the various sciences, which reveal the dialectical pattern of reality at work at each stratum of reality. This is obviously true of the objects of psychology and sociology, for instance. But it is no less true of those of the physical sciences.[14] The picture of nature revealed by the 'new physics', for example, 'sits well with Engels' arguments about all of nature having a history, how seemingly separate facets of nature are connected, and how the essence of nature is precisely its continual transformation and change':

> the development of the universe . . . is one in which matter has undergone repeated qualitative transformations when quantitative change has reached critical points . . . Differentiated facets of the totality of matter, which have an underlying unity, have been progressively transformed as they mutually interact. We have an evolution from quarks, to protons and neutrons, to neutral atoms, to gas clouds, stars and galaxies, the formation of heavier elements like carbon, the formation of planets and through a series of further transformations to the emergence of organic life. At each stage qualitatively novel behaviour of matter emerges. So quarks, having existed freely were, when the temperature of the universe fell below a critical point, permanently confined inside particles like protons, and a qualitatively new physics emerges . . . Later, below another critical point, protons and neutrons could capture electrons, and the whole possibility of the rich new arena of atomic and molecular processes emerges for the first time. It needed the first such molecules to be further transformed in the very special conditions of stellar interiors, and then those stars themselves to explode in cataclysmic events called supernovae, before the elements crucial to the formation of planets like Earth were even possible. And a further long series of transformations of matter have, billions of years later, resulted in the qualitatively new phenomena of human beings, consciousness and society.
>
> (McGarr 1994: 167)

Moreover, the development of the 'sciences of complexity' in more recent years, to offer a second example, not only supports Engels' view that 'the transformation of quantity into quality' is a universal property of natural evolution, but also shows how his 'negation of the negation' concept can be relevant to the understanding of non-linear physical systems:

> A picture of nature is beginning to emerge in which at certain points physical systems not only can undergo a transition from regular ordered behaviour to chaotic unpredictable behaviour, but of how matter, once it reaches a certain level of complexity of organisation, can spontaneously generate new higher forms of ordered behaviour. Some physical systems can be pushed from a stable ordered state into a chaotic state by

some pressure . . . or impulse (it is 'negated'). But under certain conditions some of these systems can then develop in such a way as to give rise
to new higher forms of ordered behaviour, often with novel properties
(the 'negation is negated') . . . This kind of pattern seems to be typical
of many complex systems in nature . . . There is some evidence . . . that
complex organisations of matter with genuinely novel and 'creative'
properties are those 'on the edge of chaos', systems balanced in a
dynamic tension between the tendency towards a dead, stable, repetitive
order on the one hand and an unpredictable, disordered, chaotic state
on the other.

(McGarr 1994: 166–7, 170–1)

The dialectical character of natural processes and systems has also been
revealed by contemporary work in the biological and ecological sciences.
The work of Rose (1997; Rose *et al.* 1984) and Lewontin and Levins (1986),
for example, is a brilliant application and development of Engels' dialectic
of nature in these fields. As in the work of the classical Marxists, the dialectical concepts of totality, mediation, change and contradiction are utilised as
conceptual tools, in this case to expose the shortcomings of reductionism
and dualism in biological and ecological systems theory.[15] Particularly
illuminating is Rose's discussion of the 'dialectic of life', contained in his
Lifelines. Rose's argument is that life itself is a contradictory totality, a unity
of opposites, since it 'demands of all its forms the ability simultaneously to
be and to become' (Rose 1997: 142). Thus, the organism is necessarily subject
to a dialectic of 'specificity versus plasticity', its life-process constituted by
the containment of these interdependent but contradictory pressures or
impulses within a unitary system. This understanding fits hand in glove
with, and is indeed a theoretical specification of, Engels' own summary
sketch of the dialectic of life:

The plant, the animal, every cell is at every moment of its life identical
with itself and yet becoming distinct from itself, by absorption and
secretion of substances, by respiration, by cell formation and death of
cells, by the process of circulation taking place, in short by a sum of incessant molecular changes which make up life and the sum total of whose
results is evident to our eyes in the phases of life – embryonic life, youth,
sexual maturity, process of reproduction, old age, death . . . Life therefore consists primarily in the fact that every moment it is itself and at
the same time something else; and this does not take place as the result
of a process to which it is subjected to from without . . . [O]n the contrary
[it] is a self-implementing process which is inherent in, native to, its
bearer.

(Engels, 1982: 495; Engels, 1969: 77)

Engels is thus correct to argue that nature is historically and dialectically structured, and that this structuring exhibits certain regularities or patterns ('laws'). There are, however, at least two other good reasons for endorsing a 'dialectics of nature'. First, dialectical materialism, like critical realism, provides a philosophical rationale or resource for countering reductionism and anti-scientific irrationalism or romanticism. Lacking this kind of outlook, scientists and philosophers have traditionally found themselves drawn towards reductionist world-views where science is making rapid progress and is confident (for want of a sophisticated alternative), and back towards 'the mystical path' where the contradictions of old established theories are becoming glaringly apparent and where the suspicion dawns that growing scientific knowledge of the world does not always translate into a more rational world.[16] Second, the dialectical perspective equips practising scientists and philosophers of science with the requisite flexibility of thought or 'open-mindedness' to view far-reaching transformations of scientific knowledge as a natural aspect of its internal development, not as threats to the rationality or stability of the enterprise.[17] This is because a dialectical understanding of nature is an explicit acknowledgement of its complexity, its fluidity, its capacity for endless innovation and development, of the challenge it poses to static common sense, and so of the approximate and provisional nature of scientific discoveries.

Conclusion

The fundamental aim of this chapter has been to show that a fully adequate philosophical ontology, which is capable of under-labouring the human and natural sciences, must be forged in the interface between critical realism and materialist dialectics. Thus I argue for the indispensability of materialist dialectics in philosophy and social theory, whilst recognising that realism offers ontological insights that are useful for Marxism. Overall, I want to say that philosophy and social theory require critical realism, but that critical realism requires a distinctive Marxian or materialistic application, if it is to live up to its rich promise of apprehending the social and natural worlds.

On the one hand, the critical realist concepts of 'stratification' and 'emergence' are fundamental to Marxism, because although these have their precursors in dialectical materialism, they nonetheless provide the central dialectical concept of 'differentiated totality' with much of its theoretical content. On the other hand, only a realist ontology constructed as materialist dialectic allows a constructive alternative to dualism, and avoids the danger of idealist slippage ('realist agnosticism'). Further, as Bhaskar himself recognises, only dialectic permits 'empirical "open texture"' and imparts 'structural fluidity and interconnectedness' to social and natural forms (Bhaskar 1993: 44). Dialectic is thus 'ontologically . . . the dynamic of conflict and the mechanism of change' (Bhaskar and Norrie 1998: 562). I hope

I have provided some good arguments for seeing the Marxian dialectic as still the most sophisticated conceptual and methodological tool for apprehending these processes and mechanisms. I conclude that it has not yet been 'transcended'.

Notes

1 For reason of time and space, I regret I have to focus here on the dialectic of Marx and Engels, to the exclusion of other important figures of classical Marxism, notably Lenin and Trotsky, who also made a rich contribution to dialectical philosophy and applied dialectical analysis. Nor, unfortunately, will I be considering Bhaskar's dialectical reworking of critical realism, for the same reason. My focus here is on the relationship between critical realism and materialist dialectics, on the grounds that a synthesis of the two supports a defensible philosophy and social theory that alone avoids the pitfalls of idealism, dualism, vulgar materialism and 'shamefaced materialism' (realist agnosticism).

2 D-H. Ruben (1977: 128–33) argues, successfully I think, that philosophy must base itself on the results of the empirical sciences, not simply on their rational procedures or actualities.

3 This is the argument of Rees (1998) which I endorse.

4 Rees (1998: 69–97) cogently outlines this example, and others, of the dialectical approach in classical Marxism – including the logic of capital, the theory of alienation, the dialectic of history, and the dialectic of nature.

5 For example, Marx uses these concepts to illuminate the transition from feudalism to capitalism, and from capitalism to socialism, in *Capital*.

6 This is well argued by Parekh (1979).

7 This distinction between the Marxian and Hegelian dialectic was drawn out by Lenin (1972) and theorised more precisely by Trotsky (1986).

8 The relationship between Marxism and determinism is given cogent treatment by Molyneux (1995).

9 McGarr (1994) provides an excellent overview of these developments for laypersons.

10 For example, one critical realist (Porpora 2000: 14) argues that since objective evidence is indecisive on the question of God's existence, it is therefore rational for individuals to trust their own judgement on the matter, as this is informed by subjective experience.

11 This term was coined by Trotsky (1973).

12 Teleological views of history attribute goals or purposes to evolution, which are immanent in its genesis, and towards the fulfilment of which it inevitably gravitates. Theories of natural or social development are not necessarily teleological.

13 As, for instance, Dennett (1996) argues.

14 McGarr (1994) shows how the physics of relativity, quantum mechanics, and thermodynamics support a dialectical understanding of natural evolution. Unfortunately, I cannot go into the detail of his argument here. Instead I will summarise his main conclusions.

15 Levins (1996) provides an excellent summary of these key concepts of a dialectical understanding.

16 The latter happened, for instance, when the limits of mechanical determinism were exposed by the development of quantum mechanics in the 1920s and 1930s. This led to an attack on the concept of causality in physics, and contributed to the rise of a neo-romantic intellectual culture in western Europe. This culture was also obviously shaped by the great social crises of the inter-war years, which

became interpreted as a crisis of science and technical rationality. More generally, of course, physical scientists have always been fond of invoking 'God', when dealing with the 'absences' of knowledge in their fields, precisely because their 'empiricist' disdain for philosophy creates a vacuum of ideas, which can only be plugged by idealism or mysticism, particularly when established theories are under attack.
17 As, for instance, many philosophers of science do. See especially Kuhn (1970) and Feyerabend (1975).

Bibliography

Benton, T. (1979) 'Natural Science and Cultural Struggle: Engels and the Philosophy of the Natural Sciences', in J. Mepham and D-H. Ruben (eds) *Issues in Marxist Philosophy*, vol. 2, Atlantic Highlands: Humanities Press.

Bhaskar, R. (2000) 'Introducing Transcendental Dialectical Critical Realism', *Alethia* 3, 1: 15–21.

—— (1978) *A Realist Theory of Science*, 2nd edition, Brighton, UK: Harvester Press.

—— (1986) *Scientific Realism and Human Emancipation*, London: Verso.

—— (1993) *Dialectic: the Pulse of Freedom*, London: Verso.

—— (1998) 'Philosophy and Scientific Realism', in M. Archer, R. Bhaskar, A. Collier, T. Lawson and A. Norrie (eds) *Critical Realism: Essential Readings*, London: Routledge.

Bhaskar, R. and Norrie, A. (1998) 'Dialectic and Dialectical Critical Realism', in M. Archer, R. Bhaskar, A. Collier, T. Lawson and A. Norrie (eds) *Critical Realism: Essential Readings*, London: Routledge.

Callinicos, A. (1996) 'Darwin, materialism and evolution', *International Socialism* 2, 71: 99–116.

Collier, A. (1994) *Critical Realism: An Introduction to Roy Bhaskar's Philosophy*, London: Verso.

Creaven, S. M. (2000) *Marxism and Realism: A Materialistic Application of Realism in the Social Sciences*, London: Routledge.

Dennett, D.C. (1996) *Darwin's Dangerous Idea: Evolution and the Meaning of Life*, London: Allen Lane.

Engels, F. (1982) *The Dialectics of Nature*, Moscow: Progress Publishers.

—— (1969) *Anti-Dühring*, London: Lawrence & Wishart.

Feyerabend, P.K. (1975) *Against Method: Outline of an Anarchistic Theory of Knowledge*, London: New Left Books.

Hegel, G.W.F. (1977) *The Phenomenology of Spirit*, Oxford: Oxford University Press.

Kuhn, T. (1970) *The Structure of Scientific Revolutions*, Chicago, IL: University of Chicago Press.

Lenin, V.I. (1972) *Collected Works*, vol. 38, Moscow: Progress Publishers.

Levins, R. (1996) 'When science fails us', *International Socialism* 2, 72: 59–76.

Lewontin, R.C. and Levins, R. (1986) *The Dialectical Biologist*, Cambridge, MA: Harvard University Press.

Marx, K. (1976) *Capital*, vol. I, Harmondsworth, UK: Penguin.

—— (1959) *The Economic and Philosophical Manuscripts of 1844*, London: Lawrence & Wishart.

Marx, K. and Engels, F. (1987) *Collected Works*, vol. 25, London: Lawrence & Wishart.

—— (1977) *On Religion*, New York: Schoken Books.

—— (1973) *Selected Works*, vol. 3, London: Lawrence & Wishart.

—— (1965) *Selected Correspondence*, Moscow: Progress Publishers.

McGarr, P. (1994) 'Engels and natural science', *International Socialism* 2, 65: 143–76.

Molyneux, J. (1995) 'Is Marxism deterministic?', *International Socialism* 2, 68: 37–74.

Parekh, B. (1979) 'Marx and the Hegelian Dialectic', in V. K. Roy and R. C. Sarikwal (eds) *Marxian Sociology*, vol. 1, Delhi: Ajanta Publications.

Porpora, D. (2000) 'The Sociology of Ultimate Concern', *Alethia* 3, 1: 10–15.

Rees, J. (1998) *The Algebra of Revolution: The Dialectic and the Classical Marxist Tradition*, London: Routledge.

Rose, S. (1997) *Lifelines*, Harmondsworth, UK: Penguin, Allen Lane.

Rose, S., Lewontin, R. C. and Kamin, L. J. (1984) *Not in our Genes: Biology, Ideology and Human Nature*, London: Pelican.

Ruben, D-H. (1977) *Marxism and Materialism*, Hassocks, UK: Harvester Press.

Sayer, A. (1992) *Method in Social Science: A Realist Approach*, 2nd edition, London: Routledge.

Siegel, P.N. (1986) *The Meek and the Militant: Religion and Power across the World*, London: Zed Books.

Trotsky, L. (1986) *Philosophical Notebooks 1933–35: Writings on Lenin, Dialectics and Evolutionism*, New York: Columbia University Press.

—— (1973) 'Dialectical Materialism and Science', in *Problems of Everyday Life*, New York: Pathfinder Press.

8   Dialectic in Marxism and critical realism

Andrew Collier

There is a broad sense in which the absolute idealism of Hegel and his followers, the dialectical materialism of Marx and his followers, and critical realism all belong to the family of dialectical philosophies. But this is an extended family, and it also includes Ancient Greek and medieval European philosophy. These all share an organic rather than a mechanical ontology, and an Aristotelian rather than a utilitarian conception of practical reason (for it is helpful, though anachronistic, to see the conception of practical reason in Plato's Socrates as Aristotelian). But here I want to focus on dialectic in a more exact and specific sense, centred on notions of contradiction (in several senses, including inversion), and of progress through the resolution of contradictions.

Hegel's nut and Marx's hammer

Now Hegel's version of dialectic is a unified theory, 'all one wool'. Logical contradictions, contradictions in society, progress of thought through resolution of contradictions to the Absolute, progress of humankind through resolution of contradictions to the freedom of all, these belong to a single seamless theory. But I shall argue that this is not so with Marx's dialectic, I shall then go on to ask if it is so with Roy Bhaskar's.

Hegel can treat logical contradictions as features of reality, because as an idealist he regards reality itself as having a conceptual structure. Marx does not. So when Marx, in the time-honoured metaphor, cracks Hegel's idealist nut to extract the dialectical kernel, he shatters the kernel in the process, and then picks up some of the pieces. For instance, the notions of logical contradictions and contradictions in reality come apart. I do not think that Marx ever sees dialectical contradictions as in any way related to logical contradictions (other than etymologically, in the origin of the term in Hegel). In one place, he explicitly contrasts them:

> John Stuart Mill . . . is as much at home with absurd and flat contradictions as he is at sea with the Hegelian 'contradiction', which is the source of all dialectics.

> (Marx 1976: 744 note 29)

'Absurd and flat' contradictions are presumably logical contradictions – in the case in point, between Ricardo's and Senior's theories of profit. When Engels (1969), too, wants to say what is left of philosophy after the social sciences have gone their separate ways, he says it is 'formal logic and dialectics'. Formal logic rests on the law of (non)contradiction, the principle that contradictory propositions cannot both be true. It would be strange if the other component of philosophy, dialectics, rested on the opposite principle, as virtually all those who have talked about 'dialectical logic' seem to suppose – though it must be admitted that Engels himself is not guiltless here. In fact what Marx has rescued from the fragmented Hegelian nut is not any kind of logic, but two concepts with application to some social realities:

1 Contradiction, in the sense of a structural feature of a system which necessarily generates dysfunctions for that system. It is important that these are *internal* contradictions: the dysfunctions are such not just from the standpoint of a critic of the system, but from the standpoint of the system itself. Thus class struggle and periodic crises (and today we might add environmental disasters) are necessarily generated by capitalism, but are dysfunctional for capitalist society itself. Contradiction in this sense is the fundamental concept of Marx's political philosophy, and is what enables him to avoid the utopianism of every other radical political thinker. We fight capitalism, not because we have a view from nowhere and can see what the best society for human beings would be, but because capitalism has contradictions which we can see from inside it, which hurt the people inside it, and which could be resolved with the resources produced by it, but only by its abolition. If Marx were proved wrong on every other count, he would still be the greatest political philosopher of all time, by virtue of this one discovery. And it is a discovery after all, not a mere borrowing from Hegel, for in an important respect Marx's realist conception of contradictions is the exact opposite of Hegel's idealist one. Hegel's conception is Parmenidean: what appears to be reality contains (logical) contradictions, and therefore can't ultimately be reality at all, but *mere* appearance. Marx's conception is Heraclitean: reality may appear to be free from contradictions, but this may be mere appearance, the underlying reality may be contradictory (class struggle beneath the veneer of public interest).

2 However, when Marx talks about dialectic, he is just as often referring to dialectical inversions as to dialectical contradictions. This is obviously true of the young Marx, with his idea of alienation by which the product comes to dominate the producer; but in *Capital* too the domination of living labour by dead labour (capital) is seen as an inversion. Thus he writes of 'this inversion, indeed this distortion, which is peculiar to and characteristic of capitalist production, of the relation of dead labour and living labour' (Marx 1976: 425); and again of the 'paradox that the

most powerful instrument for reducing labour time [machinery – A.C.] suffers a dialectical inversion and becomes the most unfailing means for turning the whole lifetime of the worker and his family into labour-time at capital's disposal' (ibid.: 532). The concept of inversion, unlike that of contradiction, does make an appeal to something transhistorical: in order for the domination of producer by product or living labour by dead labour to be an inversion, there has to be a natural ontological order in which producers dominate products and living labour dominates dead labour. Marx nowhere defends such a natural ontological order, but it is quite defensible, and is presupposed by what he does say.

These then are the two nut-fragments that constitute Marx's dialectic. They have roots in Hegel, but in the form they take in Marx they assume an onto-logical realism that is alien to Hegel. And they are not parts of any unified theory of dialectic.

Bhaskar's dialectic before Bhaskar's *Dialectic*

In his references to dialectic before his book *Dialectic* (1993), Roy Bhaskar seems to endorse a similar view of Marx's dialectic as non-unitary, though the particular nut-pieces with which he mainly concerns himself are not all the same as the ones I have just mentioned. By far the most thorough dis-cussion of dialectic in Roy Bhaskar's work of this period is the paper on the topic in *Reclaiming Reality* (RR) (1989: 115–25). Here he presents Marx's dialectic as fragmented:

> One possibility raised by Marx's critique of Hegel's philosophy of iden-tity is that the dialectic in Marx (and Marxism) may not specify a *unitary* phenomenon, but a number of *different* figures and topics.
>   Such dialectical modes may be related by (a) a common ancestry and (b) their systematic connections within Marxism *without* being related by (c) their possession of a common essence, kernel or germ, still less (d) one that can be read back (unchanged) into Hegel.
>
> (RR: 119)

He goes on to distinguish several distinct things within Marx's work which could be called dialectical. Most salient in this text are (1) the epistemo-logical (or methodological) dialectic (RR: 119–20) which Marx claims is the method that the St Petersburg reviewer of *Capital* has attributed to him, though Roy Bhaskar calls this description 'distinctly positivistic'. Indeed it is difficult to see what Marx means by calling his own method as it had been described 'dialectical', unless dialectic refers not to any theory but to skill in organising concepts (rather as Roy Bhaskar later describes 'thinking dialecti-cally' as 'the art of thinking the coincidence of distinctions and connections'). And (2) the theory of structural contradictions such as I have already

described, 'real inclusive oppositions, in that the terms or poles of the contradictions existentially presuppose each other' (RR: 120). Roy Bhaskar also
adds that they are 'internally related to a mystifying form of appearance',
which is the feature of what he elsewhere calls 'Colletti contradictions'.

In *Scientific Realism and Human Emancipation* (SRHE) (1987: 197), Roy
Bhaskar suggests that apart from certain similarities to logical contradictions, the various forms of contradiction discovered by social sciences
have little in common. The two sorts of contradiction that he refers to here
and in *The Possibility of Naturalism* (PN) (1979) do have closer links with
logical contractions than do structural contradictions or inversions. First,
there are 'Colletti contradictions' (PN: 70–1). These occur when the way
some social reality presents itself to us is in contradiction with the way that
reality really is. For instance the reality of money is that it is power over the
labour of others, but it presents itself as if it were a material object which
can be possessed without anyone else being affected.

The other sort of contradiction that Roy Bhaskar writes about he does not
give a name to, but since it was first pointed out in print in Roy Edgley's
(1976/1998) paper 'Reason as Dialectic', let us call them 'Edgley contradictions'. Roy Edgley drew attention to the fact that there is one very clear
sense in which there are logical contradictions in reality: people's opinions
are part of reality, and people's opinions can contradict (logically) other
opinions. Hence one way to criticise a society is to argue that the opinions
prevailing in that society are false. A social scientific discipline can arrive at
propositions which contradict those held by the people in the society studied:
hence social science can criticise its object in a way which natural science
cannot.

I don't think that when Marx uses the term 'contradiction' he ever has
Edgley contradictions in mind. But they are of fundamental importance to
critical realism, in that explanatory critiques are instances of them. In the
central case of an explanatory critique, the social science which carries out
the critique shows that an opinion about a society is prevalent in that society
and is false; furthermore that its prevalence is no accident, but is generated
by the structures of that society and is necessary to the smooth running of
that society. To show all this is not just to criticise the false opinions, but to
criticise the society and, other things being equal, to motivate the transformation of that society into one which will not necessitate falsehoods.
Explanatory critiques of this sort may or may not involve Colletti contradictions, but they necessarily involve Edgley contradictions. About all these
types of contradiction, Roy Bhaskar is quite clear that they can be described
consistently, that is, one does not have to commit logical contradictions in
order to describe them or any other kind of contradiction; for instance he
says (PN: 70) that Colletti contradictions 'can be *consistently described*, as
indeed can the more straightforward logical kind'.

Along with these valuable but distinct nut-pieces, I think that two unusable
bits of Hegelian shell have survived among some dialectical materialists.

I shall briefly discuss these before going on to see how nut and shell fare in Roy Bhaskar's *Dialectic*.

Nutshells to discard

For Hegelians, dialectic is imposed by the mind and can therefore be found everywhere. For realists, it is an empirical question whether any given bit of reality has dialectical features of one sort or another or not. The first and most common error of dialectical materialists has been so to generalise the notion of contradictions that it loses all specificity and bite. This is not done by Marx himself, but it is done by Engels, and it is quite probable that Marx approved of Engels's views on this, though his own talk of contradictions is always very specific and contentful. I am not one of those who attributes all the strengths of Marxism to Marx and all the weaknesses to Engels, but, when Engels writes about dialectic, I am constantly asking 'what is added to this description by calling this relationship a contradiction and that one the negation of a negation? Nothing but the trivialisation of those terms.' It is the same when Lenin gives as an example of contradiction plus and minus numbers (quoted by Mao 1968: 32), or when Mao himself says on the following page 'difference itself is contradiction'. If every difference is a contradiction then everyone is a dialectician because everyone (apart perhaps from Parmenides) recognises differences – and the force of Marx's discovery is lost. Mao tries to keep the distinctness of real dialectical contradictions by calling them antagonistic contradictions and other contradictions non-antagonistic.[1] But if a contradiction motivates change, it does so by virtue of the inner antagonism that it generates in the system in which it is a contradiction. And if it does not motivate change, then the concept of contradiction is idling.

The second error that dialectical materialists have occasionally committed and much more often been accused of is denying the law of (non)contradiction, that is, claiming that an inconsistent statement can describe reality. We have seen that Marxian structural contradictions, Colletti contradictions and Edgley contradictions can all be described consistently, without breaking any logical laws. One does not have to commit contradictions in order to describe them, any more than an ethologist describing canine behaviour has to bark. It seems that this is occasionally denied by dialectical materialists, and critics of dialectical materialism, including Marxists like Colletti, often think that this is essential to any dialectic. One sometimes hears it claimed that there is such a thing as dialectical logic, and that it denies the law of (non)contradiction, but no one has ever spelt out the laws of this logic or shown how it could be used for proving or disproving a point, and neither could they, for if logical contradictions are allowed, all statements lose their content, since the opposite could equally be asserted. One has to be quite careful in interpreting dialectical materialist texts on this matter, for it is often not clear whether they are denying the law of (non)contradiction or simply asserting the reality of structural contradictions. Thus Politzer tells us that one of the characteristics of 'metaphysical' (that is, undialectical) thought is 'the *abhorrence of contradiction*' (1976: 75). What he means is the view that '*two opposite things cannot exist at the same time*' (same place). But this all depends what one means by this; he has just given the example of life and death, and apparently conceded the point here: 'Indeed, in the example of life and death, there can be no third possibility.' But of course life and death can co-exist in different beings without any logical contradiction: the death of the butterfly and the life of its eggs, for instance. The 'metaphysician' does not deny this, and the dialectician, it seems, does not assert that a person can be alive and dead at the same time. What remains peculiar to the dialectician is simply the assertion of the possibility of mutually depen-dent but conflicting opposites, that is, structural contradictions. Likewise Engels' chapter on the negation of the negation in *Anti-Dühring*. Only some real 'negations' qualify for coming under this 'law of dialectic'; to say 'it is not the case that a rose is not a rose' is not a dialectical operation – these only occur when there is a real process of double negation in a sense of 'negation' in which it refers to a real process, not to a logical operation. Moreover one may negate an insect by crushing it with one's boot and, pre-sumably, negate the negation by wiping one's boot on the doormat, but this, though a real process, is not negation of the negation in the dialectical sense; the latter occurs when both negations are part of some organic process: the caterpillar negates the egg, the butterfly negates the caterpillar, the eggs negate the butterfly which dies when it has laid them (here we have a triple negation, though Engels leaves out the middle one). This dialectic is no logic, but a theory about the way things are – more precisely, the way some things are.

Those who dislike formal logic do so because they fail to see how com-pletely bland a discipline it is. It does not rule out any metaphysical (or dia-lectical) position whatever.[2] It is metaphysically neutral: it does not prevent anyone from admitting that butterflies lay eggs and then die. It should be said that analytical philosophers are largely to blame for this misunderstand-ing, since they are always presenting their metaphysical views as if they were entailed by logic, using nonsensical terms such as 'logical grammar' and 'conceptual truths' in order to do so.

A further word of clarification is needed here, in order to retrieve another good point often made by dialectical materialists and confused with the denial of the law of (non)contradiction. The law of (non)contradiction, on which not only formal logic but all informative discourse depends, says that there can be no contradictions in reality in one precise sense, and no others: it says that inconsistent propositions cannot both be true. As we have seen there are several other senses of contradiction which can exist in reality, and which can be consistently described without breaking any rules of formal logic. But dialectical materialists sometimes think that they have to challenge formal logic on different grounds: not to deny the necessary falsity of 'P and not P' but to deny 'A = A', the 'law of identity'. I think a serious and true point is being misexpressed in this denial. It is generally conceded that when one is talking about a particular being[3] at a particular time, A = A; but it does not hold for identity through time. Now what I think is really being denied here is the transitivity of identity through time. The transitivity of identity means that if A = B and B = C, then A = C. If as I write in January 2000 the leader of the Labour Party is Tony Blair, and Tony Blair is the Prime Minister, then it follows that the leader of the Labour Party is the Prime Minister. But when we are talking about identity through time, the transitivity of identity does not hold: the Holy Roman Empire destroyed by Napoleon was not the same thing as the Holy Roman Empire founded by Charlemagne, although at the end of any of the intervening centuries it would have been true that the Holy Roman Empire was the same thing as it had been at the beginning of that century. Analytical philosophers have got themselves tied up into all sorts of knots by assuming that the transitivity of identity must hold through time as well as at any given time. If, as some analytical philosophers do, one includes transitivity in the definition of identity, one must, on pain of absurdity, deny that there are any identity statements through time; but then the concept of identity loses all connection with the word 'same' in ordinary language, and indeed is rendered pointless, if not unlearnable.

But to deny the transitivity of identity through time is not to make a point about logic at all; it is not to assert A = not-A, though misguided dialecticians have sometimes thought so.[4] It is to make a point about metaphysics (in the standard sense, not the special sense that 'metaphysics' has in Hegel and Engels). It is a point about the way particulars change, and change into other things. Logic based on the law of (non)contradiction remains intact. Once again, dialectical philosophers' mistaken objections to formal logic are matched and partly excused by analytical philosophers' mistaken belief that they are doing logic when they are doing metaphysics.

Dialectical critical realism

So far, we have a list of useful concepts and theories which can be called dialectical by virtue of their common ancestry in Hegel's dialectic, but which in their demystified form do not form parts of a unitary theory of dialectic, though they are compatible and can therefore be parts of a consistent outlook. We also have a couple of bits of Hegelian nutshell which have been retained by some dialectical materialists, but which need to be discarded. By virtue of the dialectical concepts retained by critical realism (structural contradictions, inversions, Colletti contradictions, Edgley contradictions), it can be called a dialectical theory in the same sense that Marx's own work can; it may tend to be sceptical of Marx's claim to a methodological dialectic, but shares belief in three sorts of contradictions with Marx (structural contradictions, inversions, Colletti contradictions) and adds another kind (Edgley contradictions).

But with Roy Bhaskar's book *Dialectic* we come to a new departure, for it is a book centred on dialectic and aspiring to be a system. Since its publication, Roy Bhaskar and other critical realists have come to speak of 'dialectical critical realism', as a new development of critical realism, unforeshadowed by earlier work. In certain respects it is certainly a new development, for it stakes out huge areas of philosophical terrain previously unexplored by critical realism. But the question I want to ask here is: is Roy Bhaskar going 'beyond the fragments' and attempting to reassemble the shattered nut?

It is possible to have, as I have, a very high opinion of *Dialectic* as a treasure-house of insights and invaluable conceptual tools, while remaining sceptical about whether the status of system has been achieved, could have been achieved, or ought to have been aspired to. I share something of Kierkegaard's and Nietzsche's distrust of system-building and indeed think that there are grounds in critical realism for avoiding system-building. After all, critical realism explicitly shows that the multiplicity of sciences is no accident, but is founded on the stratification of nature, such that the ideal of a unitary science could not be achieved. Furthermore, it implicitly shows that sciences and the tacit knowledge that comes with everyday practices are not continuous, though they are consistent and mutually informative. Ontologically, there may be a system out there; but our knowledge of it is necessarily fragmented, and to try to make it into a system would be to fall into the error of the blind men describing an elephant: one grabs its tail and says it is like a rope, one grabs its trunk and says it is like a hose, one grabs its tusk and says it is like a spear, and so on. Each has got a perfectly good fragment of knowledge, but as soon as each mistakes the part for the whole, he says something ludicrous. Even if the blind men get together, they will advance their knowledge only if they say 'part of it is like a hose, part like a spear' and so on. To attempt a composite picture would lead to absurd results. So the prospect of a reunified dialectic does not commend itself to me: what Marx has put asunder, let no Hegelian join.

A great deal of what Roy Bhaskar says about dialectic in *Dialectic* is compatible with the fragmented dialectic in Marx and in Bhaskar's earlier work. He distinguishes logical and dialectical contradictions (1993: 56), though he says that the two classes overlap – presumably with Edgley contradictions in mind. Of dialectical contradictions, he distinguishes the views of Hegel (they are universal because necessary), Engels (they are universal because empirically general) and Marx (they are specific to certain regions of being, for instance capitalism) (ibid.: 151, diagram). A good deal of the text is taken up with the classification and subclassification of various dialectical phenomena.

The concept of dialectic, however, is extended beyond that of contradiction and the concept of contradiction is itself extended: 'The concept of contradiction may be used as a metaphor . . . for any kind of dissonance,

strain or tension' (Bhaskar 1993: 56). But in that case we have simply digni-
fied long familiar phenomena with a scholarly four-syllable word, and will
need a new word to denote Marx's discovery, namely transformation-
inducing antagonisms between internally related aspects of a whole.
Furthermore, 'dialectical contradictions > antagonisms > conflicts > overt
struggles' (ibid.: 59). Certainly there are dialectical contradictions which
don't involve conflicts between human collectivities (for instance classes) –
Engels' contradiction between organisation within the firm and anarchy in
the market, or modern environmental contradictions, for instance. But these
do involve antagonisms in the sense of mutually destructive tendencies.
Non-antagonistic contradiction, as I have suggested with reference to Mao,
is a redundant category. It would have been really helpful here if Bhaskar
could have followed the example of Engels, Lenin and Mao in one respect,
though: giving examples. On the extension of the notion of dialectic, Bhaskar
writes: "by no means all dialectics depend upon contradiction, and even less
violate the logical norms of identity and non-contradiction' (ibid.: 56).

Apart from the odd admission that *some* dialectics do violate logical norms,
this allows phenomena without contradictions to be classed as dialectical.
Which phenomena? The internal relations between aspects of a whole
which, *if* they conflict, give us dialectical contradictions are now themselves
called dialectical connections. A configuration, whether social and therefore
concept-laden or not, is said to be dialectical if it contains dialectical connections (Bhaskar 1993: 67). In fact the count-noun 'dialectic' occurs frequently
throughout the book meaning little more than 'complex developmental
process'[5] – see the list of dialectics in *Dialectic* (ibid.: 201–2). All this seems
to me to spread the concept of dialectic too widely and too thinly – the first
of the errors of which I accuse some dialectical materialists. Bhaskar generally avoids the second error, and holds to the view that dialectical contradictions can be described without committing logical contradictions: 'all
these types [of contradiction] may be described and potentially explained
(in the intrinsic aspect of science) without contradiction' (ibid.: 67 point 5).
Though in the following point he says: 'only epistemological dialectics necessarily breach, at certain critical moments, the formal principles of identity
and non-contradiction'. Though I can nowhere find an account of how
epistemological dialectics (a phrase in which 'dialectic' seems to have the
sense of 'complex developmental process') breach these principles.

On the same page he does say that dialectical critical realism 'will situate,
but not just negate, "logic"', and notes that in the chapter title ('Dialectic:
the Logic of Absence') he is using 'logic' in a different sense; so he is not
setting up dialectical logic as a rival to formal logic. Nonetheless one feels
that there is a dangerous flirtation with 'dialectical logic' here. This crops
up again in a throw-away remark: 'Marx does not breach the norm of non-
contradiction (though Marxism must, if it is to make any progress as a
science) (ibid.: 198)'. How this could help it to make such progress is not,
and could not be, specified.

On the question of the extension of the concept of dialectic, there can of course be no philosophical objection to this extension, providing it is clear to what he is extending it. What I find slightly regrettable is that the really valuable nut-pieces – the concepts of structural contradiction and inversion, on which human emancipation depends – get rather lost in this dialectical pudding, rich as it is in other ingredients. So perhaps it is time to turn to the section where Bhaskar links the essence of dialectics to emancipation, in chapter 2, section 10, 'Towards a Real Definition of Dialectic'.

The alethic truth of dialectic

In the section entitled 'Towards a Real Definition of Dialectic', Bhaskar finds the real definition or alethic truth of dialectic to be 'the absenting of absence' (1993: 176) which he later iterates as *'absenting constraints on absenting absences'* (ibid.: 177), later still specifying by means of a subscript that the constraints to be absented are socially imposed constraints (ibid.: 200).

As I have pointed out elsewhere (Collier 1995/1998) despite the abstractness of this formula, it is very easy to fill it with concrete examples: unemployment is the absence of a job; getting a job would absent that absence; but the deflationary economic policy of a government might be a constraint on absenting that absence; and removing that government might absent that constraint.

The concept which this most closely echoes from the traditional formulations of the dialectic is the negation of the negation. Like this, it is recursive; there is nothing magic about the number two or four; I have already suggested that the butterfly example is actually a treble not a double negation, and of course it is reiterated from generation to generation. Likewise, unemployment could itself be seen as a constraint on the absenting of absences of goods which it prevents the unemployed person from buying; and there may be further constraints on the absenting of the government (the atomisation of opposition forces, for instance), which can themselves be absented by a political practice. But there is a structure to the succession of absentings which is not necessarily present in the traditional succession of negations. It is a structure of alternating good and ill: the absence of a job is an ill, its absenting is a good, a constraint on that absenting is an ill, the absenting of that constraint is a good. We have first, second, third and fourth order absences, and the odd numbers are ills, the even numbers goods. But to generate this alternation there must be a terminus to the series: a first order absence, which will be an ill – 'all ills can be seen as absences' (Bhaskar 1993: 176). But since practically anything can be regarded as an absence, this must mean that first order absences are ills. This means further that, even if virtually anything can be regarded as an absence (food is the absence of famine, sight is the absence of blindness), not everything can truly be regarded as a first order absence (famine and blindness are first order absences, food and sight are not); though an absence can be a first order and a higher order absence, just as an end in itself can also be a means to other ends. Absence is not just a metaphysical shadow cast by negative judgements, which are always reversible; it belongs to ontology, and is not reversible. The medieval philosophers were right: some facts are inherently negative, privations of being, and all ills are such. This formula of fourfold absence therefore requires some such distinction as that between real and nominal absences, such as I made in my paper of that title.[6]

There is a further differentiation in the structure of this fourfold absenting. The second order absenting is an act of satisfaction; the fourth order absenting is an act of emancipation; the second order absenting ameliorates states of affairs; the fourth order absenting transforms structures. In general, the lower the order of even numbered absentings, the closer to personal fulfilment, the higher the order, the deeper the structural transformation.

Some such structure of successive absentings is just what is needed to describe those political examples that the classical dialectical materialists had in mind when they talked about the negation of the negation: the expropriation of the expropriators, for instance. To assimilate such processes to the successive negations in generations of butterflies flattens this structure. The theory of the negation of the negation can best be seen as an inadequate (because insufficiently structured) attempt to theorise emancipation, which the account of the absenting of constraints on the absenting of absences succeeds in theorising. Here we have one of the real achievements of *Dialectic.*

I have claimed that Marx's two crucial nuggets of dialectic, from the standpoint of human emancipation, are the ideas of structural contradictions and inversions. We must now ask how the alethic truth of dialectic, as defined in *Dialectic*, relates to these.

I have argued elsewhere (Collier 1989: conclusion) that the status of the 'laws of history' discovered by Marx is that they denote constraints on the reproduction and transformation of societies. Constraints on the transformation of societies are easy to understand. There are certain ways in which it is impossible to transform society, and consequently certain necessary conditions for the transforming of society. For instance it is not possible to establish equal distribution of wealth for consumption without common ownership of wealth in production. Constraints on the reproduction of societies are more complex and their theorising is more original to Marx. Capitalist society, for instance, cannot reproduce itself without progressing technologically, and hence changing in various respects consequent on that progress – an increasing organic composition of capital, concentration of capital into fewer and larger units, and so on. Among the constraints on the reproduction of capitalism are the contradictions of capitalism; capitalism cannot reproduce itself without generating certain progressively destructive tendencies: class struggle, periodic economic crises, environmental damage. These contradictions are not only constraints on the absenting of absences, but constraints to generate absences; absence of social harmony, of jobs, of life-supporting features of the environment. And there is a constraint on the absenting of these constraints: they can be absented only along with capitalist relations of production themselves. Contradictions then are not first order absences; they constrain society to produce first order absences as a necessary condition of reproducing itself. Inversions can also be seen as a kind of constraint: the inversion of producer and product constrains the producer to serve the product, not to enjoy the use of the product, and so on. But inversions can also be regarded as themselves a sort of first order absence. In the natural ontological order, rational beings take precedence over beings which lack reason, sentient beings over beings which lack sentience, living beings over beings which lack life. Inversion (colloquially: the precedence of things over people), places beings with these lacks (absences) in the place of power. There is an absence of reason, sentience and life at the heart of power in a capitalist society, and the ontological reality of these absences can be verified by their deep and wide effects.

Notes

1 There are several features of Mao's version of dialectics which suggest the influence of the Taoist classics, rather than Hegel and Marx. Thus he reduces the three 'laws of dialectics' to one, the unity of opposites, which is familiar from Lao Tzu. Likewise on the transience of all things; he praises to Taoist sage Chuang Tzu's attitude to death: 'When his wife died, he banged on a basin and sang. When people die there should be parties to celebrate the victory of dialectics, to celebrate the destruction of the old' (See his 'Talk on Questions of Philosophy' in Mao Tse-tung 1974: 227).

2 Mao Tse-tung is rather clear on this point: 'Formal logic is concerned with the form of thought, and is concerned to ensure that there is no contradiction between successive stages in an argument. It is a specialised science. Any kind of writing must make use of formal logic' (1974: 240). Mao goes on to stress the contentlessness of formal logic and its distinctness from dialectics.

3 Species-identity is not transitive even at a given time. Thus I am told there are subspecies of the Great Tit such that subspecies A interbreeds with (and is therefore part of the same species as) subspecies B, B with C, C with D, but not D with A. Hence A and D are not the same species, though by the transitivity of identity they would be.

4 For instance Sean Sayers, in a generally excellent paper 'On the Marxist Dialectic' (1980), first gives a correct characterisation of structural contradictions: 'The dialectical notion of contradiction is that such conflicts between opposed aspects are *necessary* and *essential*' (16). But unfortunately he goes on to say: 'The only correct formula to express this is "A and not-A".' But this is not so. Capitalism includes an essential conflict between bourgeoisie and proletariat, but capitalism is not both capitalism and not-capitalism, nor is the bourgeoisie the not-bourgeoisie. Sayers also commits the error of overgeneralising the dialectic: in the sentence before the two quoted he says: 'Everything is contradictory and contains negative as well as positive aspects within it.' This is not true of everything: capitalism does, oranges don't.

5 Roy Bhaskar's preliminary definition of dialectic (in the count-noun sense) at the beginning of the book is more specific than this:

> dialectic has come to signify any more or less intricate process of conceptual or social (and sometimes even natural) conflict, interconnection and change, in which the generation, interpenetration and clash of oppositions, leading to their transcendence in a fuller or more adequate mode of thought or form of life (or being), plays a key role.
>
> (1993: 3)

Unfortunately, he goes on to say that 'as we shall see', sublation, opposition and antagonism are not necessary to a dialectic. This is not something that we 'see', it is a decision to use the word 'dialectic' more loosely.

6 'Real and Nominal Absences', paper delivered at the Essex Conference of the Centre for Critical Realism, 1998; reproduced in Collier 2001.

Bibliography

Bhaskar, R. (1979) *The Possibility of Naturalism*, Brighton, UK: Harvester.

—— (1987) *Scientific Realism and Human Emancipation*, London: Verso.

—— (1989) *Reclaiming Reality*, London: Verso.

—— (1993) *Dialectic: The Pulse of Freedom*, London: Verso.

Collier, A. (1989) *Scientific Realism and Socialist Thought*, Hemel Hempstead, UK: Harvester Wheatsheaf.

—— (1995) 'The Power of Negative Thinking', in *Radical Philosophy*, no. 69; reprinted (1998) in M. Archer, R. Bhaskar, A. Collier, T. Lawson and A. Norrie (eds) *Critical Realism: Essential Readings*, London: Routledge.

—— (2001) 'Real and Nominal Absences', in G. Potter and J. Lopez (eds) *After Postmodernism: An Introduction to Critical Realism*, London: Sage.

Edgley, R. (1976/1998) 'Reason as Dialectic', in *Radical Philosophy*, no.15; reprinted in M. Archer, R. Bhaskar, A. Collier, T. Lawson and A. Norrie (eds) *Critical Realism: Essential Readings*, London: Routledge.

Engels, F. (1969) *Anti-Dühring*, Moscow: Progress.

Mao Tse-tung (1968) *Four Essays on Philosophy*, Peking: Foreign Languages Publishing House.

—— (1974) *Mao Tse-tung Unrehearsed*, Harmondsworth, UK: Penguin.

Marx, K. (1976) *Capital*, vol. I, Harmondsworth, UK: Penguin.

Politzer, G. (1976) *Elementary Principles of Philosophy*, New York: International Publishers.

Sayers, S. (1980) 'On the Marxist Dialectic', in R. Norman and S. Sayers, *Hegel, Marx and Dialectic*, Brighton, UK: Harvester.

9 Developing realistic philosophy

From critical realism to materialist dialectics[1]

Andrew Brown

1 Introduction

This chapter compares the (relatively little known) 'materialist dialectics' of E. V. Ilyenkov to the 'critical realism' and 'dialectical critical realism' of Roy Bhaskar. The latter author specifies an ontology of 'emergence' and 'stratification'. He demonstrates that, not only a critique of postmodernism, but an *outflanking* of much contemporary Marxist work can be achieved on the basis of such an ontology. For example, the 'new dialectics' interpretation of Marx and Hegel (Arthur 1993) remains largely silent on the 'emergence' of thought from material body; yet critical realism shows that a specification of the mind/body relation is of utmost importance. Not *despite*, but *because* of this great strength of critical realism, the chapter undertakes an 'immanent' critique of the critical realist ontology. Drawing upon Ilyenkov's interpretation of Spinoza, the chapter argues that the critical realist articulation of stratification and emergence collapses into (essentially Humean) scepticism. The underlying reason for this collapse is argued to be the 'non-isomorphic' and causal relationship between thought and object entailed by the critical realist theory of mind. On Ilyenkov's interpretation, Spinoza's articulation of mind and body sustains the materialist and dialectical inseparability of thought, body and object. Through this articulation, the notions of 'stratification' and 'emergence' are preserved but raised to a new level. According to this argument, Ilyenkov's novel interpretation of Spinoza provides the abstract foundation for Marxist theory and practice. It is hoped that the reader will be persuaded to refer to Ilyenkov's development of this abstract foundation found in his many writings on the subject.

The chapter is ordered as follows. Section two presents critical realism and dialectical critical realism; section three presents the Humean critique; section four demonstrates how Ilyenkov's interpretation of Spinoza can be presented as a transcendence of critical realism and dialectical critical realism. Section five concludes.

2 Critical realism and dialectical critical realism

The presentation below will, in a very stripped down way, affirm Bhaskar's own view of the nature of critical realism and of dialectical critical realism. In short, the basic tenets of critical realism are two-fold: positively, the onto-logical notions of stratification and emergence; negatively, the critique of Western thought in terms of the so-called 'epistemic fallacy'. The basic tenet of dialectical critical realism is the notion of 'real absence' (this provides a second critique of Western thought in terms of 'ontological monovalence' which simply refers to the lack of a concept of 'real absence'). With Bhaskar, it will be argued that the notion of 'real absence' is implicit in the basic tenets of critical realism. The notion crystallises and clarifies those tenets; its development deepens and extends them to yield dialectical critical realism. Thus dialectical critical realism is indeed the deepening and enrichment of critical realism that Bhaskar declares it to be (Bhaskar 1993: xiii).

Basic tenets of critical realism: stratification and emergence

The key notions for the critical realist ontology are those of 'emergence' and 'stratification' (Collier (1989, 1994) provides important discussions of emer-gence in addition to those scattered throughout Bhaskar's work). These notions provide an answer to a simple question: what is the relation between the different objects of science such as sub-atomic entities, atoms, molecules, cells, neurons, minds and social structures? One prominent answer to this question is that defining 'reductionism'. On the reductionist view, only one set of objects of science truly exist such that all other objects are completely reducible to these 'ultimate entities' and so *do not really exist*. Given the list above, then the ultimate entities are sub-atomic; all the other objects listed are no more than an agglomeration of sub-atomic phenomena and so have no real or causal status. Another answer, particularly associated with 'dual-ist' theories of the relation between mind and body, is that two (or more, in which case the answer could be deemed 'pluralist') of the objects listed above (such as mind and body) both exist but do so entirely independently of one another such that they have no necessary relation. The critical realist notions of stratification and emergence reject both the reductionist and the dualist or 'pluralist' conceptions. On the critical realist view, the different objects of science are real; established as such by their causal power. Thus reductionism is rejected. At the same time, necessary relations hold between the different objects such that dualism or 'pluralism' is rejected.

The relations between different objects of science are characterised by critical realism in terms of 'strata'. Take the important example of the emer-gence of 'mind' from body (Bhaskar 1989: 80–119). According to critical realism there exists some, as yet little understood, structure 'emergent' from the brain and central nervous system (hereafter CNS) that 'generates' thought. Humans and other thinking beings possess the 'emergent power' of thought because they possess this structure, a structure that could be labelled 'mind'. Thought is a *real* and *emergent power* generated by some complex structure emergent from the brain and CNS. Without the brain and CNS, mind (and hence the power that it generates, thought) would not exist but, at the same time, the brain and CNS are not identical to mind. Rather, mind is a (as yet unknown) structure that emerges from the brain and CNS; this structure is the 'real essence' of mind. The existence of this structure is confirmed by the power that it generates, viz., 'thought'. In critical realist terminology the emergent structure defines a new 'stratum' of reality. The stratum of 'mind' is emergent from the (presumably) neurological stratum below it, and yet 'rooted in' that stratum. Bhaskar dubs his theory of mind 'synchronic emergent powers materialism' (hereafter SEPM). The notions of 'rootedness' and 'emergence' hold for all strata.

The basic conception of stratification and emergence outlined above is intuitively appealing, especially since the invocation of any such stratified ontology is conspicuous by its absence from the elements of the mainstream philosophy and philosophy of science literature with which social scientists are familiar.[2] The absence is explained by critical realism in terms of an adherence by the mainstream to the 'epistemic fallacy' (Bhaskar 1993: 397). This is the negative defining tenet of critical realism. Bhaskar claims that, in general, Western philosophy has tacitly, or otherwise, considered statements about reality to be identical with, or at least reducible to, statements about knowledge of reality.[3] The irreducible difference between knowledge and its object, substantiated by SEPM, and the fact of scientific and human activity in general, reveals such a view to be fallacious. SEPM establishes that the 'real essence' generating thought is some (as yet little known) structure emergent from the brain and CNS. This is an essence very different to that of the objects of thought such as electrons, atoms, molecules, etc. In this almost trivial and yet fundamental way, thought is non-identical with, or 'non-isomorphic' to, its object (a 'reflection' theory of knowledge is ruled out, in any literal sense). Science and everyday activity reveal that knowledge cannot be gained merely through passive contemplation but must be worked for; reality does not readily uncover its secrets to humanity. Critical realism is thereby led to theorise the process of knowledge acquisition in terms of the causal interaction of thought and object. Thought *causes* intentional human activity. Such activity impacts upon real objects, which, in turn, causally impact upon thought. On this view, an object may be essentially independent of the process by which thought attempts to grasp it. Hence, statements referring to real objects (ontological statements) are not always reducible to statements referring to the process of knowledge acquisition (epistemological statements). It is an 'epistemic fallacy' to consider otherwise, and to focus upon epistemology at the expense of ontology.

Having outlined the defining tenets of critical realism, it remains to compare these tenets to the defining tenet of dialectical critical realism. First, it will be helpful to elaborate upon the critical realist notion of stratification. Then it will be possible to show how the basic tenet of dialectical critical realism – the notion of 'real absence' – actually crystallises and clarifies the basic tenets of critical realism. Finally, a consideration of the general dialectical critical realist understanding of processes will introduce the new terrain that the notion of 'real absence' encompasses. Thus dialectical critical realism will be argued to preserve and develop critical realism.

The 'external' relation of strata in critical realism

On the basic critical realist conception a lower stratum, such as the neurological stratum, provides the condition of existence for the stratum above it. As such the higher or emergent stratum is *necessarily* related to the root stratum. On the other hand, the root stratum can exist without the higher stratum; it is not necessary for the entities at the lower stratum to produce the higher stratum – neurons do not necessarily come together to produce 'mind'; equally, hydrogen and oxygen do not always combine to produce water. Thus, from this perspective, the relation between an emergent and a root stratum is *asymmetrically internal*. The higher stratum is necessarily (internally) related to the lower stratum but the lower stratum is only contingently (externally) related to the higher stratum. In fact, a move beyond this basic critical realist understanding of stratification reveals that the relationships between critical realist strata are subtle and complex. Collier, for example, distinguishes *three* different types of possible relationship ('ontological presupposition', 'vertical explanation' and 'composition'; see Collier 1994: 130–4). Below, a sense in which a higher stratum can be considered external to the stratum from which it emerges will be developed. Clearly, this is a different sense of 'external' to that employed above. The two senses of the term 'external' are complementary to one another in this case, despite the apparent contradiction between them. This subtle development of the critical realist conception opens the way for the subsequent presentation of dialectical critical realism, and of the relationship of dialectical critical realism to critical realism.

It is helpful to start from a familiar type of relationship, as exemplified by the landlord – tenant relationship. This is an oft-used exemplar of social relationships in critical realist literature (other typical examples include wage labour/capital and husband/wife).[4] In this type of relationship one pole of the relation 'implies' the other pole: thus, the notion of a landlord implies the notion of a tenant and the existence of a landlord implies the existence of a tenant. Note that the 'implication' holds for both thought and reality. It is possible to consider the notion of 'landlord' without *explicitly* recognising the necessary relation to a tenant but that notion *must* be at least *implicit*. In other words, it is impossible to grasp adequately one pole of this type of relationship without grasping the other pole adequately.

The critical realist conception of the relationship between strata (most clearly, natural strata) can be understood in contrast to the type of relationship just outlined. On the critical realist view, a set of powers revealed at a higher stratum, such as, for example, the powers of water (e.g. boiling at 100 degrees, transparency, ability to quench a thirst, etc.) can be understood adequately without any knowledge – implicit or explicit – of the structure, at the stratum below, that generates these powers (H_2O as it turns out, in the case of water). Thus, the notion of a molecular structure, such as H_2O, is, initially, no more than a scientific hypothesis competing with other hypotheses to explain observed powers such as those of water. 'Water', its powers (transparency, boiling point, etc.), has first to be grasped adequately at the level of the known, higher stratum, before the stratum below is uncovered (before H_2O is brought to light). There is *nothing* explicit or *implicit* in the adequate notion of powers at the higher stratum that enables the scientist to single out a unique underlying structure defining a new stratum. Instead, it is the task, ultimately, of scientific *experiment* to evaluate alternative hypotheses; hypotheses that may, without experiment, remain equally plausible. In *this specific sense* the higher stratum can be said to be 'external' to its root.[5] This sense follows from the causal and 'non-isomorphic' relationship between concept and object, outlined above. For, this non-identity entails a view of the 'fallibility' of knowledge that precludes an explicitly or implicitly necessary (one-to-one) connection between current knowledge and new knowledge.

The stratified ontology of dialectical critical realism

The subtlety of the critical realist notion of stratification is well captured and developed by dialectical critical realism; or so it is argued below.[6] The sense in which the relation between a higher (emergent) and lower (root) stratum is external gains suitably nuanced recognition through the following closely related features of dialectical critical realism (all recurrent themes in Bhaskar 1993): the emphasis on difference over unity; the stress on totalities which are 'subordinate', 'partial', 'open' or 'incomplete'; the non-linearity of the critical realist dialectic; the corresponding polemic against Hegel and 'cognitive triumphalism'; more generally, the notion of 'real absence' as the keystone of dialectical critical realism. These related features are considered in turn below.

It is well known that the relation between 'unity' and 'difference' is granted some considerable importance within the dialectical tradition. The critical realist 'stratified' ontology provides a particular slant on this aspect of dialectics. The notion of stratification gives substance to the dialectical notions of unity and difference. On the one hand, as equal members of the same hierarchy, strata have an aspect of unity (dualism or pluralism is rejected). On the other hand, the strata are not the same as, nor reducible to, one another; they have an aspect of difference (reductionism is rejected).

The question then arises: is unity or difference of greater weight or significance? The discussion above emphasised that there is nothing explicitly or implicitly present in an adequate conception of the emergent stratum that connects it uniquely to the conception of the root stratum. Each stratum is constituted by a unique type of structure (generating *sui generis* causal powers and liabilities) which is, as detailed above, adequately conceptualised in isolation from any concept of the root stratum. This is a matter of ontological significance. For, if an adequate concept of the emergent stratum does not require the presence of a concept of the root stratum, then, in *reality*, there is nothing *present* in the emergent stratum connecting it to the root stratum.[7] Because of this, then, it is the aspect of difference that requires emphasis within the critical realist ontology. At the same time it is clear that the dialectical critical realist emphasis on difference is just that: an *emphasis* rather than an absolute dichotomy. This stress upon difference is counterposed by Bhaskar to Hegel's alleged overemphasis on unity arising (according to the interpretation of Bhaskar offered here) from Hegel's failure to recognise that different respective strata can be comprehended adequately in relative isolation.

A second well-known and much contested theme within the dialectical tradition, closely related to that of unity and difference, is that of 'totality'. Once again the critical realist stratified ontology lends itself to a particular slant on this issue. Whereas Hegel allegedly champions a notion of one single, all-encompassing and 'complete' totality, Bhaskar argues for a conception of 'multiple' totalities which may be 'subordinate', 'partial', 'open' or 'incomplete'. The critical realist conception of stratification contributes to Bhaskar's argument in at least two ways. First, the sense in which a higher stratum is externally related to a lower stratum entails that there could, in principle, be an infinite number of strata below any given strata; these strata could be related in all manner of different ways and there is no reason why their character should be shaped primarily by the totality of their relations. Indeed, given that they can be grasped adequately in relative isolation then an all encompassing totality must be of secondary significance. Second, the point that a lower stratum is externally related to a higher stratum ensures that there is always the possibility, indeed likelihood, of newly emergent strata (most importantly, the possibility of new social structures brought about by human agency), so that the real totality is forever incomplete and open.

The question of the 'linearity' or otherwise of the dialectic is most easily grasped in terms of epistemological issues regarding the nature of the development of knowledge. Does knowledge display a single line of development or is it inherently multifaceted and uneven? Such epistemological considerations are addressed below. It is specifically ontological notions that are under consideration here. In ontological terms, the critical realist and dialectical critical realist stress on difference – the sense in which a stratum is such that it can be grasped in relative isolation – lends itself to the view that the relation between strata is not that of a linear development of one single thing or 'substance', rather it is non-linear; it is a 'leap' from one thing to another, reflected in the leap from a concept of a higher stratum to the concept of its root.

Finally, the keystone of dialectical critical realism, the notion of 'real absence', expresses with precision the subtle nature of the relation between strata within critical realism as elaborated above. The term 'absence' is germane because it expresses precisely (and in contradistinction to Hegel) that there is, or need be, nothing explicitly or implicitly *present* in a given stratum that is intrinsically connected to the lower stratum. The complementary sense in which a higher stratum *is* necessarily related to its root, despite the emphasis on difference, is expressed through the dialectical critical realist view that the absence of lower or higher strata is itself a matter of ontology; *absences are real*. Bhaskar expresses this idea most succinctly – if apparently contradictorily – in the view that the absence from a given stratum of the lower and higher stratum is a case of the 'presence' of an 'absence'. As in the case of linearity, the motivation for the notion of 'real absence' can best be understood from the perspective of the critical realist epistemology. This is because the move to epistemology entails consideration of the *process* of scientific development and the notion of 'real absence' is key to the dialectical critical realist understanding of any process (in terms of dialectical critical realism, the move from a focus on the notion of stratification to a focus upon the notion of process is a move from the 'first moment' of dialectical critical realism to the 'second edge' of dialectical critical realism). Once epistemology has been considered it will be possible to present the broader features of Bhaskar's polemic against Hegel and to summarise critical realism and dialectical critical realism.

The critical realist and dialectical critical realist epistemology[8]

The critical realist notion of stratification yields a conception of the nature of science and scientific progress (a conception first developed in Bhaskar 1978). On the critical realist conception, the process of scientific development consists in the theoretical move from an effect, at one stratum, to its cause at the stratum below. The sharp distinction between each stratum entails that new knowledge is not intrinsic to current knowledge; instead, new knowledge requires the effects of new strata to be perceived, at first indirectly. It is the task of scientific experiment to isolate these effects (creating a 'closure'). Once isolated, then 'old' knowledge does become important. It is not the intrinsic meaning of old knowledge that is of use. Rather, old knowledge provides the scientist with *analogies* and *metaphors* and the like. In the face of unexplained phenomena, scientists 'borrow' concepts and models from established fields and 'stretch', 'distanciate' or distort their meaning in order to produce 'hypotheses' of fundamentally new strata to be, in turn, empirically tested. This process is 'retroduction' in critical realist terminology.

Dialectical critical realism retains the critical realist conception of scientific method and progress (see, especially, Bhaskar 1993: ch. 1). The dialectical critical realist 'epistemological dialectic' is little more, in this case, than a gloss on the critical realist analysis. The dialectical critical realist notion of 'absence', highly flexible in its meaning, is introduced to stand in for both the absence from knowledge (explicit or implicit), and for the corresponding absence from actual events and the perception of those events, of deeper strata. It is thereby possible to view the process of science as driven by absence. Scientists are driven to overcome ('to absent') the anomalies, surprises and the like that arise at a particular level of stratification – these anomalies must themselves be conceived of as absences from knowledge, and from actuality, of deeper strata. The process of science thus provides one instance of the general dialectical critical realist comprehension of process in terms of 'absence' and of, in particular, human development as the 'absenting of absence'. The crucial point Bhaskar makes is that, given this view, 'absences' must have ontological status and not just epistemological status, i.e. *absences must be real*; any other way, the reality of processes in general would have to be denied and they would have to be considered as no more than constructions of the mind.

Scientific development provides also an example of the 'non-linearity' of the dialectical critical realist dialectic. The non-linearity of the 'epistemological dialectic' is reflected in the continual 'distanciation' and 'stretching' of old concepts and models indicating that the development of new knowledge is by no means a smooth and intrinsic development of old knowledge.

Summary

Critical realism and dialectical critical realism are usefully summarised through Bhaskar's critique of Hegel. Bhaskar (1993) finds a catalogue of philosophical errors in the Hegelian dialectic. Hegel is alleged to overemphasise unity; absolutise totality; linearise the dialectic; identify thought and being; and ultimately to deny the reality of absence. Hegel is further castigated by Bhaskar for his alleged 'anthropomorphic' view that totality of strata are known or fully knowable. Such 'cognitive triumphialism' must, according to critical realism, be scotched: the non-identity of subject and object ensures that there is no reason why all being must be *conceivable* being, let alone why all being must be conceived of already; the 'open totality' ensures that there is always the possibility, indeed likelihood, of newly emergent strata (most importantly, the possibility of new social structures brought about by human agency), so that reality is forever incomplete and inherently impossible to grasp fully.

There is not, it has been argued, any great gulf between critical realism and dialectical critical realism. On the contrary, dialectical critical realism clarifies, deepens, enriches, broadens and develops critical realism. The notion of 'real absence' is key to this argument. Below, critical realism and dialectical critical realism will be subjected to an immanent critique which is simple and yet, it will be argued, fundamental.

3 The immanent contradiction of critical realism and dialectical critical realism

One simple possibility serves to lead the critical realist 'open' stratified ontology into contradiction.[9] The ontology must embrace the possible existence of a structure (or force) which will cause, at some future date, the characteristic behaviour, or *defining tendencies*, of other structures to *change*. In other words the ontology opens up the possibility of a structure (or force) that will cause present scientific 'laws' to *cease to exist*. This possible structure can be termed, metaphorically, a 'time bomb'. The 'time bomb' structure envisaged here does not destroy objects in accordance with the 'known laws' of nature as would a literal 'time bomb'; rather it destroys the world as 'known' to science, by ending the 'laws' of nature 'known' by science. Though not yet discovered, the 'time bomb' could be located at a deeper stratum than hitherto uncovered by science; or it could be newly emergent; or it could be simply an isolated and, as yet, undetected entity. Bhaskar's entire polemical argument for an 'open' totality and his stress on difference collapses in the face of the sceptical consequences of the 'time bomb' possibility, or so it will be argued below.

First, it should be stressed just why the time bomb[10] cannot be ruled out. As detailed above, critical realism and dialectical critical realism articulate a particular notion of the mind-independence of the objects of thought. An object, its nature and existence, need not depend upon the conception of that object. The human process of gaining knowledge of the object is irrelevant to the nature of the object itself. In particular, the nature of the object may be such that it is inherently out of bounds of human cognition. The object could, for example, be akin to a non-spatial entity, such as a force, but one that has no effect upon spatial entities, nor on any other entities that are detectable by humanity. This indeed is the key point of the notion of 'mind-independence', as envisaged within critical realism, dialectical critical realism, and many other forms of realism. The world could exist without humanity and there could be things that exist without humanity ever being able to detect them, even in principle, regardless of spatio-temporal constraints. It is from this basic (at first sight incontrovertible) premise which, so it would seem, only an idle philosopher would have the effrontery to deny, that the notion of a metaphorical time bomb flows. For, once inherently undetectable entities are allowed for in this way, then it is equally valid to allow that entities exist that are currently undetectable but, in the future, will take effect. And this effect will be determined by the nature of the object, not by, for example, the nature of mind. Hence, the drastic effect of completely changing some or all 'known laws' must be considered a possibility, if the critical realist and dialectical critical realist (amongst other realisms) articulation of the notion of mind-independence is not to be contradicted.

Second, the nature of this 'possibility' of a time bomb must be examined. An intuitive critical realist view might be to argue that a time bomb entity is possible but unlikely (indeed this is a view that many who are not critical realists would endorse). For, the existence of such a peculiar entity would seem a remote possibility given that all fundamental laws have, apparently, not changed in the past,[11] and no structure likely to bring about such change has ever been discovered. Now, it should be stressed that the validity of this basic response *as such* is not what is at issue. Rather, the question concerns what the critical realist (or dialectical critical realist) notions of mind-independence and stratification truly validate as a response. It should be clear that the apparent lack of total change of all 'known laws' *so far* provides no evidence one way or the other as regards the likelihood of the existence of the time bomb. For, the time bomb is precisely an entity that, should it exist, will *not* and *cannot* be detected until it 'goes off' (at which point human life may cease, such that the bomb is never, in fact, detected by humanity). So the evidence shows, at best, that a time bomb has not *yet* gone off but the evidence reveals nothing about whether a time bomb exists or not. The evidence is equally compatible both with the view that the time bomb does not exist and with the view that the time bomb does exist. It must be concluded that, on critical realist and dialectical critical realist premises, it is inherently impossible to attach any possibility to the two eventualities in question. Science simply does not and cannot know *at all* whether or not a time bomb exists. The probability of a time bomb existing is inherently unknowable; it is *fundamentally uncertain*.

Exactly the same considerations apply to the question of just when the time bomb will go off, if it does exist. That is to say, if the time bomb exists, then humans must be fundamentally uncertain about when it will go off. Indeed, the bomb, if it exists, may go off *any second now*. Humans must be fundamentally uncertain as to whether or not it will do this. Let it be stressed, once more, that what is at stake here is not the question of whether or not it is *truly* the case that humans are fundamentally uncertain regarding this esoteric, if not downright ridiculous, notion of a metaphorical time bomb going off, any second. This seems patently not to be the case and, indeed, a materialist philosophy will be put forward below that is compatible with such basic intuition. Rather, the argument here is attempting to draw out the logical implications of the critical realist and dialectical critical realist ontology, based, as this ontology is, upon a particular notion of mind-independence (a notion common to many realisms).

What, then, are the implications for the status of current knowledge? There are two relevant possibilities between which humans cannot discriminate. On the first possibility, there exists a time bomb that will go off any second now. If this is true then some, or all, 'known laws' will cease to exist, any second now. On the second possibility such a time bomb does not exist. Humans are inherently incapable of having any clue as regards which of these two possibilities is the truth. It is a matter of fundamental uncertainty. Note that this fundamental uncertainty regarding the time bomb entails fundamental uncertainty regarding the existence of the 'known laws': if the time bomb exists then some or all of them are about to cease; if it does not exist then they will remain. In short, given critical realist premises, humans are inherently, eternally and fundamentally uncertain about whether or not some or all 'known laws' are about to cease to exist. A very stark conclusion.

Even so, is it not the case that, as a matter of practicality, scientists, and humans in general, just 'get on' with life, anyway? Do humans not, effectively and quite reasonably, just plump for the second of the two possibilities, viz., that there is no time bomb? Hume stresses that this behaviour cannot be considered 'reasonable' if the notion of mind-independence (as, in this case, articulated by critical realism, and in Hume's time argued by Locke and others)[12] is upheld. This is so because such a view of mind-independence leads, as argued above, to fundamental uncertainty rather than to some mere 'nagging doubt', which could reasonably be 'lived with'. Reason cannot lead to any action where it leads to total uncertainty; where there is not even a small inkling of which of the two key possibilities will occur. One response might be to accept only the view that carries a chance of survival. Certainly, this is a reasonable dictum but it does not help in the case under consideration simply because there is no way of working out which possibility carries the greatest chance of survival. For, the real outcome may entail that acting according to previously 'known laws' would lead to death, whereas acting according to some other set of laws, generated by the metaphorical time bomb, will lead to survival. Thus, it is equally as likely that acting in accordance with currently 'known laws' will lead to death, as it will not. The consequences of being inherently ignorant about the laws of nature that will exist a second from now are severe, but this is precisely the implication of ignorance regarding the time bomb.

Consider an analogy. The assertion that a time bomb does not exist, on the grounds that the non-existence of a time bomb ensures my future survival, is *partially* analogous to the assertion that I *will* win the lottery, on the grounds that I *want* to win it. The difference is that at least with the lottery there is a definite and known chance of winning, albeit a slim one. So, though I would expect to lose, it would be worth making plans for the event of winning the lottery, if this eventuality were my only hope of survival. The metaphor of the time bomb, however, indicates a situation where I do not know anything at all about the nature of the world (the laws of nature) in the immediate future; I do not know anything so specific as that there is a lottery going ahead, so I cannot make any plans at all.

Consider also the practical consequences. To argue that humans can reasonably plump for the second (non-time bomb) option, is to argue that a scientist, without any evidence on competing hypotheses, can plump for one of them, just because they happen to like it. If they do that for the case of the time bomb, if moreover they base their entire 'science' upon such an arbitrary move, then science does not have foundation in reason at all. Indeed, a 'scientist' could not coherently rule out the analogous form of 'reasoning' (arbitrarily plumping for a preferred hypothesis without a shred of evidence) for *any* set of hypotheses, if such a form of 'reasoning' has been allowed in the time bomb case. That is to say the mode of 'argument' in question is the very *antithesis* of science; to adopt it, is to make science an unintelligible activity, to collapse critical realism by removing its cornerstone, the intelligibility of science. Thus, these apparently esoteric philosophical concerns turn out to impinge directly upon concrete and practical matters. The practising scientist, given the critical realist articulation of mind-independence, cannot in fact practise at all. For, that scientist would have to face the question of the time bomb, and would have to admit that it cannot be satisfactorily answered. The scientist would have to admit to ignorance regarding what things will be in the immediate future. Despite what appeared to be a wealth of knowledge regarding the essential structure of things, the scientist would have to admit to being ignorant of the 'essential structure' of anything because s/he would not have any clue as to what the laws of nature, in the immediate future, will be.

What if, despite all that has been argued above, the reader should feel that the idea of a time bomb is simply too ridiculous to worry about? And that anyone who does worry about it should just go and get medical help! Undoubtedly such a view is quite correct. But the *point* of the argument has not been to convince anyone that a time bomb really exists, far from it. Rather, the point has been to demonstrate that critical realism and dialectical critical realism (indeed, many other forms of realism) collapse due to the failure to rule out, in any way whatsoever, the evident nonsense of a time bomb. The critical realist articulation of 'mind-independent' reality (in terms of a 'non-isomorphic' and causal relation between thought and its object) leads to the self-contradictory notion that a time bomb structure could exist somewhere in the universe. Any attempt to rule out the time bomb structure, on the ground that it leads to scepticism, would flatly contradict this articulation of the mind-independence of reality. There is, quite simply, no way out for critical realism and dialectical critical realism. If the deep insights of critical realism and dialectical critical realism are to be salvaged, then a fundamental reworking of the notion of 'realism' must be undertaken. A reworking which is able to cope with the evident nonsense of the time bomb possibility. Before embarking upon just such a reworking, the basis upon which it will be made is clarified below.

In effect, the argument thus far provides a set of criteria for any coherent philosophy. First, the articulation of 'mind-independence' in terms of a non-isomorphic and causal relationship between thought and its object has turned out to be self-contradictory because it leads to scepticism. So in one way or another it must be replaced. Second, the critical realist articulation of mind-independence represents an attempt to uphold evident facts about reality. Thus critical realism appears to be difficult to deny without taking a position which is in flat and disingenuous contradiction with the practicalities of everyday life. The conception of mind (SEPM) is tied to a definite conception of ontological 'emergence' without which, as critical realism shows, it is very difficult to maintain a coherent philosophy. Furthermore, there is, quite evidently, a big ontological difference between thought and the objects of thought. This difference would seem to entail a notion of 'mind-independence' along precisely the lines critical realism suggests. For, it seems quite evident that a 'thought' does not possess the same shape as its object; that, quite to the contrary, a thought is emergent from a very different structure than its object. Any attempt, against critical realism, to uphold an isomorphism of thought and its object, must deal with the evident ontological difference between the two. It must also deal with the evident practical, active nature of humanity and the process of knowledge. How, for example, can the process of science, and indeed any human act at all, be grasped, if the critical realist attempt to do so fails? The causal theory of mind put forward by critical realism attempts to capture the active nature of science and humanity. What place for such activity in a non-causal theory of mind, and/or in a theory which takes object and concept to be directly identical? What place for Marx's famous dictum that *practice* is fundamental to knowledge, if practice cannot be articulated in terms of the causality of mind?

4 Spinoza's transcendence of critical realism and dialectical critical realism

This section draws upon Ilyenkov's interpretation of Spinoza (Ilyenkov 1977: 11–74) in order to transcend Bhaskar's philosophy. Spinoza bases his theory upon a critique of Descartes and it is with Descartes that the exposition below begins.

As is well known, Descartes was acutely aware of the dangers of scepticism as captured in the notion of 'Cartesian doubt' (there are some similarities between Descartes' 'evil demon' and the 'time bomb' invoked above). Hence, amongst other things, Descartes aimed to avoid the pitfalls of scepticism. Descartes developed a materialist principle that can be seen, in the terms of the critique above, as an attempt to exclude the possibility of a 'time bomb' from the material world. According to Descartes, the material world is constituted by definite structures. A common principle underlies these structures, such that to know any one structure is enough to know the principle common to all structures. This common principle, necessarily possessed by any object, is not possessed by a 'time bomb'. The 'time bomb' is thereby ruled out. In other words all individual and particular objects instantiate a universal, such that knowledge of any object assures knowledge of the universal. The 'time bomb' is defined as an entity that does not possess the universal and hence cannot exist.

The problem, for Descartes, lay in his grasp of just what the common principle consists in. More specifically, it lay in his inability to square the principle, as he understood it, with thinking beings (a category which, for Descartes, excluded animals). For, Descartes grasped the principle in 'mechanistic' terms closely analogous to the pioneering conceptions of the natural science of his day (to which Descartes made, himself, major contributions).[13] According to this conception, all material structures behave according to a simple 'stimulus-response' schema. Any impulse (stimulus) to a structure will set in play a chain of movement within the structure producing a definite response of that structure; a response predetermined by the particular structural configuration involved. More complex behaviour, on this view, is nothing but the result of a more complex structural configuration and, whatever the apparent complexity, is thereby fixed and predetermined such that the same stimulus, to the same structure, will always produce the same response.

Descartes well recognised that such a schema of action does not fit the behaviour of thinking bodies. For, as Descartes carefully described, the behaviour of thinking bodies is characterised by a break between stimulus and response. Thinking bodies reflect before acting in response to a stimulus such that their behaviour in the face of the same stimulus may change and adapt through time. Descartes noted the consequential characteristic trait of the thinking body. The activity of the thinking body is not fixed to a limited range of objects. Rather, the thinking body continually and fluidly strives to embrace *any* object that it may come into contact with. The activity of the thinking body thus has a *universal* character in contradistinction to the particular activities of non-thinking bodies. This meant, for Descartes, that the search for some structural configuration constituting thought must be fruitless because the associated activity is, precisely, *not fixed* and so can have no fixed structural 'determination' (limitation). Any structure constituting thought would have to contain equivalent structural complexity to all other structures – a structure equivalent, in the limit, to the universe, packed somewhere within one thinking body; a structure that would, in other words, contradict the very principle of structural determination.

It was the impossibility of any structural constitution that led Descartes (on Ilyenkov's interpretation) to argue that thought instead belongs to a separate substance, viz., 'mind'. As is well known, Descartes could not explain how two things without anything essential in common, mind and matter, interact and accord with one another. So in the final analysis Descartes could not provide an account of mind and body any more rational than SEPM. He ultimately took refuge in 'God' to connect what cannot conceivably be connected. On Ilyenkov's interpretation it was Spinoza who first overcame rationally the contradiction of SEPM and of Cartesian dualism.

Spinoza by no means discards, *in toto*, the reasoning behind Descartes' system. This has the relevant implication that Spinoza develops the resolution of the problem of scepticism contained in Descartes' philosophy. For Spinoza, as for Descartes, material structures constitute the universe, and the principle that is universally tied to structures rules out scepticism (in the terms set out above, it excludes the possibility of a 'time bomb' from material reality). Where Descartes had gone astray was in his conception of this common principle. Spinoza transcends Descartes' system fundamentally through recognising the true materialist principle constituting objects, a principle that encompasses thinking bodies.

Spinoza recognises that matter is not limited solely to the mechanistic principle recognised by Descartes. Rather, with greater structural complexity, the mechanistic form of motion is superseded. In other words the basic material principle that would today be described as *emergence* is recognised by Spinoza. However, this notion of emergence is not precisely the same as that of critical realism. Spinoza stresses that the totality of matter ('substance') constitutes the identity of all objects. The 'attributes' of this totality of matter are, for Spinoza, preserved and developed through all of its transformations. They thereby constitute universal laws of matter. As in the case of Descartes, elementary aspects of these laws are grasped (in a way to be outlined below) once any specific object is grasped and, as for Descartes, these aspects exclude any possibility of a 'time bomb'. For, this 'time bomb' is defined precisely as that which can completely change all laws, whereas the elementary attributes of the totality of matter are both known and eternally unchanging.

In effect, and in terms of the critique above, Spinoza excludes a 'time bomb' from his philosophy. The presentation above demonstrates that Spinoza must provide an account of knowledge that is able to justify this exclusion. Furthermore this account must embrace the manifest phenomena of scientific practice and of human activity in general. Spinoza's articulation of both knowledge and practice arises out of a revolutionary account of thought and body as will be outlined below.

The fundamental breakthrough made by Spinoza lies in his reconceptualisation of the relation between knowledge (thought), human practical activity and the material objects towards which that thought and activity are addressed. Instead of holding that thought *causes* intentional human activity (as does critical realism), Spinoza argues that thought is *inseparable* from that activity. What is the nature of this inseparability? Well, to focus on the crucial feature of thought, viz., knowledge, or 'adequate' ideas, Spinoza holds that such ideas consist in awareness of the spatiotemporal form of the thinking body; in other words they consist in self-awareness. Self-awareness not of the inner structure and motion of the thinking body but of the outer movement of that body; self-awareness of the movement of the hands, arms, legs, head, etc., of the thinking body amongst the other bodies of the universe.

Bhaskar (1989, and elsewhere) notes, as must any enquirer into this issue, that thinking beings continually self-monitor their external activity; self-awareness being an emergent property of thinking bodies. What Bhaskar does not recognise, however, and what is not readily apparent to any enquirer into the issue, is the characterisation of adequate ideas as consisting in self-awareness of outer bodily activity. In particular, an adequate idea of an object, in Spinoza's view, is nothing but self-awareness of the form of the thinking body, where that body is isomorphic to, i.e. in correspondence to, or moving in accordance with, the object. This is a subtle and strange twist, or reworking, of the relationship between knowledge, human activity and object on Spinoza's part. Intentional human activity is still associated with thought, inseparable from it, but not in terms of a causal relationship. Rather, the relationship is one of self-awareness; a different kind of inseparability to that entailed in a causal relationship.

The beauty of this conception is that it makes human practice vital to knowledge, inseparable from it, whilst being able to resist the sceptical consequences of the causal and non-isomorphic conception of critical realism. Thus the critical realist analysis of experiment can be re-conceptualised in terms of Spinoza's reworking of the relationship between knowledge, practical activity and object. In Spinoza's conception, practice is indeed necessary in order for the thinking body to achieve accordance with, or correspondence to, the objects that it comes into contact with. Through continual and fluid spatial activity, and through the revision of the schema of that activity in response to the reciprocal impact of the object of activity, the thinking body achieves spatio-temporal correspondence with the object. There is a 'mirroring' of the thinking body's activity with its object. The actions of the thinking body correspond to, or map, the form of the object, such that the object is brought under the control of the thinking body. In an experiment, therefore, the object under study is isolated and its characteristic activity induced, at will, by the scientist, once the scientist has fathomed the requisite activity to yield this desired result. Technically speaking, the body achieves a (spatio-temporal) isomorphism, or identity (iso-) of shape (morph), with the object. *Simultaneously* as it does this, the thinking body achieves an adequate idea of the object, since such ideas consist in self-awareness of the isomorphism.

Thinking bodies are able to reflect and accordingly self-transform their inner bodily structure, hence their outer bodily activity, so as to act in accordance with, and comprehend, the material world. The development of human spatial activity within the objective material environment is simultaneously expressed for humans in the form of their ideas (their knowledge). Conversely, this practice is the objective, outer, expression of their developing knowledge. Crucially, knowledge is not determined (delimited) by the thinking body. Rather, knowledge is determined by the objects of thought. The thinking body must subordinate its will and consciousness to the dictates of the object, in ongoing material practice. In this way an adequate idea of an object is determined independently of the consciousness and will of the thinking body. Knowledge is guided, not by the thinking individual's consciousness and will, but by the material objects of practice, which forever serve to correct mistakes and to provide new puzzles, as actions run up against the palpable material barrier of objects, in unexpected ways. Hence, Spinoza's philosophy cogently sustains the mind-independence of the objects of thought. The thinking body is progressively able to improve its grasp of these mind-independent objects, through ongoing practical engagement with them.

The 'time bomb' cannot exist because, by definition, it lacks the elementary and universal attributes of matter, present (not 'absent', as in dialectical critical realism) in all objects, hence grasped by all thinking bodies (a grasp implicit in their ongoing activity, even if denied explicitly). However, it is one thing to have certainty regarding aspects common to all material objects, so ruling out the idle concoction of a 'time bomb', but it is quite another to grasp the specific developing forms of matter that constitute the specificity of objects encountered in everyday life. In other words, the knowledge that there is a developing and interconnected material universe, not a universe inhabited by 'time bombs', knowledge which is obvious to a small child (though not explicitly articulated by a small child), is hardly sufficient to grasp the specific material forms that constitute objects. It is in no way a *full* conception of matter. Such a full conception of the totality of matter ('substance'), hence of all possible specific objects that may be encountered in everyday life, is a far cry from the knowledge that humanity will ever possess. Only through ongoing practical engagement with the world is the partial knowledge that humans do possess developed further. Thus Spinoza refutes scepticism whilst upholding practice, through a materialistic reworking of the relation of thought, practice and object.

5 Conclusion

From Ilyenkov's perspective, it does not appear that Hume would have had great difficulty in refuting either Bhaskar or contemporary Hegelian Marxists ('new dialecticians'). The critical realist conception of the causal and non-isomorphic relation between thought and object is an easy target for Hume's sceptical argument. Contemporary Hegelian Marxism of the 'new dialectical' variety does not even recognise the full philosophical significance of the mind/body relation, and so does not begin to justify the claims to knowledge that it makes.[14] In neither case is a rational warrant provided for rationality itself, i.e. self-contradiction is not, finally, overcome. The paramount importance of Spinoza's notion of substance (as interpreted by Ilyenkov) and related notions lies, it has been argued, in the upholding of a materialist and dialectical theory of mind, body and object that is uniquely able to salvage rationality.

However, the development of this abstract foundation was not a task achieved by Spinoza. On Ilyenkov's interpretation, Marx goes beyond

Spinoza by noting that the mode of human activity is not merely one of accordance with the object; humans transform not only themselves but also the object in the course of their labour i.e. in the process of social production. On Marx's conception, it is through labour that nature (substance) transforms itself, given that humans are as much part of nature as are the objects of their labour. The exposition of Spinoza remains vital because it clearly reveals the true significance of Marx's well-known remarks on labour and nature. Most importantly, it reveals that the notion of labour incorporates a materialist account of the inseparability of thought, practice and object, captured in Spinoza's concept of substance. A development of such a Spinozist based Marxism is beyond the scope of this chapter. The interested reader is referred to Bakhurst (1991) for an account, and full bibliography, of Ilyenkov's life's work, which was dedicated to just such a development.

Notes

1 Especial thanks to Andrew Mearman for his ongoing e-mail commentary on previous drafts of this chapter. A version of the paper was presented at the King's College Seminars in Critical Realism. I should like to thank Alan Norrie, for inviting me to present at the seminar, and the seminar participants. Thanks also to the participants at the presentation of the paper given at the Annual Conference for the International Association for Critical Realism, Lancaster University, August 2000. Many thanks to the editorial board of *Historical Materialism* for their encouragement and stimulating comments (I hope to publish a companion article to this chapter in that journal). Thanks also to members of the Bhaskar e-mail list. I am very grateful to the following people for their comments on earlier drafts: Andrew Chitty, Hans Despain, Paul Dunne, Howard Engelskirchen, Adrian Haddock, Nick Hostettler, Mervyn Hartwig, Martin Jenkins, Clive Lawson, Corrina Lotz, Warren Montag, John Roberts, Alfredo Saad-Filho, Simeon Scott, Gary Slater, Tony Smith and David Spencer. Few, if any, of the above named people agree with the argument herein!

2 Thus social scientists are most likely to be aware of philosophers of science such as Popper, Kuhn and Lakatos. These philosophers do not dwell upon the notion of 'emergence'.

3 The clause 'tacitly, or otherwise' is important. Bhaskar is not claiming that all philosophers *intentionally* commit the fallacy.

4 Almost invariably, one or more of these examples is used in expositions of the critical realist conception of social structures.

5 This sense is implicit in the critical realist literature but has not previously been made explicit to the author's knowledge.

6 The presentation below attempts to strip the relationship between critical realism and dialectical critical realism down to its bare essence. At no point, does Bhaskar (1993) offer such a presentation.

7 Note, first, that the lower stratum is 'absent' from the higher stratum and that this absence is a facet of reality according to dialectical critical realism, as will be explained below. Second, it is important to stress that the status of a concept as 'adequate' has, for critical realism, ontological connotations. Hence ontological conclusions can be drawn from an adequate concept without committing the epistemic fallacy.

8 In addition to Bhaskar's work, that of Tony Lawson (e.g. 1997) and Andrew Sayer (e.g. 1992) is especially useful in detailing the critical realist conception of epistemology and of methodology.
9 The critique in this section can be seen as a recapitulation of Hume's famous sceptical argument as, for example, contained in Hume (1975: sections II–IV).
10 For the sake of readability, the term 'time bomb' will not be placed within quotation marks for the remainder of this section of the chapter.
11 Thus, the fundamental laws of physics and chemistry are ordinarily presumed to be universal through time and space. Of course, the nature and extent of scientific *knowledge* of them has changed and will continue to do so. Note that the 'time bomb' envisaged above could possibly change all of the 'known laws' fundamentally and within a negligible (practically instantaneous) time period, or the time bomb could change just a few of them over time. The problem is that humans have no way of knowing either of its existence or of its impending effect.
12 Right from the inception of critical realism Bhaskar (1978) makes explicit the Lockean heritage of the critical realist notion of 'real essences'.
13 It is a mechanistic conception analogous, also, to the mechanistic division of labour already present in early capitalism and to the machinery that later arises as capitalism becomes more developed.
14 A recent special issue of *Science and Society* (1998) on Marxist–Hegelian dialectics contained not one direct reference to the mind/body problem.

Bibliography

Arthur, C. (1993) 'Review of Ali Shamsavari's *Dialectics and Social Theory: The Logic of Capital*', *Capital and Class* 50: 175–80.
Bakhurst, D. (1991) *Consciousness and Revolution in Soviet Philosophy: From the Bolsheviks to Evald Ilyenkov*, Cambridge: Cambridge University Press.
Bhaskar, R. (1978) *A Realist Theory of Science*, 2nd edition, Hemel Hempstead, UK: Harvester Press.
——— (1989) *The Possibility of Naturalism*, 2nd edition, Hemel Hempstead, UK: Harvester Wheatsheaf.
——— (1993) *Dialectic: The Pulse of Freedom*, London: Verso.
Collier, A. (1989) *Scientific Realism and Socialist Thought*, Hemel Hempstead, UK: Harvester Wheatsheaf.
——— (1994) *Critical Realism: An Introduction to Roy Bhaskar's Philosophy*, London: Verso.
Hume, D. (1975) *An Enquiry Concerning Human Understanding*, in K. A. Selby-Bigge and P. H. Nedditch (eds) *Enquiries Concerning Human Understanding and Concerning the Principles of Morals*, 3rd edition, Oxford: Clarendon.
Ilyenkov, E.V. (1977) *Dialectical Logic: Essays on its Theory and History*, translated by H. Campbell Creighton, Moscow: Progress.
Lawson, T. (1997) *Economics and Reality*, London: Routledge.
Sayer, A. (1992) *Method in Social Science: A Realist Approach*, 2nd edition, London: Hutchinson.
Special Issue (1998) 'Dialectics: the new frontier', *Science and Society* 62 (3).

10 From spaces of antagonism to spaces of engagement[1]

Noel Castree

Geographical space is always the realm of the concrete and particular. Is it possible to construct a theory of the concrete and the particular in the context of the universal and abstract determinations of Marx's theory of capital accumulation? This is the fundamental question to be resolved.

David Harvey (1985a: 144)

Theorising about space itself largely requires an abstraction from particular spatial configurations . . .

Andrew Sayer (2000: 128)

Thinking space

Does space make a difference and, if so, what kind of difference does it make? In just a few short years, this has become one of the most important and difficult questions confronting workers in the human sciences. At first the question of space seemed rather trivial and even irrelevant. As recently as a decade ago, most economic, political and social theorists abstracted from space without so much as a second thought. The predominant view, more implicit than explicit, was that while socio-economic and political processes necessarily assumed a spatial form, this form did not in itself enter into the constitution of those processes. Space was thus seen as a consequent domain, the study of which was best left to geographers 'dutifully mapping the outcomes of processes which it was the role of others to study' (Massey 1985: 12). From the mid-1980s, though, the matter of space began to be viewed differently. A new generation of geographers, less parochial than their disciplinary forebears, made the argument that space is more than a passive outcome or container of 'aspatial' processes and relations. For them, economies, polities and societies were *intrinsically* spatial, meaning that they could not be comprehended without reference to geography. At the same time, social theorists like Giddens and Urry began to take space seriously, while the publication of Soja's (1989) *Postmodern Geographies* and Lefebvre's (1991) *The Production of Space* showed why 'the question of space is . . . too important to be left exclusively to geographers' (Harvey 1989a: 5). Today, the spatial vogue is such that literal and metaphorical references to 'location', 'terrain', 'positionality', 'site', 'region', 'locale' and the like have become commonplace in the human sciences. This burgeoning interest in spatiality has served as a vital corrective to the space-blind worldviews that have animated critical and mainstream theoretical work for so long. However, it is not in my view an unalloyed good. Ironically, the more that space has become the focus of debate within and between disciplines, the less we know about the difference it makes. So many and varied are contemporary theoretical references to space that it has become something of a chaotic concept – or, more precisely, a cluster of competing concepts each with different meanings and referents which ought to be carefully distinguished (cf. Crang and Thrift, 2000).

This brings me, in a roundabout way, to my concerns in this chapter. In the pages that follow I want to stage an encounter between the work of two figures who have been central to the debates over the difference that space makes: David Harvey and Andrew Sayer. Their work on space warrants close attention for several reasons. First, it has been uncommonly original, clear and influential.[2] Second, in the context of this volume, the differences (real and apparent) between the two authors are particularly interesting. Harvey, as is well known, is a Marxist in (for want of a better term) the 'full-blooded' sense: that is, he insists on the continued relevance of historical materialism in the twenty-first century and adheres to a version of Marxism that is peculiarly 'classical'. By classical I mean a form of Marxism directly indebted to the later Marx rather than to later interpreters of Marx (though Harvey has, at times, drawn upon the work of Lefebvre, the regulation theorists and several process-philosophers for inspiration). Harvey's signal contribution over the last twenty-plus years has been to upgrade historical materialism to historical-*geographical* materialism by integrating 'the production of space and spatial configurations as an active element within the core of Marxian theorising' (1989a: 4). In other words, Harvey's project has been to add space into Marxism at the level of abstract theory. Sayer, by contrast, is decidedly neo- or post-Marxist. His research, alone and with Kevin Morgan and Dick Walker (1995, 1988 and 1992 respectively), has been syncretic and multi-paradigmatic. Moreover, where Harvey's work has, predominantly, been substantive-theoretical,[3] Sayer has also ventured into the realms of social philosophy, drawing upon the realism of Bhaskar and Harré. Now in its second edition, his *Method in Social Science* (1992) has sought to tackle a set of persistent epistemological and ontological problems and confusions afflicting social scientific inquiry. Underlabouring on behalf of those theoretical and empirical researchers interested in space, one of Sayer's key objectives has been to put space in its proper place (1992: 146–51). In this regard, he has (in)famously become associated with the argument that while space matters the difference it makes is contingent. First elaborated sixteen years ago (Sayer, 1985), this claim has been interpreted as meaning that space cannot enter into the construction of economic, social and political theory. For many commentators (e.g. Peet, 1998: 176), therefore, Sayer's realism makes space a legitimate subject mostly or only for concrete research rather than theoretical inquiry.

It is this different stance on the difference that space makes that I want to focus on in this chapter. Harvey and Sayer have been seen as leading proponents of what, respectively, we might call an 'essential' and 'conditional' view of the difference that space makes. Yet, surprisingly, there has been no real attempt to bring their arguments into some sort of productive conjunction. Beginning with an oblique and slightly ill-tempered exchange back in the mid-1980s (Harvey, 1987; Sayer, 1987), both authors have steadfastly held to their respective positions on space.[4] In the case of Harvey this has involved a string of papers and books that make virtually no reference to Sayer or to critical realism and concede no ground to them either. In Sayer's case this has involved several indirect and direct refutations of Harvey's position, most recently in his *Realism and Social Science* (2000, in which a whole chapter is devoted to further elaborating the arguments on space first made in the 1985 essay). Meanwhile, though many commentators have analysed Harvey's and Sayer's works separately, virtually none have sought to consider them together. This lack of a sustained Sayer–Harvey dialogue about space is a third reason why I seek to forge one in this chapter.[5]

But what kind of dialogue? Clearly, my title speaks to a desire to move beyond the seeming stand-off between Harvey and Sayer. I use the word 'seeming' advisedly. Much of the recent discussion about the Marxism-critical realism relation – particularly as it has appeared in the pages of *Capital and Class* – has been fairly antagonistic, with Marxists in particular taking an aggressive stance towards their perceived critical realist 'rivals' – see, for example, Gunn (1989) and Roberts (1999). While Harvey and Sayer are hardly representative of the wider currents of either Marxism or critical realism, I want to use this opportunity to suggest that, on space at least, their positions are not necessarily antithetical. My strategy, broadly speaking, will be to 'split the difference' between the two thinkers in order, however modestly, to generate less heat and more light in the debate over space (cf. Couzens-Hoy, 1989). At first sight this may seem an unlikely strategy: after all, aren't Harvey's and Sayer's views on space mirror opposites? As we'll see, my answer to this question is 'no' because (i) Sayer's arguments about space have been routinely misunderstood and misrepresented (not least by Harvey) and because (ii) once Sayer's actual position is established the remaining differences with Harvey can be seen as synergistic not simply antithetical. Splitting the difference between Harvey and Sayer does not, therefore, imply some woolly compromise or hasty synthesis in which the insights of each are watered down and diluted with generous doses of the other. Rather, as we shall see, my tack is to argue that *both* thinkers are saying something right about space: that is, the difference that space makes can be necessary *and/or* conditional since there is nothing contradictory about holding to either or both positions simultaneously.[6]

My argument is organised as follows. I begin with some general comments about space in order to identify those conceptions Harvey and Sayer both dissent from. Having thus narrowed the terrain of discussion, I then go on to summarise the different views of both men. This done, I show that (i) many of the differences between the two on the difference that space makes are more apparent than real and (ii) that we do not have to conceive of their remaining disagreements as an either/or choice between rival conceptions of space. At a more general level, I hope to show that Harvey and Sayer actually have something useful to learn from each other, in Harvey's case regarding the limits of his own views on space, and in Sayer's case regarding the limits and possibilities of relational and dialectical thinking.

Conceptions of space

In order to lay the groundwork for the discussion to follow, it is worth reflecting on what we might mean by the term 'space'. If, as Soja (1989, 1996) insists, space is now 'on the agenda' among an unprecedented number of social researchers, then presumably they have a fairly secure understanding of what the spatial is all about. Would that this were so. Ironically, the proliferation of references to space across the human sciences has been achieved through attachment to an unexamined and problematic conception of spatiality. This is clearest in the current penchant for spatial metaphors – particularly among analysts of culture and identity – where terms like 'displacement', 'location', 'positionality' and 'nomadism' have become common currency. As Smith and Katz (1993: 69) observe, 'Metaphor works by invoking one meaning system to explain or clarify another': it assumes that the 'source domain' for the metaphor – in this case space – is well understood. But space is arguably not at all well understood by many of those who are currently so fond of talking about it. In fact, though it is frequently not realised, many of the metaphorical and literal references to space that currently abound are rooted in a hoary and seemingly common-sense conception of spatiality: that is, 'space as a field, [a] container, [and] a co-ordinate system of discrete and mutually exclusive locations' (ibid.: 75). Arguably, it is precisely because the discourse about space is so underdeveloped that this notion of *absolute space* is rearing its head again some two centuries after Descartes, Kant, Newton and others first formalised it. This notion is problematic for several reasons, but chief among them is the fact that space is severed from socio-economic and political processes (which are deemed merely to occur 'in and across' space); consequently, it makes no difference at all (since it is seen as simply an 'empty' matrix).

So what alternative conceptions of space are available? One well-known (though seemingly not well used) alternative is a *relative* view of space, tracing a lineage back to Einstein, Bohm and other physicists. As Harvey (1997: 22) observes, 'In this view, space . . ., although . . . still [a] container . . ., [is] not neutral with respect to the processes . . . [it] contain[s]'. Since space is, here, 'seen to vary depending upon the nature of the processes under consideration' (ibid.), the relative view has two advantages over the absolute view from the perspective of someone insistent that space matters. First, space is seen as a mutable social construction, not something passive *vis-à-vis* the processes it serves as an 'arena' for. Second, space is therefore seen to be internally related to these processes not an optional or external 'add-on'. However, this said, the difference that space makes from the relative perspective is still rather weak. First, as in the absolute view, space remains a container. Second, as such it is seen to express but not to modify the processes producing it.

This brings us to perhaps the 'strongest' conception of space currently available and the one which, as we shall see, Harvey and Sayer both adhere to (despite their other differences). It is a conception of space which, despite being fairly old, is favoured by only a few researchers in social science today. This *relational* view of space can be traced back to (at least) Leibnitz and finds twentieth-century expression in the work of A. N. Whitehead and other process-philosophers. Here different economic, social and political processes are seen to produce their own spaces. But, in turn, space is not seen simply as the 'outcome' of these essentially non-spatial processes. Instead, space (like time) is also considered 'constitutive *of* [these] . . . processes' (Harvey, 1997: 23): that is, space is seen to materially affect and alter the way these processes actually work. There is, incidentally, no question here of implying that space has effects 'in and of itself'. This would be to flip from seeing space as a reflex of supposedly 'deeper' processes to an equally extreme position that we might call 'spatial fetishism' (Anderson, 1973). Against such antinomian thinking, the relational view asks us to see space as *both* medium and outcome, as consequence *and* cause – which is why Soja (1980), for example, chooses throughout his work to talk of an indissoluble 'socio-spatial dialectic'. Clearly, the relational view makes a set of ontologically bold claims about the difference that space makes. If human activities of all kinds are considered to be always already spatial *to their very core*, then the relational view mandates at least two possible epistemological-cum-theoretical stances on space's material significance. The first stance is to say that 'since it is impossible to conceptualise . . . processes and structures outside their spatial form and spatial implications, then the latter must also be incorporated into our initial formulations and definitions, into our basic concepts' (Massey 1985: 18).[7] The second, less exacting stance is to say that while space matters it must be possible to abstract from space in order to specify the nature of economic, social and political processes. Otherwise, analysts are faced with so many geographical contingencies, variations and modifications at the start of the analysis that they are forced to wallow in an idiographic morass. In this view, then, it is frequently necessary and permissible to theorise relations, processes and structures *as if* they had little or no spatial integument, prior to investigating the particular configurations those relations, processes and structures assume in given times and places.[8]

So far so good. We are now in a position to look more closely at what is at stake in the differences between Harvey and Sayer on space. Of the two stances on space mandated by the relational view, Harvey takes the former and Sayer the latter. As we shall see, from the perspective of Sayer it is Harvey's Marxism that leads him to draw erroneous conclusions about the difference space makes. Likewise, we'll see that from Harvey's vantage point it is Sayer's critical realism that forces him to under-estimate the difference that space makes. This Marxism–critical realism stand-off is, I think, more apparent than real in this particular instance. Though Harvey's specific brand of Marxism is, philosophically speaking, irreducible to the tenets of Sayer's realism, there is a far larger middle ground on the question of space than there at first sight seems.

Marxism, Harvey and the theorisation of space

Preliminaries

Harvey's *oeuvre* is, as already noted, doubly distinctive. First, he is one of a very few living Marxists who bases his work almost exclusively on insights drawn directly from Marx's later political economic writings.[9] Since his first formal engagement with Marx in *Social Justice and the City* (1973) Harvey has, if you like, chosen to bypass much of twentieth-century Marxist thought in the belief that the *Grundrisse, Capital, Theories of Surplus Value* and other late Marxist texts can still speak to us powerfully today without the benefit of interpretations provided by his epigones.[10] Second, Harvey is one of an even smaller number of Marxists to take space seriously – indeed, he is perhaps the pre-eminent Marxist theorist of space in the Anglophone world. Within geography several Marxists have directly followed his lead – chief among them Neil Smith and Erik Swyngedouw – and he is perhaps the discipline's most celebrated intellectual. However, it is a testament to the extraordinary space-blindness of the Marxist tradition that it is only in the last few years that his ideas have had a major impact outside geography and urban studies.[11] Indeed, when, some two decades ago, he published what remains one of the most complete and original studies in Marxist political economy – *The Limits to Capital* (Harvey, 1982/1999)[12] – most Marxists passed over the geographical aspects of the book as if puzzled and bemused by them. So how does Harvey view space and its importance? And how does he integrate it into Marx's political economy?[13]

Marx, like virtually all his epigones, tended to bracket out questions of geography and theorised capitalism as if it operated in a spaceless world.[14] Though his writings are peppered with comments and asides about localities, regions and nations, geography tends to be treated as an 'unnecessary complication' that can be abstracted from in formal theory construction. Marx was not necessarily wrong to treat it in this way. First, the dynamics of capital accumulation appear to make time, temporality and change – rather than geography – the fundamental dimension of economic and social life. As Harvey (1985a: 144–5) avers,

> The aim and objective of those engaged in the circulation of capital must be, after all, to command surplus labour *time* and convert it into profit within the *socially necessary turnover time*. From the standpoint of the circulation of capital, therefore, space appears in the first instance as a mere inconvenience, a barrier to be overcome.

Second, as Harvey (1989a: 5) readily admits,

> the insertion of concepts and space relations . . . into any social theory has the awkward habit of paralysing that theory's central propositions . . . Whenever social theorists actively interrogate the meaning of . . . spatial categories either they are forced to [make] so many ad hoc adjustments that their theory splinters into incoherency or they are forced to rework very basic propositions.

In light of all this, Harvey's long-standing ambition to show that 'space relations and geographical phenomena are fundamental material attributes that have to be present at the very beginning of the analysis' (Harvey, 1985b: 33) may seem extraordinarily difficult to realise. The key challenge, as Harvey recognises in most of his published writings, is threefold. First, how can space be integrated into Marx's political economy in non-arbitrary ways so that geography becomes genuinely *internal* to the argument? Second, how can space be shown to be not just internal to capital accumulation but also a 'fundamental and "active moment"' (ibid.): that is, a *necessary* aspect of the way capitalism works and might be transcended? Finally, and most challenging of all, given that space is about difference and particularity – London, for example, is not Lahore – how can it be incorporated into a general theory of capital accumulation without rendering such a theory incoherent? In Harvey's estimation, the work he's published since *Social Justice and the City* addresses all three challenges in defensible and illuminating ways. As he puts it in a recent reflection (Harvey, 1999a: xxvii), his Marxism has 'pioneered [an] . . . understanding . . . of how capital accumulation operates not only in but through the active production of . . . space.' In the remainder of this section I want to take up each challenge in turn and show what makes Harvey's take on space so distinctive. First, though, we need to make a philosophical detour. For without saying something about Harvey's self-declared ontology and epistemology it becomes difficult to grasp how he works space into Marx's substantive theory of capitalism.

Philosophical precepts

Until relatively recently, Harvey was like the later Marx when it came to specifying his own philosophical commitments: that is, these commitments were implicit and had to be teased out of his substantive work. Thus, in the introduction to *The Limits* for example, he preferred not 'to puff... [it out] ... with learned-sounding comments on . . . epistemology and ontology, . . . [and] on the "true" nature of dialectics . . . [but] to let the methods of both enquiry and presentation speak for themselves' (1982: xxxi). Similarly, on those rare occasions where he did venture opinion on his way of working his comments were typically brief (cf. Harvey, 1985b: Introduction; Harvey and Scott, 1987; Harvey, 1989a: Introduction). However, this all changed with the publication of *Justice, Nature and the Geography of Difference* (1996) where Part I is given over entirely to the precepts of historical-geographical materialism. Of course, we cannot assume that Harvey's philosophical self-assessment is accurate or complete (indeed Sayer, as we'll see, thinks Harvey does not fully understand his own onto-epistemology). However, because my aim in this sub-section is simply to explain Harvey's conception of space as *he* understands it, I shall take him at his word for the time being.[15]

Since most of Harvey's work is geared to making sense of political economic realities, his various comments on ontology and epistemology are not offered as *a priori* or 'first philosophical' statements. Rather, they are *a posteriori* statements about what must be the case if Marx's and his own ideas are to be about a capitalist world that is real not just some figment of the Marxist theoretical imagination (cf. Gibson-Graham, 1996). At the heart of Harvey's worldview is the idea that knowledge and the realities it purports to conceptually capture are related but not the same. For example, recalling Marx's distinction between the method of inquiry and the mode of presentation, Harvey (1982/1999: 38) reminds readers of *The Limits* that the task is 'to appropriate the material in detail to trace out their inner connexion. Only after this work is done can the actual movement be adequately described.' For Harvey this difference-in-relation between the world and knowledge of the world must hold for several reasons. First, 'to superimpose a particular mental logic on the world as an act of mind *over* matter' (Harvey, 1996: 56) amounts to an idealism wherein thought makes the world in its own image – a patently absurd position. Though Harvey readily – and correctly – concedes that knowledge is performative ('Observation of the world is . . . inevitably intervention in the world', ibid.) and while he acknowledges that what 'we call "facts" and "data" are by no means independent of the theories which inform them' (Harvey, 1989a: 7), he is nonetheless critical of the kind of full-blooded nominalism in which theorists are deemed to be trapped in their own conceptual universes. Second, Harvey is equally critical of the idea that the world compulsively determines thought about it (what Bhaskar (1989: 157) has called the 'ontic fallacy'). If, in this way, knowledge (the transitive dimension) is seen to lack even relative autonomy from the world (the intransitive dimension), then the researcher becomes nothing more than a passive conduit of sense experiences. Moreover, this kind of crude realism – in which, effectively, thought and reality are collapsed one into the other – potentially encourages a shallow, fetishistic knowledge of the world which is limited to 'surface appearances'. If the realm of observable, empirical things were synonymous with the real *tout court* then such knowledge might be adequate. But for Harvey, as for Marx, it is precisely because there is *more* to reality than this that the thought-real distinction is as irreducible as it is vital. For the power of careful theoretical work, in Harvey's view, is that it can help us to see non-observable processes that *are ontologically real but really invisible*. Consequently, Harvey sees the knowledge–reality relation as recursive: 'we think before we act but learn to think through doing' (1989a: 3). That is, experience and practice tell us that while theory and theorists are part of the world, they are always non-identical with it. It is this difference-in-relation that sets parameters to the possibilities of knowledge.

More technically, Harvey's epistemology and ontology are <u>avowedly dialectical</u>. Since dialectics is 'possibly the most contentious topic in Marxist thought' (Bhaskar, 1989: 115), it is as well to be absolutely clear about what the term means in this particular context. Drawing upon Ollman's (1980, 1993) germinal interpretations of Marx, leavened with the process-philosophy of Leibnitz, Whitehead and others, Harvey argues that social reality is – or at least significant portions of it are – dialectical. In the chapter devoted to dialectics in *Justice, Nature and the Geography of Difference*, he explains this as follows: 'there is a deep ontological principle involved here, for dialecticians in effect hold that elements, things, structures and systems do not exist outside of or prior to the processes, flows and relations that create, sustain or undermine them' (Harvey, 1996: 49). For Harvey at least three things follow. First, the 'things' and 'structures' we see in the world are in fact particular 'permanences' that have crystallised out of ongoing processes and flows (economic, social, political, etc.). That is, 'the material world is *simultaneously* both a thing and a process' (Merrifield, 1993: 320). Second, flows and things, fluxes and permanences are internally related (which is why Ollman (1980) has famously referred to Marx's concepts as being like bats: for in them one can see both birds and mice, they're neither one thing nor the other). That is, the material world is relationally constituted; it is not a collection of discrete things, events and entities which just happen to 'interact'. Finally, for Harvey the motor of change in this gestalt process–thing/flux–permanence world is contradiction: 'In the dialectical view, opposing forces, themselves constituted out of processes, in turn become particular nodal points for further patterns of transformative activity' (1996: 54). Where analytical ontologies look for causes and their effects (relations of *betweenness*), Harvey's looks for tensions and feedbacks emergent from complex, continuous processes and their material forms (relations of *withinness*).

Clearly, whether or not Harvey has 'correctly' grasped Marx's own ontological stance is a moot point. More interesting is Harvey's treatment of
Hegel. Perhaps concerned that any close association with the 'mighty
thinker' is strategically bad for the image of historical-geographical materialism, Harvey has long maintained that Marx's dialectics has a 'different
grounding' (1989a: 10) to that of Hegel's.[16] At one level, of course, this
claim is perfectly reasonable. After all, Hegel was an idealist whereas Marx
was a materialist who insisted on the difference between the real and thought
about the real (Murray, 1988). But more than this, Harvey seems to regard
the Hegelian dialectic as closed, rigid and 'rock-ribbed' (Ollman, 1993: 10;
see Harvey, 1989a: 10–11, 1996: 48–9, 57, 1999b: 558). Ontologically this
means that, for Harvey, Marx accents process, change and complexity far
more than Hegel ever did. Likewise, epistemologically, any attempt to represent this dialectically dynamic world must, he maintains, be supple enough
to constantly 'spin out new lines of argument' (Harvey, 1989a: 11) and 'preclude . . . closure . . . at any particular point' (1982/1999: 446). Implicitly,
Harvey sees Hegel's dialectical method as too static and too committed to
mapping an *already*-constituted 'whole' to be serviceable for his historical-
geographical materialism.

However, it is precisely in his epistemological dialectics that, in my view,
Harvey is most productively influenced by Hegel. In brief, it seems to me
that Harvey takes important lessons Marx learned from Hegel's *Logic* and
builds them directly into his dialectical epistemology. Because Harvey has
never been a close student of Hegel, I doubt whether he's completely aware
of the influence the *Logic* has had – via Marx – on his own work (particularly
in *The Limits* and *The Urbanisation of Capital*). Accordingly, I have elsewhere
drawn upon Chris Arthur, Patrick Murray and Tony Smith, to show in
detail the Hegelian provenance of Harvey's dialectical method (Castree,
1995). Put simply, Harvey follows Marx in seeking to show *systematically* the
internal and necessary relations between what, at first sight, might appear to be
quite distinct people, processes, places and things. As we'll see momentarily,
Harvey incorporates space into Marx's political economy in precisely this
systematic-dialectical way. The essence of this approach is neither inductive
nor deductive. Instead it works in something like the following way.

It is a truism to say that social life is what Harvey (1989a: 8) calls 'a complex configuration' or what Marx famously described as 'the unity of the
diverse'. Accordingly, theorists and researchers have only the power of
abstraction to make sense of this complexity. Here it is important to recognise
the non-identity of thought and the real. For Harvey (1982: 450), theory
aims 'to create frameworks of understanding, an elaborated conceptual
apparatus, with which to grasp the most significant relationships at work
within the intricate dynamics of social transformation'. This must proceed
by *abstracting from* 'the particularities of historical geography' (Harvey and
Scott, 1987: 224). So how are we to represent a changing world of internally
related phenomena, particularly one where many key processes are not

phenomenally apparent? Harvey's answer, discernible both from his scattered comments on epistemology (especially 1989a; and Harvey and Scott, 1987) and his theoretical practices, is as follows. First, *after* the process of inquiry – 'the detailed appropriation of historical-geographical materials' (Harvey and Scott: 225) – is complete, the analyst traces 'the path of *descent* from the complexity of everyday life to a simple set of concrete representations of the way material life is reproduced' (Harvey, 1989a: 9). By concrete representations, Harvey means concepts like commodity and money that refer to phenomenally observable things. Second, though, close scrutiny of these concepts reveals a set of 'contradictions, antagonisms and oppositions' (ibid.: 11) which imply that the phenomena to which they refer are not self-sufficient. That is, the theoretical analysis is *necessarily* propelled forward in order to seek out things, processes and relations that *must* exist to 'deal' with the 'in-sufficiency' of the initial concepts posited. As Harvey (1982: xvi) puts it in *The Limits*, 'At each step in the formulation of the theory, we encounter antagonisms that build into intriguing configurations of . . . contradictions. The resolution of each merely provokes the formulation of new contradictions or their translation onto some fresh terrain.' In particular, the analysis of concrete representations is led to identify 'non-observable concepts . . . such as value' (Harvey, 1989a: 9) that describe virtual relations which, while invisible, can account for or arise from already-identified contradictions: 'explanatory power becomes the central criterion of acceptability' (ibid.: 10). Finally, because this systematic-dialectical method is a 'logical device' (ibid.) it should not – as a mode of presentation and explanation – be conflated with the reality it represents. After all, the cognitive content of the concepts Marx and Harvey throw out early on in texts like *Capital* and *The Limits* is necessarily incomplete. It is only as the theoretical account unfolds dialectically that 'what appears as a secure conceptual apparatus from one vantage point turns out to be partial and one-sided on further investigation' (ibid.: 11). As Chris Arthur (1993: 86) has observed, collapsing epistemological into ontological dialectics risks 'positing as real . . . [w]hat are in truth insubstantial phases of a dialectical presentation'. The dialectical presentation is thus emphatically *about* the world but not *isomorphic with it*.[17]

Theorising space: three moves

Our philosophical detour complete, we are now in a position to fully grasp Harvey's conception of space. I want to explicate the three elements of this conception by reference to just one aspect of Harvey's wide-ranging attempt to spatialise historical materialism: that concerning what he has famously called capitalism's 'spatial fix'.[18] The argument is worked out most fully in *The Limits* (chs 13 and 14) but can be found in summary form in 'The geopolitics of capitalism' and 'The geography of capital accumulation' (Harvey, 1985a and b; see also Harvey, 1988).

(i) First, why is space internal to the dynamics of capital accumulation? Harvey's answer is straightforward and relatively uncontroversial. Summarising Marx, he argues that capitalism takes the following contradictory form:

$$M - C \ldots P \overset{LP}{\underset{MP}{\ldots}} C' - M + m, \text{ etc.}$$

This system of production is (i) inherently growth orientated (ii) rests on inter-capitalist competition and class struggle and (iii) is necessarily technologically and organisationally dynamic. For Harvey, Marx's genius was to develop a battery of concepts (value, abstract and concrete labour, labour power, etc.) which showed that the 'inner contradictions' of this system made it intrinsically prone to crises of over-accumulation. There's nothing surprising in any of these claims. Geographically speaking, Harvey's first move is to simply point out that this system of production – like any other – must take on a spatial form at any given historical moment. In basic terms, this means a set of territorial production complexes (cities, regions, nations, etc.) and a transport and communications network linking them. If, as Harvey insists, capital is a process then it can only circulate in and through a material landscape which, if you like, act as its arteries. In the words of one of Harvey's former students, Andrew Merrifield (1993: 521):

> Capital is an inexorably circulatory process . . . which fixates itself as a thing in space and so begets a built environment. The fixity nature (the thing quality) of the geographical landscape is necessary to permit the flow . . . of capital; and vice versa . . . [H]ence . . . [sp]ace can be taken as a specific *form* emergent from an apparent stopping of, or as one specific *moment* in, the dynamics of capitalis[m].

Or, to put it more plainly, 'Capital . . . must represent itself in the form of a physical landscape created in its own image' (Harvey, 1985b: 43). In effect, one fraction of capital (infrastructures, built environments, etc.) must circulate at a much slower pace than fixed capital if the other fractions are going to be able to circulate at all.

(ii) To say that space is internal to capitalism in this way is relatively unproblematic. But it is also to say very little substantive about capitalist space since, presumably, *all* modes of production construct their own 'rational' and distinctive landscapes. This brings us to Harvey's second thesis on space: that it is – in a non-trivial sense – a *necessary* aspect or moment of capital accumulation. This thesis devolves into two others: first, that capitalism's survival is partly *dependent* upon the production of space; and second that produced space decisively *alters* the course of capitalist development.[19] Harvey makes good on the first argument in the following way. Since 'the tendency towards over-accumulation can never be eliminated under capitalism . . . The only question . . . is how [it] . . . can be expressed, contained, absorbed or managed in ways that do not threaten the . . . social order' (1988: 177). So how is over-accumulation dealt with? One strategy – and a painful one – is devaluation of the sort most Western nations experienced for two decades post-1973. Another is macro-economic management of the kind that, in its Keynesian incarnation, sustained the long post-war boom up until the early 1970s. Then, third, there's temporal displacement or what Harvey calls capital's 'temporal fix'. Here crises are staved off by switching capital from immediate uses into longer-term investments like lending/debt. But where does space figure in all this? Centrally in Harvey's view. Historical evidence suggests that during periods of actual or incipient over-accumulation large quantities of capital are 'switched' into constructing built environments of production and consumption (what Harvey (1985b: 6) calls the 'secondary circuit of capital'). This can take the form of external geographical expansion (capital lent or invested in new markets and new production centres) or internal reorganisations of the capitalist space economy (the rise and fall of established cities and regions or investment in new transport and communications infrastructures). In effect, then, 'capital buys itself time out of the space it conquers' (Harvey, 1985a: 156). The contradictions of capital accumulation *compel* structural tendencies to produce space as a strategy of crisis-avoidance.

Once produced though, space is not passive in regard to the processes it arises from. Rather (and this, for Harvey, is the second aspect of space's 'necessary' role), it becomes an 'active moment' within the dynamics of accumulation. To begin with, the landscapes inherited from earlier rounds of accumulation can ultimately act as material barriers to further accumulation. We have here a contradiction between capital fixity and capital motion. As Harvey (1985b: 43) puts it, 'The produced geographical landscape constituted by fixed and immobile capital is both the crowning glory of past capitalist development and a prison that inhibits further progress of accumulation precisely because it creates spatial barriers where there were none before'. Capital must thus devalue a part of itself if crises – regional or even global – are not to take hold. However, this said, in the long run the reorganisation of the space economy only widens and deepens the terrain upon which capitalism's contradictions unfold. Since, for Harvey, crises cannot in the end be avoided, the 'spatial fix' ultimately entails the production of multiple regional and national production-consumption centres warring one against the other 'over who is to bear the brunt of the crisis [: T]he search for a "spatial fix" takes a viciously competitive and perhaps even violent turn' (1985a: 157).

(iii) Finally, if, in the two ways explained immediately above, Harvey integrates space as a necessary aspect of Marx's general theory of capital, how does he deal with the fact that space is, in his view, 'always the realm of the concrete and the particular'?[20] For some commentators, it is simply incoherent to 'make universal generalisations about the evident unique particularities of space' (1985b: 45). For Harvey, though, it is not. His point is not that theory should be able to comment *in detail* on each and every locally/regionally/nationally embedded capitalist economy. The level of abstraction at which he himself has worked typically precludes such specificity.[21] Rather, his point is that a study of the way 'processes of capital circulation bring the unique qualities of . . . given places . . . into a framework of universal generality' (ibid.) allows us to see how the *same* processes work themselves out in *different* places. As Harvey's own work suggests, peppered as it is with supporting empirical evidence, it is possible to see how general tendencies towards 'capital switching', 'spatial fixes', 'spatial competition' and the like can be seen to underlie similar developments in seemingly distinct places. To regard particular spaces as *simply* separate and unique one from another is, for Harvey, to miss the 'phantom-like' value relations and processes conjoining the here and there in a contradictory global unity.

Realism and Sayer: the theoretical indifference of space?

Preliminaries

Like Harvey, Andrew Sayer has made a series of outstanding contributions to the recent development of political-economic thought. And, like Harvey, Sayer's geographical background has disposed him to look closely at the difference that space makes.[22] However, these similarities aside, his contributions have been of a rather different order to those of Harvey. First, though broadly sympathetic to Marxism, Sayer's substantive theoretical and empirical research has sought to disclose the limits of historical materialist thinking. His major statement in this regard – *Radical Political Economy: A Critique* (Sayer, 1995) – is an exceptionally lucid attempt to show how Marxism gets us so far *and* falls apart.[23] Second, where only a small part of Harvey's corpus has been given over to an explicit consideration of philosophical questions, Sayer is well known for his deep and sustained engagement with such questions. Together, his influential *Method in Social Science* (1992) and his new book *Realism and Social Science* (2000) are an effort to place social research on firmer intellectual foundations. Through a careful analysis of the practice of social research, what Sayer aims for in both books is a philosophy *of* and *for* the human sciences. Like one of his mentors, Roy Bhaskar, Sayer concludes that only a critical realist philosophy can help us make proper sense of what both the social world and research upon it are all about. Unlike Bhaskar though (*Reclaiming Reality* (1989) excepted), Sayer's writings are a model of accessibility and he has become a leading advocate of critical realism in Anglophone social science today.

One of his most distinctive, influential and even controversial philosophical arguments relates to space. The controversy, as I will show in this section of the chapter, stems less from what Sayer has actually said and more from how he has been interpreted by various commentators. For these commentators, the essence of Sayer's argument is this: the ontological nature of space is such that it is virtually impossible to theorise about space. As he puts it (2000: 128), in seeming confirmation of this argument, 'theorising about space largely requires an abstraction from particular spatial configurations'. In other words, Sayer is frequently seen to advocate the view that the difference that space makes is largely *contingent*; its effects, supposedly, cannot be theorised in any substantive sense as part of the necessary properties of things, relations or processes. Consequently, in Sayer's view (or so it is often claimed), space's influence can *only* be disclosed through concrete research on a case-by-case basis.

If Sayer did indeed hold to this 'conditional' view of space then it would clearly stand in sharp contrast with Harvey's 'essential' view of space. What is more, because Sayer derives his argument not from first principles but by looking at existing attempts to understand the difference that space makes, the implication is that Harvey has misunderstood his own philosophical positions and theoretical practices. Though I do want to insist that Harvey has, in part, misrepresented his own conception of space, I also want to argue that Sayer does *not* simply see space as a contingent domain which cannot be theorised. His view of space is, in fact, more complex and nuanced than this. In clearing the ground for (in his terms) a less 'chaotic' and more 'rational' conception of space, Sayer's arguments can only be grasped once we lay to rest the myth that his is a purely conditional view. Let's now try to understand these arguments on their own terms.[24]

Philosophical precepts

As with Harvey, it is useful to begin with Sayer's philosophical commitments. These are far easier to identify than in Harvey's case (see Sayer, 1992, 2000). Indeed, because Sayer's popularisation of critical realism is now so well known I'll take the liberty of offering a highly succinct restatement of his epistemological and ontological beliefs. Like Bhaskar, Sayer insists on a fundamental distinction between the transitive and intransitive domains. Seeking to avoid both the epistemic and ontic fallacies, Sayer argues that the social world exists independently of what social researchers happen to think about it even though (i) it can only be known under particular socially-constructed descriptions and (ii) those descriptions may materially alter the world they purport merely to 're-present'. This combination of ontological realism and epistemic relativity does not, however, leave Sayer stranded on the horns of a philosophical dilemma. In his view, it is precisely the intransigence of the world – and our experience of having some of our beliefs rendered practically incorrect – that permits us to adjudicate among competing theories and representations of the same reality (and thus avoid judgemental relativism). Drawing on Bhaskar's stratified, depth-ontology,

Sayer makes a now familiar distinction between the real, the actual and the empirical, the implication being that wholly observation-based epistemologies are misleading in a world where myriad processes and relations are not phenomenally apparent. Moreover, this ontology is non-atomistic. It posits a relationally constituted world of *internal* and *external* relations. The former refers to entities whose existence and nature is attributable to their relations with other entities; the latter refers to the (usually contingent) coming together of nominally independent entities in a particular situation. Both types of relation are substantial rather than merely formal. The powers and liabilities of a specific entity or process arising by virtue of its internal relationality (the real) may (or may not) be activated depending on the external relations it enters into in specific geo-temporal settings (the actual). Moreover, 'emergent' effects may arise from the articulation of two or more different entities or processes. Whether or not any of this is observed in research (the empirical) is a separate question.

Because this complex, layered and only partly observable social world is an 'open system', Sayer (1995: 5) emphasises the use of 'abstractions [to] give us a grasp of one kind of complexity by abstracting from another'. Here his thinking resonates with Harvey's in all sorts of ways. 'Rational abstractions' should, as it were, cut into reality 'at the joints' and 'distinguish incidental from essential characteristics' (Sayer, 1992: 88). This is what defines both their cognitive power and epistemic limits. For they identify ontologically coherent 'lumps' of reality but also, necessarily, abstract *from* that reality and so, at one level, do violence to that which is represented. Thought and the world are, in other words, related but different. Indeed, because social reality is typically so complex, 'neither objects nor their relations are given to us transparently; their identification is an achievement and must be worked for' (ibid.). 'Abstract research' – that is, theoretical research – should thus be geared to dissecting social reality into its constituent parts, processes, relations and systems. This involves the quest for 'necessary relations' which *must* be part of the thing being analysed. As part of this, 'retroduction' is used to identify-in-thought the usually invisible causal powers and affordances intrinsic to particular parts, processes, relations and systems.[25] Whether and how these powers and affordances are realised is a contingent question which it is the job of 'concrete research' – that is, theoretically informed empirical research – to fathom. Here, we should note, causality in the world is not about the 'interaction' of different 'variables' or 'things'. Rather, it is a relational outcome wherein multiple mechanisms act in concert to produce specific events. Overall, then, in explaining these events, the research process passes through a concrete → abstract → concrete movement. Starting with a reality that is a 'unity of the diverse', abstraction is used to disaggregate the situation into its 'one-sided' aspects prior to returning to the concrete armed with concepts able to make sense of its complexity.

As noted, there is much here that resonates with Harvey's worldview. However, there are also important points of difference – both apparent and real – and several of them concern space. It is to Sayer's realist view of space that I now turn.

Putting space in its place

If, as Sayer insists, theory ought to grasp the 'necessary relations' or properties that are an indissoluble – or internal – part of an entity or process, can space be theorised? In the interests of clarity (and symmetry) I'll unfold Sayer's answer in relation to the three aspects of space I explored in Harvey's case. Along the way, I will endeavour to correct a common misunderstanding of Sayer on space. It should be noted at the outset that where Harvey's argument is adumbrated in substantive-theoretical terms, Sayer's is expounded in a more philosophical register.

(i) Like Harvey, Sayer is critical of the absolute view of space (1985: 51). He sees space as both a relational entity (e.g. 'Space only exists through its constituents' (2000: 111)) and one which is always already an aspect of social life (e.g. 'there is no such thing as non-spatial processes' (ibid.: 121)). This spatiality of social life includes the physical form of things (people, built environments, etc.) and the relations between them. Indeed, following Harré (1970), Sayer makes the case that space is both cause and effect in social life.[26] His argument, explicated in highly abstract terms, is as follows. Consider entities **ABC**. Each entity has shape and extension and, together, they stand in a 'spatial relationship' (Sayer, 2000: 111). We cannot, Sayer argues, understand the difference the space constituted by and between **ABC** makes 'until we know what kinds of things, with what causal powers or liabilities, A, B or C are' (ibid.). But, whatever their nature, it remains the case that 'although space only exists through its constituents, it is not reducible to them' (ibid.). Thus **BAC** is not the same as **ABC** even though the constituents are. For Sayer it is the nature of **ABC** in conjunction with their spatial relations that defines the difference that space makes. 'Aspatial' processes, relations or entities are, therefore, literally unthinkable and, '*depending on the nature of the constituents*, their spatial relations may make a crucial difference' (1985: 52). So, to summarise, at a general level Sayer agrees with Harvey that space is internal to all aspects of social life and that it *may* make a real difference to how social life unfolds. But the similarities, it seems, end here because as we'll now see Sayer argues that this is not quite the same as saying that space can – or should – be theorised.

(ii) Where Harvey claims that space is – in a non-trivial sense – ontologically necessary to capitalism's survival, Sayer argues that claims to necessity about space usually cannot be made in this way. Note that, contra his critics,

Sayer does not deny the possibility that space can or should be theorised as a necessary aspect of social life. On the contrary, he maintains that space may be essential to the powers and effects of some things. In these cases, theory can either include information about actual spatial extensions, forms or relations or else 'build . . . in . . . an assumption about the form of the particular . . . spatial setting that happens to exist, so as to work out what would happen to a process of interest'[27] (Sayer, 2000: 122–3); on this latter kind of theoretical work in political economy see Sheppard and Barnes (1990). However, these cases excepted, Sayer's point is that claims to necessity about space in social, economic and political theory are 'characteristically vague' (Sayer, 2000: 123). That is, one can rarely say anything *substantive* about the difference that space makes at the theoretical level.

Sayer bases this argument on the way space has been treated in a plethora of substantive studies. Reviewing the work of leading socio-spatial theorists such as Castells, Lefebvre, Soja and, of course, Harvey, Sayer insists that they 'have found it difficult to say much that is specific about space' (2000: 109). Concepts like the 'spatial fix', he goes on, are effectively 'contentless abstraction[s]' (1985: 59) that make claims about necessity in only the most general[28] of senses. The reason for this is not any intellectual inadequacy on the part of theorists like Harvey but – and here Sayer makes a particularly strong claim – 'an inevitable consequence of the nature of space' which poses 'ontological limits to theorising' (2000: 109, 126).

What does Sayer mean? Following Harré's (1970) 'principle of spatial indifference', Sayer (2000: 116) explains that 'one of the main lessons of attempts to theorise . . . spatiality has been the recognition of the "spatial flexibility" of most actors and institutions, that is, their ability to maintain their integrity and operate in a variety of different settings' (ibid.). Put differently, in Sayer's estimation the fact that the *same* sorts of processes or entities can survive in *different* contexts means that the latter cannot, *inter alia*, be factored into theoretical work. For instance, on this view, while capitalism undoubtedly has a geography that is internal – and even necessary in a non-trivial sense – to its functioning, Sayer's point is that theory can say little specific about this geography. Capitalism can exist in and through a virtually endless array of spatial forms and relations meaning that it is, for Sayer, 'in a sense . . . context-*in*dependen[t]' (ibid.: 117).

None of this, it should be noted, means that space is unimportant or that one can never make theoretical claims about space (though Sayer's critics have often imputed this position to him). On the contrary, 'space *is* certainly important, but to say what that importance consists in we normally have to move to a more concrete kind of analysis where we identify particular kinds of objects, relations and processes constituting it in concrete spatial conjunctures' (ibid.: 112). In short, for Sayer the importance of space is often – but not only – a *contingent* question and it is the task of concrete research to figure out the difference it makes. Contingency here means one or both of two things: first, the specific spatial form a particular thing, relation or process assumes, even though it did not have to assume that form; and second, the particular conjunction of spaces associated with nominally distinct things, relations or processes. It follows from this that, depending on the situation, space may be a wholly contingent and unimportant factor or else a crucial determinant that is a necessary and consequential aspect of something *and* contingently related to other relatively autonomous entities and their spaces.

(iii) In light of (ii) above it is plain to see why Sayer believes it impossible to, in Harvey's words, 'construct a *theory* of the concrete and the particular' (1985a: 144, emphasis added). Quite simply, precisely because space is – ontologically – concrete, particular or otherwise complex and irregular, theory usually cannot 'anticipate its form with some degree of specificity' (Sayer, 2000: 124). Since the necessary relations, powers and liabilities which abstract research seeks to capture can be realised in 'a wide variety of spatial forms' (ibid.: 128) then, ultimately, only concrete research can adequately account for the particular difference that space makes. In terms of representing-in-thought the nature and role of space, for Sayer it is only after abstracting from geography theoretically that we can then return to it (the concrete → abstract → concrete movement) to grasp its true importance.

From antagonism to engagement

So who's right, Harvey or Sayer? Can space be theorised substantively as Harvey insists? Or, as Sayer argues, is it in the nature of space typically, though not always, to preclude such substantive theorisation? Sayer (2000: 128–9) has recently confessed to being 'disappointed by the fact that while [his] formulation [on space] . . . has provoked many brief mentions in the literature, most of them have . . . omitted to provide an argued reply'. Indicative of this is Harvey's reaction to Sayer. Aside from a couple of dismissive rebuffs (Harvey, 1987; Harvey and Scott, 1987), in which Sayer is clearly the target though not mentioned by name, Harvey has made no real attempt to engage with his stance on space. By contrast, we have seen above that Sayer has been very willing to offer an explicit critique of attempts – like Harvey's – to fashion a theory of space. As a result, the debate on space seems to be at something of an impasse. In Harvey and Sayer we have two of the clearest extant statements about the difference that space makes. But, in the absence of attempts to stage a dialogue between the two thinkers, we are, it seems, left with an either/or choice, with little in the way of a middle ground.

Or are we? Having outlined their respective positions on space at length, I now want to suggest that *both* Harvey and Sayer may, in certain crucial respects, be right and that to say this is not at all contradictory. Indeed, this argument is only contradictory if two highly questionable assumptions are made: first, that Harvey and Sayer do, in fact, advocate an essential and conditional view of space respectively; and second, that these two views are, in any case, incompatible. In the previous section I sought to dispel the idea that Sayer only sees space as a conditional factor in social life. On the basis of this, I want, in this section, to look at the remaining real – as opposed to apparent – differences between Harvey and Sayer on space with a view to 'splitting them'.

My argument begins with a simple statement about what, intellectually, both men have in common. Philosophically, both insist on a thought–reality distinction and the irreducibility of epistemology to ontology (and vice versa). Ontologically, both adhere to (i) a relational perspective in opposition to 'common-sense' Cartesian worldviews, (ii) a depth ontology which sees empirical events as but one 'layer' of reality, and (iii) a form of ontological essentialism wherein objects or processes have particular ways of acting as a consequence of their structure or intrinsic nature. Epistemologically, both regard knowledge as being about a material world that it is not, by its very nature, homologous with. Indeed, for both men one of the key 'powers' of disciplined inquiry is to make visible ontologically hidden processes and capacities through the force of abstraction. Finally, in theoretical terms, Harvey and Sayer both distinguish conceptual from empirical research, seeing them as linked but also distinct. By abstracting from a multifaceted world, both see theoretical work as a search for necessary relations internal to ontologically meaningful 'chunks' of reality.

So far so good. What, though, of the remaining philosophical differences? One of these, which I have only alluded to thus far, concerns Harvey's and Sayer's relational ontologies. Throughout his writings Sayer has sought to distinguish a 'bad' from a 'good' notion of internal relations (see especially Sayer, 1995: 26–33). The former he attributes to Marxists like Harvey and Ollman, wherein 'ubiquitous internal relations' are assumed 'in Hegelian fashion' (ibid.: 29). For Sayer, this 'universal internal-relations ontology' (ibid.: 28) is at once exorbitant ('every object is internally related to every other one' (2000: 127)) and 'dogmatic and silly' (1995: 27). As with Harvey's reading of Hegel, whether or not Sayer is right to ultimately attribute this 'universal' notion of internal relations to the German philosopher is moot. What is more important, as I now want to show, is that Sayer has arguably misunderstood the notion of internal relations, at least as it appears in Harvey's work.

Let us look at the supposed shortcomings of the 'bad' version of internal relations. Here, it seems to me, Sayer enters into some confusion even as he makes a set of erstwhile valid arguments. First, Sayer is right to deride the idea that ontologically *everything* is related to everything else. Even if it were true, this idea is banal. However, to my knowledge Harvey and like-minded Marxists have nowhere disagreed with Sayer on this. Second, Sayer argues that such a promiscuous notion of internal relations 'pushes one to the . . . absurd extreme of assuming that everything is . . . specific to the point of being unique, or entirely context dependent' (1995: 28). Again, though,

Marxist geographers like Harvey are very clear that their theoretical claims about space apply to *a multitude of different geographical situations*. Third, as a corollary of his second complaint, Sayer argues that the likes of Harvey misunderstand their own ontology since they theorise a system – capitalism – which has a large 'degree of context independence', existing as it does 'in a vast range of situations' (ibid.). However, once again this is, I think, to misapprehend the Marxian ontology at work here. For it seems to me that one of Harvey's key points is not that a 'context independent' process – capital accumulation – just happens to work itself out in a set of different, contingent settings but, rather, that it *only exists in and through those settings*. In other words, the specific and unique *makes* the general and the universal, and vice versa.

There is, we should note, nothing in this implying that *everything* in the social universe is internal to capital. More straightforwardly, the argument is that myriad different people and things can and do become caught up in general processes of capital circulation – processes that cannot exist except in and through these concrete particulars. We should note also that this notion of internal relations does not at all mitigate against one of the features of Sayer's 'good' version: the ability to distinguish 'external' relations. Nowhere, to my mind, has Harvey ever said or implied that the ontological properties of those peoples and spaces internal to capital are *exhausted* by their capitalist colouration. Indeed, those properties may enhance or counteract pressures arising from the role these peoples and spaces play within capitalism. All Harvey has done throughout his work is to bracket these non-capitalist influences (much like Marx did), not deny their importance.

In light of this, we are better able to appreciate just how (in)accurate Sayer's insistence that space cannot be meaningfully theorised is. As we have seen, Harvey uses systematic dialectics to bring space within the horizon of Marx's political economy. This entails making a set of claims about the necessary and active role space plays within the dynamics of capital accumulation. In Harvey's corpus, space comes to be seen as one key 'moment' within the contradictory logics of capital. Sayer has no particular problem with dialectical reasoning *per se* (indeed, he has never offered any in-depth consideration of it), perhaps because it is a rigorously effective way of exploring those necessary relations existing in the social world. His beef, as noted, is that because the necessary relations that make capital what it is can occur in multiple settings these settings cannot be considered necessary aspects of capital. But it seems to me that this view goes awry in two ways. First, it severs content and form. If, as Harvey insists, geographical space is the material condition and outcome of an ongoing circulation and accumulation process then it *must* be a key element of capitalism. Capital simply could not function without space. Contra Sayer, space is not predominantly the realm of the concrete and particular but a phenomenal form that general processes necessarily assume. Second, I think Sayer is wrong to imply that claims about necessity entail having to say something very *specific* about the things deemed necessary. He is quite right that detailed claims about space cannot be made at the theoretical level (especially the macro-theoretical level). But this does not mean that theoretical statements about space are invariably 'contentless abstractions'. If one thinks it through, for example, Marxian abstractions like commodity, value or labour power are no more 'thick' or 'thin' than an abstraction like 'the spatial fix'. As Harvey's work shows, it is possible to theorise space *and* it is possible to say something meaningful and illuminating about space in the process.

One suspects that the roots of Sayer's misapprehension of Harvey on space is his failure to engage the question to dialectics in any sustained way. Sayer typically employs a rather prosaic, non-technical concept of dialectics in his own work and, instructively, has not thus far heeded Bhaskar's (1993) injunction to take dialectics seriously. Ill-equipped to grasp Harvey's systematic dialectics – with its non-dualistic, synthetic appreciation of content and form/universality and particularity, and its non-linear mode of presentation – Sayer arguably reads him in an overly analytical way.

So, it seems to me that Harvey is right: it is *not* misguided to believe that space can be theorised. More particularly, Harvey shows why Marxists simply must take space seriously. His theoretical statements about spatiality are no more or less substantive than other Marxian ideas. However, if I've been somewhat critical of Sayer in the paragraphs above, I now want to suggest that he too has something important to tell Marxists (and others) about space. In his thinly veiled asides about Sayer, Harvey, it seems, has little time for realist distinctions between abstract and concrete research, necessity and contingency and so on. This, I think, is unfortunate. One of the virtues of much critical realist scholarship is its exceptional attention to the meaning and coherence of concepts. In general, realists have helped do away with much fuzzy (or just plain misguided) thinking in the conduct of social scientific research. In this respect, Sayer's insistence that the *full* effects of space can only be appreciated through concrete research strikes me as correct. One of the strengths of Harvey's work on space (see, especially, Harvey, 1985b) is that it reveals the general logics that can explain geographical shifts in all manner of seemingly different cities, regions and nation states. But the problems are twofold. First, because these claims about space are abstract they are necessarily at one remove from the spaces they purport to cognitively represent.[29] Harvey's is a theory of the concrete and particular in, if you like, a relatively non-concrete, non-particular way. As I noted above, this doesn't mean his theoretical claims about space are vague, but it does mean they can only say so much. Second, because Sayer is correct in that the ontological properties of space will always *exceed* those attributable to capitalism (or any other process), then a full appreciation of the difference space makes requires contextual analysis of concrete situations. After all, if Harvey is right the capital entrains all manner of otherwise unique people, materials, environments and objects, then these various particulars will always have their own specific powers and liabilities. Depending on their spatial patterning within global capitalism, all sorts of unexpected and emergent effects may occur that enhance, contradict or remain indifferent to the geographical imperatives of the accumulation process.

What are the implications of these two problems for the study of space? One is that a proper appreciation of the necessary role of space in social, economic, and political life *requires theoretical work at a variety of levels of abstraction.* Harvey, in his theoretical work, has tended to work with a set of rather 'abstract abstractions'. This no doubt accounts for Sayer's charge that he and other spatial theorists appear rather vague about space. As Cox and Mair (1989) argue, the essential role space plays in a system like capitalism can only be understood theoretically by working at different levels of abstraction simultaneously. Thus within any given theory – be it Marxism or some other – it is necessary to develop a plethora of abstractions in order to understand space's essential role. Second, though, questions of necessity aside, the effects of space are *also* in part contingent, such that abstract research will never be able to tell us all we need to know about space. This follows from Sayer's proper insistence that social life, while structured, is ineluctably over-determined: that is, it's a complex constellation of multiple processes, peoples, events, mechanisms and structures. It is one thing to undertake careful theoretical work into the role space plays within capitalism, say, or the perpetuation of homophobia. But it's quite another to understand how the spaces of capital and heteronormativity interact, synergise or contradict. Thus, however insightfully someone like Harvey might theorise the geography of capital accumulation, only concrete research will be able to account for how capital, patriarchy, racism, the division of labour, etc. *articulate* in and through particular geographical landscapes. It is at this level it seems to me that Sayer is right. It is, *contra* Sayer, possible to make theoretical claims about space. But, *contra* Harvey, we have to recognise that, in practice, the necessary properties of space are realised in and through contingent conditions. That is, one has to recognise that space is always implicated in a *multitude* of processes, power relations and systems. This means that claims to necessity about space – which are theoretical claims internal to particular perspectives (Marxist or otherwise) – can never address the contingent question of how real spaces are necessarily co-determined by and co-determining of a plethora of relatively autonomous relations and structures.

Conclusion

This chapter has been a long and dense one, so I'll keep my conclusion brief. The Marxism of Harvey and the realism of Sayer seem, at first sight, to be at loggerheads over the question of space. But the two bodies of thought are not necessarily antithetical. In staging an encounter between two influential analysts of space, I've tried to show that it is possible to 'split the difference' between them concerning the difference geography makes. In this respect, Harvey's Marxism and Sayer's realism may have something to learn from each other. Harvey, I've suggested, is right that space is integral to capitalism and thus to Marx's substantive economic theory. But Sayer is right that space is not always essential for all types of social relations, processes and objects. Moreover, questions of necessity aside, because the spaces of capital combine in uneven and unpredictable ways with spaces of sexism, racism, cultural identity, political authority and the like, then the precise nature of the difference that space makes is a contingent question.[30] Battered and bruised by over two decades of neo-liberalism, Leftists need, wherever possible, to make common cause, not engage in pointless in-fighting. By taking the best – or most defensible – elements from Harvey's and Sayer's views on space, perhaps we can now go beyond academic debates to figure out what a lived, revolutionary *politics of space* might be about in the twenty-first century.

Notes

1 By arguing that space is both necessary and conditional and that space may or may not make a difference depending, I realise that I'm likely to be misunderstood or accused of being inconsistent and contradictory. I therefore want to thank two people for their careful readings of the first draft. Andrew Sayer's candour helped me to avoid at least one serious misrepresentation of his work and I'm grateful for his critical comments. I must also thank John Roberts for his principled objection to the arguments I put forward. Even though he dissents from my 'third way' resolution of the Sayer–Harvey debate on space, the chapter is all the better for his input. Kevin Cox kindly allowed me to read his unpublished essay on the geographical imaginations of Harvey, Sayer and Doreen Massey. This proved to be very helpful in reworking the first draft. Finally, I'm grateful to my colleagues Neil Coe and Kevin Ward. They kindly commented on an earlier version of the chapter and assured me that splitting the difference between Harvey and Sayer was not, after all, a wholly implausible endeavour.
2 As we'll see, in Sayer's case clarity of expression has not engendered clarity of interpretation. Several commentators – including myself in an earlier draft of this essay – have routinely misread Sayer's arguments on space.
3 The early philosophical chapters of *Justice, Nature and the Geography of Difference* form the notable exception to this, along with the empirical essays in *Consciousness and the Urban Experience*.
4 Clearly, my working assumption in this essay is that both Harvey and Sayer have distinct and coherent positions on space. In other words, I am deliberately bracketing the question as to whether, in reality, their positions have varied over time or might be internally inconsistent. A far more in-depth analysis of each thinker's *oeuvre* would be required to answer this question.
5 To my knowledge, this is the first published essay to forge some kind of Harvey–Sayer dialogue on space. Kevin Cox (1999) has written on the Harvey–Sayer–Doreen Massey relation, but his essay remains unpublished. More generally, it must be said that the intellectual projects of Harvey and Sayer have not received the kind of close, critical, book- or essay-length scrutiny that those of 'key thinkers' in other disciplines have in recent years (I'm thinking, for example, of Giddens in sociology or Derrida in philosophy). Though many particular aspects of their

work have proven inspirational for other social and economic researchers, rarely have their *oeuvres* been taken as a whole and subject to critical scrutiny. I'm slightly at a loss to explain this omission since the work of both men has, by any standards, been enormously original and influential.

6 Sayer, as we'll see, has been very explicit about this. As I'll explain, his position in space is as follows: (i) space is a necessary property of myriad processes and things which can be theorised but (ii) most theoretical claims about space are characteristically vague, which is why (iii) to understand the difference that space makes, researchers need to turn to more concrete kinds of analysis wherein one finds that (iv) space's role is at once necessary and contingent, depending on the situation.

7 Here, then, all theory must be 'configurational' and grasp the world in its immediate spatial integument (see Thrift, 1983).

8 For an excellent, introductory exploration of different conceptions of space see Gregory (2000). At the most general level, we can make a heuristic distinction between *material space* (geographical forms and relations), *representations of space* (discourses and depictions of space, lay and specialist) and *spatial practices* (routinised or transformative activities in and on space). For more on how space has been conceived in social, economic and political theory see Smith (1984: ch. 3) and Massey (1999).

9 Harvey has not always been a Marxist. During the early part of his career as a geographer he was deeply influenced by the tenets of positivism (see, for example, Harvey, 1969).

10 In this respect, other like-minded Marxists include Chris Arthur, Alex Callinicos, Fred Moseley, Moishe Postone, Derek Sayer, Ali Shamsavari and Tony Smith.

11 This wider recognition was in large part due to the success of *The Condition of Post-modernity* (Harvey, 1989b), since when Harvey has published in avowedly inter-disciplinary journals such as *Public Culture, Rethinking Marxism* and *Social Text*. Even so, some Marxists still seem to display an ignorance of Harvey's seminal work when it comes to theorising space (see, for example, Wilson, 1999).

12 This title has a double-meaning, referring not just to the limits to Marx's key text – *Capital* – but the structural limits of capitalism as a functioning economic system.

13 Unless otherwise specified all quotations in this section come from Harvey's published writings.

14 Of course, this rather bold statement needs some qualification. Some of Marx's writings – such as the *Communist Manifesto* – are rich with geographical references and many a post-Marx Marxist has taken geography seriously (think of Lenin, Luxemburg and Amin, for instance). Swyngedouw (2000) offers a useful intro-duction to Marxist thought in the discipline of geography.

15 John Roberts, I think rightly, has suggested to me that Harvey's philosophical position has shifted of late. Where his 'middle work' – that is, after *Social Justice* but before *Justice, Nature and the Geography of Difference* – was systematically dia-lectical, his more recent writing has adopted a more open and fluid conception of dialectics that perhaps lacks the rigour of his earlier dialectical worldview. In this essay, I'm going to focus on Harvey's systematic dialectics and thereby side-step the question of whether or not Harvey in fact works with *several* dialectical models.

16 On top of this, Harvey is highly critical of Hegel's treatment of space, which he sees as regressive and reactionary (see Harvey, 1981).

17 To render this in the language of mainstream social theory, Harvey's theor-etical work is an abstract account of 'system (dis)integration' that exists at several removes from the messy particularities of quotidien existence ('social [dis]-integration').

18 In one sense, I'm taking the 'spatial fix' as broadly emblematic of the way Harvey works space into historical materialism. This, I realise, may be an illicit move since some critics argue that Harvey works with *several* conceptions of space. The geography of Harvey's Marxism is clearly rich and multi-faceted. A full account would, therefore, have to address the whole sweep of his thought from *The Limits* through to his recent *Spaces of Hope* (2000), identifying any changes and inconsistencies in his notion of space.

19 By 'production of space' Harvey means the ongoing constitution, reconstitution and destruction of the built environments for production, consumption and communication. The concept can tell us nothing about the specific geographical forms assumed by political economic processes.

20 Andrew Sayer (pers. comm.) has usefully reminded me that space may also be the realm of generality and sameness, depending on the objects and relations in question.

21 Only concrete research can account for these specifics in all their complexity, as Sayer (below) insists.

22 Though his academic training was not *exclusively* geographical. His long residency at Sussex University entailed inter-disciplinary teaching and research formalised in a 'school' rather than 'department' structure.

23 Sayer's particular contribution has been to distinguish capitalism ontologically from the division of labour and to insist on the intractability of the latter.

24 Unless otherwise specified, all the quotes below are drawn from Sayer's published writings.

25 This is not the place to offer a detailed account of retroduction. Roberts (1999) claims that Marx 'retroacts' rather than retroduces and so is not a realist. Whether or not Harvey retroacts must be the subject of another paper.

26 Note that at this stage no claims are being made about how *important* space is as a cause or effect.

27 For instance, in economics the aspatial theory of perfect competition is simply implausible because the location of business makes a big difference to how competition works. To render the theory more accurate, a set of different geographical assumptions would have to be made in order to see how competition operates (viz., for example, spatial monopolies, geographical barriers to market entry etc).

28 'General', incidentally, should not be confused with the extra-local. As Cox and Mair (1989) show, theory can make claims about local phenomena as much as non-local ones.

29 Here I use the polysemic word 'abstract' to mean 'at a distance from' the world.

30 Cf. Bob Jessop's idea of contingent necessity?

Bibliography

Anderson, J. (1973) 'Ideology in geography', *Antipode* 5, 1: 1–6.

Arthur, C. (1993) 'Hegel's *Logic* and Marx's *Capital*', in F. Moseley (eds) *Marx's Method in* Capital, Atlantic Highlands: Humanities Press, pp. 67–83.

Bhaskar, R. (1989) *Reclaiming Reality*, London: Verso.

—— (1993) *Dialectic: The Pulse of Freedom*, London: Verso.

Castree, N. (1995) 'Birds, mice and geography: marxisms and dialectics', *Transactions of the Institute of British Geographers* 21, 3: 342–62.

Couzens-Hoy, D. (1989) 'Splitting the difference: Habermas's critique of Derrida', *Praxis International* 8, 1: 447–64.

Cox, K. (1999) 'Spatial imaginaries and reconceptualising human geography', unpublished MS, Dept. of Geography, Ohio State University.

Cox, K. and Mair, A. (1989) 'Levels of abstraction in locality studies', *Antipode* 21, 2: 121–32.

Crang, M. and Thrift, N. (eds) (2000) *Thinking Space*, London: Routledge.

Gibson-Graham, J-K. (1996) *The End of Capitalism (As We Knew It)*, Oxford: Blackwell.

Gregory, D. (2000) 'Space', in R. J. Johnston *et al.* (eds) *The Dictionary of Human Geography*, Oxford: Blackwell, pp. 767–73.

Gunn, R. (1989) 'Marxism and critical realism: the same, similar, or just plain different?', *Capital and Class* 68: 21–49.

Harre, R. (1970) *Principles of Scientific Thinking*, London: Macmillan.

Harvey, D. (1969) *Explanation in Geography*, London: Edward Arnold.

—— (1973) *Social Justice and the City*, London: Arnold.

—— (1981) 'The spatial fix', *Antipode* 13, 3: 1–12.

—— (1982/1999) *The Limits to Capital*, Oxford: Blackwell, London: Verso.

—— (1985a) 'The geopolitics of capitalism', in D. Gregory and J. Urry (eds) *Social Relations and Spatial Structures*, London: Macmillan, pp. 128–63.

—— (1985b) *The Urbanization of Capital*, Oxford: Blackwell.

—— (1987) 'Three myths in search of a reality in urban studies, *Society and Space* 5, 4: 367–76.

—— (1988) 'The geographical and geopolitical consequences of the transition from Fordism to flexible accumulation', in G. Sternlieb and J. Hughes (eds) *America's New Market Geography*, New Brunswick: Rutgers University Press, pp. 101–35.

—— (1989a) *The Urban Experience*, Oxford: Blackwell.

—— (1989b) *The Condition of Postmodernity*, Oxford: Blackwell.

—— (1996) *Justice, Nature and the Geography of Difference*, Oxford: Blackwell.

—— (1997) 'Contested cities: social process and spatial form', in N. Jewson and S. MacGregor (eds) *Transforming Cities*, London: Routledge.

—— (1999a) 'Foreword' to *The Limits to Capital*, 2nd edition, London: Verso.

—— (1999b) 'On fatal flaws and fatal distractions', *Progress in Human Geography* 23, 4: 557–66.

—— (2000) *Spaces of Hope*, Edinburgh: Edinburgh University Press.

Harvey, D. and Scott, A. (1987) 'The practice of human geography: theory and empirical specificity in the transition from Fordism to flexible accumulation', in B. Macmillan (ed.) *Remodelling Geography*, Oxford: Blackwell, pp. 217–29.

Lefebvre, H. (1991) *The Production of Space*, translated by D. Nicolson-Smith, Oxford: Blackwell.

Massey, D. (1985) 'New directions in space', in D. Gregory and J. Urry (eds) *Social Relations and Spatial Structures*, London: Macmillan, pp. 9–19.

—— (1992) 'Politics and space/time', *New Left Review* 196: 65–84.

—— (1999) 'Space-time "science" and the relationship between physical and human geography', *Transactions of the Institute of British Geographers* 24, 2: 261–76.

Merrifield, A. (1993) 'Space and place: a Lefebvrian reconciliation', *Transactions of the Institute of British Geographers* 18, 4: 516–31.

Murray, P. (1988) *Marx's Theory of Scientific Knowledge*, Atlantic Highlands: Humanities Press.

Ollman, B. (1980) *Alienation*, Cambridge: Cambridge University Press.

—— (1993) *Dialectical Investigations*, London: Routledge.

Peet, R. (1998) *Modern Geographical Thought*, Oxford: Blackwell.

Roberts, J. (1999) 'Marxism and philosophy: a critique of critical realism', *Capital and Class* 37: 86–116.

Sayer, A. (1985) 'The difference that space makes', in D. Gregory and J. Urry (eds) *Social Relations and Spatial Structures*, London: Macmillan, pp. 47–66.

—— (1987) 'Hard work and its alternatives', *Society and Space* 5, 4: 395–9.

—— (1992) *Method in Social Science*, 2nd edition, London: Routledge.

—— (1995) *Radical Political Economy: A Critique*, Oxford: Blackwell.

—— (2000) *Realism and Social Science*, London: Sage.

Sayer, A. and Morgan, K. (1988) *Microcircuits of Capital*, Oxford: Polity Press.

Sayer, A. and Walker, R. (1992) *The New Social Economy*, Oxford: Blackwell.

Sheppard, E. and Barnes, T. (1990) *The Capitalist Space Economy*, Boston: Unwin Allen.

Smith, N. (1984) *Uneven Development*, Oxford: Blackwell

Smith, N. and Katz, C. (1993) 'Grounding metaphor: spatialising politics', in M. Keith and S. Pile (eds) *Place and the Politics of Identity*, London: Routledge, pp. 67–83.

Soja, E. (1980) 'The socio-spatial dialectic', *Annals of the Association of American Geographers* 70, 2: 207–25.

—— (1989) *Postmodern Geographies*, London: Verso.

—— (1996) *Thirdspace*, Oxford: Blackwell.

Swyngedouw, E. (2000) 'The Marxian alternative', in E. Sheppard and T. Barnes (eds) *A Companion to Economic Geography*, Oxford: Blackwell, pp. 41–59.

Thrift, N. (1983) 'On the determination of social action in space and time', *Society and Space* 1, 1: 23–57.

Wilson, H. T. (1999) 'Time, space and value', *Time and Society* 8, 1: 161–81.

11 The spectral ontology of value

Christopher J. Arthur

Introductory remarks

There is a void at the heart of capitalism. It arises because of the nature of commodity exchange, which abstracts from, or absents, the entire substance of use value. What is constituted therewith is a form of unity of commodities that does not rest on any pre-given common content – which does not exist, it will be argued. The historical specificity of capitalism is that an 'ontological inversion' occurs whereby (exchange) 'value', immediately just the negation of use value, gains self-presence, real 'Being', albeit that of an empty 'Presence'. Thus value emerges from the void as a 'spectre' that *haunts* the 'real world' of capitalist commodity production. This original *displacement* of the material process of production and circulation by the ghostly objectivity of value, is supplemented when the spectre (in the shape of self-positing capital) takes *possession* of it.

In a short paper such as this, such large claims necessarily take on a programmatic character. Only the barest indications of the argument are given, in the hope of stimulating thought and discussion.[1] It might be useful first to contextualise what is said by remarking on some ideas drawn upon here.

a In Roy Bhaskar's *Dialectic* (1993) it is argued that ontological monovalence, a purely positive account of reality, cannot account for *real* negation or absence. It must be admitted that absence is a reality as much as presence. Moreover, since 'absenting' is certainly a real process, what has become absent through such a process leaves not simply 'nothing', but a 'determinate nothing' structured by the specific process that brought it about. The present paper will situate value theory in this context through establishing that value is constituted in the exchange process by a determinate negation of use value. Although it is the thesis of this paper that exchange and circulation set up an 'ideal world' of pure forms, empty of content, which then take hold of production, this is consistent with, indeed depends upon, an *emergent powers materialism*.[2]

This chapter was first published as an article in *Radical Philosophy* (May 2001).

The focus is on the emergent properties of the determinate absence of use value. In virtue of the mechanism of emergent powers it is possible to suppose that, if there is at the base level real determinate non-being, then a more complex practice might *redetermine* this as a pseudo-positive *presence*.

b   What is constituted when the heterogeneous material features of commodities are declared absent from their identity as 'values' is a form of unity of commodities lacking pre-given common content, it will be argued. It can only be characterised as form as such, the pure form of exchangeability. In advancing this argument the paper draws upon a relatively new tendency in Marxian theory, which puts at the centre of its critique Marx's notion of 'value form'. It is the form of exchange that is seen as the prime determinant of the capitalist economy rather than the content regulated by it; thus some theorists postpone consideration of the labour theory of value until the value form itself has been fully developed. (Relevant here is the work of I. I. Rubin, A. Sohn-Rethel, K. Uno and H-G. Backhaus.)

c   Hegel is an important reference for value form theorists because his logic of categories is well suited to a theory of form and of form determination. Moreover Hegel is important methodologically in that his systematic dialectical development of categories, especially in his logic, is directed towards articulating the structure of a totality, showing how it supports itself in and through the interchanges of its inner moments. The first to use the term 'systematic dialectic' with reference to Marx's method may have been Bhaskar (1991: 147, 1993: 346). (Prominent exponents are T. Smith, T. Sekine, G. Reuten and M. Williams.)

d   The most important single influence on this paper is Marx's insight into the 'metaphysical' character of capitalist commodity production. Throughout the first chapter of *Capital* there are references to 'ghostly objectivity'; 'sensuous supersensuousness'; 'mysteriousness'; 'turns into its opposite'; 'stands on its head'; 'metaphysical subtleties and theological niceties'; 'fantastic'; 'absurd'; and so on. This language I take to be much more than rhetoric. Many have complained that Marx's concept of 'value' is metaphysical. They have not seen that Marx himself said this, but saw it as a feature of reality. Such a 'metaphysical theory of value' is what I aim to vindicate. Capitalism is marked by the subjection of the material process of production and circulation to the ghostly objectivity of value. Our title, and text, flirt with the language of Jacques Derrida's (1994) commentary on this aspect of Marx's work. (But it has to be said that Derrida vastly overgeneralises the purchase of his 'hauntology'. Here we take 'hauntology' to be a specific region within ontology, characterised by inversion.)

In sum the paper aims at a new synthesis of dialectical critical realist themes with (Hegelian inspired) Marxian value-form theory. First a form-theoretical account of commodity exchange is given; then the fundamental ontology of value is outlined, founded on 'Nothing' contrasted with Hegel's 'Being'; finally the spectre of this 'Nothingness' is claimed to be hegemonic.

Commodity exchange

In this first substantive section of the paper the nature of commodity exchange is analysed, using the categories of 'use value' and 'exchange value'. I follow here Marx's terminology so it should be explained that in his usage 'use value' is identified with the natural body of the good concerned. It is the various properties inherent in it that allow it to have various uses, but rather than focusing on such *relations* Marx employs the term *substantively*, such that it is possible to speak of a commodity as 'a' use value. Putting the point this way heightens the sense of paradox when it is contrasted with its 'value', because, again, Marx takes this too not in a relational sense in which it stands for an exchange ratio, but substantively again, such that the commodity is 'a' value. There is thus consubstantiation here. Every commodity 'contains', as it were, two substances in its body, its use value and its value; the former is specific to each type of commodity, but the latter is a (capitalistically produced) universal substance of which each commodity is an instance or certain amount.

Now, while speaking of a commodity as 'a use value' might be deemed a somewhat peculiar locution, there can be little objection, in that the natural body of the commodity taken under this description is clearly a substance present to inspection. To speak of 'value' as a substance, by contrast, could be taken as highly objectionable. From the time of Samuel Bailey's attack on Ricardo, such a view has been rejected (other than by Marx) in favour of an account in which there is no value substance, and insofar as it appears as a property of commodities, something they 'have', this has been analysed as a purely relational property identical with 'value in exchange', and accordingly labile. Thus it is problematic simply to assert that value is a substance inherent to the commodity. The argument below represents the first steps in a chain designed to *ground* such a presupposition through a dialectical development of the form of exchange.

It will be argued that (monetary) exchange gives rise *immediately* to a world of pure form empty of content. The two major schools that claim to be able peremptorily to reduce 'value' to a definite content are those adhering to the labour theory of value and to the marginal utility theory. These will be briefly considered, and rejected for failing to grasp the objective validity of the 'real abstraction' predicated on exchange relations.

Whatever may be true before and after exchange, in the sphere of exchange itself the commodity is entirely abstracted from its character as a use value. It is of great importance here that this abstraction, and the 'nominalist' (i.e. empty) universal it yields, are not effects of consciousness but objectively constituted in the real process of exchange. This is a *material* abstraction from the character of the commodities as use values, which is 'absented' for the period of exchange; the commodities acquire as a new determination the character of values; and the natural bodies of the commodities concerned play the role of bearers of this determination imposed on them while passing through this phase of their life-cycle. They become subject to the *value form*.

What is at issue in the value form abstraction is by no means the same sort of abstraction as natural science employs when it studies mass, for example, and treats bodies under this description regardless of their other properties. For mass is indeed a given property of the bodies concerned, inhering in each. But value is a socially imputed property; as Marx says, not 'an atom of matter' enters into it (Marx 1976a: 138). There seems no natural limit in the *form* of exchange itself to *what* people might take to exchanging. At first sight, therefore, it seems an empty mediator, tailor-made to registering various heterogeneous relations. The key advance of value form theory is the insight that the value form develops to the point at which, with self-valorising value, it is constituted as a *self-relation*, and 'takes over' the world of production and consumption given to it.

The exchange determinations are dimensionally incommensurable with use. Notice that to say 'we *abstract* from use' is very different from generating the abstraction 'utility' from heterogeneous use values, by disregarding the *particularity* of use. Böhm-Bawerk was correct to notice, although wrong to complain, that Marx abstracts even from the genus itself, when he abstracts from the use value of commodities (Böhm-Bawerk 1975: 74). Exchange is certainly not an *actualising* of the 'common property' of utility. As Marx rightly pointed out, the thing must be realised as an exchange value *before* it can be as a use value. It might be said that exchange is underpinned by the comparative preferences for A and B by the parties, but in this case what is actualised is some weight of such preferences in the minds of the exchangers rather than an identity *in the commodities* A and B. The latter identity, i.e. of A and B, is the *value* in exchange of *them*, whatever external conditions shape the ratio of exchange. Moreover, exchange could not be based on *their* identity as use values, or it would have no point; rather they must be different, so that one person's preference may be for A and one for B. The non-identity of the commodities as use values is set aside then in their identity as Beings of Exchange (as we shall call them later).

If use value is 'suspended' for the duration of exchange this 'absenting' is equivalent not to destruction but to 'distantiation', so that use value remains potent at a level removed from exchange determinations; the natural body of the commodity appears in exchange, but merely as a 'bearer' of value, its use value having been substantively displaced. As Bhaskar says, what is absent at one level, region or perspective may be present at another. This is 'the duality of absence' (Bhaskar 1993: 60, 346). Value and use value are not two polar properties of a commodity like North and South. They are immediately contraries. Where value *is*, use value *is not*: if use value *is*, value is nothing: two different regions of being in which what is present in the one region is absent in the other. It is a feature of the structure of commodity relations that use value and value exhibit such duality (yet eventually inter-penetrate).

Having rejected the relevance of 'utility' to exchange value let us turn to 'labour'. It should be remembered that Marx does not succeed in *Capital*, chapter 1, in *demonstrating* the labour theory of value. He simply stipulates that value relations pertain to exchange of products of labour, and that other exchangeable things have price but not value. Nor is it just a problem that the deduction (if it is one) given in chapter 1 is insufficient, it is that the nature of exchange is such that at this level of abstraction *nothing* determinate can be posited without arbitrary foreclosure of the dialectic of the value form. Those who do insist on the labour content cannot explain why this form should be so void of determinacy that anything and everything can be inscribed in it.

It is certainly justifiable to claim that an accidental universal (in this case exchangeability) must be disaggregated so as to focus on a real universal (in this case labour products) but this must be justified explicitly, and, moreover, it is still necessary then to explain how other things can appear as identical in form to the chosen class. If this can only be done by granting that the commodity form is not peculiar to products, and that its abstractly general character allows it to cover other content, that answer shows this form can be analysed on its own account. So the argument that there is indeed a con-tent to the value form in labour cannot be correct as far as the pure form of exchange is concerned because many non-products are coherently inscribed within the form. It requires an additional argument to secure a version of the labour theory of value (such as I have provided elsewhere: Arthur, 2000, 2001), and, in this paper, so far from value being treated simply as the social form of appearance of labour, it will be shown that value is an unnatural form that clings, vampire-like, to labour and feeds off it.

As Marx rightly said in his *Grundrisse*, it is impossible to start with labour and show the commodity is a form it takes on. Because this form is an alien *imposition* on labour, one has to start from circulation in its developed form he says (Marx 1973: 259). It is *through* exchange that abstraction imparts itself to labour, making it abstract human labour, because it is the form of exchange that establishes the necessary social synthesis in the first place before labours expended may be commensurated in it.

But Marx failed to grasp that this implies a method of exposition which engages the value form first, and then provides reasons to narrow the focus of the enquiry to products, rather than one that starts from production, i.e. 'value', and then inexplicably allows the scope of the commodity form to include non-values. In dialectical terms, Marx has a dogmatic beginning insofar as he initially presupposes the items exchanged are labour products. This could be justified externally by appeal to the broader concerns of historical materialism with modes of production. But for any attempt to follow the model of Hegel's dialectic an absolute beginning without imposed conditions is needed. Only after developing the forms of circulation can one give grounds for picking out as systematically important those commodities which are products of labour.

To sum up: exchange brings about a *sui generis* form without any given content, because *all* use value is absented, not merely all *determinate* utility but the *category* itself. It is presupposed *to* exchange and actualised *after* exchange but simply not present *in* exchange.

Money

When exchange 'absents' the use value inherent in the natural body of the commodity it does so by asserting that all commodities are identical as exchangeables, but, since this last is *not* a property inherent as such to commodities, rather one which is imposed on them, to hypostatise it, as if it were, is to posit some *imputed* universal – whether property or substance. Thus, if exchange declares all commodities identical as 'values', it cannot do so on the basis of abstracting a common property already present within the realm of use value because there is no such commonality. *Only the very fact of being exchanged unites the commodities generically.* Since the range of exchangeables is unlimited, to characterise anything thus is not to pick out something belonging to the nature of the object but a reference to the operation on it. Exchange does not flow from an *inherent* power of exchange *in the commodities*. Rather, the operation of gathering them into the class of exchangeables reflects itself into them, imputing value as the substance of them, which then appears fetishistically as an inherent power. More precisely it is money that is socially imputed with the power of immediate exchangeability, and commodities are classed as exchangeable in virtue of the worth imputed to them in their price.

Money, as a medium of circulation, seems simply to 'stand for', stand in the place of, commodities, for reasons of convenience. On such a view theory would give this metal mediator short shrift, treating it as a veil behind which lies the 'real economy', whose laws are investigated in abstraction from their current forms of appearance. Such an approach would be mistaken for failing to grasp the nature of money, and its central place in a capitalist economy.

Let us borrow an example from Marx to illustrate the peculiarity of money. Whereas 'animal' 'stands for' cats and dogs etc., it is merely our concept of them, but when money 'stands for' commodity value it is objectively present, and enters into objective relations with the said commodities; it is 'as if' 'the animal' existed *beside* the cats and dogs, and entered into relations with them (Marx 1976b: 32). What is absurd when we hypostatise 'animal' is nonetheless objectively valid when money 'stands for' commodities. Their concept is incarnate in coin. Moreover, this 'convenience' of the exchange system takes over from what it is supposed to mediate reducing the extremes to *its* supports in *its* activity, namely the *making* of money.

Since money represents the emptiness of commodities as value-bodies, it need share no common property with them, and, indeed, need have hardly any 'natural body' at all, an electronic charge will do. It is true that money is supposed to represent in external form the essence of commodities but since there *is no* common essence (other than their relation to money) money represents the presence of this absence! Albeit some use value (e.g. gold) may be selected to play the role of its visible body, this clothing is contingent. But since it is the function that counts, not the particular body of money, it can be replaced by a symbol of itself.

To sum up, money 'stands for' commodities not because it represents some common property in them (which in some theories of money must also be shared by it), but rather contrariwise, money takes it upon itself to stand in place of them, therewith *imposing* this common relation on them, putting as their essence this ideal signification, of being worth so much money. The common content is therefore not a pre-given one but a dialectically developed one, introjecting the *form* of value.

The ontology of value

We have explicated the doubleness of the commodity (as use value and value) and described monetary exchange so as to situate the dialectic of capital, to be discussed shortly. This dialectic will be modeled on that of Hegel, with the most important categories being those of 'Nothing' and 'Being'. Value will be shown to mark an 'empty presence', and yet, it will be argued, this spectral objectivity prevails over the material of economic life.

First we must explain that a *specific* domain of reality, namely capitalist commodity exchange, can yet give rise to the most abstract categories, homologous with those of Hegel's logic, the most abstract part of his *universal* philosophy. Although our implicit starting point, namely 'the commodity produced by capital', appears as a concrete one, the real abstraction, imposed in exchange, from every given feature of it leads to a dialectic of 'pure form' homologous with the 'pure thoughts' of Hegel's logic.[3] Whereas Hegel abstracts from everything through the power of thought, exchange abstracts only from what is presented to it, a delimited sphere of use values. So we have in the dialectic of capital one that is less general than Hegel's in its scope, but within its own terms equally *absolute* in so far as it is founded on all round abstraction to leave quasi-logical primitives.

Now the exposition of the argument proper begins by first presenting a table of categories and then a commentary upon it (see Table 11.1). The focus here is on exchange; terms in quotation marks are overly concrete for this level of the exposition, but used to help give a more accessible 'picture' of what is going on; the capitals head the key categories the scheme is

Table 11.1 The spectral ontology of value

		'Production' →	Exchange →	'Consumption'
A	'Value' as absence	real being	Nothing	real being
B	'Value' as presence	non-being	Being	non-being

intended to explicate; line A is understood as originating the dialectic, through absenting real being (use value) during exchange, and line B is derived from A as a quasi-inversion of it. At A, then, 'production' and 'consumption' (or, more abstractly, the presenting of goods for exchange and their removal) are presupposed to exchange as realities, and a wealth of use values gets transferred through exchange from one hand to another. While use value is here presented *to* exchange it is suspended for the period *of* exchange; this absenting of use value while commodities cross the space of exchange constitutes their 'value' as all that is not use value, sheer nothingness. This line, therefore, is characterised by 'the positing of value as absence (of use value)'. Immediately, the exchanging commodity is simply predicated as 'not use value' but this absence 'makes space' so to speak for the emergence of 'Nothing' into positive self-presence (as illustrated in Table 11.1).

The movement from A to B is a switch to an inverted world in so far as line B is itself a determinate negation of the whole of line A. Whereas at A 'value' is nothing but absence of use value, in accordance with Bhaskar's opposition to ontological monovalence it is here taken as a reality axed around the *presence* of absence grasped as resulting from *the negation* of use value. The 'ontological inversion'[4] is the moment of 'negation of negation', but whereas the first negation is brought about *by* exchange, the second negation is effected *in the space of exchange*, a space predicated on absence of the 'real being' of commodities as use value. So, instead of returning to the starting point, and recollecting that the commodity is, after all, use value, 'absenting the absence' results in the (abstract) 'Nothing' becoming its opposite, (abstract) 'Being'. At B therefore the space is filled by . . . what? Sheer 'Being': the Being of exchange. At B, 'value' makes itself *present* to us through *displacing*[5] the real being of commodities, which are hence posited prior to exchange as the 'non-being' of 'value', before they are present *in* exchange *as* 'value', only to be 'devalorised' as they pass beyond it. So this inverted world of 'value' transforms real being (use value) into 'non-being', and 'Nothing' into 'Being' ('value'). Hence Line B is characterised by 'the positing of value as presence'.

Notice that the movement *across each line* is characterised by ontological reversal but that *from line to line* by ontological inversion. The difference is that the reversal maintains the original presupposition, and posits in the same 'universe', so to speak, the opposite. But the ontological inversion supplants the entire 'universe' together with its existing regional presences and absences such that *all* is represented as other than it is, as standing on its head.

In explicating 'the presence of value', I draw attention to two different distinctions: first, between the sheer 'Nothing' of line A and the sheer 'Being' of line B indicative of a transition from one world to another, and, second, between the 'Being' and the 'non-being' of line B where the latter has no capital letters, indicating that 'non-being' is here a correlative moment of 'Being' and hence implicated in the world of exchange even if only in the mode of being denied, of absence. Thus, following Hegel (1969: 83), I shall distinguish between a structure characterised by the *correlative* moments 'Being' and 'non-being', and the unstructured immediacy of 'Being' and 'Nothing', where 'Nothing' does not refer to the absence of some related term but a sheer void, an immediacy, unrelated to anything outside itself; 'Being' likewise in Hegel is such an immediacy, sheer indeterminacy, and as such indistinguishable from 'Nothing'. (In a moment I shall explain why such immediacies are justified.)

It follows that I distinguish value *as* Nothing from the non-being *of* value. The former lies always at the heart of the dialectic of value, even where 'value as presence' veils this emptiness. The latter refers to value's determinate negation, namely use value, a sphere where considerations *other* than value are in play (see line B): 'non-being' might be thought a strange way to refer to the visible reality, use value;[6] but what is meant is that there is *nothing of value* in it as such a visible reality, that 'turn and twist it as we may' we can never find 'value' there. (Considered as something destined *for exchange* its 'Being' in exchange may be ideally anticipated, but here is only a potential.)

Now why should there be any inversion of line A into line B in the first place? It must be emphasised that this 'perspectival switch'[7] from A to B is as such only a presentiment of the reality of the inverted world of capitalism (where, as Marx said, everything is 'topsy-turvy'); as such it is merely a shadow cast by exchange. To give the shadow substance would involve a long development, in which new, more concrete, categories are brought to birth, precisely through the consideration, at each stage, of the *insufficiency* of the shape of value under consideration to prove that it has *made itself present*. Thus this argument can follow somewhat the same lines as that of Hegel's onto-logic, his attempt to constitute the universe out of the self-movement of thought; however in this case it is the self-movement of capital that has to be shown to constitute the universe of value.

So I stress there is no 'proof', here at the start, of value as a positive presence; it is rather the completely ungrounded indeterminate beginning of the 'spirit world of capital' (as I shall develop it); it stands in need of grounds and it must be legitimated *retrospectively* when the 'Being' of value borne by commodities is conceived as a moment of the capitalist totality.[8]

An absence in Hegel's dialectic

Since the categories 'Nothing' and 'Being' are reminiscent of Hegel let us turn aside to consider this. One significant disanalogy is in the *starting point*. Hegel starts by reducing real being to (abstract) 'Being', passes to 'Nothing' and back again, resolving this instability in 'Becoming' and collapsing this to '*Dasein*' (usually translated as 'determinate Being', or, literally, Being-There).

On the basis of the absenting of use value we start from sheer 'Nothing', but then make a transition, through the consideration that this is a determinate nothingness, to its possible inversion as 'Being'. What corresponds to the Hegelian instability of 'Being' and 'Nothing' is the wavering of value between absence and presence. This might be called the 'transitoriness' of value, which has the advantage of connoting both the shifting of 'value' from 'Nothing' to 'Being' and back *and* the predication of 'value' on the *transit* of commodities across exchange. Let us examine more closely the movement of exchange. Although commodities pass *across* this space, nonetheless something is posited *in* this sphere. When a commodity is exchanged its duality as a 'Being' *of* exchange, value, and a 'non-being' of exchange, use value, bifurcates. One use value is replaced by another use value, but the very same value persists *in* exchange. It is the 'Being Present' of value, the equivalent of Hegel's *Dasein*, mentioned above.

However, we must explain that this '*Dasein*' is not the same as Hegel's, and redeem our earlier pledge to justify our originating category, 'Nothing'. It is worth pondering why Hegel, whose dialectic is pervaded by determinate negation, starts from terms (namely 'Being' and 'Nothing') lacking any determinacy. This is bound up with his methodological principle that in philosophy nothing at all may be presupposed, for that would amount to dogmatism. So the beginning should not commit him to anything, and as a true beginning must not refer back beyond itself, it must not itself be mediated. An obvious objection is that his beginning is indeed a mediated result, for Hegel arrived at it through a complete abstraction from all determinate principles. Hegel, himself, however, insists that this fact lies 'outside the science' (Hegel 1969: 99). He brackets the abstract negativity of the thought process that produced it, and takes as absolute beginning the immediacy of 'Being', leaving until the result of its dialectical development the mediations grounding this beginning. If it is accepted that such 'clearing of the ground' may be left aside so that 'science' itself begins with pure immediacy, and develops immanently, there remains a tricky problem. For Hegel does not clearly distinguish between a beginning that strips away all determinacy from being leaving the indeterminate immediate 'Being', and a more radical abstraction from being itself, as a genus, to leave nothing at all. While admitting this, namely 'Nothing', could have been the beginning and end of the dialectic, he dismisses it by saying that the 'Nothing' would itself have being and so this beginning would join with his in an unstable identity of 'Being' and

'Nothing' (Hegel 1969: 99–100). But Hegel dissimulates, because within a couple of moves he has definitely prioritised 'Being' over 'Nothing', so his starting point was not innocent after all. Let us see how this happens.

It seems to happen immediately with the transition to 'Becoming', but Hegel again argues this category is understood by him to comprehend a movement of both coming to be and ceasing to be, indifferently. Cynthia Willett has used the image of a circle to illustrate this; one can move round in either direction even though the same thing is the ground of the movement. Hegel's 'option for the positive' comes out only with the next category, '*Dasein*', referring to Being-There or determinate Being in general. This, he admits blandly, resolves the opposed moments of 'Becoming' in a stable result that is a 'one-sided unity' favouring 'Being' (Hegel 1969: 106, 110). What is lost here is the logical alternative 'one-sided unity': 'determinate Nothing', or the self-presence of Nothing. While Hegel gives no reason for his choice, it is in fact legitimate in so far as he takes for granted that his project is a reconstruction of reality, assumed of course to embody the truth of Being.[9] But, as Willett argues in her brilliant paper on the subject, if Hegel resolves the circle of coming and going into an upward pointed spiral, its shadow side, logically equally possible, is a downward pointed spiral (Willett 1990: 92).

The circle needs a shove to get it moving orthogonally. The shove 'upwards' is justified only because of Hegel's reconstructive method. His concern is with *truth* (the usual philosophical topic) and since truth is the whole, only the *whole truth* retrospectively explains the transition. But if we deconstruct Hegel's dialectic, a certain 'prejudice-for-truth' is revealed. Occluded is another possibility: a world of falsity, where everything is inverted. This would be a 'downward' spiral, the concretisation of nothingness, the apotheosis of the false, insofar as 'Being' is denied, and demoted to the other of 'Nothing'. No doubt such a hellish dialectic, in which, contrary to the vision of 'the whole as the true', the whole is the false, could not occur to Hegel. But it is precisely the case in capitalism, we argue. Living as we do in the belly of the 'rough beast' born in Manchester, this possibility must be taken seriously.

Since the downward spiral, concretising 'Nothing', reflects the upward spiral, concretising 'Being', all the more determinate categories of the downward spiral may be expected to develop in parallel to the upper, with the understanding that they qualify the 'Nothing'. It is rather like the physicists' hypothesis of a world of 'anti-matter'. It is important to Hegel's onto-logic that the stages gone through, in developing the Absolute Idea, are *constitutive of it*, not abandoned husks of its immature shapes. They are *preserved*, albeit as sublated moments of the self-comprehending Absolute. This is why even the most primitive, 'Being', is itself a way of referring to the Absolute, albeit very abstractly; for the Absolute certainly *has* being; indeed, in a way, it is nothing other than the fullest expression of 'Being'. As a *dialectical* development, this concretisation of 'Being' is equally always constituted at each stage with reference to its opposite, at the start sheer 'Nothing'; but in Hegel's dialectic 'Being' encloses this 'Nothing', albeit Nothing is carried along 'within' *Dasein*.

In the dialectic of capital are shapes of its 'Idea' homomorphic with those of Hegel (as I have argued elsewhere: Arthur 2000),[10] but with an inverted meaning. 'Nothing' is at the origin, and encloses 'Being'. The more concrete and complex shapes of the onto-logic are likewise posited as the building-up of the shadow world of nothingness.

This 'negative teleology' (Backhaus 1992: 85) must be distinguished from simple inadequacy, lack, or conflict, characterising pre-capitalist formations. What is historically specific to capitalism is that 'Nothing' perfects itself when it develops its 'Presence', whereas generally Hegel would be right to give a positive exposition merely marred by the negative as when he notes the unassimilability of mass poverty to his positive dialectic of the modern state.

Let us return to the status of our own founding category 'Nothing'. In accordance with the above exegesis of Hegel in which attention was drawn to the fact that Hegel set aside the activity of abstraction giving rise to his originating category 'Being', our category 'Nothing' is not to be understood merely as the non-being of use value, but in its own terms as an immediacy. What lies 'outside the science' for the project of reconstructing the inner dialectic of the 'Substance-Subject' capital, is the external force (exchange) that took hold of goods – against their will so to speak – and transformed them into commodities, comprehensively negating their use value.[11] *Within* the space of exchange, then, this leaves us with this immediacy, namely 'Nothing', as the point of origin of the dialectic of capital. But if this 'Nothing' is not able to affirm itself as a 'Being' of exchange, it loses any ontological standing. To put it another way, without line B as its concretisation, line A would refer solely to use value and would read; real being – non-being – real being; 'value' would be meaningless.

For Hegel 'Nothing' is reduced, in effect, to the lack of determinacy of his 'Being', and a signal that the latter requires concretising until it has achieved plenitude in the Absolute. For us, 'Nothing' is the more abstract category; hence it is logically prior to its immediate 'Being' as such a beginning. (It will be recalled that I drew attention to Marx's abstracting from the genus 'use value' altogether.) This 'value as absence', then, is what is concretised in the dialectic of capital. When it becomes absolute it becomes its opposite 'value as presence' (but an *empty* presence because it is the fullest expression of its *origin*). However 'full of itself' it is, it must yet *prove* itself as *present to* its world, through inverting its constitutive context, i.e. *effecting* line B, as opposed to line A.

The spectre

The remainder of this paper sketches the way this 'Nothing' claims to make itself present to itself, and its others, rather than stay as the mere absence of use value. It must be capable of determining itself to be-ing there, a negative form of the *Da-Sein* of Hegel's onto-logic, an *empty presence*. In further determining itself to concrete actuality and power the same stages would have to be traced as those of Hegel's logic, up to the Absolute Idea. Only at that point is 'value as presence' conceivable as *making itself present*, rather than merely haunting a fetish form of consciousness.

It follows from the argument thus far that there is a void at the heart of capitalism, that the circulation of commodities and money as seemingly material objects supports a world of pure form. In proportion as the Being of Exchange develops (see line B in Table 11.1) the 'real being' of commodities itself becomes merely the shadow of value, its other being, its *non-being* – at best the material bearer of value; but the real *substance* of every commodity would be its value, which displaces its natural substance; the commodity is a 'sensuous-supersensuous thing' ('*ein sinnlich übersinnliche Ding*': Marx 1962: 85). This 'presence' at their heart is *there* in the value form taken by commodities. Yet it *is not*. It is a spectre. Derrida rightly distinguishes between the ideality of spirit and its embodiment as a spectre (Derrida 1994: 126, 136). If we treat value as the spiritual essence of the capitalist economy, its range of incarnations all centre on a single origin, namely money, the transubstantiated Eucharist of value; 'the spectre' is this hollow armour, at once mute metal and possessor of the magical power to make extremes embrace. The spirit is made metal and stalks among us. The spectre interpellates all commodities as its avatars – a spectral phenomenology. This negative presence, posited thus, fills itself out through emptying them of all natural being, and forming for itself a spectral body, a body of spectres. In capitalism all is *always* 'another thing' than what it is.

So far, then, from 'value' being some mundane material property or stuff, it is a shape opposed to all materiality, a form without content, which yet takes possession of our world in the only way it can, through draining it of reality, an ontological vampire that bloats its hollow frame at our expense.

'Value as presence' *contrasts* immediately with the spheres where it is not, positing them as its non-being. But the result of the systematic development of the value form is to *subsume* them under it. The name of this active negativity is ultimately 'capital'. Only the emergent powers characteristic of this form of value can *effect* the inversion and reduce use value to a moment of valorisation. Value is a *sui generis* form arising from capitalist commodity exchange, sinking into production, and then reflecting back on exchange so as to accomplish its *self-production*. This movement 'Being – non-being – Being' is parallel to that of Hegel's absolute negativity; value negates itself but then recovers itself in fuller form. So, even when the value form grounds itself on production, the former is not reduced to the mere appearance form of the latter, a previously empty form seized by this content; rather, the form of self-determination achieved by this ideality maintains itself, takes production *within* its power, thereby *form-determining* production so as to shape it into its own content (real subsumption of labour for example). The empty presence of value gains a content when it produces itself – but this is a strange sort of content we shall see.

The value form, following its development to the general formula of capital, gives itself reality through sinking into production and *making* products the incarnation of value. But, whereas Hegel has the Absolute Idea itself originate the reality its categories inform, capital confronts production and consumption as alien domains that it must subdue and actively seek to *in*form with its shapes. It must *take charge* of presenting commodities to exchange through shaping industry as capitalist industry so as to guarantee that there *be* commodities for exchange, that there be *new value*. So the forming of existent commodities as values in exchange is not enough; there must be real *positing* of value, occurring in real time and space 'prior' to exchange. Then value as *presence* overlaps (*übergreifen*: an important term in Marx) constellationally (Bhaskar's term[12]) what is outside exchange, subsuming it, 'formally' and then 'really', to the self-production of value. If this form has sufficient determinacy to be a power in the world then an ontological *inversion* obtains.

But it is important to realise the domain that objectively predicates itself on this inversion is the pure form of exchange. Such ontological inversion does not, and could not, abolish the reality outside exchange, which still stands (on its own feet, so to speak); but it is *haunted* by it; still worse, at the emergent level of ontological complexity achieved by capital (self-valorising value) the spirit of capitalism *takes possession* of the real world of production and consumption. When capital attempts to ground itself *on* production, it runs into economic determinations springing from use value. This should have dethroned value; but instead the opposite happens; the spectre prevails. The spectre 'takes possession' of use value, estranges its meaning, drains away its truth, and substitutes a new one. Just as those 'possessed' by spirits use their own larynx and tongue but speak in another's voice, so use values are 'possessed' by capital, in the spiritual as well as the legal sense. Capital speaks through them only of its own concerns, profit and accumulation.

The positing of value

This raises the question of how exactly to connect categorially the value endorsed in exchange with the positing of value as a result of the activity of production.

A clue is given in the *language* of Marx's *Capital* when he first introduces the topic of the labour process. Here he gives an 'idealist' reading even of concrete labour, as a form-giving fire that freezes into fixity:

> What on the side of the worker appeared in the form of unrest [*Unruhe*]
> now appears, on the side of the product, in the form of being, as a fixed,

immobile [*ruhende*] characteristic. The worker has spun and the product is a spinning.

(Marx 1976a: 287)

The proper place for such metaphysical considerations is really the other section (on the valorisation process) of that chapter, where the idea of an activity passing into fixity makes good sense of the relation between the activity of value-positing and the resulting value. This result must have a material product to inhabit but what counts is its conceptual form as value, hence absenting its determinate material features and reducing it to nothing more than the *abstract result* of activity. Thus the value 'substance' is nothing other than the *condensation of the activity* that posited the commodity as a value; the *act* of positing value results in its own fixity. In the passage quoted earlier there is an unmistakable reminiscence of Hegel's language of 'Becoming' determining itself to 'Being'. Hegel writes: 'Becoming is an unstable unrest [*Unruhe*] which settles into a stable [*ruhiges*] result' (Hegel 1969: 106). So Marx deliberately identifies the process of production with Hegel's restless 'Becoming'. However, there is an inflexion of this category to be noted; originally when discussing the 'Becoming' of value in the space of exchange, its inner moments were identified as 'Being' and 'Nothing'. Now, as already something, value is grappling with the sphere of its *non-being*, the domain of production as a real process of determinate transformation of use values. What was an inner relation is here external, such that 'Being' *faces* its non-being and must internalise it. This more concrete level of 'Becoming' is an unstable unity of 'Being' and 'non-being'.

When 'Becoming' *comes to rest* in a result, namely a marketable commodity, value is *posited*. The result value, abstracted from its contingent use value support, has to be considered simply as *what has become* from the unrest of its becoming, simply as its conclusion in finite determination.

The difficult problem is to understand production as at one and the same time a labour process and the bearer of value in motion. At the level of the production of real being, use value undergoes a determinate transformation from raw material to goods, mediated by labour. Now the absolute negativity of capital takes this within its grasp such that concrete labour is reduced to the bearer of the abstract activity of transformation, namely negating of use value. Capital is not interested in the particularities of the determinate transformation of material, only in the reproduction of value. In accord with the earlier mentioned structure of inversion this negating of use value simply *is* the positing of value. The use value positing of labour is abstracted from so that in itself it counts as the activity of value positing insofar as all concrete determinacy involved in use value positing is absented leaving the logical category of positing *per se*.

Self-valorising value posits itself in comprehending within itself production, through negating *dialectically* (i.e. *preserving* the material side within it) the realm of the real labour of production. So far from labour embodying itself in commodities and thereby constituting them as values, the value form embodies itself in production, subordinates its purposes to value creation, and realises itself in the product, posited as nothing but its own othering, when it successfully gains control of the labour process.

With this sinking of the value form into production, such that production is formed as production *for exchange*, the empty presence of value appears to gain a material filling. But this is not quite so; for the manner in which the spectre (capital) takes possession of the labour crystallised in products is such that this too becomes, as the stuff of an ideal objectivity (value), itself constituted as a 'spectral objectivity' (Marx: '*gespenstige Gegenständlichkeit*'), reduced to 'pure jelly' (Marx: '*eine blosse Gallerte*'), ectoplasm (Marx 1962: 52; 1976a: 128).[13]

The abstract objectivity of value mediates itself in the abstract activity of value positing. Conversely what abstract labour 'produces' can be only an abstract product such as value, whose magnitude is a function of the amount of spectralised labour absorbed.

This raises the issue of determining the magnitude of value. Money is its measure, but what is the immanent determinant of the magnitude measured in money terms? We have defined value as an empty presence; but how can there be 'plenty of nothing'? The answer is that this is a determinate nothing resulting from the passing into fixity of the restless process of its becoming, a cessation that sublates its origin, i.e. preserves the process in the product as a definite magnitude. Value posits itself as a quantity of negating activity fixed as what *is posited*. The only possible measure of such negating activity is the time it goes on for.

When we examine a product we may judge that 'a lot of work has gone into it' but such work is generalised concrete labour evident in the carving, polishing, etc. However if we have as product only a *spectral* 'body of work', how can that be represented as 'six hours worth'? It can – simply *as* mediated result: mediated in *what*? It does not matter! as long as the result of six hours can be represented as twice that of three hours: hence the peculiar immaterial dimensionality of money. The dimensionality of the source (time) is simply given a different categorial status in the product as finite result of so much time that *has* passed. (Hegel points out that the 'Essence' is a past tense of Be-ing: 'The truth of *being* is *essence* [*Wesen*]. . . . The [German] language has preserved essence in the past participle [*gewesen*] of the verb *to be*; for essence is past – but timelessly past – being' (Hegel 1969: 389).) A crystal of accumulated time, the fixing of time that passed, is the magnitude represented in money.

'Nothing' nothings

The commodity understood as the *result* of capitalist production is not merely the visible immediacy of use value, but a truly metaphysical entity, as Marx promised. The void at the heart of bourgeois life results in the most accomplished irony: accumulation as an infinite increase in emptiness is mistaken for a plenitude of wealth. What capitalist accumulation is (un)really about is the sublimation of material wealth into a ghost of itself. Capital is a spectre in that through it the originally posited 'Nothing' gains *its determinacy*, subsuming, transforming and negating the 'real being' of the capitalist economy. But is it really *present*? Is it not rather a halo, a mirage, a semblance of actuality? To those who doubt that 'Nothing' can have agency and power I reply: 'It acts therefore it exists.' That it acts is demonstrated by the impossibility of trying to say what is going on in a factory without referring to valorisation; and what is that but increase in money? And what is money but the empty universal that not only 'stands for' real wealth but elbows it aside and takes precedence? In money-making the spirit of capitalism is able to enter into commerce with the earthly reality of production and consumption.

The spectre inhabits such material as a secret subject, animating it, and, vampire-like, communicating spectrality to all with which it has intercourse. Under the hegemony of the spirit world of capital, the phenomenal subject is itself a spectre. We exist for each other only as its instances, its 'personifications', 'masks', 'supports', to use Marx's terms. A world of spirits is therewith incarnated in us, 'our' activity, and 'our' products. 'Now nothing but Spirit rules in the world' said the post-Hegelian Max Stirner.[14] He knew this, but he could not elucidate it. Instead he blamed our 'fixed ideas', as if the fault were in us. But the fault is in reality; hence the needed critique is not critique of a false view of the world, but one that moves within the object itself, granting its objective validity, epochally speaking: in the society of the spectre the false is *out there*.[15]

Notes

1 I thank for comments on the first draft Andy Brown, Geert Reuten and Nick Hostettler.
2 '*Emergence*: A relationship between two terms such that one term . . . arises out of the other, but is capable of reacting back on the first and is in any event causally and taxonomically irreducible to it' (Bhaskar 1993: 397).
3 I have elsewhere argued for this homology and given a detailed account of the parallels between the categories of Hegel's *Logic* and those of Marx's *Capital* (see Arthur 2000).
4 The Marxian notion of ontological inversion presupposes a stratified ontology obtains, rather then the 'flat' ontology of empiricism (Bhaskar 1991: 147).
5 *Verrückung* (= displacement; derangement) is an important term in Marx, as Backhaus has pointed out (Backhaus 1992: 61–2). In his usage of *Verrücktheit* Marx draws on its double meaning as 'dis-placement' and 'madness'. For example, he says that in the value form the relation between private labour and the collective labour of society appears '*in dieser verrückten Form*', translated by B. Fowkes as 'this absurd form' (Marx 1976a: 169).
6 I distinguish value's origin in 'Nothing' from the non-being of value. The latter is how the dialectic of capital posits the realm of use value. R. Albritton, following Sekine, grasps this but, from my standpoint, confuses this *non-being* of value with

the *Nothing* of the dialectic of value itself (Albritton 1999: 70). I take the dialectic to begin from the value-form; if so, then *both* the initial moments (Being and Nothing) must be moments of value. Incidentally, Sekine and Albritton see 'reification' (rather than 'inversion') as the crucial critical category; value is taken in a positive sense as a social reality, albeit reified.

7 '*Perspectival switch*. The switch from one transcendentally or dialectically necessary condition or aspect of a phenomenon, thing or totality to another which is also transcendentally or dialectically necessary for it' (Bhaskar 1993: 401).

8 The method of systematic dialectic depends in my view on the possibility of such retrospective validation (see Arthur 1998).

9 Bhaskar (1993: 337) identifies '*Dasein*' as a crucial moment of Hegel's uncritical positivism.

10 Although I now contextualise the dialectic of capital differently, this previous work detailing the homology between Hegel's categories and those of Marx may still be affirmed, in virtue of the aforementioned reflection of their 'spirals'.

11 Notice that, just as Hegel's Logic ends with Absolute Method, which in effect reinstates the mediating activity bracketed at the absolute beginning, so the perfected value form, capital, realises itself in a *circuit of exchanges*, so this (seemingly external) condition of existence of value is then *internal* to its completed concept.

12 '*Constellationality*: A figure of containment within an over-reaching term . . . from which the over-reached term may be diachronically or synchronically emergent. It may take the form of identity, unity, fluidity etc.' (Bhaskar 1993: 395).

13 Re: '*gespenstige*'. This has the same root as the 'spectre' of communism announced in the first sentence of the *Communist Manifesto*. Notice that, for Marx, communism is not of course a 'spectre' but 'the *real* movement which abolishes the present state of things' (Marx and Engels 1976: 49). However, the beginning of the *Manifesto* reports the experience of the bourgeoisie. For them, who take the spectrality of capital *for reality*, everything must be inverted and the truth of communism seen as an unnatural abomination.

14 Quoted in Marx and Engels 1976: 190.

15 'What is false is in the ontological order itself' (Bhaskar 1993: 110).

Bibliography

Albritton, R. (1999) *Dialectic and Deconstruction in Political Economy*, Basingstoke, UK: Macmillan, and New York: St. Martin's.

Arthur, C. J. (1998) 'Systematic dialectic', *Science & Society* 62, 3: 447—59.

—— (2000) 'From the Critique of Hegel to the Critique of Capital', in T. Burns and I. Fraser (eds) *The Hegel–Marx Connection*, Basingstoke, UK: Macmillan.

—— (2001) 'Value, Labour and Negativity', *Capital & Class* 73 Spring: 15—39.

Backhaus, H-G. (1992) 'Between Philosophy and Science: Marxian Social Economy as Critical Theory', in W. Bonefeld, R. Gunn and K. Psychopedis (eds) *Open Marxism: Volume I Dialectics and History*, London: Pluto.

Bhaskar, R. (1991) 'Dialectics', in Tom Bottomore (ed.) *A Dictionary of Marxist Thought*, 2nd edition, Oxford: Blackwell.

—— (1993) *Dialectic: The Pulse of Freedom*, London: Verso.

Böhm-Bawerk, E. von (1975) *Karl Marx and the Close of his System*, London: Merlin.

Derrida, J. (1994) *Specters of Marx*, New York: Routledge.

Hegel, G. W. F. (1969) *The Science of Logic*, translated by A. V. Miller, London: George Allen & Unwin.

Marx, K. (1962) *Das Kapital: Erster Band, Marx–Engels Werke 23*, Berlin: Dietz Verlag.

—— (1973) *Marx's Grundrisse*, translated by M. Nicolaus, Harmondsworth, UK: Penguin.

—— (1976a) *Capital*, vol. I, translated by B. Fowkes, Harmondsworth, UK: Penguin.

—— (1976b) *Value: Studies by Karl Marx,* translated by A. Dragstedt, London: New Park.

Marx, K. and Engels, F. (1976) *The German Ideology, Marx–Engels Collected Works 5,* London: Lawrence & Wishart.

Willett, C. (1990) 'The Shadow of Hegel's *Science of Logic*', in G. di Giovanni (ed.) *Essays on Hegel's Logic*, Albany, NY: SUNY Press.

12 Abstracting emancipation

Two dialectics on the trail of freedom[1]

John Michael Roberts

Introduction

In his justly famous essay, Isaiah Berlin (1969) sketched out two definitions of the concept 'freedom'. According to Berlin, 'negative liberty' refers to those actions or forms of regulation that might interfere with my own acts. Negative liberty is concerned with the question, 'what is the area within which the subject – a person or group of persons – is or should be left to do, or be what he is able to do, or be, without interference by other persons?' By way of contrast Berlin suggested that 'positive liberty' is directed towards the establishment of self-government. The most salient question to ask here is, 'what, or who, is the source of control or influence that can determine someone to do, or be, this rather than that?' (Berlin 1969: 121–2). The main difference between these two concepts of 'freedom' is therefore this. Whereas negative libertarians base themselves within a classical liberal account of freedom and seek to justify a space within society where a 'free individual' can exist without interference from the state, society and other individuals, positive libertarians seek to justify state intervention within society in order to enhance, develop and promote those abilities, powers, capacities, opportunities and resources deemed necessary for self-determination. Thus, as Ramsay (1997: 39) argues in her excellent critique of liberal political thought, negative liberty is at the same time an ideological justification for private property because it maintains that the free market is the ideal social arena for the pursuit of individual autonomy and free action. State intervention merely hinders the rational workings of free competition and trade. Only if state intervention ensures the adequate functioning of the market can it be justified.

One of the most original contributions to this ongoing debate has been that developed by critical realists. Adopting what is plainly a positive concept of liberty, critical realists have been at pains to point out that a social analysis of the freedom to act must take account of the often non-observable causal powers which may (or may not) inhibit or obstruct potential courses of action. By taking seriously the impact that these underlying powers have on individual actions, critical realists begin to address the crucial issue of how such causal properties either promote or impede the necessary abilities, powers, capacities, opportunities and resources which go towards assessing whether an act can be said to be free. Three advantages can be flagged up here for a critical social theory if we take on board these observations.

The first advantage is that we can begin to overcome an empiricist account of human agency. Empiricism holds an essentially passive view of human agency based upon a sensory theory of causality. At its simplest, a sensory theory of causality reduces the independent causal production of objects to observational statements about causality between objects. Causality, on such an account, rests upon the ability of *individuals* to understand the cause and effect relationships between themselves and objects in the world. This is the usual theory of causality applied by many thinkers in the liberal theory tradition (Hoffman 1986). Yet this theory of causality cannot, according to critical realists, adequately explain the internal structure and causal powers of the *real* domain of objects. The real domain refers to the intrinsic powers of objects that exist irrespective of whether they generate events for the human senses to directly observe (Bhaskar 1978: 56).

The second advantage relates to the possibility of generating knowledge about underlying causal powers which can be used to *transform* those causal powers which we believe oppress us in some way or another. Applying critical realism in this manner therefore involves the possibility of *emancipating* ourselves from those very powers that oppress us.

The third advantage rests upon the insistence by critical realists that an integral link exists between facts and values. According to critical realists, a social analysis concerned with the freedom to act must also consider the link between causal powers of the world and the causal powers bound up with human agency. Included in the latter set of causal powers are those beliefs and values guiding human agency. On this understanding, our beliefs about the social world are bound up in some way or another by the way the world is structured. Under this definition, freedom becomes the freedom to understand the complexly structured causal nature of the world through the beliefs and values we hold about it. The dialectisation of critical realism by Bhaskar (1993) enriches this account of emancipation by placing freedom within an interconnected totality along with their associated sub-totalities. This enables Bhaskar to provide a much more complex and precise account of freedom, an account that recognises the different dimensions of freedom.

In this chapter I wish to critically explore the emancipatory project of critical realism as regards the concept of freedom. While I believe that critical realists make some astute observations around this subject matter, and while they are clearly concerned to construct a social theory which is directed towards the Left of the political spectrum, I also believe that critical realists are in danger of developing a somewhat general-historical account of freedom. Focusing primarily upon the work of Bhaskar, I hope to demonstrate that both critical realism and dialectical critical realism violently abstract the concepts 'freedom' and 'emancipation' from specific ideological social relations. As a result, both concepts are explored at too high a level of abstraction to be meaningful for political action. I make these observations through a comparative analysis with Marxism. This seems a particularly apt approach to take if for no other reason than because Bhaskar has explicitly suggested that Marx is a closet critical realist (cf. Bhaskar 1986, 1989).

By basing my observations within Marxism I am able to compare the emancipatory claims of critical realism to a similar though, as I hope to demonstrate, substantially different social theory. Through this comparative procedure I can also begin to construct a base through which to pose an alternative way of thinking about emancipation and its relationship to freedom. Even though these alternative insights should be taken as preliminary and as in no way representing a detailed account, I believe that they do nevertheless open the way for a more satisfactory way of thinking about the historical and ideological form of emancipation and freedom. This has profound consequences for the issues of emancipation and freedom. I begin first by outlining a dialectical critical realist take on these two essentially contested concepts.

Emancipation and freedom: a dialectical critical realist perspective

In *Scientific Realism and Human Emancipation*, Bhaskar defines emancipation along the following lines:

> It is my contention that that special qualitative kind of becoming free or liberation which is *emancipation*, and which consists in the *transformation*, in self-emancipation by the agents concerned, *from an unwanted and unneeded to a wanted and needed source of determination*, is both causally presaged and logically entailed by emancipatory theory, but that it can only be effected in *practice*. Emancipation, as so defined, depends upon the transformation of structures, not the alteration or amelioration of states of affairs. In this special sense an emancipatory politics or practice is necessarily both grounded in scientific theory and revolutionary objective or intent.
>
> (Bhaskar 1986: 171)

Here Bhaskar clearly outlines a positive concept of freedom. This is because freedom, to become meaningful, is also:

> (1) to know one's real interests; (2) to possess both (a) the ability and the resources, i.e. generically the power, and (b) the opportunity to act in (or towards) them; and (3) to be disposed to do so.
>
> (Bhaskar 1986: 171)

To understand Bhaskar's particular take on positive freedom we need to say more about the specificity of a critical realist position.

The first observation to make in this respect is that critical realists defend a 'naturalist theory of knowledge'. This is based upon the premise that adequate knowledge of the social world can be gained by transferring to a significant extent the methods of the natural sciences to the social sciences. To understand how we might go about transforming an unwanted and unneeded 'source of determination' to a wanted and needed one it is necessary to explore the structured and layered properties of the social world – 'social structures' – beyond that which is immediately visible to the senses. Thus, like natural science, social science should aim to take seriously the structured and layered properties of the world beyond that of human consciousness. Unlike natural science, however, social science cannot afford to ignore human consciousness but must include the ideas, beliefs, etc., with which individuals act upon when they interact within society and social structures. Simply stated, human consciousness is the characteristic 'causal power' that separates the social world from the natural world. This being the case, human consciousness must form part of the explanation about society and social structures.

Due to the fact that social science must take account of human consciousness Bhaskar insists that the explanatory work of social science differs from natural science in three ways: (i) social structures, unlike natural structures, do not exist independently of the activities they govern; (ii) social structures, unlike natural structures, do not exist independently of the agents' conceptions of what they are doing in their activity; (iii) social structures, unlike natural structures, may be only relatively enduring (so that the tendencies they ground may not be universal in the sense of space-time invariant) (Bhaskar 1989: 79). According to Bhaskar, these principles demonstrate ontological, epistemological and relational limits to naturalism.

Yet it is also part of Bhaskar's naturalist account of the social world that human consciousness can direct individuals to an emancipatory path to freedom. This can be seen in his earlier exposition of the 'transformational model of social activity' (TMSA). This model revolves around the claim that society is both the condition and outcome of human praxis, while praxis is the (conscious) production and (unconscious) reproduction of society (Bhaskar 1989: 92). By adopting the TMSA we gain adequate knowledge of the 'motivated productions' of society along with the 'unmotivated conditions' necessary for these productions. In line with his 'limits to naturalism', however, Bhaskar strongly urges us to follow an 'epistemological relativism' – objects and structures can only be known under particular definitions (Bhaskar 1978: 249). This is an anti-foundationalist theory of knowledge insofar that 'being' is only *contingently* related to knowledge (Outhwaite 1987: 36–44; Pratt 1995: 65). We can now return to Bhaskar's definition of freedom as outlined in *Scientific Realism and Human Emancipation*.

As we have already seen, in *Scientific Realism* Bhaskar suggests that an emancipatory critique must be reflexive of its location within its own pre-determined surroundings. If an emancipatory critique also aims to develop 'a revolutionary object or intent', then freedom, as part of this revolutionary object and intent, can only be meaningful to the extent that it too is situated within the predeterminations of the world around us. Bhaskar expresses this point about an emancipatory critique with the following observation:

> I want to insist that social science always happens in a context which is at once always understood, preconceptualised, and codetermined by non-cognitive factors too. So that, on this stance, social science appears, at its best, in the form of *conditioned critique*. As critique, it presupposes and engages with those preconceptualisations; as conditioned, it is subject in its genesis, reception and effect, to extra-scientific, extra-cognitive and non-ideational, as well as scientific, cognitive and ideational, determinations (whose critical understanding is itself part of the business of theory).
>
> (Bhaskar 1986: 170)

To be conscious of freedom is to be conscious of those 'non-cognitive' and 'cognitive' predeterminations in order to transform them into a 'wanted and needed source of determination'. We could also add from the overall discussion so far that these predeterminations exist at a number of levels of abstraction because the social world is complexly structured and layered. Freedom is thus an integral moment of Bhaskar's idea of emancipation.

Bhaskar deepens his account of freedom by insisting that three additional ideas about human agency are linked to an emancipatory critique. First, intentional human agency is caused, in a large measure, by *reasons*. Second, reasons are bound up with 'preconceptualisations' and 'predeterminations'. This being the case, reasons have an ontological identity to the extent that they are defined through their intrinsic relationship with the ontological structure of the world. As such our reasons can help us to change the onto-logical structure of the world in whatever measure. Third, the freedom to act is based upon the principle that reason is a causal mechanism and upon the principle that reason can be undetermined by physical bodily states. Reasons are real in their own right and are therefore not reducible to purely physical phenomenon such as the brain (cf. Bhaskar 1979/1998: ch. 3). This 'emergent powers materialism' (Bhaskar 1979/1998: 97 ff.) is aptly summed up by Benton through his following example:

> A certain structure of the central nervous system, vocal and auditory organs, in working order, is a necessary condition for speech . . . However the position is not reductionist, in that I do not *reduce* the ability to speak to its organic condition.
>
> (Benton 1997: 87)

Causal connections may very well exist between the structure of psycho-logical abilities and the structure of organic processes, but both are still distinct causal mechanisms – they are both ontologically real – in their own right.

Causality, or 'causal powers', is taken by critical realists to mean something different to more mainstream accounts of causality such as that found within empiricism. According to critical realists, an object can be said to possess a set of causal powers in its status as an object. Causal powers thereby refer to an object's *power to* act in a particular manner irrespective of their empirical effects in the contingent conditions of the everyday world. A causal power is therefore best seen as a complexly layered feature of an object. As a causal power reason is likewise complexly structured and layered and this further implies that a person's conscious reason for an action may not be their *real* reason. Rather, and in keeping with a critical realist explanatory framework, the *real* reason for an action may be based upon an unconscious desire, unacknowledged conditions and tacit skills. All of these elements may not be readily apparent to an individual and yet they all contribute to an individual's *agency*; an agency which in turn produces unintended consequences.

Freedom, upon this understanding, turns upon the capacities bound up within agency. In particular, freedom is coming to understand the causal powers of reasons and their relationship to intentional human behaviour. By becoming conscious of reasons as causes we become conscious of the fact that we are 'free to act otherwise' (Bhaskar 1979/1998: 114). This is especially the case when we realise, with Bhaskar, that intentional human behaviour operates in 'open systems'. These are systems in which unpredictability, uncertainty and contingency reign supreme implying that all we can ever really know about a causal power in such circumstances are their *tendencies* to operate in a certain manner. An agent is therefore also free in the sense that s/he 'could have acted otherwise' in a world that is open and undetermined (cf. Bhaskar 1979/1998: 114).

In the next section I want to begin to critically assess the emancipatory critique developed by Bhaskar. I wish to do this in the first instance by focusing upon emergent powers materialism. By comparing Bhaskar's *realist* theory of human consciousness to Marx's *materialist* theory of human consciousness, I will try to show why Bhaskar has come to be accused by some theorists of propagating a dualist theory of mind and matter and why there is some justification in this accusation. Primarily Bhaskar does not understand the relationship between mind and matter as one being mediated through a historical realm. In the section that immediately follows I suggest that Bhaskar's recent dialectisation of critical realism is an attempt, in part, to overcome this type of accusation. However, I do not believe that Bhaskar is successful in this.

Exploring a dualism: mind and matter

As we have already seen, Bhaskar (e.g. 1989: 73–4) is quite explicit in his insistence that Marx is a closet critical realist. Certainly it is possible to detect similarities between both Bhaskar and Marx. For example, both view human consciousness as being predetermined by the non-cognitive realm. Correspondingly, both suggest that how the world appears is often a distorted expression of the underlying structures of this predetermination. Thus both likewise argue that this distorted appearance may serve to mask exploitative power relations associated with the predetermined non-cognitive realm. However, I think it is also true to say that a major difference separates both thinkers. While Marx, like Bhaskar, takes seriously the need to sketch out some of the universal characteristics of human activity, Marx, unlike Bhaskar, ensures that these universal characteristics have a historical dimension attached to their very core. I will expand upon this point through a brief discussion of Marx's early work in the *Economic and Philosophic Manuscripts of 1844*.

In the *Economic and Philosophic Manuscripts of 1844* Marx seeks to provide, amongst other things, an account of the estrangement of human nature. Marx prefers the term 'species-being' to that of 'human nature'. Marx defines species-being in the following manner:

> Man is a species-being, not only because in practice and in theory he adopts the species (his own as well as those of other things) as his object, but – and this is only another way of expressing it – also because he treats himself as the actual, living species; because he treats himself as a *universal* and therefore a free being.
>
> (Marx 1844/1981: 67)

Marx suggests that a defining characteristic of being human, of being a species-being, is driven by the activity of producing for the species as a whole. Species-being is a social activity whereby each individual produces for their own needs and for the needs of others and vice versa (cf. Chitty 1993). But Marx also suggests that through social activity individuals gain a sense of freedom. This freedom is based upon the ability of individuals to *consciously* direct production to meet collective needs.

> The animal is immediately one with its life activity. It does not distinguish itself from it. It is *its life activity*. Man makes his life activity itself the object of his will and of his consciousness. He has conscious life activity. It is not a determination with which he directly emerges. Conscious life activity distinguishes man immediately from animal life activity. It is just because of this that he is a species-being. Or it is only because he is a species-being that he is a conscious being, i.e., that his

own life is an object for him. Only because of that is his activity free activity.

(Marx 1844/1981: 68)

Freedom, according to Marx, is in the first instance bound up with a specific social activity, namely the collective and conscious labouring capacity of individuals and society as a whole. As a result, Marx believes that consciousness is an integral part of labouring upon the objective world. 'It is just in his work upon the objective world, therefore, that man really proves himself to be a *species-being*. This production is his active species-life' (Marx 1844/ 1981: 69). This leads Marx to further assert that there is no *ontological* distinction between mind and matter. 'Thinking and being are thus certainly *distinct*, but at the same time they are in *unity* with each other' (Marx 1844/ 1981: 93). Mind is a *form* of matter, though a distinct one at that. That is to say, Marx views the relationship between mind and matter as a monism.

Yet it is also important to note that an historical dimension figures strongly in Marx's account. Matter, for Marx, is in a constant state of motion. Consciousness can be seen to exist as a qualitative manifestation of this motion and, as a form of matter, consciousness assists labour in thinking about the appropriation of this motion to meet changing human needs. Even universal human needs are a historical product. For example, Marx and Engels argue in *The German Ideology* that the first historical act of humanity is the satisfaction of basic, fundamental human needs such as eating, drinking, habitation, clothing, etc. However, basic human needs lead to the creation of new needs. These new needs are also an integral 'moment' of the 'first' historical act. Through this natural, social and historical relation there develops co-operation amongst individuals as is evident in the development of the family structure and modes of production (Marx and Engels 1845–6/1994: 48–50).

To suggest that species-being is rooted within history obviously tells us very little about the nature of specific historical relations such as capitalism. Species-being is, in other words, a concept located at a high transcendental level of abstraction. Even so, the discussion so far indicates that at this level a historical dimension still figures strongly in Marx's account in two complementary ways. First, Marx insists that the ontological unity between mind and matter is based upon the premise that matter is in a constant state of motion – matter changes – and consciousness, as part of matter, changes its form also. This is why mind can be said to be a qualitatively distinct *form* of matter in motion.

Second, Marx argues that species-being develops through distinct forms of labouring activity. Marx terms these forms of labouring activity as 'modes of production'. A mode of production is characterised by the unity of forces of production (those instruments through which concrete, everyday human labour produces useful products) and relations of production (the form which labour takes for it to engender surplus extraction within historical periods). When *class* societies are the object of analytical attention then the relationship between forces and relations of production assumes a *contradictory* unity because this relationship is defined primarily through opposing class forces that encapsulate a form of *exploitation*. 'Mode of production' is therefore a useful term because it prompts us to begin to think about the total experience of specific and historical forms of contradiction and exploitation.

Summarising the observations so far we can say that both senses of the term 'historical' opens up a space for Marx to show how species-being is (i) an integral moment of the material world, which is (ii) bound up with a form of consciousness that develops by interacting with the changing nature of the material world through the labouring activity of individuals, so that (iii) distinctively human creative powers change their form during distinct historical modes of producing wants and needs.

While I believe that both historical dimensions are integral to Marx's development of historical materialism, I am not convinced that they are integral to Bhaskar's emergent powers materialism perspective. As we have seen, this perspective is based upon the idea that mind *emerges from* the material world, but that mind is also ontologically *distinct* to the material world. There is no necessity in such a perspective for mind to constantly change over time nor is there a necessity for mind to be the outcome of specific modes of production. From a Marxist perspective, therefore, Bhaskar constructs a thoroughly confusing and question-begging materialist account of the mind in both senses of the term 'historical' outlined above. That is to say, Bhaskar constructs a more invariant and non-historical account of mind than that of Marx.

If we take the first sense of the term historical, then the following observations can be made. To begin with, what does it mean to say that mental capacities cannot be reduced from the physical states from which they emerged? How are they therefore to be grounded in the physical world? If causal powers associated with reasons are simply seen as part of the essence of being 'human', then we are in danger of adopting an extreme individualist and voluntarist position in which the structures of the world are *reduced* to the essence of human causal powers (Suchting 1992: 28). If, on the other hand, emergence is read as an intransitive and ontological category so that the emergence of mind from matter is ontologically though irreducibly real, then all we can really do is to understand the interaction between mind and matter as one of 'constant-conjunction'. Yet such a position obviously strays close to an empiricist account of mind and matter (Pleasants 1999: 109). As critics have suggested, on Bhaskar's account we are left in a dualist minefield and the notion of *duality*, the idea that it is possible for two ontological realms to interact causally, presents more problems than it solves (Bryant 1995; Roberts 1999).

If we take the second sense of the term historical, then the following observations can be made. In the first instance, if mind does not emerge from particular modes of production then how are we to account for the specific historical and *ideological* limits to human activity? This becomes a particularly problematic question for Bhaskar because he argues that the social world is 'open' and that individuals can always 'act otherwise'. The social world is 'open' to the extent that both structures and agents interact with each other in contingent and open contexts. Thus although Bhaskar does stress that agents always operate within a predetermined world, he has a weak sense of what this predetermination entails because he has no *ground* in which to say how freedom is constrained by a specific set of ideological social relations such as a mode of production. Thus structures and agents remain, on Bhaskar's understanding, 'undetermined' by 'open systems' (agents are free to the extent that they can 'always act otherwise'). It would seem to be the case that Bhaskar ultimately believes that human agency is just as undetermined as much as everything else in the world is 'undetermined'. As a result, as Pleasants (1999: 116) notes, freedom is grounded 'in ignorance' because we have no real way of saying how a specific ideological form of historical determinism must *necessarily* interact with an historically specific ideological form of freedom.

To sum up the main points of the argument in this section we can say that for Marx consciousness is both a social *and* historical product. This differs from the emergent powers materialism perspective as developed by Bhaskar. As we have seen, Bhaskar argues that it is possible to identify a transcendental and abstract 'essence' of human beings. In contrast, the Marxist position defended in this chapter argues that distinctively human attributes – those attributes which coalesce into 'species-being' – are historical products which emerge from the ability of individuals to labour upon the world in order to meet their needs. As new needs are satisfied and new ones develop, consciousness changes and alters its form. Through this combination, namely the development of new needs and the development of new forms of consciousness, we increase our skills and abilities to rationally control and organise society to meet human needs. As a result we also increase our freedom and autonomy insofar that we develop the basis to overcome *forced* labour driven by distinctive relations of exploitation (cf. Sayers 1998: 40, 65).

In the next two sections I wish to explore these preliminary points in more detail. By turning my attention to dialectical critical realism I will suggest that the concept of unity-in-opposite is a crucial one for a dialectical emancipatory theory because it incorporates the idea of 'essential, internal and determining contradiction'. Once this element has been brought into the analytical picture we can begin to see how and why the *meaning* of freedom is itself contradictory because it is entwined within a set of *specific* exploitative social relationships in which different classes attach different interpretations to its significatory power. I argue that these crucial insights are missing from dialectical critical realism. By neglecting these insights it is not at all clear how dialectic is to be conceived as, in Bhaskar's words, 'the pulse of freedom'.

Hegel, freedom and the question of dialectics

The dialecticisation of critical realism by Bhaskar in his monumental *Dialectic: The Pulse of Freedom* (1993) places the emancipatory project of critical realism onto a new metatheoretical level. Such is the breadth and scope of *Dialectic* that a full and detailed account of the themes contained in that work can not realistically be presented here. Rather I will briefly say something about the enriched account of freedom that Bhaskar presents here.

In *Dialectic* Bhaskar suggests that emancipation and the freedom which it encapsulates both become embroiled within the logic of 'absence'. Absence is Bhaskar's defining category (or 'the second moment' which is abbreviated to 2E) of dialectical critical realism. According to Bhaskar absence demonstrates that the stratification, emergence and ground of a causal power (the 'first moment' of dialectical critical realism which is abbreviated to 1M) is only possible through the absence of some other causal power (the moment of 2E), and so on. Simply stated, the stratified nature of the world implies that each causal power is dependent upon an emergent causal power not yet known. However, the critical realist view that the world is complexly layered and stratified means that the absence of knowledge concerning the dependence of a causal power upon another causal power is an ontological question. Seen in this way it is possible to say that absence is real.

Bhaskar also suggests that agency is characterised by action against some constraint or another. This, as we have seen, is central to the critical realist notion of agency and freedom. From this seemingly simple observation Bhaskar goes on to make a stronger claim which revolves around a universality principle. Due to the fact that each person aims at 'absenting some constraint', then it follows (on Bhaskar's reckoning) that each person is simultaneously and universally committed to the goal of freedom from the external constraint in question. 'So the goal of universal human autonomy is implicit in every moral judgement' (Bhaskar 1993: 264).

In order to overcome what Bhaskar readily admits is a somewhat formal criterion of freedom (1993: 264), a more substantive basis is required. Bhaskar develops this through his '*naturalistically grounded* four-planar theory of the possibilities of social being' (Bhaskar 1993: 264). This four-planar account comprises:

[a] = plane of material transactions with nature
[b] = plane of inter/intra-subjective [personal] relations
[c] = plane of social relations
[d] = plane of subjectivity of the agent.

(Bhaskar 1993: 160)

According to Bhaskar, these four planes 'generalise, dialecticise and substantialise the TMSA' (Bhaskar 1993: 160). They do so because they situate the characteristics of the TMSA within a relational and absenting totality. This can be seen more readily once we take account of the enriched theory of power encapsulated within the four planes.

Bhaskar makes the distinction between power 1 relations and power 2 relations. The first, power 1 relations, relate to 'the transformative capacity intrinsic to the concept of agency as such' (Bhaskar 1993: 153). The second, power 2 relations, relate to 'the . . . transfactually efficacious capacity to get one's way against either (i) the overt wishes and/or (ii) the real interests of others (grounded in their concrete singularities); and to thematise the plurality, which approximates to a *potential transfinity* of power 2 or *generalised master–slave-type relationships* from class and gender to age and ethnicity' (Bhaskar 1993: 153–4). Thus Bhaskar wishes to differentiate between a type of power which merely stipulates 'power to' (power 1) from a more dominant type of power (power 2) which seeks to control and manipulate. This is a type of power related to structures and ideology.

Bhaskar's main point is that all power 2 relations are of a type of power 1 relation, but the reverse is not the case. Not all power relations are necessarily founded upon control, manipulation, ideology, etc. Moreover, power 1 relations can be found at plane a, but power 2 relations are found mainly at planes b, c and d. At each plane there can be distinguished a further set of power relations. So, for example, Bhaskar suggests at plane c it is possible to distinguish hegemonic/counter-hegemonic forces, discursive and normative relations. At plane b Bhaskar distinguishes communicative and moral relations (Bhaskar 1993: 153). A dialectic of freedom is therefore concerned with the absenting of power 2 relations and such a freedom is really found at planes b, c and d. These planes can be broken down into further realms of power.

Undeniably, and as a result of the dialecticisation of the TMSA, Bhaskar provides a more thorough and discriminating analysis of the negation of power and constraints and this development enriches his earlier work on critical realism. Notwithstanding this, there is still a real sense in which Bhaskar still fails to take fully into consideration the two senses of the term 'historical' which were so integral to Marx's ideas on similar theoretical issues. As I have suggested, Marx takes very seriously the idea that individuals are unique creatures to the extent that they embody a distinct historically evolving 'essence' within specific ideological and historical modes of production. But because Marx's thinking about these issues is rooted within Hegelian philosophy, I will now begin to critically explore dialectical critical realism by first, though briefly, discussing this Hegelian legacy. This move is justified not only because Marx was influenced by Hegel, but also because Bhaskar quite explicitly engages with Hegel himself. It is in part through this engagement that Bhaskar constructs dialectical critical realism.

Certainly it is true to say that many similarities can be noted between Bhaskar and Hegel. For example Hegel, like Bhaskar, is interested in theoretically exploring the underlying 'essences' of the world and how these essences appear to us in our everyday activity. According to Hegel the essence of an object must *necessarily* appear to human consciousness. However, its appearance can only ever reveal partial aspects of an essence. This means that appearance may provide us with an illusionary picture of an essence. However, such illusions are still aspects of an essence. 'Essence *appears*, so that it is now *real* illusory being, since the moments of illusory being have Existence' (Hegel 1812–1816/1969: 499–500). Appearance is at the same time a real illusion because it reveals something about the nature of the essence of an object. The reality, or existence, of an object is therefore comprised by the unity-in-opposite of essence and appearance.

But Hegel also suggests that essence *must* reveal itself through appearance. The primary reason for Hegel's conviction here is his belief that essence was structured by a set of internal and essential *contradictions*. According to Sayers (1994) there are two elements to an internal and essential contradiction.

> (1) (T)o stress that concrete things are not indifferent to one another, but rather in interaction and conflict with each other . . . (2) The concept of contradiction is required in order to stress that such concrete opposition is not external and accidental to things, but rather essential and necessary: it is internal to things and a part of their nature.
>
> (Sayers 1994: 8; see also Hunt 1993; Johnson 1982; Ollman 1993)

More importantly, Hegel argues that contradictions reside in real, concrete objects and not just in the way we think about them. Objects are structured by a *real* set of internal and essential contradictions, and through such contradictions objects gain movement and change. Indeed, according to Hegel, internal and essential contradictions mean that an essence develops through *self-movement* as the contradictions within an object transform into new determinations, possibilities and, eventually, new contradictions. This being the case, each pole within the opposition not only produces itself through the other, it also produces the totality of which it is a moment. Even so, the totality, as a collection of such moments, reproduces itself through its moments (Arthur 1995: 6). Moreover, even though essence dialectically unfolds into a contradictory totality it is nevertheless possible to distinguish a *determining moment* of a totality based within a set of determining contradictions. At the start of *The Science of Logic* Hegel announces that pure being is both something and nothing; it is positivity and negativity.

> (I)n the beginning, being and nothing are present as *distinguished* from each other; for the beginning points to something else – it is a non-being which carries a reference to being as to an other; that which begins, as yet *is* not, it is only the way to being. The being contained in the beginning is, therefore, a being which removes itself from non-being or sublates it as something opposed to it.
>
> (Hegel 1812–1816/1969: 73–4)

These twin moments endow being with a determining contradiction. From this determining contradiction Hegel seeks to understand the movement and change which result within concrete objects. Thus for Hegel contradiction is the driving force of the world (cf. Hegel 1812–1816/1969: 439).

Even so, Hegel's characterisation of Being is still incomplete. This is because Being is a simple immediate. Therefore Hegel has not at this stage of his analysis suggested how Being has a sense of universality related to its own determinations. That is to say, Hegel has not as yet demonstrated to us how Being develops through its own determinations into a universal, though contradictory, totality. What is required for further scientific analysis, according to Hegel, is an appreciation of the internal *mediation* of Being through concrete relationships. To trace this mediation is to trace an essence that connects Being through its various stages of development. Thus the idea of 'concrete' being developed here is one which seeks to trace the 'richest determinations' of an object as this relates to the developed essence of a contradictory starting point (in this case the contradictory starting point of Being). The term, Notion, captures for Hegel this sense of 'concrete' because it manages to convey the sense that thinking about the world seeks to uncover internal, developing contradictions of a systematic totality. Thus Notion operates as the universal element of thinking. Moreover, Notion *unites* the starting point of analysis and its end result by showing that they are both moments of the same contradictory totality (Shamsavari 1991: 126 ff.).

The foregoing discussion builds upon the critical observations already levelled against critical realism. For Hegel shows us that there is a complex process of determination related to a constituting structural contradiction at work within an object of analysis (cf. Hegel 1812–1816/1969: 121). Thus an object is a moment within the developing totality of a constituting contradiction. Certainly Bhaskar takes the question of an interconnected totality seriously in *Dialectic*. Yet he also constructs a somewhat weak theory of totality to the extent that he neglects the Hegelian idea that a totality is structured by a constituting contradiction. What Bhaskar constructs instead is a *relational* theory of a totality. Simply stated, a relational theory of a totality explores the interconnections and links that reside between the 'essences' or 'causal powers' of different objects. Yet on such an understanding there is no intrinsic mechanism to *force* the movement of an essence. According to Bhaskar's dialectic, we can see that objects are always partially constituted by something other than themselves and thus are 'fluid' and subject to 'change' because of this. But this tells us very little about the 'motor' of such change and fluidity, and tells us very little about how such fluidity and change are connected to one another. There is no sense of objects sharing an internal identity through the same *specific* determining contradiction. Implicit in Bhaskar's account, therefore, is the idea that the identity of an object is based upon its own distinctive causal power. This distinctive identity is, in turn, situated upon its *external* absence as this is mediated through its relationship to another object. This is an external absence in the sense that each object is not seen to be a moment of the unfolding of a specific constituting contradiction.

This is not to deny that Bhaskar does develop some sense of an interconnected totality through the partial 'absence' of an object. This is based primarily upon an object's shared *identity* with another object. An object will never experience completeness because it will always be defined, in part, through its relationship to other objects. It is in this sense that Bhaskar now redefines how a system is 'open' because the precise establishment of an object's limits are endlessly deferred due to the 'absenting' constraints imposed through the relationship with new objects.

My point is therefore not to deny that Bhaskar does develop the idea of an interconnected totality in *Dialectic*. But I would want to say that the 'open' nature of the totality of which Bhaskar is now interested is, like its critical realist forebears, characterised by a rather non-discriminating theory of determination. For Bhaskar now transfers his earlier exposition of 'open systems' to a much more 'totalising' level. An object through its absence eventually passes into an 'existential' relationship with another object and thus the totality in which it resides is increasingly complexified. But to reiterate my earlier point, it is difficult to see why there is a *necessity* for each object to transform itself into another object (see also Roberts 2001).

As a result, the 'pulse of freedom' identified within the critical realist dialectic is a rather weak pulse. Power 2 relations, those relations based by Bhaskar upon master–slave-type relationships, are so general and trans-historical that their use for analytical purposes must be questioned. For example, the idea that freedom is based within the 'absenting of absences' by an agent merely places the transcendental status of freedom within the original critical realist conception of agency upon more grandiose philosophical foundations. We can see this more readily in Bhaskar's four-planar account of social being. Each plane stipulates a very general and trans-historical characteristic of human agency. For example, plane d, the plane of the subjectivity of the agent, tells us very little about subjectivity within, say, capitalist social relations. Indeed, Bhaskar leaves us guessing at how we might say something meaningful about subjectivity within capitalism because his description of plane d contains no immediate ground within itself through which we might proceed to explore subjectivity within capitalist social relations.

To make progress in the positing of an emancipatory social theory I believe that we must construct an emancipatory critique from *within* a set of historically specific social relations rather than from without. In practice this would entail the isolation of the normative content of the structure of rights, freedoms, entitlements, duties, privileges, immunities, etc. constitutive of a specific set of social relations. To say that rights, etc. are constitutive of a set of social relations is to say that they are essential elements of the social relations in question. If the social relations in question lack one of these essential elements which contributes to its defining identity then we can say that these particular social relations are incomplete (Taiwo 1996).

This normative standpoint stresses two interconnected points. First, the identity of a set of social relations is arrived at, in part, through its constitutive structure of rights, etc. Second, this structure offers a yardstick in which to measure the extent to which individual societies embody the rights, etc. of a particular set of historical social relations in practice (Taiwo 1996: 66). But these observations are also important because they encourage us to identify the constitutive ideological structure binding a particular set of social relations together. This is because the normative standpoint argued for here invites us to try to discover the 'essence' – those specific properties and powers that go to give a social entity its unique identity – of the particular set of social relations in question (Meikle 1985). As I have argued from a Hegelian–Marxist position, essence is structured along lines of contradiction, exploitation, power, inequality, etc. Thus this structuring moment must be included in any discussion about rights, etc. In other words, a normative content must be alive to the contradictory rights, etc., which structure the very essence of a specific set of historical social relations at different levels of abstraction. This observation, I believe, goes some way in allowing us to keep hold of a normative and emancipatory standpoint whilst recognising that the rights, etc. structuring that standpoint are themselves contradictory.

In the next section, which draws heavily upon the discussion in Arthur (1995; see also Arthur 1993, 1997; cf. Smith 1990, 1999), I briefly try to show how a Hegelian–Marxist standpoint might conceptualise freedom in capitalist social relations. We will see that such a standpoint can situate freedom within a specific set of contradictory social relations. As such it simultaneously rejects a formalist definition of freedom in favour of a dialectical and contradictory definition. By highlighting the inner contradiction bound up within 'capitalist freedom' a Hegelian–Marxist standpoint also stipulates the negation of the capitalist character of that specifically inverted and fetishistic freedom. However, it must be borne in mind that the comments made are preliminary rather than substantive. They are used merely for illustrative purposes (but see Roberts forthcoming for a more substantive presentation).

Capitalist rights and freedom

Capitalism, according to Marx, is characterised by its own peculiar right claims. In order to understand the ideological nature of these right claims Marx isolates their determining properties at different levels of abstraction. Following the comments made in the previous sections, we can say that a dialectical materialist approach seeks to isolate the determining contradictory moment of right claims as this moment manifests itself within a specific set of social relations. However, the determining moment is not necessarily placed as the starting point of analysis. Nonetheless, the starting point must *presuppose* the determining moment so that the starting point necessarily is transformed from conditions to consequences (see the previous section).

Marx begins his analysis of capitalism with the commodity. The commodity, according to Marx, is the 'cell-form' of capitalist society because it is the most simple appearance of capitalist society. Yet the commodity is also characterised by an internal and essential contradiction between use-value and exchange-value. What this contradiction means in practice is that the value of a single commodity lacks the 'internal independence' required for its transformation into self-subsisting entity because it is one-side of a contradictory relationship with use-value. Only through money acting as a reflected form of value (objectified abstract labour) can exchange-value gain an 'external independence'. Through money, therefore, exchange-value overcomes its contradictory relationship with use-value to gain an illusionary appearance of an independent entity. Money is therefore transformed into, as Elson (1979) says, '(the) externally independent expression, in objectified form, of a one-sided abstraction, the abstract aspect of labour, which is the fetishism of commodities' (Elson 1979: 165).

But this objective relationship also has an alienated subjective side. Commodities cannot enter into an exchange relation of their own free will. As a necessity, commodities require individuals who are willing to enter into a relationship of exchange to the extent that each individual stands in a relationship with the other and recognises that the will of the other resides within the object to be exchanged. Each individual must:

> behave in such a way that each does not appropriate the commodity of the other, and alienate his own, except through an act to which both parties consent. The guardians must therefore recognise each other as owners of private property. This juridical relation, whose form is the contract, whether as part of a developed legal system or not, is a relation between two wills which mirrors the economic relation.
>
> (Marx 1867/1988: 178)

As Pashukanis (1929/1978) observes, in this passage Marx describes two separate though interconnected forms of the term 'abstract' in capitalist society. First, commodity production transforms social life into a totality of reified relations such as profit rates, price level, rate of surplus value, etc. Second, individuals discover that they are defined as an abstract object, namely as a subject endowed with abstract rights freely disposing of what is theirs (Pashukanis 1929/1978: 112–13). Power itself becomes a thing that can, in principle, be privately possessed by everyone (Sayer 1991: 67).

Three observations are worth making at this point. First, both forms of 'abstractness' within commodity production are in contradiction with one another. This is because abstract rights provide the basis for each subject to enter the exchange process as an individual freely disposing of that which is theirs.

Never, in any earlier period, have the productive forces taken on a form so indifferent to the intercourse of individuals as individuals, because their intercourse itself was formally a restricted one. On the other hand, standing over against these productive forces, we have the majority of the individuals from whom these forces have been wrested away, and who, robbed thus of all real life-content, have become abstract individuals, but who are, however, only by this fact put into a position to enter into relations with one another *as individuals*.

(Marx and Engels 1845–6/1994: 92)

The universal forces of private property under commodity production inaugurate a universal discourse of rights that can be used against the fetishistic nature of commodity production. Thus an emancipatory logic runs through commodity production, even if it is essentially an inverted topsy-turvy logic.

Second, both forms of abstractness are derived from the same structuring substance, namely the objectification of abstract labour. Both forms of abstractness are therefore integrally part of the same specific set of social and historical relations. We thus escape from the trans-historical dualism embedded within the critical realist conceptualisation of freedom. Third, and related to the previous two points, we provide a point of departure for further investigation simply because we have isolated the most abstract and contradictory form of right within the historical system of capitalism.

So far in the analysis the key to understanding both forms of abstractness has been 'objectified abstract labour'. But what are the presuppositions for the historical emergence of this form of labour? Marx claims that commodity production itself cannot obtain this status. As we have seen, commodity production requires money in order to overcome its internal contradiction between use-value and exchange-value. But Marx also suggests that money as value is itself contradictory. This is so because money must act as both a universal commodity for exchange and as a particular unit withdrawn from circulation to hoard for future value. To overcome this contradiction, so Marx suggests, money must become the source of value itself, to produce more value than that which originally entered circulation. But, as Arthur (1997: 28) indicates, Marx discovers that money as circulation cannot itself ground surplus value because money as value is predicated upon an exchange of equivalents or non-equivalents. Obviously if commodities are exchanged as equivalents it is difficult to see how surplus value arises. As regards exchange of non-equivalents, this is itself premised upon the idea that buyer and seller must change places if exchange is to continue i.e. a seller must become a buyer at some point in the circulation of commodities. Yet through this 'role reversal' the gain made from being a seller is easily wiped out as a buyer simply because a person must now purchase a commodity at the price at which a profit was originally made. For Marx, therefore, surplus value cannot be derived from circulation. Rather, surplus value emerges from production; or more precisely, from the producing power of alienated labour.

The discovery of labour-power allows Marx to reconcile the enigma of how profit is produced through a seemingly equal exchange between capital and labour. Labour-power is a particular form of alienation. Tied to the ability of a labourer to work for a certain length of time, labour-power exacts from the worker the right of entitlement to her product because she sells her labour to the capitalist in return for a wage. Each worker is thereby indifferent to their potential and capacity to labour. The capitalist, on the other hand, has to try and guarantee that the value he has laid out in capital increases. He can only achieve this if he subordinates the will of the labourer to his own will. It is important to note that this subjective struggle is mediated through the social form of capitalist production. Clarke makes a shrewd observation on this point when he says:

> (T)he theory of surplus value does not depend on the determination of value by labour-time, but on the analysis of the social form of capitalist production, based on the distinction between labour and labour-power, the value of which is determined quite independently of one another. Surplus value derives from the quantitative relationship between the two quite distinct magnitudes, as the difference between the sum of value acquired by the capitalist for the sale of the product and the sum paid out in the purchase of labour-power and the means of production.
>
> (Clarke 1991: 116)

Labour-power subsequently exhibits specific spatial and temporal dimensions. Spatially, the worker is now positioned in a particular location for a certain amount of time. During the period in which the worker is positioned, she must labour for the capitalist. Temporally, the worker must give up her labour-time to the capitalist. During this specified period, the capitalist gains a surplus through the *compression* of labour-time to a bare minimum. By utilising the worker's *capacity* to labour, the capitalist can produce more value than it costs to pay the worker a living wage.

But in order for labour-power to be transformed into a commodity the labourer must be free to sell her product to whoever s/he so wishes. Yet this freedom must be linked to freedom from ownership of the means of production by the labourer. Advanced capitalism is thereby characterised by the increasing separation of the labourer from the means of production (Marx 1867/1988: 270 ff.). This double-form of freedom denotes the specific class relationship under capitalism and signifies a specific relationship of exploitation based upon the extraction of surplus-value. In part eight of *Capital* vol. I, Marx (1867/1988) makes it clear that primitive accumulation lays the basis for the conditions necessary for capital accumulation. These conditions are based upon the historic separation of the producer from the means of production. This separation perpetuates the double-form of freedom. The labourer now has the right to sell labour-power to whoever s/he wishes and has the right to be free from the ownership of production. Advanced capitalism is therefore based upon the constant *reproduction* of both this separation and this double-form of freedom. Both forms are 'not the result of the capitalist mode of production but its point of departure' (Marx 1867/1988: 873; cf. 270 ff.).

What this analysis tells us is that freedom under capitalism has a distinctive meaning within a specific set of historical social relations. At the same time, this double-form of freedom is based upon 'abstract right' as found within the commodity form. The discovery of the ideological nature of freedom does not extinguish the ideological nature of right. Rather, the double-form of freedom *grounds* the alienated nature of abstract right within *capitalist* society. This is because the separation of the labourer from the means of production is accompanied by a change in the public–private relationship. Abstract right no longer represents the right of individuals existing within a commodity producing society. Instead we now discover discursive claims and rights representative of a class society. On the one hand we have the right of capital to gain a surplus through the acquisition of labour-power. On the other hand we have the right of the labourer to sell labour-power to whoever will purchase it. Labour is thus transformed from an owner of a commodity into a commodity itself.

> He must constantly treat his labour-power as his own property, his own commodity, and he can do this only by placing it at the disposal of the buyer, i.e. handing it over to the buyer for him to consume, for a definite period of time, temporarily. In this way he manages both to alienate (*veräussern*) his labour-power and to avoid renouncing his rights of ownership over it.
>
> (Marx 1867/1988: 271)

This is an interesting passage. Marx seems to be saying that the labourer is compelled to alienate herself whilst simultaneously holding onto certain rights over her product. At the same time these rights can only be validated publicly through a relationship with the capitalist. Both the labourer and the capitalist are *forced* to publicly interact in order to establish dialogue between one another on the question of the rights associated with the social product. At first glance all of this seems very similar to the foregoing discussion of abstract right as this exists in commodity production. There is, however, a subtle though significant shift in Marx's thinking here. Marx no longer talks about the division between the abstract individual and the reified social domain as was the case under simple capitalist production. The main object of Marx's concern under advanced capitalism is, rather, the division between the *class* individual and *class* society. This new exploration does not abolish the emphasis upon the abstract individual and abstract social relations, but rather takes that particular division down to a more complex level. At the same time we alter our understanding accordingly of abstract right. For abstract right can now be placed within its proper historical and class context. Unlike dialectical critical realism, therefore, historical materialism situates an emancipatory project within its own historical conditions of existence and posits a negating agent, the proletariat, as the resolution of the contradictions immanent within those historical conditions of existence. Only through the collective power of the proletariat will the *necessity* of an emancipatory project dissolve and an alternative form of freedom without alienation be realised.

Conclusion

Hodgson (1999: 3) has claimed that some of the titles and content of Bhaskar's works (e.g. *Scientific Realism and Human Emancipation* and *Dialectic: The Pulse of Freedom*) and those of other critical realists (e.g. Collier 1989, 1994; Lawson 1997; Sayer 2000) 'betray a driving concern with the topic of human emancipation'. Hodgson (1999: 3) goes on to argue that the main problem with this emancipatory project is that it contains no clear normative evaluation or operational criterion as to what is a 'false' or 'true' belief.

I think that Hodgson touches upon a major problem with critical realism and dialectical critical realism. As I have argued in this chapter, (dialectical) critical realism bases its emancipatory claims, in part, upon a trans-historical and general concept of human freedom. Such a concept cannot account for the form of freedom and, hence, emancipation, within historical and ideological social relations because it contains no sense of being theoretically embedded within a self-moving systematic and historical totality characterised by a determining contradiction. Hence the theoretical development of emancipation thus derived is too general and trans-historical to act as a guide for political practice. To therefore say, as critical realists do, that emancipation might follow from the transformation of underlying structures provides us with no normative grounds in itself to separate out those more ideologically determining structures from those that have less effect within society. A comparison can be made with Marxism on this point.

Larrain (1979) argues that Marx suggests in various places that we should have a discriminating account of ideology. According to Marx, ideology relates to a limited social practice whereby the failure to solve contradictions in reality leads to an epistemological distortion concerning solutions about those contradictions. This distortion is not simply false but is itself a real manifestation of a contradictory essence. Correspondingly if ideology inverts the world in which we live, this is only because the social relations of which ideology plays a part are themselves already inverted. By negating the inverted world of social relations in this manner, ideology imbues appearances with an autonomous existence. Within specific class relations, therefore, ideology conceals objective contradictions that emanate from those relations. Under these conditions ideology can be said to benefit the interests of a ruling class. We arrive at a 'critical' theory of ideology (Larrain 1979: 35 ff.).

This is a discriminating account of ideology because it does not assume that all ruling class ideas are necessarily ideological. Rather, it enables us to comprehend how one set of historical ideas within a set of social relations represent more insidious forms of thinking about the world than is the case with another set of historical ideas evident in those same social relations. For the reasons stated throughout this chapter, I do not believe that the same discriminating emancipatory critique can be found within critical realism. What we get instead from critical realism is a far more general and non-committal emancipatory critique in which the ideology concept is present, but in an all too embracing sense.

Note

1   I would like to thank Steve Fleetwood for his detailed comments on an earlier draft. Conversations with Andrew Brown and Jonathan Joseph have also helped me enormously to clarify my own thoughts on the subject matter discussed in this chapter. However all errors remain my own.

Bibliography

Arthur, C. J. (1993) 'Hegel's *Logic* and Marx's *Capital*', in Fred Moseley (ed.) *Marx's Method in Capital*, New Jersey: Humanities Press.
—— (1995) 'Negation of the negation in Marx's *Capital*', *Studies in Marxism* 2: 1–12.
—— (1997) 'Against the logical-historical method: dialectical derivation versus linear logic', in F. Moseley and M. Campbell (eds) *New Investigations of Marx's Method*, New Jersey: Humanities Press International.
Benton, T. (1997) 'Response to Cecile Jackson', in *Economy and Society* 26(1): 81–91.
Berlin, I. (1969) *Four Essays on Liberty*, London: Oxford University Press.
Bhaskar, R. (1978) *A Realist Theory of Science*, 2nd edition, London: Verso.
—— (1979/1998) *The Possibility of Naturalism*, 3rd edition, London: Routledge.
—— (1986) *Scientific Realism and Human Emancipation*, London: Verso.
—— (1989) *Reclaiming Reality*, London: Verso.
—— (1993) *Dialectic: The Pulse of Freedom*, London: Verso.
Bryant, G. A. (1995) *Practical Sociology: Post-Empiricism and the Reconstruction of Theory and Application*, Cambridge: Polity Press.
Chitty, A. (1993) 'The early Marx on needs', *Radical Philosophy* 64 (Summer): 23–31.
Clarke, S. (1991) *Marx, Marginalism and Modern Sociology: From Adam Smith to Max Weber*, 2nd edition, London: Macmillan.
Collier, A. (1989) *Scientific Realism and Socialist Thought*, Hemel Hempstead, UK: Harvester Wheatsheaf.
—— (1994) *Critical Realism: An Introduction to Roy Bhaskar's Philosophy*, London: Verso.
Elson, D. (1979) 'The value theory of labour', in D. Elson (ed.) *Value: The Representation of Labour in Capitalism*, London: CSE Books.
Hegel, G. W. F. (1812–1816/1969) *The Science of Logic*, trans. by A. V. Miller, London: Allen & Unwin.

Hodgson, G. (1999) 'Marching to the promised land? Some doubts on the policy affinities of critical realism', *Alethia* 2(2): 2–10.

Hoffman, J. (1986) *The Gramscian Challenge*, Oxford: Basil Blackwell.

Hunt, I. (1993) *Analytical and Dialectical Marxism*, Aldershot, UK: Avebury.

Johnson, R. (1982) 'Reading for the best Marx: history-writing and historical abstraction', in R. Johnson, G. McLennan, B. Schwarz and D. Sutton (eds) *Making Histories: Studies in History-Writing and Politics*, London: Hutchinson.

Larrain, J. (1979) *The Concept of Ideology*, London: Hutchinson.

Lawson, T. (1997) *Economics and Reality*, London: Routledge.

Marx, K. (1844/1981) *Economic and Philosophic Manuscripts of 1844*, Moscow: Progress Publishers.

—— (1867/1988) *Capital* vol. I, London: Penguin.

Marx, K. and Engels, F. (1845–6/1994) *The German Ideology*, edited by C. J. Arthur. London: Lawrence & Wishart.

Meikle, S. (1985) *Essentialism in the Thought of Karl Marx*, Illinois: Open Court Publishing.

Ollman, B. (1993) *Dialectical Investigations*, London: Routledge.

Outhwaite, W. (1987) *New Philosophies of Social Science: Realism, Hermeneutics and Critical Theory*, London: Macmillan.

Pashukanis, E. V. (1929/1978) *Law and Marxism: A General Theory*, translated by B. Einhorn, edited by C. J. Arthur, London: Pluto Press.

Pleasants, N. (1999) *Wittgenstein and the Idea of a Critical Social Theory: A Critique of Giddens, Habermas and Bhaskar*, London: Routledge.

Pratt, A. C. (1995) 'Putting critical realism to Work: the practical implications for geographical research', *Progress in Human Geography* 19(1): 61–74.

Ramsay, M. (1997) *What's Wrong with Liberalism?*, London: Leicester University Press.

Roberts, J. M. (1999) 'Marxism and critical realism: the same, similar, or just plain different?', *Capital and Class* 68: 21–49.

—— (2001) 'Critical realism and the dialectic', *British Journal of Sociology*, forthcoming.

—— (forthcoming) *Rethinking the Public Sphere: The Aesthetics of Free Speech*, Liverpool: Liverpool University Press.

Sayer, A. (2000) *Realism and Social Science*, London: Sage.

Sayer, D. (1991) *Capitalism and Modernity: An Excursus on Marx and Weber*, London: Routledge.

Sayers, S. (1994) 'On the Marxist dialectic', in R. Norman and S. Sayers *Hegel, Marx and Dialectic: A Debate*, Aldershot, UK: Gregg Revivals.

—— (1998) *Marxism and Human Nature*, London: Routledge.

Shamsavari, A. (1991) *Dialectics and Social Theory: The Logic of Capital*, Braunton, UK: Merlin.

Smith, T. (1990) *The Logic of Marx's Capital: Replies to Hegelian Criticisms*, Albany, NY: SUNY Press.

—— (1999) 'The relevance of systematic dialectics to Marxian thought: a reply to Rosenthal', *Historical Materialism* 4: 215–40.

Suchting, W. (1992) 'Reflections upon Roy Bhaskar's "critical realism"', in *Radical Philosophy* 61: 23–31.

Taiwo, O. (1996) *Legal Naturalism: A Marxist Theory of Law*, Ithaca and London: Cornell University Press.

Index